The Encyclicals and Other Messages of John XXIII

The Encyclicals and Other Messages of John XXIII

With Commentaries by
REV. JOHN F. CRONIN, S.S.
REV. FRANCIS X. MURPHY, C.SS.R.
REV. FERRER SMITH, O.P.

Arranged and Edited by
THE STAFF OF THE POPE SPEAKS MAGAZINE

TPS PRESS
Washington, D.C.

Nihil obstat:

    Reverend Harry A. Echle

    Censor Librorum

Imprimatur:

    ✠ Patrick A. O'Boyle

    Archbishop of Washington

November 3, 1964

Copyright © 1964 by TPS Press

PRINTED IN THE UNITED STATES OF AMERICA BY
GARAMOND/PRIDEMARK PRESS, BALTIMORE, MARYLAND

TABLE OF CONTENTS

Preface ix
Introduction and Biography 1

PART I: *The Early Months*

THE NAME "JOHN"
   Address to the Cardinals on the Day of his Election 9
THIS ANXIOUS HOUR
   His First Public Address 11
POPE AND PASTOR
   His Coronation Address 15
ANNOUNCEMENT OF ECUMENICAL COUNCIL
   From an Address to the Roman Cardinals 20
TRUTH, UNITY, AND PEACE
   His First Encyclical, "Ad Petri Cathedram" 24
DEVOTION TO THE ROSARY
   The Encyclical "Grata Recordatio" 57

PART II: *On the Priesthood*

A Commentary on Pope John and the Priesthood 65
ST. JOHN VIANNEY, MODEL FOR PRIESTS
   The Encyclical "Sacerdotii Nostri Primordia" 68
COUNSELS FOR SEMINARIANS
   An Address to Seminarians in Rome 102
THE ROMAN SYNOD AND THE PRIEST
   An Address to the Clergy of Rome 112
THE ART OF SPIRITUAL DIRECTION
   An Address to Spiritual Directors of Seminaries 129

PART III: *On Church Unity*

ONE FOLD, ONE SHEPHERD
   An Excerpt from the 1958 Christmas Message 139
ST. LEO THE GREAT AND CHURCH UNITY
   The Encyclical "Aeterna Dei Sapientia" 140

Contents

ONE, HOLY, CATHOLIC, APOSTOLIC
An Address after a Mass in the Byzantine-Slav Rite 160
THE MISSIONS
The Encyclical "Princeps Pastorum" 168

PART IV: On Peace

TRUE CHRISTIAN PEACE
The 1959 Christmas Broadcast 201
THE WAY TO PEACE
A Radio Address to the World 212
THE FIFTH COMMANDMENT
An Address at a Time of International Strife 219
A CALL FOR NEGOTIATIONS
A Broadcast to World Leaders 222

The Spirit of Pope John
An Essay in Pictures and His Own Words

PART V: Two Great Encyclicals

A PREVIEW OF "MATER ET MAGISTRA"
An Address to an Audience of Workers 227
A Commentary on "Mater et Magistra" 240
MATER ET MAGISTRA
The Encyclical on Christianity and Social Progress 250
A Commentary on "Pacem in Terris" 316
PACEM IN TERRIS
His Last Encyclical 327
THE SPIRIT OF "PACEM IN TERRIS"
Reflections on the Encyclical, from Five Addresses by Pope John 374

PART VI: The Great Council of Renewal and Reunion

A Commentary on Pope John and the Council 381
PROCLAMATION OF THE SECOND VATICAN COUNCIL
The Apostolic Constitution "Humanae Salutis" 386

PENANCE FOR SUCCESS OF THE COUNCIL
  The Encyclical "Paenitentiam Agere" 397
THE CONTRIBUTION OF NUNS TO SUCCESS OF THE COUNCIL
  A Letter to All Women in Religious Life 409
OPENING ADDRESS TO THE COUNCIL
  His Address Opening the First Session 423
TO THE OBSERVER DELEGATES
  An Address to Non-Catholics at the Council 436
TOWARD A NEW PENTECOST
  Address at the Close of the Council's First Session . . . 439
THOUGHTS FOR THE COUNCIL'S RECESS
  A Letter Sent to Each of the Fathers of the Council . . . 447

PART VII: *A Spiritual Testament*

A LETTER TO HIS FAMILY
  From Pope John XXIII to His Brother and Intended for All
  Members of the Roncalli Family 461
LAST WILL AND TESTAMENT
  His Spiritual Testament and Last Wishes 465
RETREAT NOTES
  Selections from Notes of Pope John Made on Several Retreats
  During His Pontificate 470
DIARY PAGES AND FINAL REFLECTIONS
  Excerpts from His Diary and Some Random Meditative Notes 490

Appendix
  A. Bibliographic Data and Notes 501
  B. Commentators and Editors 509
Index 511

PREFACE

THE ASTONISHING IMPACT which Pope John made on the world and on history calls for this book. It would be wrong to say that this impact was due solely or even primarily to his public speeches and letters—millions loved him who may never have heard or read a single one of them. Yet to us who were reading his words day by day, not only the profound wisdom and insight but also the warm personality of this great man came through, even in his most formal addresses. Hence this book, which is truly "Pope John's book."

The importance of these documents being indisputable and the desirability of collecting them into a book obvious, the only questions for any publisher were where to get the best translations and which of his hundreds of talks and letters to include.

As publishers of *The Pope Speaks* magazine, which is devoted entirely to providing translations of papal documents, we were in a unique position for solving the problem of translations: they were already at hand in our periodical and, we felt, they were the best available.

The problem of making the wisest selection from the many published addresses and letters of Pope John was more difficult. In solving it we were helped by a number of people familiar with his talks and letters. The long familiarity of our own staff with papal documents was also of great help.

Our choice was based primarily upon what we judged to be the importance of a particular subject to Pope John, an importance indicated for the most part by the frequency with which he spoke on it. And so we chose to group the messages into sections, each section corresponding to one of these topics. Thus the priesthood, Church unity, peace, and the Ecumenical Council were so often his topics that we have separate sections on each, with several messages in each section. His eight encyclicals were an obvious choice and they appear here, each in an appropriate topical section, with the two most famous in a section of their own.

Finally, we placed at the beginning several messages (including two encyclicals) from the early months of his reign that set the tone for his whole pontificate—and at the end, as a fitting climax, some writings of a very personal nature: a letter to his family, notes made while on retreat and at other times, his last will and testament.

A selective anthology rarely satisfies every reader. Each will no doubt deplore the absence of a letter or address he believes too important to have been left out. We can only say that within the limits imposed by the practical problem of book size we have tried our best to do full justice to this remarkable man. (Those who wish to see letters or addresses not in this book are referred to *The Pope Speaks* magazine, which has published over two hundred of his messages in full and many others in part or in summary form. It has also listed chronologically practically every published message of Pope John, with reference data on each.)

To what use should this book be put? It will be a reference work for students of papal teachings, one link in the long chain of papal documents stretching back to Peter. For a Catholic reader, a Christian reader, it will be a continuation and deepening of his religious education, a lifelong spiritual companion. For any reader it will be a place to browse and catch at every point the true spirit of Christianity. Perhaps what sets it apart from other collections of papal documents is the deeply personal quality that Pope John managed to inject into all his messages, a quality that leaves the reader feeling that he has gotten to know the man himself, as well as his ideas.

To help the reader use the book more fruitfully we have included several features besides the Pope's own words. Each section is prefaced by our own note to cast some light on the contents of the section, as well as to place the section in the context of the whole book. Special commentaries have been prepared for Pope John's messages on the priesthood and on the Council, and for each of his two best known encyclicals, "Mater et Magistra" and "Pacem in Terris." A biographical essay introduces the book and a "picture essay" with selected quotations adds a visual dimension.

We are very grateful to Fathers Cronin, Murphy, and Smith for writing commentaries. Assistance and suggestions were gladly received from friends too many to name, particularly from those who have been helping *The Pope Speaks* magazine over the years.

Finally, our deep thanks go to the translators, whose work made this book possible. (We have indicated in the bibliographic section the translators for each document.) In this regard, we owe a special debt of gratitude to the Catholic Truth Society, London, and to their Latin expert, Rev. H. E. Winstone, for the translations of "Mater et Magistra" and "Pacem in Terris," used in both our magazine and this book.

In his words and example, in his entire life as in his pontificate, Pope John has truly left us a priceless spiritual testament. We are happy to play our small role in helping pass it on, through this collection of his own words.

THE EDITORS

INTRODUCTION AND BIOGRAPHY

by

Rev. Francis X. Murphy, C.SS.R.

POPE JOHN XXIII reigned as Vicar of Christ and supreme pastor of the Catholic Church for less than five years, from October 28, 1958, to June 3, 1963. He had the shortest pontificate of any pope in the last 150 years. Yet, in that brief interval he so impressed not only the Christian world but the whole of mankind with the sincerity and personal holiness of his life that when he died, a Washington newspaper printed a drawing of the earth shrouded in mourning and put over it the simple caption "A Death In the Family."

Characteristic of Pope John was his unfeigned interest in everybody and in everything that happened in this world, as well as his effortless ability to draw the attention of everyone he encountered to the world beyond. He had lived a busy and eventful life throughout his career as priest, apostolic diplomat and pastor of souls. And while his role in the Church's affairs frequently seemed a relatively minor one to many of his contemporaries, the importance of each of his assignments is now clear. Divine Providence had so arranged his life's pattern that each part became an essential factor in the formation of the man who was to succeed the brilliant and ascetic pontiff, Pius XII, as Supreme Pastor in an age that will prove to have been crucial in world affairs and revolutionary in the history of the Church. The whole of Pope John's life thus prepared him for the singular accomplishments that marked his pontificate, and in particular for the holding of Vatican Council II.

Born Angelo Giuseppe Roncalli in the little village of Sotto il Monte outside of Bergamo on November 25, 1881, he made his earlier clerical studies in that northern Lombard town, before being admitted to the Lombard College in Rome on a burse that enabled him to complete his theological preparation in the Roman Seminary. At an early age he encountered several important churchmen who were to have a decisive influence on his life. As a young cleric in minor orders he had been introduced to Monsignor Giacomo Radini-Tedeschi, then an official in the Roman Curia, noted for his ardent interest in social justice. The day he took his doctoral examination in theology at the Roman Seminary of the Apollinare, one of the professors on his board was Don Eugenio Pacelli (the future Pope Pius XII); and the day he said his first Mass in St. Peter's Basilica, he encountered Pope Pius X, who spoke to him encouragingly and gave him his blessing. Meanwhile he had completed a year of military service (November 1901-1902) and had demonstrated an aptitude for languages by taking a prize in Hebrew, and by participating in the annual polyglotic academies held at the *Propaganda Fide,* the famous Roman seminary for the training of priests for the foreign missions.

Immediately after ordination his competence and general bearing recommended him to his old friend, the newly elected Bishop of Bergamo, Monsignor Radini-Tedeschi, and he was taken on as that dynamic prelate's secretary. He had assisted at Bishop Radini-Tedeschi's episcopal consecration in the Sistine Chapel on January 29, 1905, which was performed by Pope Pius X, and, after returning to Bergamo, accompanied the Bishop on his official visitations of the diocese, and also on trips to France and the Holy Land.

Meanwhile he was given a post teaching Church History in the diocesan seminary at Bergamo and was asked to give conferences and preach on special occasions. For a young priest, such an experience was exceptional, but Don Angelo Roncalli took it in stride, even finding time to turn his hand to literary work. He published a brochure on the Church historian, Cardinal Cesare Baronio in 1907, and the following year inaugurated a small diocesan monthly called *La Vita Diocesana.* Stirred by the Bishop's concern for the social, economic and political problems affecting the Lombard plains, as well as Italy in general, Don Roncalli began to take an active interest in Catholic Action movements himself, and gained firsthand knowledge of the circumstances and difficulties attendant upon the condemnation of the heresy of Modernism by Pope Pius X in 1908. In 1910 he served as secretary for the diocesan Synod of Bergamo and was responsible for editing its Acts. He also travelled widely in Central Europe, combining pilgrimages and visits to local shrines with a search for information about current social and religious problems. And through his bishop he had met both Cardinal Giacomo della Chiesa, who became Benedict XV, and Monsignor Achille Ratti, the future Pius XI.

Bishop Radini-Tedeschi died in August 1914, two days after Pius X, and in May 1915 Don Roncalli was called into military service, where he served first as a sergeant with the medical corps, and then as a chaplain in the military hospital at Bergamo. On leaving the Army in 1918 he was made spiritual director of the Seminary. He also found time to promote the welfare of Bergamo's growing student population. He had utilized his introduction to Monsignor Ratti, then the curator of the Ambrosian Library in Milan, to locate documents for his *History of the Effects of the Episcopal Visitation of Bergamo by Cardinal Charles Borromeo Immediately after the Council of Trent*—a study that he continued to work on during his long diplomatic career. This work enabled him to become familiar with the inner history of that great reform Council of the sixteenth century, and inspired in him a great devotion to the saintly Cardinal Charles Borromeo who had been instrumental both in closing the Council which had lasted eighteen years (1545-1563), and later, in implementing its decrees in northern Italy.

Summoned to Rome in early 1921, he was personally commissioned by Pope Benedict XV to reorganize the Society for the Propagation of the Faith. In four years time he visited every diocese in Italy and most of the major centers in Europe, arousing interest in the foreign missions and eliciting financial support for them, while managing between times to take part in the spiritual and intellectual life of the Eternal City. On March 3, 1925, he was nominated Apostolic Visitator to Bulgaria. This position not only brought him into contact with the Orthodox Churches of the East, but also gave him a keener insight into the sorrier side of life, including nationalistic and religious enmity, hunger and natural disaster, political intrigue and war. He was transferred to Turkey and Greece as Apostolic Delegate in 1939, and in 1945 was personally picked by Pius XII for the delicate task of presiding over the Church's tremendous effort at renewal in France after World War II.

In 1953 he became Cardinal and Patriarch of Venice and upon assuming possession of the patriarchial archdiocese in the Cathedral of St. Mark, begged the people, *"Per carità*—in your charity—do not look upon your patriarch as a politician or a diplomat. But rather, find in him the servant of God. Look for the pastor of souls called to exercise his mission among the humble, a pastor indeed completely unworthy of the great Pastor, who is Christ, whom he represents on earth." Thus, at the age of 73 he seemed destined to end his days serving as an active pastor of souls in one of the great Italian sees. In November 1957 he held a diocesan Synod, and was in the process of putting the synodal program to work in his vast Archdiocese, known as the Queen of the Sea, when Providence decreed that he personally was not to finish the program he had outlined: he was correcting the printer's proofs of the synodal Acts when he was called to Rome for the conclave following the death of Pius XII in October 1958.

It is quite certain that Cardinal Roncalli had no thought when he left Venice that he would be the next Pope. Yet when he realized that Providence was pointing uncomfortably in his direction, he accepted his fate, took the name of John, and in his first public address set the mark for his pontificate. It would be a pastoral reign, directed toward bringing a dynamic peace to the world and a new order to the Church.

John's predecessor, Pope Pius XII, in a remarkable series of encyclicals, allocutions and letters, had proposed the principles for solving the many grave problems facing the Church and the world. And Angelo Roncalli had been listening attentively. When he himself became Pope he determined to put these principles into effect and bring about a renewal of the Church in the twentieth century. It was while talking to Cardinal Tardini, his new Secretary of State, on this topic a month or two after his election that, as he described it, there suddenly came to him the idea of holding a council. It is clear that the idea was spontaneous and the suggestion immediate. And Cardinal Tardini's agreement was equally spontaneous. Pope John made up his mind to prosecute the idea at once, taking it as a sign from the Holy Spirit. Cardinal Tardini, realizing the tremendous work and risk involved in such a move, suggested a Roman Synod as a sort of pilot venture. Pope John accepted this proposal gladly and held his Roman Synod in January 1960. The monumental work entailed by the Synod was scarcely a novelty for him; as we have seen, he had already been through at least two synods— one in Bergamo, the other in Venice. Then he turned with full eagerness and seriousness to the problems of the whole Catholic world and began the countdown on Vatican Council II.

In his first extensive comment on the Council, in the encyclical *Ad Petri Cathedram* of June 29, 1959, Pope John told the world:

> Bishops from every part of the world will gather there to discuss serious religious topics. They will consider, in particular, the growth of the

Catholic faith, the restoration of sound morals among the Christian flock, and appropriate adaptation of Church discipline to the needs and conditions of our times.

This event will be a wonderful spectacle of truth, unity, and charity. For those who behold it but are not one with this Apostolic See, We hope that it will be a gentle invitation to seek and find that unity for which Jesus Christ prayed so ardently to His Father in heaven.

Of all the magnificent things that can be said about Pope John, perhaps the most pleasing to him, and the most just, is the fact that, in accepting the burden of the papacy at the obvious urging of the Holy Spirit, he did have a program. He announced that he would be called John, and immediately demonstrated the double significance of his choice, in his determination to "make straight the way of the Lord" as a true pastor, and in his immense goodness and kindliness as a Good Shepherd. For all his gentleness and the informality of his ways, he fixed a definite goal for his pontificate, and his basic objectives were achieved.

It is all but incredible, nevertheless, that in pursuing his goal he was able to preserve all the qualities associated with his outward appearance. He was gentle almost to a fault, unhurried, and so courteous as to be apparently beyond losing his temper. Despite age and portliness, or perhaps because of these qualities, he evinced an energetic interest in everything. He visited every nook and corner of Vatican City during his pontificate, spoke to all its employees and inhabitants, raised their salaries in keeping with present-day economic standards, examined its institutions from the museums to the local fire department.

Nor did he hesitate to sally forth to revive old pastoral customs in Rome and its environs, calling on the sick and imprisoned, visiting the cemetery, and taking part in the stational processions on the Sundays of Lent in the parishes at the outskirts of the city. He did not hesitate to depart from the policies of his predecessor in dealing with matters bordering on the political, gradually urging Italy's priests and prelates to disengage from any close association with the country's political alignments.

In dealing with the hierarchies behind the Iron Curtain, he sought the advice of men directly involved in the situation there, and adopted what looked like an "opening to the left" despite the dire predictions of some of his advisers. He set an eirenic and ecumenical goal for Vatican Council II, and only occasionally admitted that he was *"addolorato"*—somewhat saddened—by the intransigent attitude of certain advisers.

The reason why Pope John appeared to be such a magnificent enigma is that he had within himself qualities the modern world considers hopelessly incompatible. He was efficient without being ruthless. He was completely spiritual-minded without once taking his eyes from the most temporal of this world's problems. His physical appearance was not at all formidable and his kindly garrulousness disarmed critics. The manner in which he met people overwhelmed them: his attention was immediate and absolute, his words and bearing comfortably informal. Within hours after assuming the papacy, he had won the respect and affection of almost the entire world. Following the lead of his saintly predecessor, he completed the transformation of the image of the papacy in the modern world, and showed to an ever more receptive world that the claim of his office as pastor, teacher and father to all mankind was really capable of fulfillment.

Obedience was a strong force in the life of Angelo Roncalli and he cheerfully accepted all his assignments. In the course of a talk in St. Mark's in Venice he said:

> What made me secretary to Bishop Radini in 1905 was obedience; what brought me into the seminary to teach, to take charge of the spiritual direction of future priests, to give assistance to soldiers, was obedience. Benedict XV called me to Rome. Pius XI sent me to Bulgaria, and then pushed me on to Constantinople. Pius XII personally sent me to Paris.

And on the eve of his death, having become Supreme Pastor of the Church, he obediently awaited God's final call, reassuring his physician, Professor Gasbarrini, with these words: "Do not be concerned about me. I have my bags packed and am ready to go."

Pope John's pontificate has without a doubt made a permanent impression on the life of the Church. History will record that what he did for the Church in the twentieth century was similar to what Leo the Great did for it in the fifth, Gregory the Great in the seventh and Gregory VII in the eleventh centuries. Above all else he desired to return the Church to the spirit which animated the earliest Christian communities. That was why he chose the name of John and declared both the Precursor and the Beloved Disciple to be his models. Although Pope John occupied the papal throne for but a brief five years, the memory of his reign will live in the annals of the Church forever.

I

*The Early
   Months*

From the very beginning of Pope John's pontificate, his words hinted at the dynamic things that were to come in the reign of this supposedly "interim" pope. In fact, the messages which we have selected here from the early months are almost a "preface" to his entire pontificate.

His burning desire for reunion with separated Christians, his great concern for peace, his desire to be a pastoral Pope, all were revealed in the very first days of his Pontificate—as was his habit of doing the unexpected. And, the surprising announcement of an ecumenical council came when he had been Pope less than three months. Also apparent throughout these early messages (six of which, including two encyclicals, appear here), were his deep concern for the material as well as spiritual lot of man in this world, the "scriptural savor" that permeated all his talks and letters, and his lifelong devotion to Mary and the rosary.

Clearly he was a man who had long pondered the anguish of the Church and the world. Now, after a lifetime spent, all unknowingly, in preparation for just this opportunity, he was in the supreme position for bringing aid and comfort to both. In a phrase he loved to employ, the time had come to "launch out into the deep."—Ed.

THE NAME "JOHN"

Address to the College of Cardinals on the Day of his Election

- *Associations of the name*
- *Two Johns of the Bible*
- *A prayer*

I SHALL BE CALLED JOHN. This name is dear to Us, for it was the name of Our Father. It is a name that provokes pleasant memories, for it is the name of the tiny parish in which We were baptized. It is a solemn name, for it is the name of many cathedrals throughout the world, particularly of Our own cathedral, the holy Church of the Lateran. It is a name that has been borne more often than any other in the long history of the Roman Pontificate. Twenty-two of the popes whose title to this office is beyond legitimate dispute have had this name. Almost all of them led short lives as pontiffs. We prefer to hide the insignificance of Our name behind this imposing array of Roman pontiffs.

John was also the first name of Saint Mark the Evangelist, the pride and protector of Our beloved Venice, whom Saint Peter, prince of the Apostles and first bishop of the Roman Church, loved as a son.

The two Johns

But We have a special reason for choosing the name John, a name so especially dear to Us and to the whole Church. For it is the name of two men who were and are close to Christ the Lord, the divine Redeemer of the whole world and Founder of the Church.

One of these men is John the Baptist, precursor of the Lord, who was not, to be sure, the light, but bore witness to the light—and indeed bore invincible witness to truth, justice, and liberty in his preaching, in his baptism of penance, in the shedding of his blood.

The other is John the disciple and evangelist, loved by Christ and by His dear mother, the same John who reclined at Jesus' bosom during the last supper and drank deep of that love of which he was to be a burning and apostolic flame even to his old age.

God grant that the voices of these two Johns may be heard in the Church through Our humble pastorship, which follows on those of Our mourned predecessor Pius XII and the other Roman pontiffs, whose praises are sung in the Church. May these two Johns announce to the clergy and to all the people this work of Ours whereby We long "to prepare for the Lord a perfect people, to make straight his paths, that the crooked ways might be made straight and the rough ways smooth, that all mankind might see the salvation of God."[1]

A message of love

And may John the Evangelist, who—as he testifies himself—took into his home Mary the mother of Christ and our mother, continue to preach, along with her, that message of exhortation that is so essential to the life and happiness of the Catholic and Apostolic Church and to the peace and prosperity of all mankind: "My little children, love one another; love one another, for this is the greatest commandment of the Lord."

May God in His goodness grant, venerable brothers, that, with the help of His grace, We, who have the same role as the first in this line of sovereign pontiffs, might be able to reflect the same holiness of life and the same steadfastness of spirit—even, if it should please God, to the shedding of Our blood.

—October 28, 1958

[1] *Luke* 3, 4-6.

THIS ANXIOUS HOUR

The First Public Address of Pope John XXIII

- *Reunion with separated Christians*
- *Concern for world peace*

IN THIS anxious hour We first address Our prayers to God. May He deign to strengthen Us in Our weakness and frailty, to enlighten Our mind, to direct Our will. For Our predecessor of immortal memory, Pius XII—to whom the Catholic Church owes so much—is dead, and a provident God has, in accord with His mysterious designs, laid on Us the burden of this supreme pontificate, which weighs heavily on Our heart and almost crushes it.

Next We greet with affection Our sons of the Sacred College of Cardinals, whose spiritual gifts and virtues are well known to Us. In particular We greet those who are unfortunately far from Us and whose sufferings and hardships trouble Us deeply.

Workers in the vineyard

We wish also to express Our fatherly goodwill and affection for all Our venerable brothers in the episcopacy, who are tireless in their efforts to cultivate the Lord's vineyard throughout the world. And there are others whom We must mention: the priests, dispensers of God's mysteries, and especially the missionary priests, heralds of the divine word, who expend every effort to bring the truth of the Gospel to far-off lands; the religious, men and women, who are so zealously accomplishing great things; those who serve under the captaincy of the bishops in the peaceful militia of Catholic Action, and all others who assist in any way in the apostolate of the hierarchy. With deep affection We bless each and every one of these.

Finally, for all Our children in Christ, especially those who suffer from poverty or any sort of sorrow, We pray and beseech God in His goodness to grant each and every one of them in abundance the help and divine consolation they need.

Venice and Bergamo

Among these children of Ours, those are particularly dear to Our paternal heart who live in the region of Venice, where We have exercised the pastoral ministry, and in the diocese of Bergamo, where We first saw the light of this mortal life. Although We are now far from them, We always are and always will be with them in the love of Jesus Christ. We are confident that their prayers will rise to God with Ours and win many heavenly graces.

The Church persecuted

And now Our thoughts turn in a special way to the bishops, priests, religious, and faithful who dwell in those lands where the Catholic Church is not given, or is not given fully, the freedom she deserves, where the rights of the Church are trampled under foot with reckless daring, where her lawful pastors are exiled, or held in custody, or so impeded that they cannot perform their duties with due freedom.

We want them all to know that We share their sorrows, their hardships, and their sufferings, and We pray that God, the giver of all good things, may soon put an end to these cruel persecutions, which are inconsistent, not only with international peace and prosperity, but with civilization itself and the basic rights of man.

May God pour forth His divine light into the minds of those who rule these nations. May He pardon the persecutors. May He grant better and happier days, in which all will enjoy the blessings of true liberty.

"That they may be one"

We embrace the whole Church, Western and Eastern, with warm

fatherly love. We open Our loving heart and extend Our outstretched arms to all who are separated from this Apostolic See, where Peter lives in his successors "even to the consummation of the world"[1] and fulfills Christ's command to bind and loose on earth[2] and to feed the Lord's entire flock.[3]

We long for their return to the house of the common Father and repeat the words of the divine Redeemer: "Holy Father, keep in thy name those whom thou hast given me, that they may be one even as we are."[4] For thus "there shall be one fold and one shepherd."[5] We pray that they may all return freely and gladly; may this come to pass soon through the inspiration and assistance of God's grace. They will not find it a strange house, but one that is truly their own, a house which has from time immemorial been enlightened by the teachings and adorned by the virtues of their forefathers.

The rulers of nations

Now, however, We would like to address the rulers of all nations, men into whose hands have been placed the lot, fortune, and hopes of their people. Why do they not settle their differences and disputes at last on an impartial basis? Why are the powers of human ingenuity and material resources so often directed to the production of weapons—grim instruments of death and destruction—rather than to the advance of prosperity among the various classes of citizens, especially among those who live in want?

We know that great and complex difficulties stand in the way of realizing this worthy objective and settling these disagreements, but they must be surmounted and overcome, for this is a most serious matter and a serious goal, intimately involved with the happiness of the whole human race.

Peace

Take action, then, boldly and with confidence. Heavenly light will shine upon you; God's help will be granted you. Look at the people who are entrusted to you! Listen to them! What do they

---

[1] *Matt.* 28, 20. [2] *Matt.* 16, 19. [3] *John* 21, 15-17.
[4] *John* 17, 11. [5] *John* 10, 16.

want? What do they ask you for? Not for the new weapons our age has begotten for fratricide and general slaughter! But for *peace,* in which the human family may live, thrive, and prosper freely; for *justice,* by which the classes can adjust equitably their mutual rights and duties; for *tranquility and harmony,* from which genuine prosperity rises.

For in peace based on lawful individual rights and fostered by brotherly love, the finest arts thrive, talents merge into virtue, public and private resources grow. You know what great men of the past have said on this topic: Peace is the "ordered harmony of men"[6]; "peace is the tranquility of order"[7] and "the name of peace is sweet, and peace itself is a blessing; but there is a great deal of difference between peace and slavery. Peace is tranquil liberty."[8]

We must ponder and consider with care the words the angels sang as they hovered over the Divine Infant's crib: "Glory to God in the highest and on earth peace to men of good will."[9] But there is no real peace among men, peoples, or nations unless peace has first been implanted in the hearts of individuals. There can be no outward peace unless it reflects and is ruled by that interior peace without which the affairs of men shake, totter, and fall. And only God's holy religion can foster, strengthen, and maintain such a peace.

Let all take note of these facts who scorn God's name, trample on His holy rights, and boldly endeavor to withdraw men from worship of Him!

At this somber moment We repeat our divine Redeemer's words of promise: "Peace I leave with you; my peace I give you."[10]

May the Apostolic Blessing which We impart with fervent love upon the City and the World betoken and win this real peace, as well as other heavenly gifts.

—October 29, 1958

[6] St. Augustine, *De Civitate Dei,* XIX, ch. 13.
[7] *Ibid.* and *Summa Theologica* II-II, 29, 1, ad 1.
[8] Cicero, *Second Phillipic,* 44.
[9] *Luke* 2, 14.
[10] *John* 14, 27.

POPE AND PASTOR

The Coronation Address of Pope John XXIII

- *A promise to be a pastoral pope*
- *Concern for those outside the Church*
- *Devotion to principles of humility, gentleness*
- *The need for renewal*

WE GREET with a father's affection the cardinals, archbishops, and bishops of the Holy Roman Church who are present either in person or in spirit at these sacred rites in which We, though unworthy, are solemnly entering upon the office of supreme pontiff; and We greet all of you, Our dear children among all the classes of men throughout the world, who are troubled by the cares and anxieties of this present life but are mindful, nonetheless, of those eternal goods which merit particular attention.

We are assembled before a great monument to the Prince of the Apostles. His august office has been entrusted to Us as his successor. At this memorable moment We seem to hear the voice of Peter, coming to Us across the centuries; We seem to hear the voices of those two Johns, brethren of our Lord, whose dear and honored name We have chosen to bear.

Joy and perturbations

In these days that are so full of strange happenings and of anxiety, We have received the congratulations of a great number of men. We are consoled by the expressions of joy with which Our elevation to the pontificate has been hailed. But, on the other hand,

We are troubled and perturbed by the great variety of complex tasks that have been placed upon Our shoulders. We refer to tasks which have been described to Us in various ways, set forth by many men in many ways—within certain definite limits—according to their own personal inclinations, practical experience, and the particular perspectives from which they view the life of individuals or society. Some believe the pope should busy himself in guiding the affairs of nations, that he should be a seasoned diplomat or universal genius, that he should be wise in directing the day-by-day life of man, or that he should be the sort of pope whose spirit embraces all the advances of this modern age without exception.

A new pontiff

But, venerable brothers and beloved sons, they are not on the right track, since they fashion an image of the supreme pontiff which is not fully consistent with sound thinking or the purpose of this office.

For a new pontiff, in the trials of this life, is like the son of the patriarch Jacob, who welcomed his suffering brothers and showed his love and compassion for them, saying: "I am Joseph . . . your brother."[1] By this We mean that a new pontiff embodies that clear image set forth in the Gospel when St. John describes the good shepherd in the Savior's own words.[2] No one can enter the sheepfold of Jesus Christ except under the guidance of the supreme pontiff. Only when men are in union with him can they safely attain salvation, since the Roman pontiff is the vicar of Christ and represents Him on earth. How fine it is to bear in mind this picture of the good shepherd which the Gospel narrative sets out in such exquisite and attractive terms!

The good shepherd

Venerable brothers and beloved sons, the Roman pontiffs through the ages, and particularly Our predecessor Pius XII, have issued warnings on this matter and We now do the same. We assert vigorously and sincerely that it is Our particular intention to be the

---
[1] *Gen.* 45, 4.   [2] Cf. *John* 10, 1-21.

shepherd, the pastor, of the whole flock. All other human gifts and accomplishments—learning, practical experience, diplomatic finesse—can broaden and enrich pastoral work, but they cannot replace it.

A special place must be given the zeal and concern of the good shepherd who is ready for the most difficult tasks, who is outstanding for his prudence, uprightness, and steadfastness, who does not fear danger. "The good shepherd gives his life for his sheep."[3] With what beauty is the Church of Christ, "the sheepfold,"[4] resplendent! The shepherd "goes before the sheep,"[5] and they all follow him. To defend them he is not afraid to ward off the attacks of the wolf by fighting.

And then the mind turns to even deeper thoughts: "Other sheep I have that are not of this fold. Them also must I bring, and they shall hear my voice, and there shall be one fold and one shepherd."[6] These words sum up the scope and the splendor of all missionary work. This activity is certainly the first concern of the Roman pontiff, though not the only one, for even of itself it involves many other cares that are no less important.

The countenance of Christ

But over and beyond external activity, it is important to know the spirit and the policies with which things are done. No doubt, a sovereign pontificate takes its character from the pontiff who conducts it and imparts a particular personality to it. But it is evident that the countenances of all the Roman pontiffs who have through the centuries succeeded to the height of apostolic power, have reflected, or should have reflected, the countenance of Jesus Christ, the divine Master, who undertook his earthly journeys in order that he might sow the seed of divine learning and shed the light of good example.

Of these divine teachings, certain words of the Gospel are the central point and precept which comprehends and embraces in itself all the others: "Learn from me, for I am meek and humble of heart."[7] This is the great principle of gentleness and humility.

---

[3] *John* 10, 11. [4] *John* 10, 1. [5] *John* 10, 4. [6] *John* 10, 16.
[7] *Matt.* 11, 29.

All of you throughout the world, devout and "fervent in spirit,"[8] should pray assiduously to God for your pontiff, with this intention: that he might advance more and more in the gentleness and humility of the Gospel. We are convinced that many benefits will follow from the exercise of these virtues, and if they become the customary manner of the Father of all the faithful, important advantages will result even by way of those human needs which pertain to the social and terrestrial order.

Saint Charles Borromeo

Finally, venerable brothers, cardinals, and bishops of the Holy Roman Church, and beloved sons, priests and members of the faithful, We are pleased to direct your attention to a circumstance that gives Us great pleasure: the fact that this celebration falls upon a day which has a joyful meaning for Us as a priest and a bishop.

On this feast day, November 4th, on which the coronation of a new sovereign pontiff will henceforth be commemorated, the universal Church celebrates each year in her sacred liturgy the feast of Saint Charles Borromeo. We have long had a special affection for this bishop of Milan who must be numbered among the greatest shepherds of the flock. For it was thirty-four years ago that We were consecrated an archbishop, amid solemn ecclesiastical services, in the church dedicated at Rome to his honor, where his heart is kept as a precious relic.

You know that God's Church has at times amid the trials of the centuries lost some of her vigor but she has always found new strength again. It was in such a period of ecclesiastical decline that Saint Charles was called in the wisdom of a provident God to the high task of restoration. Since he labored with might and main that the decrees of the Council of Trent might have the greatest possible efficacy and strove by his example to enforce them in Milan and throughout Italy, he well deserves the distinguished title "Master of Bishops." Sovereign pontiffs took counsel of him; he was to a marvelous degree a model of episcopal holiness.

During the religious services which accompany the coronation of

[8] *Rom.* 12, 11.

a sovereign pontiff, it is permissible to add to the litanies the names of those saints for whom the new pope has special devotion. And so when the invocation *"Saint Charles help him"* was raised today, you prayed fervently, We are sure, that heavenly blessings might descend upon Us in abundance through the intercession of Saint Charles, Our patron, on whose support We rely now and for the future. Amen.

—November 4, 1958

Announcement of Ecumenical Council

From an Address of Pope John XXIII
to the Roman Cardinals

- *The disheartening condition of the world*
- *A council and synod for the welfare of the Church*
- *His trust in heaven*

VENERABLE brethren and beloved sons: This festive occasion, commemorating the conversion of St. Paul, has gathered us around the tomb of the Apostle in his illustrious basilica and offers Us an opportunity to confide to your kindness and understanding some of the most noteworthy aspects of apostolic activity which have come to Our attention during these first three months of Our presence here in Rome in close contact with Roman ecclesiastical society.

Our sole concern is the *"bonum animarum"*[1] and Our wish is to see the new pontificate meet the spiritual demands of the present time accurately and forcefully.

We are aware that the new pope is watched with friendship and warmth in some quarters, and with uncertainty, even with hostility, in others, with everyone waiting to see what can be expected from him.

It is only natural that, among everyday activities which include both the loftiest and the most ordinary manifestations of the pastoral task, observers will try to single out the most important, and

---

[1] "The good of souls."—Ed.

perhaps the only distinctive feature of a pontificate which is more or less happily taking its place in history.

Twofold role

Venerable brethren and beloved sons, if we consider the twofold task which is entrusted to a successor of Saint Peter, we immediately notice his double responsibility: he is Bishop of Rome and Pastor of the Universal Church. These are two expressions of one, single supernatural investiture; two titles which cannot be separated, but must be taken together, for the encouragement and edification of the clergy and the whole Christian world. . . .

World problems

The Bishop of Rome contemplates the whole world, for whose spiritual rule he is responsible as a consequence of the divine mission entrusted to him by his succession to the supreme apostolate, and his eye is caught by two different spectacles: on one side he sees the grace of Christ spreading its marvelous fruits of spiritual elevation, health, and holiness to the whole world; on the other side, alas, he sees the misuse and deprivation of human freedom by certain men. Oblivious of the open gates of heaven and rejecting faith in Jesus Christ, Son of God, Redeemer of the world and founder of the Church, these men are striving only toward the so-called goods of this world, inspired by him whom the Gospel calls prince of darkness, prince of this world—as Jesus Christ Himself defined him in His words after the Last Supper—and are contradicting and fighting against truth and goodness. Their attitude widens the gulf between the two cities—as St. Augustine calls them—while they increase their efforts to deceive, if possible, even the elect, to drag them to ruin.

The cup of misfortune confronting the sons of God and of the Holy Church is filled to the brim by temptations in the material order, which are increased and magnified by the progress of modern technology—in itself morally indifferent.

All of this—this progress, as it is called—distracts men from the quest for superior spiritual goods and is conducive to a weakening of spiritual energies and to a relaxation of the old discipline and order. As a result, grave obstacles arise to confront the Church and her children in her fight against errors which, throughout history, have always brought about fatal and evil divisions, spiritual and moral decay, and the destruction of nations.

This most disheartening sight has caused this humble priest (whom divine Providence singled out, although unworthy, for the exalted mission of the supreme pontificate) to make a decision intended to recall certain ancient forms of doctrinal affirmation and of wise arrangements for ecclesiastical discipline. These forms, in the course of Church history, have yielded the richest harvest of results because of their clarity of thought, their compactness of religious unity, and their heightened flame of Christian fervor, which we acknowledge (with reference to our temporal welfare, too) as abundant wealth *"de rore coeli et de pinguedine terrae."*[2]

A synod and a council

Venerable brethren and beloved sons! Trembling a little with emotion, but with humble firmness of purpose, We now tell you of a twofold celebration: We propose to call a diocesan synod for Rome, and an ecumenical council for the Universal Church. . . .

To you, venerable brethren and beloved sons, We need hardly elaborate on the historical significance and juridical meaning of these two proposals. They will lead to the desired and long awaited modernization of the Code of Canon Law, which is expected to accompany and to crown these two efforts in the practical application of the rules of ecclesiastical discipline, applications the Spirit of the Lord will surely suggest to Us as We proceed. The coming promulgation of the Code of Oriental Law foreshadows these events. . . .

Trust in heaven

Our knowledge and experience, which has been strengthened and increased during the past three months of Our initiation into the

---

[2] "Dew of heaven, and of the fatness of the earth." (*Gen.* 27, 28)—Ed.

service *"servorum Dei,"*[3] encourages Us to place Our trust in the benevolence of heaven: first of all, in the mediation of the Immaculate Mother of Jesus and Our Mother, and then in the protection of Saint Peter and Saint Paul, *"Apostolorum Principum,"*[4] and in the protection of Saint John the Baptist and Saint John the Evangelist, Our special patrons, and of all the saints of the heavenly court. We entreat all of them to grant Us a good beginning and continuation, and final success, in these projects (all of which require hard work) to the enlightenment, edification, and happiness of the whole Christian world, and to the inducement of the faithful of the separated communities to follow Us amicably in this quest for unity and for grace, to which so many souls aspire from all corners of the earth. . . .

—January 25, 1959

[3] "Of the servants of God."—Ed.
[4] "Princes of the Apostles."—Ed.

TRUTH, UNITY, AND PEACE

The Encyclical "Ad Petri Cathedram" of Pope John XXIII to the Entire Catholic World

- *Importance of scriptural truths*
- *Power of the press*
- *His horror of war, love of peace*
- *Distribution of the world's wealth*
- *Church unity, Christian reunion*
- *Renewal of the Church through the Council*

WE WHO have been elevated despite Our unworthiness to the Chair of Peter have often reflected on the things We saw and heard when Our predecessor passed from this life. Virtually the entire world, regardless of race or creed, mourned his passing. And then when We were summoned to the dignity of Sovereign Pontiff, great numbers of people, although occupied with other things or weighed down with troubles and difficulties, turned their thoughts and affections to Us, and placed their hopes and expectations in Us.

From these reflections of Ours, We have drawn comfort and instruction. For this experience certainly is clear indication that the Catholic Church is forever young and is indeed a standard raised before the nations.[1] From her come a pervading light and a gentle love which reach all men.

Then We revealed Our plans to summon an ecumenical council

---

[1] Cf. *Isa.* 11, 12.

and a Roman synod, as well as to revise the Code of Canon Law in accordance with present needs and to issue a new Code of Canon Law for the Church of the Oriental Rite. This announcement received widespread approval and bolstered the universal hope that the hearts of men would be stirred to a fuller and deeper recognition of truth, a renewal of Christian morals, and a restoration of unity, harmony, and peace.

Truth, unity, peace

Today as We address Our first encyclical letter to the entire Catholic world, Our apostolic office clearly demands that We discuss three objectives—truth, unity, and peace—and indicate how they may be achieved and advanced in a spirit of charity.

May the light of the Holy Spirit come upon Us from on high as We write this letter, and upon you as you read it. May the grace of God move all men to attain these objectives, which all desire, even though prejudices, great difficulties, and many obstacles stand in the way of their achievement.

I

All the evils which poison men and nations and trouble so many hearts have a single cause and a single source: ignorance of the truth—and at times even more than ignorance, a contempt for truth and a reckless rejection of it. Thus arise all manner of errors, which enter the recesses of men's hearts and the bloodstream of human society as would a plague. These errors turn everything upside down; they menace individuals and society itself.

And yet, God gave each of us an intellect capable of attaining natural truth. If we adhere to this truth, we adhere to God Himself, the author of truth, the lawgiver and ruler of our lives. But if we reject this truth, whether out of foolishness, neglect, or malice, we turn our backs on the highest good itself and on the very norm for right living.

Revealed truth

As We have said, it is possible for us to attain natural truth by virtue of our intellects. But all cannot do this easily; often their efforts will result in a mixture of truth and error. This is particularly the case in matters of religion and sound morals. Moreover, we cannot possibly attain those truths which exceed the capacity of nature and the grasp of reason, unless God enlightens and inspires us. This is why the Word of God, "who dwells in light inaccessible,"[2] in His great love took pity on man's plight, "became flesh and dwelt among us,"[3] that He might "enlighten every man who cometh into the world"[4] and lead him not only to full and perfect truth, but to virtue and eternal happiness. All men, therefore, are bound to accept the teaching of the Gospel. For if this is rejected, the very foundations of truth, goodness, and civilization are endangered.

Truth and error

It is clear that We are discussing a serious matter, with which our eternal salvation is very intimately connected. Some men, as the Apostle of the Gentiles warns us, are "ever learning yet never attaining knowledge of the truth."[5] They contend that the human mind can discover no truth that is certain or sure; they reject the truths revealed by God and necessary for our eternal salvation.

Such men have strayed pathetically far from the teaching of Christ and the views expressed by the Apostle when he said, "Let us all attain to the unity of the faith and of the deep knowledge of the son of God . . . that we may no longer be children, tossed to and fro and carried about by every wind of doctrine devised in the wickedness of men, in craftiness, according to the wiles of error. Rather are we to practice the truth in love, and so grow up in all things in him who is the head, Christ. For from him the whole body (being closely joined and knit together through every joint of the system according to the functioning in due measure of each single part) derives its increase to the building up of itself in love."[6]

Anyone who consciously and wantonly attacks known truth, who arms himself with falsehood in his speech, his writings, or his conduct in order to attract and win over less learned men and to

[2] *1 Tim.* 6, 16.   [3] *John* 1, 14.   [4] *John* 1, 9.   [5] *2 Tim.* 3, 7.
[6] *Eph.* 4, 13-16.

shape the inexperienced and impressionable minds of the young to his own way of thinking, takes advantage of the inexperience and innocence of others and engages in an altogether despicable business.

The duties of the press

In this connection We must urge to careful, exact, and prudent presentation of the truth those especially who, through the books, magazines, and daily newspapers which are so abundant today, have such a great effect on the instruction and development of the minds of men, and especially of the young, and play such a large part in forming their opinions and shaping their characters. These people have a serious duty to disseminate, not lies, error, and obscenity, but only the truth; they are particularly bound to publicize what is conducive to good and virtuous conduct, not to vice.

For We see with deep sorrow what Our predecessor of immortal memory Leo XIII lamented: "Lies are boldly insinuated . . . into weighty tomes and slender volumes, into the transient pages of periodicals and the extravagant advertisements of the theater."[7] We see "books and magazines written to mock virtue and exalt depravity."[8]

Modern media of communication

And in this day of ours, as you well know, venerable brethren and beloved sons, we also have radio broadcasts, motion pictures, and television (which can enter easily into the home). All of these can provide inspiration and incentive for morality and goodness, even Christian virtue. Unfortunately, however, they can also entice men, especially the young, to loose morality and ignoble behavior, to treacherous error and perilous vice.

The weapons of truth, then, must be used in defense against these weapons of evil. We must strive zealously and relentlessly to ward off the impact of this great evil which every day insinuates itself more deeply.

We must fight immoral and false literature with literature that is

---

[7] Letter *Saepenumero considerantes: Acta Leonis* 3 (1883) 262.
[8] Letter *"Exeunte iam anno," Acta Leonis* 8 (1888) 396.

wholesome and sincere. Radio broadcasts, motion pictures, and television shows which make error and vice attractive must be opposed by shows which defend truth and strive to preserve the integrity and safety of morals. Thus these new arts, which can work much evil, will be turned to the well-being and benefit of men, and at the same time will supply worthwhile recreation. Health will come from a source which has often produced only devastating sickness.

Indifference to truth

Some men, indeed, do not attack the truth wilfully, but work in heedless disregard of it. They act as though God had given us intellects for some purpose other than the pursuit and attainment of truth. This mistaken sort of action leads directly to that absurd proposition: one religion is just as good as another, for there is no distinction here between truth and falsehood. "This attitude," to quote Pope Leo again, "is directed to the destruction of all religions, but particularly the Catholic faith, which cannot be placed on a level with other religions without serious injustice, since it alone is true."[9] Moreover, to contend that there is nothing to choose between contradictories and among contraries can lead only to this fatal conclusion: a reluctance to accept any religion either in theory or practice.

How can God, who is truth, approve or tolerate the indifference, neglect, and sloth of those who attach no importance to matters on which our eternal salvation depends; who attach no importance to the pursuit and attainment of necessary truths, or to the offering of that proper worship which is owed to God alone?

So much toil and effort is expended today in mastering and advancing human knowledge that our age glories—and rightly—in the amazing progress it has made in the field of scientific research. But why do we not devote as much energy, ingenuity, and enthusiasm to the sure and safe attainment of that learning which concerns not this earthly, mortal life but the life which lies ahead of us in heaven? Our spirit will rest in peace and joy only when we

---

[9] Encyclical *"Humanum genus," Acta Leonis* 4 (1884) 53.

have reached that truth which is taught in the Gospels and which should be reduced to action in our lives. This is a joy which surpasses by far any pleasure which can come from the study of things human or from those marvelous inventions which we use today and are constantly praising to the skies.

II

Once we have attained the truth in its fullness, integrity, and purity, unity should pervade our minds, hearts, and actions. For there is only one cause of discord, disagreement, and dissension: ignorance of the truth, or what is worse, rejection of the truth once it has been sought and found. It may be that the truth is rejected because of the practical advantages which are expected to result from false views; it may be that it is rejected as a result of that perverted blindness which seeks easy and indulgent excuses for vice and immoral behavior.

Truth, peace, prosperity

All men, therefore, private citizens as well as government officials, must love the truth sincerely if they are to attain that peace and harmony on which depends all real prosperity, public and private.

We especially urge to peace and unity those who hold the reins of government. We who are placed above international controversy have the same affection for the people of all nations. We are led by no earthly advantages, no motives of political dominance, no desires for the things of this life. When We speak of this serious matter Our thoughts can be given a fair hearing and judged impartially by the citizens of every nation.

The brotherhood of man

God created men as brothers, not foes. He gave them the earth to be cultivated by their toil and labor. Each and every man is to enjoy the fruits of the earth and receive from it his sustenance and the necessities of life. The various nations are simply communities of men, that is, of brothers. They are to work in brotherly co-operation for the common prosperity of human society, not simply for their own particular goals.

A journey to immortal life

Besides this, our journey through this mortal life should not be regarded as an end in itself, entered upon merely for pleasure. This journey leads beyond the burial of our human flesh to immortal life, to a fatherland which will endure forever.

If this teaching, this consoling hope, were taken away from men, there would be no reason for living. Lusts, dissensions, and disputes would erupt from within us. There would be no reasonable check to restrain them. The olive branch of peace would not shine in our thoughts; the firebrands of war would blaze there. Our lot would be cast with beasts, who do not have the use of reason. Ours would be an even worse lot, for we do have the use of reason and by abusing it (which, unfortunately, often happens) we can sink into a state lower than that of beasts. Like Cain, we would commit a terrible crime and stain the earth with our brother's blood.

Before all else, then, we must turn our thoughts to sound principles if we wish, as we should, to guide our actions along the path of justice.

We are called brothers. We actually are brothers. We share a common destiny in this life and the next. Why, then, do we act as though we are foes and enemies? Why do we envy one another? Why do we stir up hatred? Why do we ready lethal weapons for use against our brothers?

There has already been enough warfare among men! Too many youths in the flower of life have shed their blood already! Legions of the dead, all fallen in battle, dwell within this earth of ours. Their stern voices urge us all to return at once to harmony, unity, and a just peace.

All men, then, should turn their attention away from those things that divide and separate us, and should consider how they may be joined in mutual and just regard for one another's opinions and possessions.

Unity among nations

Only if we desire peace, as we should, instead of war, and only if we all aspire sincerely to fraternal harmony among nations, shall it come to pass that public affairs and public questions are correctly understood and settled to the satisfaction of all. Then shall international conferences seek and reach decisions conducive to the longed-for unity of the whole human family. In the enjoyment of that unity, individual nations will see that their right to liberty is not subject to another's whims but is fully secure.

Those who oppress others and strip them of their due liberty can contribute nothing to the attainment of this unity.

The mind of Our predecessor Leo XIII squares perfectly with this view: "Nothing is better suited than Christian virtue, and especially justice, to check ambition, covetousness, and envy, which are the chief causes of war."[10]

But if men do not pursue this fraternal unity, based on the precepts of justice and nurtured by charity, then human affairs will remain in serious peril. This is why wise men grieve and lament; they are uncertain whether we are heading for sincere, true, and firm peace, or are rushing in complete blindness into the fires of a new and terrible war.

We say "in complete blindness," for if—God forbid!—another war should break out, nothing but devastating destruction and total ruin await both victor and vanquished. The monstrous weapons our age has devised will see to that!

We ask all men, but particularly rulers of nations, to weigh these considerations prudently and seriously in the presence of God our protector. May they enter with a will upon those paths which will lead to the unity that is so badly needed. This harmonious unity will be restored when hearts are at peace, when the rights of all are guaranteed, and when there has dawned that liberty due everywhere to individual citizens, to the State, and to the Church.

Unity in society

The harmonious unity which must be sought among peoples and nations also needs ever greater improvement among the various classes of individuals. Otherwise mutual antagonism and conflict can result, as we have already seen. And the next step brings rioting

[10] Letter *"Praeclara gratulationis,"* Acta Leonis 14 (1894) 210.

mobs, wanton destruction of property, and sometimes even bloodshed. Meanwhile public and private resources diminish and are stretched to the danger point.

On this point Pope Leo XIII made apt and appropriate comment: "God has commanded that there be differences of classes in the human community and that these classes, by friendly cooperation, work out a fair and mutual adjustment of their interests."[11] For it is quite clear that "as the symmetry of the human frame results from suitable arrangement of the various parts of the body, so in a body politic it is ordained by nature that . . . the classes should dwell in harmony and agreement, so as to maintain the balance of the body politic. Each needs the other: capital cannot do without labor, nor labor without capital. Their mutual agreement will result in the splendor of right order."[12]

Anyone, therefore, who ventures to deny that there are differences among social classes contradicts the very laws of nature. Indeed, whoever opposes peaceful and necessary cooperation among the social classes is attempting, beyond doubt, to disrupt and divide human society; he menaces and does serious injury to private interests and the public welfare.

As Our predecessor Pius XII wisely said, "In a nation that is worthy of the name, inequalities among the social classes present few or no obstacles to their union in common brotherhood. We refer, of course, to those inequalities which result not from human caprice but from the nature of things—inequalities having to do with intellectual and spiritual growth, with economic facts, with differences in individual circumstances, within, of course, the limits prescribed by justice and mutual charity."[13]

The various classes of society, as well as groups of individuals, may certainly protect their rights, provided this is done by legal means, not violence, and provided that they do no injustice to the inviolable rights of others. All men are brothers. Their differences, therefore, must be settled by friendly agreement, with brotherly love for one another.

---

[11] Letter *"Permoti Nos," Acta Leonis* 15 (1895) 259.
[12] Encyclical *"Rerum novarum," Acta Leonis* 11 (1891) 109.
[13] Christmas Message, 1944, *Discorsi e radiomessaggi di S.S. Pio XII*, v. 6, 239.

Improved relations among the classes

On this point it should be noted, and this gives rise to hope for a better future, that in some places in recent days relations among the classes have been less bitter and difficult. As Our predecessor, addressing the Catholics of Germany, expressed it: "The terrible disasters of the recent war plunged you into hardship, but produced at least one blessing among the many classes of your population: prejudices and exaggerated ambitions for personal advantage have subsided; the conflicting interests of the classes are nearer to reconciliation. Closer association with one another since the war has done this. Hard times borne together have taught you all a helpful, though bitter, lesson."[14]

As a matter of fact, the distances which separate the classes of society are shrinking. Since it is no longer a matter merely of "capital" and "labor," the number of classes has multiplied, and all of them are readily accessible to all men. Anyone who is diligent and capable has the opportunity to rise to higher levels of society. As for the condition of those who live by their daily toil, it is consoling to note that recently undertaken improvements in working conditions in factories and other places of employment have done more than give these workers a greater economic value; they have made their lives nobler and more dignified.

A long way to go

But there is still a long way to go. For there is still too much disparity in the possession of material goods, too much reason for hostility among various groups, because of opinions on the right to property (opinions sometimes unsound, sometimes not entirely just) held by those who desire unfair advantages and benefits for themselves.

There is also the threat of unemployment, a source of anxiety and unhappiness for many men. And this problem can entail even greater difficulties today, when men are being replaced by all sorts of advanced machines. Of this kind of unemployment, Our prede-

---

[14] Radio address to the 73rd Congress of German Catholics, *Discorsi e radiomessaggi di S.S. Pio XII*, v. 11, 189.

cessor of happy memory Pius XI uttered this complaint: "There are," he said, "honest workingmen almost beyond number who want only an opportunity to earn by honest means that daily bread for which, by divine command, we entreat our Father in heaven. But, instead, they are reduced to idleness and, along with their families, reach the very depths of privation. Their unhappiness touches Our heart; We are constrained to take pity and to repeat the merciful words that came from the heart of our Divine Master when He saw the multitude languishing in hunger: 'I have compassion on the crowd' (*Mark* 8, 2)."[15]

Indeed, if we long hopefully—as we should—for realization of this mutual union among the classes of society, then we must do all that we can to bring it about by public and private endeavor and cooperation in courageous undertakings, that all men, even those of the lowest classes, can obtain life's necessities by their toil and by the sweat of their brow, and that they can provide, in an honorable manner and with some degree of sureness, for their future and that of their families. In addition, contemporary progress has made many conveniences an integral part of everyday life; even the poorest citizens may not be excluded from the enjoyment of these advantages.

Moreover, We earnestly exhort all those who have responsible positions in the various areas of human endeavor and on whom the lot of the workers and sometimes their very lives depend, not only that they pay the just wages due to the labors of their workers or simply safeguard their rights so far as wages are concerned, but also that they really consider them as men, or rather, as brothers. And so they should see to it that in some suitable way their employees are able to share more and more in the fruits of their labor and come to regard themselves as partners in the entire enterprise.

We give counsel in order that the rights and duties of employers may more and more be harmonized and reconciled with the rights and duties of employees, and that the associations representing the interests of each "will not seem like armies ready to make or repel attacks in such wise as to make the enemy more resolute or

---

[15] *AAS* 23 (1931) 393-94.

to incite counterattack, or like a river which engulfs every obstacle in its course; but like a bridge which joins opposite shores."[16]

It is very important, however, that moral progress should not lag behind economic progress. Anything else would be unworthy of men, not to say of Christians. If the working classes have an abundance of material goods and enjoy all the benefits of civilization while losing or neglecting those higher goods which pertain to the immortal soul, what does it profit them?

Christian charity

But all will come out well if the social teaching of the Catholic Church is applied as it should be to the problem. Everyone then must "strive to preserve in himself and to arouse in others, be they of high or low degree, the queen and mistress of all the virtues, charity. The salvation we hope for is to be expected primarily from a great outpouring of charity. We refer to that Christian charity which is a principle synthesizing the entire Gospel. That charity is always ready to spend itself in the interest of others and is the surest remedy against worldly pride and immoderate self-esteem. St. Paul the Apostle described the characteristics of this virtue when he said: 'Charity is patient, is kind; is not self-seeking; bears with all things, endures all things' (*1 Cor.* 13, 4-7)."[17]

Unity within the family

We have called nations, their rulers, and all classes of society to harmonious unity. Now We sincerely urge families to achieve and strengthen this unity within themselves.

For unless peace, unity, and concord are present in domestic society, how can they exist in civil society?

This harmonious unity which should exist within the family circle rises from the holiness and indissolubility of Christian marriage. It is the basis of much of the order, progress, and prosperity of civil society.

Within the family, the father stands in God's place. He must

---

[16] "*Per un solido ordine sociale,*" *Discorsi e radiomessaggi di S.S. Pio XII*, v. 7, 350.
[17] Letter *"Inter graves,"* Acta Leonis 11 (1891) 143-44.

lead and guide the rest by his authority and the example of his good life.

The mother, on the other hand, should form her children firmly and graciously by the mildness of her manner and by her virtue.

Together the parents should carefully rear their children, God's most precious gift, to an upright and religious life.

Children must honor, obey, and love their parents. They must give their parents not only solace but also concrete assistance if it is needed.

The charity which burned in the household at Nazareth should be an inspiration for every family. All the Christian virtues should flourish in the family, unity should thrive, and the example of its virtuous living should shine brightly.

We earnestly pray God to prevent any damage to this valuable, beneficial, and necessary union. The Christian family is a sacred institution. If it totters, if the norms which the divine Redeemer laid down for it are rejected or ignored, then the very foundations of the state tremble; civil society stands betrayed and in peril. Everyone suffers.

III

Now We shall discuss a unity which is of particular concern to Us and is closely connected to the pastoral mission which God has entrusted to Us: the unity of the Church.

One fold and one shepherd

Everyone realizes, of course, that God our Redeemer founded this society which was to endure to the end of time, for as Christ said, "Behold, I am with you all days, even unto the consummation of the world."[18] For this intention He addressed ardent prayers to His Father: "That all may be one, even as thou, Father, in me and I in thee; that they also may be one in us."[19] Surely this prayer was heard and granted because of His reverent submission.[20] This is a comforting hope; it assures us that some day all the sheep who are

[18] *Matt.* 28, 20.   [19] *John* 17, 21.   [20] Cf. *Heb.* 5, 7.

not of this fold will want to return to it. Then, in the words of God our Saviour, "there shall be one fold and one shepherd."[21]

An ecumenical council

This fond hope compelled Us to make public Our intention to hold an ecumenical council. Bishops from every part of the world will gather there to discuss serious religious topics. They will consider, in particular, the growth of the Catholic faith, the restoration of sound morals among the Christian flock, and appropriate adaptation of Church discipline to the needs and conditions of our times.

This event will be a wonderful spectacle of truth, unity, and charity. For those who behold it but are not one with this Apostolic See, We hope that it will be a gentle invitation to seek and find that unity for which Jesus Christ prayed so ardently to His Father in heaven.

Movements toward union

We are already aware, to Our great joy, that many of the communities that are separated from the See of Blessed Peter have recently shown some inclination toward the Catholic faith and its teachings. They have manifested a high regard for this Apostolic See and an esteem which grows greater from day to day as devotion to truth overcomes earlier misconceptions.

We have taken note that almost all those who are adorned with the name of Christian even though separated from Us and from one another have sought to forge bonds of unity by means of many congresses and by establishing councils. This is evidence that they are moved by an intense desire for unity of some kind.

A mark of Christ's Church

When the divine Redeemer founded His Church, there is no doubt that He made firm unity its cornerstone and one of its essential attributes. Had He not done this—and it is absurd even to make

[21] *John* 10, 16.

such a suggestion—He would have founded a transient thing, which in time, at least, would destroy itself. For in just this way have nearly all philosophies risen from among the vagaries of human opinion: one after another, they come into being, they evolve, they are forgotten. But this clearly cannot be the history of a divine teaching authority founded by Jesus Christ, "the way, the truth, and the life."[22]

But this unity, venerable brethren and beloved sons, must be solid, firm, and sure, not transient, uncertain, or unstable.[23] Though there is no such unity in other Christian communities, all who look carefully can see that it is present in the Catholic Church.

Three unities

Indeed, the Catholic Church is set apart and distinguished by these three characteristics: unity of doctrine, unity of organization, unity of worship. This unity is so conspicuous that by it all men can find and recognize the Catholic Church.

It is the will of God, the Church's founder, that all the sheep should eventually gather into this one fold, under the guidance of one shepherd. All God's children are summoned to their father's only home, and its cornerstone is Peter. All men should work together like brothers to become part of this single kingdom of God; for the citizens of that kingdom are united in peace and harmony on earth that they might enjoy eternal happiness some day in heaven.

Unity of doctrine

The Catholic Church teaches the necessity of believing firmly and faithfully all that God has revealed. This revelation is contained in sacred scripture and in the oral and written tradition that has come down through the centuries from the apostolic age and finds expression in the ordinances and definitions of the popes and legitimate ecumenical councils.

Whenever a man has wandered from his path, the Church has

---
[22] *John* 14, 6.
[23] Cf. the encyclical of Pope Pius XI fostering true religious unity, *"Mortalium animos," AAS* 20 (1928) 5 ff.

never failed to use her maternal authority to call him again and again to the right road. She knows well that there is no other truth than the one truth she treasures; that there can be no "truths" in contradiction of it. Thus she repeats and bears witness to the words of the Apostle: "For we can do nothing against the truth, but only for the truth."[24]

Religious controversy

The Catholic Church, of course, leaves many questions open to the discussion of theologians. She does this to the extent that matters are not absolutely certain. Far from jeopardizing the Church's unity, controversies, as a noted English author, John Henry Cardinal Newman, has remarked, can actually pave the way for its attainment. For discussion can lead to fuller and deeper understanding of religious truths; when one idea strikes against another, there may be a spark.[25]

But that common saying, expressed in various ways and attributed to various authors, must be recalled with approval: in essentials, unity; in doubtful matters, liberty; in all things, charity.

Unity in organization

That there is unity in the administration of the Catholic Church is evident. For as the faithful are subject to their priests, so are priests to their bishops, whom "the Holy Spirit has placed . . . to rule the Church of God."[26] So, too, every bishop is subject to the Roman pontiff, the successor of Saint Peter, whom Christ called a rock and made the foundation of His Church.[27] It was to Peter that Christ gave in a special way the power to bind and loose on earth,[28] to strengthen his brethren,[29] to feed the entire flock.[30]

Unity of worship

As for unity of worship, the Catholic Church has had seven sacraments, neither more nor less, from her beginning right down to

---
[24] *2 Cor.* 13, 8.
[25] Cf. J. H. Newman, *Difficulties of Anglicans*, v. 1, 261 ff.
[26] *Acts* 20, 28.   [27] Cf. *Matt.* 16, 18.   [28] Cf. *ibid.* 16, 19.
[29] Cf. *Luke* 22, 32.   [30] Cf. *John* 21, 15-17.

the present day. Jesus Christ left her these sacraments as a sacred legacy, and she has never ceased to administer them throughout the Catholic world and thus to feed and foster the supernatural life of the faithful.

All this is common knowledge, and it is also common knowledge that only one sacrifice is offered in the Church. In this Eucharistic sacrifice Christ Himself, our Salvation and our Redeemer, immolates Himself each day for all of us and mercifully pours out on us the countless riches of His grace. No blood is shed, but the sacrifice is real, just as real as when Christ hung from a cross on Calvary.

And so Saint Cyprian had good reason to remark: "It would be impossible to set up another altar or to create a new priesthood over and above this one altar and this one priesthood."[31]

Obviously, of course, this fact does not prevent the presence in the Catholic Church of a variety of approved rites, which simply enhance her beauty. Like a king's daughter, the Church wears robes of rich embroidery.[32]

All men are to have part in this true unity; and so, when a Catholic priest offers the Eucharistic Sacrifice, he presents our merciful God with a spotless victim and prays to Him especially "for Thy holy Catholic Church, that it may please Thee to grant her peace, to protect, unite, and govern her throughout the world, together with Thy servant our Pope, and all who truly believe and profess the Catholic and Apostolic faith."[33]

An invitation to union

We address Ourselves now to all of you who are separated from this Apostolic See. May this wonderful spectacle of unity, by which the Catholic Church is set apart and distinguished, as well as the prayers and entreaties with which she begs God for unity, stir your hearts and awaken you to what is really in your best interest.

May We, in fond anticipation, address you as sons and brethren? May We hope with a father's love for your return?

Once when a terrible schism was rending the seamless garment of

---

[31] Letter 43, 5: *Corp. Vind.* III, 2, 594; cf. letter 40: Migne, *PL* 4, 345.
[32] Cf. *Ps.* 44, 15.   [33] Canon of the Mass.

the Church, Bishop Theophilus of Alexandria addressed his sons and brethren with words of pastoral zeal. We take pleasure in addressing these same words to you: "Dearly beloved, we have all been invited to heaven. Let each, then, according to his abilities imitate Jesus, our model and the author of our salvation.

"Let us embrace that humility of soul which elevates us to great heights, that charity which unites us with God; let us have a genuine faith in revealed mysteries.

"Avoid division, shun discord, . . . encourage charity toward one another. Heed the words of Christ: 'By this will all men know that you are my disciples, if you have love for one another.' "[34]

When We fondly call you to the unity of the Church, please observe that We are not inviting you to a strange home, but to your own, to the abode of your forefathers. Permit Us, then, to long for you all "in the heart of Christ Jesus,"[35] and to exhort you all to be mindful of your forefathers who "preached God's word to you; contemplate the happy issue of the life they lived, and imitate their faith."[36]

There is in paradise a glorious legion of saints who have passed to heaven from your people. By the example of their lives they seem to summon you to union with this Apostolic See with which your Christian community was beneficially united for so many centuries. You are summoned especially by those saints who in their writings perpetuated and explained with admirable accuracy the teachings of Jesus Christ.

We address, then, as brethren all who are separated from Us, using the words of Saint Augustine: "Whether they wish it or not, they are our brethren. They cease to be our brethren only when they stop saying 'Our Father.' "[37]

"Let us love God our Lord; let us love His Church. Let us love Him as our father and her as our mother. Him as our master and her as His handmaid. For we are the children of His handmaid. This marriage is based on a deep love. No one can offend one of them and be a friend of the other. . . . What difference does it make that you have not offended your father, if he punishes offenses

---

[34] Cf. *Hom. in mysticam caenam: PG* 77, 1027.   [35] *Phil.* 1, 8.   [36] *Heb.* 13, 7.
[37] Saint Augustine, *In Ps.* 32, *Enarr.* II, 29: Migne, *PL* 36, 299.

against your mother? . . . Therefore, dearly beloved, be all of one mind and remain true to God your father and your mother the Church."[38]

A crusade of prayer

We address suppliant prayers to our gracious God, the giver of heavenly light and of all good things, that He safeguard the unity of the Church and extend the fold and kingdom of Christ. We urge all Our brethren in Christ and Our beloved sons to pray fervently for the same intentions. The outcome of the approaching ecumenical council will depend more on a crusade of fervent prayer than on human effort and diligent application. And so with loving heart We also invite to this crusade all who are not of this fold but reverence and worship God and strive in good faith to obey His commands.

May the divine plea of Christ further and fulfill this hope and these prayers of Ours: "Holy Father, keep in thy name those whom thou hast given me, that they may be one even as we are. . . . Sanctify them in the truth. Thy word is truth. . . . Yet not for these only do I pray, but for those also who through their word are to believe in me . . . that they may be perfected in unity. . . ."[39]

We repeat this prayer, as does the whole Catholic world in union with Us. We are spurred by a burning love for all men, but also by that interior humility which the gospel teaches. For We know the lowliness of him whom God raised to the dignity of the sovereign pontificate, not because of Our merits, but according to His mysterious designs. Wherefore, to all Our brethren and sons who are separated from the Chair of Blessed Peter, We say again: "I am . . . Joseph, your brother."[40] Come, "make room for us."[41] We want nothing else, desire nothing else, pray God for nothing else but your salvation, your eternal happiness.

The peace of Christ

Come! This long-desired unity, fostered and fed by brotherly love, will beget a great peace. This is the peace "which surpasses all

---
[38] Saint Augustine, *In Ps.* 82, *Enarr.* II, 14: Migne, *PL* 37, 1140.
[39] *John* 17: 11, 17, 20, 21, 23.   [40] *Gen.* 45, 4.   [41] *2 Cor.* 7, 2.

understanding,"[42] since its birthplace is in heaven. It is the same peace which Christ promised to men of good will through the song of the angels who hovered over His crib;[43] it is the peace He imparted after instituting the Eucharistic Sacrament and Sacrifice: "Peace I leave with you, my peace I give to you; not as the world gives do I give to you."[44]

Peace and joy! Yes, joy—because those who are really and effectively joined to the Mystical Body of Christ, which is the Catholic Church, share in that life which flows from the divine Head into each part of the Body. Through that life, those who faithfully obey all the precepts and commands of our Redeemer can enjoy even in this mortal life that happiness which is a foretaste and pledge of heaven's eternal happiness.

And yet, as long as we are journeying in exile over this earth, our peace and happiness will be imperfect. For such peace is not completely untroubled and serene; it is active, not calm and motionless. In short, this is a peace that is ever at war. It wars with every sort of error, including that which falsely wears the face of truth; it struggles against the enticements of vice, against those enemies of the soul, of whatever description, who can weaken, blemish, or destroy our innocence or Catholic faith. This peace combats hatred, fraud, and discord, which can impair and cripple our faith.

This is why our divine Redeemer left *His* peace with us, gave *His* peace to us.

The peace, then, which we must seek, which we must strive to achieve with all the means at our disposal, must—as We have said—make no concessions to error, must compromise in no way with proponents of falsehood; it must make no concessions to vice; it must discourage all discord. Those who adhere to this peace must be ready to renounce their own interests and advantages for the sake of truth and justice, according to the words: "Seek first the kingdom of God and his justice."[45]

We pray earnestly to the Blessed Virgin Mary, to whose Immaculate Heart Our predecessor Pius XII consecrated the entire human race. May she seek and obtain from God this harmonious unity, this true, active, and militant peace, on behalf of Our children in

---

[42] *Phil.* 4, 7.   [43] Cf. *Luke* 2, 14.   [44] *John* 14, 27.   [45] *Matt.* 6, 33.

Christ and all those who, though separated from Us, cannot help loving truth, unity, and peace.

IV

Now We wish to address a few fatherly words specifically to each of the ranks within the Catholic Church.

Bishops

First of all, "our heart is wide open to you,"[46] venerable brethren in the episcopacy of both the Eastern and Western Church. As guides with Us of the Christian people, you have borne the burden of the day's heat.[47] We know your diligence. We know the apostolic zeal with which, in your respective dioceses, you strive to advance, strengthen, and spread the kingdom of God.

And We also know your hardships, your sorrows. You grieve that so many of your children are lost, pathetically duped by falsehood; you are confronted by a lack of material means, which sometimes makes impossible a wider spread of Catholicism in your dioceses; and the number of priests at your disposal is in many places inadequate to the mounting demands for their services.

But trust in Him from whom comes "every good gift and every perfect gift."[48] Have confidence in Jesus Christ; pray without ceasing to Him, without whom "you can do nothing."[49] By His grace you may each repeat the words of the Apostle, "I can do all things in Him who strengthens me."[50]

"But may . . . God supply your every need according to his riches in glory in Christ Jesus,"[51] that you may reap rich harvests and gather rich crops from the fields you have cultivated by your toil and your sweat.

The clergy

We also address Ourself with a father's love to the members of the diocesan and religious clergy: those who are your close assist-

[46] *2 Cor.* 6, 11.   [47] Cf. *Matt.* 20, 12.   [48] *James* 1, 17.
[49] *John* 15, 5.   [50] *Phil.* 4, 13.   [51] *Ibid.*, 4, 19.

ants in your Curia, venerable brethren; those who toil in seminaries at a very important work, the formation and education of youths called to the Lord's service; those, finally, who are parish priests in crowded cities, in towns, or in distant and lonely outposts and whose mission today is very difficult, very demanding, and of the utmost importance.

We are sure it is unnecessary for us to mention it, but priests should be careful to be always obedient and submissive to their bishop. As Saint Ignatius of Antioch said: "Since you are subject to your bishop as to Jesus Christ, . . . whatever you do must be done in union with your bishop."[52] "All who belong to God and Jesus Christ are in union with their bishop."[53]

Priests should also be mindful that they are more than public dignitaries; they are sacred ministers. And so, as they work to bring God's light to the minds of men, to re-direct the wills of sinners with heaven's help and with brotherly love, as they work to advance and spread the peace-bringing kingdom of Jesus Christ, they must never think that there is a fixed limit to their labors, or to the outlay of their time and belongings, their expenditures, or of their personal inconvenience. They must seek God's grace in humble and ceaseless prayer, and they must rely on this grace far more than on their own toil and labor.

Religious men

We also extend Our paternal best wishes to Our sons in religious orders and congregations. These men have embraced the various states of evangelical perfection and live according to the particular rules of their institutes in obedience to their superiors. We urge them to strive tirelessly and with all their strength for the achievement of the goals their founders have set forth in those rules. They should, in particular, be fervent in prayer and assiduous in works of penance; they should undertake the sound formation and education of the young and assist, so far as they can, those who are beset in any way by want or distress.

---

[52] Funk, *Patres Apostolici*, I, 243-245; cf. Migne, *PG* 5, 675.
[53] *Ibid.* I, 267; cf. Migne, *PG* 5, 699.

We know, of course, that due to various conditions many of these beloved sons of Ours are frequently called upon to undertake the pastoral care of the faithful; and this has redounded to the benefit of the Christian name and Christian virtue. Although We are sure they need no such admonition, We again exhort these religious to meet the present-day needs of the people spontaneously and enthusiastically, cooperating zealously and energetically with the efforts of the other clergy.

Missionaries

And now Our thoughts turn to those religious who have left the homes of their ancestors and their beloved countries and have gone to foreign lands where they experience serious inconveniences and overcome all sorts of difficulties. Today, in distant fields, they toil to impart the truth of the gospel and Christian virtue to the people who dwell there, that "the word of the Lord may run and be glorified" among them.[54]

A tremendous task is entrusted to these missionaries. To fulfill it and expand its scope, all Christians must cooperate by prayer and such contributions as their means permit. There is, perhaps, no undertaking that pleases God more than this one; it is an integral part of the duty all men have to spread the Kingdom of God.

Ambassadors of Christ

These heralds of the Gospel dedicate and consecrate their lives to God in order that the light of Jesus Christ may enlighten every man who comes into the world,[55] that the grace of God may enter and support every soul, and that all men may be aroused to a life that is good, honorable, and Christian. These men seek not their own interests, but those of Jesus Christ.[56] They have answered with generosity the call of their divine Redeemer and can apply to themselves the words of the Apostle of the Gentiles: "On behalf of Christ . . . we are acting as ambassadors,"[57] and "though we walk in the flesh, we do not make war according to the flesh."[58] They regard as

[54] *2 Thess.* 3, 1.   [55] Cf. *John* 1, 9.   [56] Cf. *Phil.* 2, 21.   [57] *2 Cor.* 5, 20.
[58] *2 Cor.* 10, 3.

a second fatherland and love with an active charity the land to which they have come to bring the light of the Gospel's truth. Although they will always have deep affection for their native land and their diocese or religious institute, they regard it as clear and certain that the good of the universal Church must be preferred and they must give it their first and wholehearted service.

We wish, therefore, to say that there is a special place in Our heart for these beloved sons, and for all who generously assist them in their fields of labor by teaching catechism or in other ways. Every day We offer humble prayers to God for them and their endeavors. We wish to confirm with Our authority, and with like affection, all that Our predecessors—especially Pius XI[59] and Pius XII[60]—have seen fit to set down on this subject in their encyclical letters.

Religious women

We must also write of those holy virgins who by their vows have consecrated themselves to God that they might serve Him alone and unite themselves closely with their divine Spouse in mystic nuptials.

They may lead hidden lives in cloistered convents or dedicate themselves to the works of the apostolate. In either case, they can pursue their salvation the more easily and happily and also be of pre-eminent assistance in Christian countries and in those lands where the light of the Gospel has not yet shone.

How much these holy virgins accomplish! They render extensive and distinguished service which no one else could perform with the same blend of virginal and maternal concern! They do this not in one, but in many fields of endeavor. They attend to the sound formation and education of the young. They teach religion to boys and girls in parochial schools. They tend the sick in hospitals and lead their thoughts to heavenly things. They care for patients in homes for the aged with cheerful and merciful charity and move them in a wonderful and gentle way to a desire for eternal life. In homes for orphans, and for children born out of wedlock they stand

[59] Encyclical *"Rerum Ecclesiae," AAS* 18 (1926) 65 ff.
[60] Encyclical *"Evangelii praecones," AAS* 43 (1951) 497; Encyclical *"Fidei donum," AAS* 49 (1957) 225 ff. *TPS,* IV, 295-312.

in the place of a mother and cherish with a mother's love children who have lost their parents or been abandoned. They care for them, nurse them, and hold them dear.

These holy virgins have rendered outstanding services not only to the Catholic Church, to Christian education, to what are called the works of mercy, but to civil society as well. At the same time, they are winning for themselves that imperishable reward which lies ahead in heaven.

Catholic Action

But as you well know, venerable brethren and beloved sons, the problems that beset men today—and affect Christianity also—are so vast and varied that priests, religious men, and holy virgins seem now unequal to the task of providing the complete remedy. Priests, religious men, and virgins consecrated to God cannot make contact with every class of person. All paths are not open to them. Many men ignore or avoid them; some, alas, even despise and abhor them.

This is a serious matter that has occasioned much sorrow and unhappiness and induced Our predecessors to summon the laity to the ranks of a peaceful militia, Catholic Action. It was their wise intention that the laity should cooperate in the apostolate of the hierarchy. In this way, what the hierarchy could not do under present circumstances, these Catholic men and women would accomplish in a spirit of generosity. They would work, of course, in union with their bishops and in constant obedience to them.

Over the years the bishops and priests of lands that are still mission territories have been assisted by laymen of every rank and condition. It gives Us great comfort to recall the projects they have undertaken and carried forward with swift and energetic resolution in order that all men might recognize the truth of Christianity and feel the force and attraction of Christian virtue.

The needs of our age

But vast areas still await their efforts. Great numbers of men have not had the benefit of their shining example and apostolic labor. We think this matter is so serious and important that We intend at some other time to discuss it at greater length.

Meanwhile, We are confident that all who serve in the ranks of Catholic Action, or in the many pious associations which flourish in the Church, will pursue this apostolate with very great diligence. The more overwhelming the needs of our age, the greater should be their efforts, concern, industry, and zeal.

Let all be of one mind, since—as all know well—in unity there is greater strength. When it is a matter of the cause of the Catholic Church they must be ready to sacrifice personal whims, for nothing is of more value and importance. This should be their attitude, not only in doctrinal matters but also in matters of ecclesiastical and Christian discipline, to which all must submit.

The members of Catholic Action must marshal their ranks; they must align themselves beside their bishops and be ready to obey every command. They must advance to ever greater achievements. They must shirk no hardship, shun no inconvenience, that the cause of the Church may be triumphant.

But they will accomplish all this as they should only if each of them pays particular attention to his personal formation in Christian wisdom and virtue. They are certainly aware of this fact. For it is obvious that they can impart to others only what, with the help of God's grace, they have won for themselves.

These last remarks are meant particularly for the young. They are easily aroused to eager enthusiasm for the highest ideals, but it is most important that they learn prudence, self-restraint, and obedience to authority. We wish to express Our deep gratitude and love for these beloved children of Ours. In them the Church places her hope for the future. We have complete confidence in their industrious and effective service.

The sick and suffering

And now We hear voices that fill Us with sorrow. We hear those who are sick in mind or body, afflicted by terrible suffering. We hear those who are so beset by economic hardship that they have no home fit for human habitation and cannot by any effort of their own obtain the necessities of life for themselves or their families. Their cries touch Our heart and move Us to the depths of Our being.

We wish first to give the sick, the infirm, and the aged that comfort which comes from heaven. They should remember that we have here no permanent city, but must seek for the city that is to come.[61] They should recall that the sufferings of this life serve to purify the soul; they elevate and ennoble us and can win us eternal joy in heaven. Our divine Redeemer bore the yoke of the cross to wash away the stains of our sins; to this end He endured abuse, torture, and agonizing pain, all by His free choice. Like Christ, we are all called to light, by way of the cross, for He has told us: "If anyone wishes to come after me, let him deny himself, and take up his cross daily, and follow me,"[62] and he shall have a treasure unfailing in heaven.[63]

We have another recommendation also, and We are sure that it will be warmly received. We wish these sufferings of mind and body not only to be steps in the sufferer's ascent to his eternal fatherland, but also to contribute greatly to the expiation of others, to the return to the Church of those who unfortunately are separated from her, and to the long-desired triumph of Christianity.

Social justice

Those citizens of straitened fortune who are dissatisfied with their very difficult lot in life may be sure that We deeply regret their condition. With respect to social matters: it is Our paternal desire that relations among the various classes come under the guidance, control, and direction of the Christian virtue of justice. We are especially concerned here because the Church's enemies can easily take advantage of any unjust treatment of the lower classes to draw them to their side by false promises and deceptive lies.

We ask these dear children of Ours to realize that the Church is not hostile to them or their rights. On the contrary, she cares for them as would a loving mother. She preaches and inculcates a social doctrine and social norms which would eliminate every sort of

---

[61] Cf. *Heb.* 13, 14.   [62] *Luke* 9, 23.   [63] Cf. *Luke* 12, 33.

injustice and produce a better and more equitable distribution of goods, if they were put into practice as they should be.⁶⁴ At the same time, she encourages friendly cooperation and mutual assistance among the various classes, so that all men may become in name and in fact not only free citizens of the same society but also brothers within the same family.

Anyone who considers without bias the opportunities and advantages which have recently come to the working classes must admit that they are in great part the result of persistent and effective social measures taken by Catholics in accord with the wise directives and repeated exhortations of Our predecessors. The social teachings of Christianity, then, contain sure and sound principles which will make very adequate provision for the rights of the lower classes if those who endeavor to defend these rights only put those principles into practice.

False teachings

There is never any need, therefore, to turn to proponents of doctrines condemned by the Church; for they only draw men on with false promises and when they obtain control of the state, try boldly and unscrupulously to deprive men of their supreme spiritual goods —the Christian commandments, Christian hope, and Christian faith. Those who adhere to the doctrines these men propose, minimize or eliminate all that our present age and our modern civilization hold dearest: true liberty and the authentic dignity of the human person. Thus they attempt to destroy the bases of Christianity and civilization.

All, therefore, who wish to remain Christians must be aware of their serious obligation to avoid those false principles, which Our predecessors—especially Popes Pius XI and Pius XII—have condemned in the past, and which We condemn once again.

We know that many of Our children who live in want or great misfortune often protest that the social teachings of Christianity have not yet been fully put into practice. Private citizens, and more particularly public officials, must take steps to see that the Christian

---
⁶⁴ Cf. the encyclical *"Quadragesimo anno," AAS* 23 (1931) 196-8.

social doctrine which Our predecessors have often clearly and wisely taught and decreed, and which We have confirmed, is really given full effect.[65] Although this will have to be done gradually, no time should be wasted.

Emigrants and exiles

We are also and equally concerned for the lot of those who are forced to leave their native lands because they cannot earn a living there or because of intolerable conditions and religious persecution. They must undergo many inconveniences and hardships when they go from their native land into foreign countries. Oftentimes, in crowded cities and amid the noise of factories, they must lead a life very different from the one they once knew.

At times, and this is more serious, they find themselves in an environment that is hostile and hurtful to Christian virtue. In such surroundings many are led into serious danger, and step by step turn away from the wholesome way of life and the religious practices which they learned from their elders. Since husbands are often separated from their wives and parents from their children, the bonds and ties that hold them together are stretched thin and serious injury is done to the family.

We give Our paternal approval to the competent and effective work of those priests who have become voluntary emigrants out of love for Jesus Christ and in obedience to the instructions and wishes of this Apostolic See. These priests have spared no effort to ascertain and serve, so far as they can, the social and spiritual needs of their flocks. Thus, wherever the emigrant may journey, he sees the Church's love for him and discovers that this love is even more evident and more effective when his need for care and aid is greatest.

We have also observed with great pleasure the praiseworthy steps various nations have taken with regard to this important matter. A number of countries have recently adopted a common plan and program to bring this critical problem to a swift and happy conclusion. We trust that these measures will make it possible for

---

[65] Cf. the allocution of Pius XII to members of Italian Christian trade unions, March 11, 1945: *AAS* 37 (1945) 71-2.

emigrants to enter those lands in greater numbers and with greater ease, but We are even more concerned that they provide for the happy reunion of parents and children as a family unit. Once these sound steps are taken, it will certainly be possible to make adequate provision for the needs of the emigrants, in religion, in morals, and in economic matters; and this, in turn, will benefit the countries which receive them.

The Church persecuted

We have exhorted all Our children in Christ to avoid the deadly errors which threaten to destroy religion and even human society itself. In writing these words Our thoughts have turned to the bishops, priests, and laymen who have been driven into exile or held under restraint or in prison because they have refused to abandon the work entrusted to them as bishops and priests and to forsake their Catholic faith.

We do not want to offend anyone. On the contrary, We are ready to forgive all freely and to beg this forgiveness of God.

But We are conscious of Our sacred duty to do all that We can to defend the rights of Our sons and brethren. Time and time again, therefore, We have asked that all be granted the lawful freedom to which all, including God's Church, are entitled. Those who support truth, justice, and the real interests of men and nations do not refuse liberty, do not extinguish it, do not suppress it. There is no need for them to act this way. The just prosperity of their citizens can be achieved without violence and without oppressing minds and hearts.

A self-evident truth

There is one truth especially which We think is self-evident: when the sacred rights of God and religion are ignored or infringed upon, the foundations of human society will sooner or later crumble and give way. Our predecessor of immortal memory Leo XIII expressed this truth well: "It follows . . . that law becomes ineffective and all authority is weakened once the sovereign and eternal rule of God, who commands and forbids, is rejected."[66] Cicero expressed

[66] Letter *"Exeunte iam anno,"* Acta Leonis 8 (1888) 398.

the same idea when he wrote, "You, the priests, are protecting Rome with religion more effectively than she is protected with walls."[67]

As We reflect on these truths, We embrace with deep sorrow each and every one of the faithful who is impeded and restricted in the practice of his religion. They indeed often "suffer persecution for justice' sake,"[68] and for the sake of the Kingdom of God. We share their sorrows, their hardships, their anxieties. We pray and beseech heaven to grant at length the dawn of a happier day. We earnestly desire all Our brethren in Christ and Our children throughout the world to join Us in this prayer. For thus a chorus of holy entreaties will arise from every nation to our merciful God and win a richer shower of graces for these unfortunate members of the Mystical Body of Christ.

A renewal of Christian life

But We ask Our beloved children for more than prayers; We wish to see a renewal of Christian life. This, far more than prayer, will win God's mercy for ourselves and our brethren.

We wish to repeat to you again the sublime and beautiful words of the Apostle of the Gentiles, "Whatever things are true, whatever honorable, whatever just, whatever of good repute, if there be any virtue, if there be anything worthy of praise, think upon these things."[69] "Put on the Lord Jesus Christ."[70] That is to say, "Put on therefore, as God's chosen ones, holy and beloved, a heart of mercy, kindness, humility, meekness, patience. . . . But above all these things have charity, which is the bond of perfection. And may the peace of Christ reign in your hearts; unto that peace, indeed, you were called in one body."[71]

If anyone is so unfortunate as to wander far from his divine Redeemer in sin and iniquity, let him return to Him who is "the way, and the truth, and the life."[72] If anyone is lukewarm, slothful, remiss, or neglectful in the practice of his religion, let him arouse his faith and, by the grace of God, nurture, rekindle, and strengthen

[67] *De Natura Deorum* III, 40. [68] *Matt.* 5, 10. [69] *Phil.* 4, 8.
[70] *Rom.* 13, 14. [71] *Col.* 3, 12-15. [72] *John* 14, 6.

his virtue. He who "is just, let him be just still, and he who is holy, let him be hallowed still."[73] This is Our earnest plea.

There are many today who need our counsel, good example, and assistance, for their lot in life is unhappy and miserable. Do you all, therefore, within the limits of your abilities and resources, perform the works of mercy, for they are most pleasing to God.

The Christian

If each of you strives to accomplish all this that We have recommended, there will shine forth anew in the Church that which was expressed so wonderfully about Christians in the *Epistle to Diognetus*: "They are in the flesh, but do not live by the flesh. They dwell on earth, but they are citizens of heaven. They obey valid laws, and even go beyond the demands of law in the conduct of their lives. . . . They are not understood, and yet they are condemned; they are put to death, and yet their life is quickened. They are poor, and yet they make many wealthy. They lack all things, and yet they have all in abundance. They are dishonored, and yet in the midst of dishonor they find honor. Their good name is railed at, and yet is presented as evidence of their justice. They receive rebukes and give blessings in return. They suffer abuse and offer praise. When they conduct themselves like honest men, they are punished like criminals. While they are being punished, they rejoice as though they are being rewarded. . . . To express the matter simply: what the soul is to the body, Christians are to the world."[74]

Many of these sublime words apply in a special way to those who are members of the "Church of Silence," for whom we are all especially bound to pray to God, as We recently urged in Our addresses to the faithful in Saint Peter's Basilica on Pentecost Sunday[75] and on the feast of the Sacred Heart of Jesus.[76]

We anticipate that all of you will achieve this renewal of the Christian life, this holiness and virtue—not only you who remain

---
[73] *Apoc.* 22, 11.
[74] Funk, *Patres Apostolici*, I, 399-401; cf. Migne, *PG* 2, 1174-75.
[75] Cf. *AAS* 51 (1959) 420 ff.; *L'Osservatore Romano*, May 18-19, 1959. *TPS*, V, 403-06.
[76] *L'Osservatore Romano*, June 7, 1959.

steadfastly in the unity of the Church, but all you who with love of truth and with a sincere goodwill are striving to attain it.

With all the love of a father, We impart the Apostolic Blessing to each and every one of you, venerable brethren and beloved sons. May it be the occasion and forerunner of heaven's blessings.

Written in Rome, at Saint Peter's, on the 29th day of June, the feast of the Apostles Peter and Paul, in the year 1959, the first of Our Pontificate.

JOHN PP. XXIII

Devotion to the Rosary

The Encyclical "Grata Recordatio" of Pope John XXIII to Catholic Bishops

- *His own love of the rosary*
- *Missionaries and the future of the Church*
- *An appeal to world leaders*
- *Hope for the end of false philosophies*

AMONG THE pleasant recollections of Our younger days are the encyclicals which Pope Leo XIII used to write to the whole Catholic world as the month of October drew near, in order to urge the faithful to devout recitation of Mary's rosary during that month in particular.[1]

These encyclicals had varied contents, but they were all very wise, vibrant with fresh inspiration, and directly relevant to the practice of the Christian life. In strong and persuasive terms they exhorted Catholics to pray to God in a spirit of faith through the intercession of Mary, His Virgin Mother, by reciting the holy rosary. For the rosary is a very commendable form of prayer and meditation. In saying it we weave a mystic garland of *Ave Maria*'s, *Pater Noster*'s, and *Gloria Patri*'s. And as we recite these vocal prayers, we meditate upon the principal mysteries of our religion;

---

[1] Cf. the following encyclical letters in *Acta Leonis XIII*, in the volumes indicated: "*Supremi Apostolatus*," III, 280 ff.; "*Superiore anno*," IV, 123 ff.; "*Quamquam pluries*," IX, 175 ff.; "*Octobri mense*," XI, 299 ff.; "*Magnae Dei Matris*," XII, 221 ff.; "*Laetitiae sanctae*," XIII, 283 ff.; "*Iucunda semper*," XIV, 305 ff.; "*Adiutricem populi*," XV, 300 ff.; "*Fidentem piumque*," XVI, 278 ff.; "*Augustissimae Virginis*," XVII, 285 ff.; "*Diuturni temporis*," XVIII, 153 ff.

the Incarnation of Jesus Christ and the Redemption of the human race are proposed, one event after another, for our consideration.

Pope John's devotion to the rosary

These pleasant memories of Our younger days have not faded or vanished as the years of Our life have passed. On the contrary, We want to declare in complete frankness and simplicity that the years have made Mary's rosary all the dearer to Us. We never fail to recite it each day in its entirety and We intend to recite it with particular devotion during the coming month.

During Our first year as pope—a year which is almost over—We have several times had occasion to urge the clergy and laity to public and private prayer. But today We make this same request with even greater emphasis and earnestness, for reasons which this encyclical will set out very briefly.

I

This coming October will mark the end of the first year since the saintly departure of Our predecessor Pius XII from this mortal life in which he had distinguished himself by so many glorious achievements.

Twenty days after his death, We, though all unworthy, were raised to the sovereign pontificate in accord with God's mysterious designs.

An unbroken succession

One pope bequeathed, as it were, to another pope, as a sacred legacy, the care of the whole Christian flock; with the same pastoral concern each of them declared his paternal love for all mankind.

These two events—the one full of sorrow, the other full of joy—attest clearly to the world that while all things human gradually decline and decay, the Roman pontificate withstands the rush of centuries, even though the visible heads of the Church must, one after another, leave this mortal exile as they complete the span of days which God in His providence has set for them.

But all Christians should turn their thoughts to the late Pope Pius XII and to his lowly successor, in whom blessed Peter continues his eternal mission as supreme pastor, and they should address this prayer to God: "To preserve in holy religion the pope, and all clerics in holy orders, we beg Thee hear us."[2]

A call to the rosary

And now it is a pleasure also to recall that this same predecessor of Ours urged all the faithful to pious recitation of the rosary during October in the encyclical *Ingruentium malorum*.[3] We would like to repeat one admonition[4] from that encyclical: "Turn in spirit with ever greater confidence to the Virgin Mother of God, the constant refuge of Christians in adversity, since she 'has been made a source of salvation for the human race.'"[5]

II

On October 11, 1959, We shall have the great pleasure of presenting mission crucifixes to a large group of Catholic missionaries who are about to leave their beloved homes and undertake the heavy responsibility of bringing the light of Christianity to distant people.[6] On the same day, in the afternoon, We are scheduled to visit the North American College on the Janiculum and there joyously celebrate with its superiors, faculty, and seminarians the completion of that college's first century.[7]

Although these two celebrations fall only by coincidence on the same day, they have the same meaning and importance: in all that she does the Catholic Church is motivated by heaven's inspiration and drawn on by the principles and precepts of eternal truth; all of her children contribute with a selfless and dynamic will to mutual respect, the fraternal union of mankind, and solid peace.

---

[2] Litany of the Saints.
[3] On September 15, 1951: *AAS* 43 (1951) 577 ff.
[4] *Ibid.*, 578-579.
[5] St. Irenaeus, *Adv. haer.* III, 22: Migne, *PG* VII, 959.
[6] A précis of the talk given on this occasion appears in *TPS* VI, 46.
[7] A translation of the talk given on this occasion appears in *TPS* VI, 37-42.

Hope for the future

These young men present such a wonderful spectacle that We must be optimistic for the future. They have overcome many obstacles and inconveniences and given themselves to God that other men might gain Christ,[8] whether in foreign lands as yet untouched by the light of truth or in those immense, noisy, and busy cities in which the pace of daily activity, rapid as a whirlwind, sometimes makes souls wither and become content with earthly goods. From the lips of their elders, who have labored long in the same cause, comes the ardent prayer of the Prince of the Apostles: "Grant to thy servants to speak thy word with all boldness."[9]

We trust that the apostolic labors of these young men will be commended to the Virgin Mary in your devout prayers through the month of October.

III

There is another matter also which compels Us to ask that the Sacred College of Cardinals, you, venerable brethren, all priests and nuns, the sick and disabled, our innocent children, and all Christians address earnest and suppliant prayers to Jesus Christ and His most loving Mother. It is this: that those who, in great measure, hold the future of nations in their hands consider attentively the dangerous pass to which our age has come. Be these nations large or small, their legitimate rights and their inheritance of spiritual riches are sacred and must be safeguarded.

A prayer for rulers

Therefore We pray God that their rulers may carefully weigh and consider the causes of dissension and endeavor in good faith to remove them. They must, above all, realize that war (God keep it from us!) can have only one result, vast ruins everywhere, and thus cannot be the object of anyone's reliance. They must adapt to the needs of men of today the laws which regulate the state and society

---

[8] Cf. *Phil.* 3, 8.   [9] *Acts* 4, 29.

Devotion to the Rosary 61

and which bind together nations and classes of society. They must be mindful of the eternal laws which come from God and are the bases and pivots of all government. Finally, they must be ever aware that the individual souls of men are created by God and destined to possess and enjoy Him.

False philosophies

It must also be remarked that there are current today certain schools of thought and philosophy and certain attitudes toward the practical conduct of life which cannot possibly be reconciled with the teachings of Christianity. This impossibility We shall never cease from asserting in firm and unambiguous, though also calm terms.

But God made men and nations curable![10]

And so We hope that men will set aside those sterile postulates and assumptions, hard as rock and just as inflexible, which rise from a way of thinking and acting that is infected with laicism and materialism, and that they will find a complete cure in that sound doctrine which experience makes more certain with every day that passes. We mean that doctrine which attests that God is the author of life and its laws, that He is guarantor of the rights and dignity of the human person. God then is "our refuge and our redemption."[11]

The coming of God's Kingdom

Our thoughts turn to all the lands of this earth. We see all mankind striving for a better future; We see the awakening of a mysterious force, and this permits Us to hope that men will be drawn by a right conscience and a sense of duty to advance the real interests of human society. That this goal may be realized in the fullest sense—that is, with the triumph of the kingdom of truth, justice, peace, and charity—We exhort all Our children in Christ to be "of one heart and one soul"[12] and to pour out ardent prayers in October to our Queen in heaven and our loving Mother, re-

---

[10] Cf. *Wisd.* 1, 14.   [11] Sacred Liturgy.   [12] *Acts* 4, 32.

flecting upon the words of the Apostle: "In all things we suffer tribulation, but we are not distressed; we are sore pressed, but we are not destitute; we endure persecution, but we are not forsaken; we are cast down, but we do not perish; always bearing about in our body the dying of Jesus, so that the life also of Jesus may be made manifest in our bodily frame."[13]

The Synod and the Council

Before We conclude this encyclical We also wish to ask you, venerable brethren, to recite Mary's rosary through the month of October with particular devotion, and to entreat the Virgin Mother of God in suppliant prayer, for another intention which is dear to Our heart: that the Roman Synod may bring many blessings and benefits upon this city; that the forthcoming ecumenical council, in which you will participate by your presence and your advice, will add wondrous growth to the universal Church; and that the renewed vigor of all the Christian virtues which We hope this council will produce will also serve as an invitation and incentive to reunion for Our brethren and children who are separated from this Apostolic See.

In this fond hope, We lovingly impart the Apostolic Blessing to each and every one of you, venerable brethren, to the flocks entrusted to your care, and to those individuals especially who will respond to Our entreaties in a devout and zealous spirit.

Given at Rome, in St. Peter's, on the 26th day of September, in the year 1959, the first of Our Pontificate.

JOHN PP. XXIII

[13] *2 Cor.* 4, 8-10.

II

On the Priesthood

So important did Pope John consider the priesthood and religious life that in the course of his brief pontificate he spoke or wrote on these topics some fifty times. This section of the book contains only four of those messages but, we believe, four that are among the most important and most representative. We have included, too, a commentary on them by Rev. Ferrer Smith, O.P.

Pope John's encyclical "Sacerdotii Nostri Primordia" describes the priestly virtues of St. John Vianney and holds him up as a model for all priests. In "The Synod and the Priest" Pope John, while instructing the Roman clergy on the meaning of their diocesan synod, says much that is vitally important to the priesthood generally. His "Counsels for Seminarians" advises those preparing for ordination, and his "The Art of Spiritual Direction" is addressed to those in charge of the formation of future priests.—Ed.

A Commentary on

POPE JOHN AND THE PRIESTHOOD

by Rev. Ferrer Smith, O.P.

MILLIONS OF WORDS in scores of languages have described the impact of Pope John XXIII upon his time. In a brief reign he spoke often, he did much. Yet, not what he said nor even the magnificence of his deeds account for his impact upon men everywhere. In a thousand different ways men reached to what he was, in himself, and responded to the goodness and love, the humility and simplicity they found within him. For them he lived in a world that was not, tragically, their world yet which he demonstrated convincingly could be, should be. He gave new dimensions to the well worn phrase, "in the world, not of it." He was unmistakably, even dramatically, in the world but he caught the world to himself, lifted it to new heights, gave to it new horizons; he would make it to be his, of him. So he would give it to God.

Of all the words he spoke and wrote none take us more deeply into himself, enable us to breathe so refreshingly of his world, as those spoken to priests and of priests. As a priest, John saw himself, as parish priest for all men, everywhere. He spoke wistfully of his own Bergamo, of the tiny village of Salzano administered by St. Pius X, of the little town of Ars with St. John Vianney as its "very humble Curé." The very smallness of Bergamo, of Salzano, of Ars appealed to him, not only to his humility, but especially to his love. He was the good shepherd who wanted to know each of his sheep and so he envied St. Pius and St. John. Yet his thirst to know each of his flock was not in vain nor entirely frustrated; men everywhere, knowing him, felt in a measure known.

In this he was, in St. Catherine of Siena's happy description of every pope, quite literally "Christ on earth." Like Christ he is the instrument of divine love for men; as Christ he prays and teaches; in Christ he suffers, with Him he dies. The unity and peace he seeks are of the kingdom of Christ. The Synod of Rome, the Second Vatican Council, the renewal of the Church, all have but one motive, the fulfilling of the Cross, the triumph of the Resurrection.

In those who shared his vocation as priest he sought to bring forth

Christ. The way he would bring forth Christ in others reveals the sources of his own Christliness. The way cannot be other than the way of Christ Himself; the sources must be those of the saints. Whether it be Peter in the first papal encyclical or John XXIII through the legislation of the Synod, what is to be grasped is "the same heavenly doctrine, the same spiritual direction, the same sound discipline."[1] To other priests also called to form Christ in their brothers he says: "You must be firmly convinced that the basic principles, without which the whole edifice would crumble and fall into ruins, retain their full force."[2]

The basic principles of holiness, penance, prayer, life centered upon the Cross and the Mass, are presented by the Pope with the richness and vitality, the suffusing charity, the culminating serenity of his own living. In him their eternal newness, and so renewal, find eloquent voice and forceful actuality. For John the Sacred Scriptures are vibrant with the loving voice of God; dwelt upon, they enable him to think the thoughts of God, to see himself, all men, all reality with divine eyes. Penance is the Passion; by it he leaves behind himself and enters ever new and widening vistas of the love of God for men. With St. John Vianney he daily finds in the sacrifice of self not only courage but an inner, urging need to do more, "to try everything" to bring the souls of men to union with their God.[3]

At once simplifying and unifying, giving to all the balance of wisdom, yielding gentleness and dignity, is the penetration by Pope John of Christ as the only-begotten Son sent by His Heavenly Father. Two traits which are in the end one make this manifest: John's sense of divine providence and his concept of himself as father.

Look behind Pope John's frequent reference to his early days, to the men who influenced him, to incidents in Bergamo, Rome, Paris and Venice. These are not simply the stories of an old man reminiscing. They are the loving tracing of the ways of divine providence, uttered in a profound sense of God's plan for men, for all and for each. John was surrounded by, immersed in God's presence, God's love, protecting, guiding, prodding. So he could not forbear to testify to his wonderment, to point out to others what daily became ever more clear to him.

"I came to do the will of Him that sent me," are the familiar words of Christ.[4] As the Son sent by the loving mercy of the Father He is the

---

[1] *The Roman Synod and the Priest*, p. 123.
[2] *The Art of Spiritual Direction*, p. 131.
[3] *The Encyclical Letter, Sacerdotii Nostri Primordia*, p. 91.
[4] *John* 5, 30.

revelation of the Father. In Him John beheld the Father and found the meaning of his life as priest, as pope. All his words as priest to priests, all his deeds as Pope, were those of the universal father. "I speak to you as a father"; he urges "in the name of Jesus Christ from the depths of a father's heart"; "be firm but fatherly."[5] He reached out to all men to will with the Father the salvation, the sanctification of all. He would use all science, all literature, all culture as of man made in the image of God, ruling the world under the provident Fatherhood of God. Above all he saw himself and every priest as sent by the love of the Father, as instrument of His mercy, as Christ revealing Him to men. So he would teach and preach; so he would pray; so he would love. The goodness in him, emphasized by Pope Paul VI, as the cause of his attractiveness, was the overflowing, creative goodness of God.

The words of Pope John to follow constitute a selected yet rounded and integral totality. The complete dedication of St. John Vianney mirrors the priest who is Christ and Christ only. To those approaching ordination Pope John shows the way to become such a priest; to the priests of his own diocese of Rome he would impart the generosity of spirit to be such a priest; with the spiritual directors of seminaries he would unite in love to beget generations of new saints in the priesthood. In all he is transcending the present, seeing all that he is doing, that is being done by Synod and by Council, in terms of the immortal Church giving life, the eternal life of God, to men through men who are more than men, who are Christ.

[5] The Encyclical Letter, *Sacerdotii Nostri Primordia*, pp. 88, 97, 98.

St. John Vianney, Model for Priests

The Encyclical "Sacerdotii Nostri Primordia"
of Pope John XXIII to Catholic Bishops

- *Personal holiness in priests*
- *The pastoral zeal of St. John Vianney*
- *His care in preaching, teaching*
- *A plea for kindness to sinners*

WHEN We think of the first days of Our priesthood, which were so full of joyous consolations, We are reminded of one event that moved Us to the very depths of Our soul: the sacred ceremonies that were carried out so majestically in the Basilica of St. Peter's on January 8, 1905, when John Mary Baptist Vianney, a very humble French priest, was enrolled in the lists of the Blessed in Heaven. Our own ordination to the priesthood had taken place a few short months before, and it filled Us with wonder to see the delight of Our predecessor of happy memory St. Pius X (who had once been the parish priest of the tiny town of Salzano), as he offered this wonderful model of priestly virtues to all those entrusted with the care of souls, for their imitation. Now as We look back over the span of so many years, We never stop giving thanks to Our Redeemer for this wonderful blessing, which marked the beginning of Our priestly ministry and served as an effective heavenly incentive to virtue.

It is all the easier to remember, because on the very same day on which the honors of the Blessed were attributed to this holy man, word reached Us of the elevation of that wonderful prelate, Giacomo M. Radini-Tedeschi, to the dignity of bishop; a few days later, he was to call Us to assist him in his work, and We found him a most loving teacher and guide. It was in his company that, early in

1905, We made Our first pious pilgrimage to the tiny village called Ars, that had become so famous because of the holiness of its Curé.

Again, We cannot help thinking that it was through a special design of God's providence that the year in which We became a bishop—1925—was the very one in which, toward the end of May, the Supreme Pontiff of happy memory, Pius XI, accorded the honors of sainthood to the humble Curé of Ars. In his talk of that occasion, the Supreme Pontiff chose to remind everyone of "the gaunt figure of John Baptist Vianney, with that head shining with long hair that resembled a snowy crown, and that thin face, wasted from long fasting, where the innocence and holiness of the meekest and humblest of souls shone forth so clearly that the first sight of it called crowds of people back to thoughts of salvation."[1] A short while after, this same predecessor of Ours took the occasion of the 50th anniversary of his own ordination to the priesthood to designate St. John Mary Vianney (to whose patronage St. Pius X had previously committed all of the shepherds of souls in France) as the heavenly patron of all "pastors, to promote their spiritual welfare throughout the world."[2]

A time for tribute

We have thought it opportune to use an encyclical letter to recall these acts of Our predecessors that are so closely bound up with such happy memories, venerable brethren, now that We are approaching the 100th anniversary of the day—August 4, 1859—on which this holy man, completely broken from forty years of the most tireless and exhausting labors, and already famous in every corner of the world for his holiness, passed on most piously to his heavenly reward.

And so We give thanks to God in His goodness, not only for seeing to it that this saint would twice cast the brilliant light of his holiness over Our priestly life at moments of great importance, but also for offering Us an opportunity here at the beginning of Our pontificate to pay solemn tribute to this wonderful shepherd of souls on this happy 100th anniversary. It will be easy for you to

[1] *AAS* 17 (1925) 224.   [2] Apostolic letter *"Anno Iubilari," AAS* 21 (1929) 313.

see, venerable brethren, that We are directing this letter principally to Our very dearest sons, those in sacred orders, and urging each and every one of them—especially those engaged in pastoral ministry—to devote all their attention to a consideration of the wonderful example of this holy man, who once shared in this priestly work and who now serves as their heavenly patron.

Earlier popes on the priesthood

The Supreme Pontiffs have issued many documents reminding those in sacred orders of the greatness of their priestly office, and pointing out the safest and surest way for them to carry out their duties properly. To recall only the more recent and more important of these, We would like to make special mention of the apostolic exhortation of St. Pius X of happy memory entitled *Haerent Animo*,[3] issued early in Our priesthood, which urged Us on to greater efforts to achieve a more ardent devotion, and the wonderful encyclical of our predecessor of happy memory, Pius XI, that began with the words "*Ad catholici sacerdotii*,"[4] and finally the apostolic exhortation *Menti Nostrae*[5] of Our immediate predecessor, along with his three allocutions on the occasion of the canonization of St. Pius X that give so clear and complete a picture of sacred orders.[6] Undoubtedly you are familiar with all of these documents, venerable brethren. But permit Us also to mention a few words from a sermon published after the death of Our immediate predecessor; they stand as the final solemn exhortation of that great pontiff to priestly holiness: "Through the character of Sacred Orders, God willed to ratify that eternal covenant of love, by which He loves His priests above all others; and they are obliged to repay God for this special love with holiness of life.... So a cleric should be considered as a man chosen and set apart from the midst of the people, and blessed in a very special way with heavenly gifts—a sharer in divine power, and, to put it briefly, another Christ.... He is no longer supposed to live for himself; nor can he devote himself to the interests of just his own relatives, or friends or native

---

[3] *Acta Pii X*, IV, pp. 237-264.   [4] *AAS* 28 (1936) 5-53.
[5] *AAS* 42 (1950) 657-702.
[6] *AAS* 46 (1954) 313-317; *TPS* I, pp. 147-158.

land. . . . He must be aflame with charity toward everyone. Not even his thoughts, his will, his feelings belong to him, for they are rather those of Jesus Christ who is his life."[7]

Subject of the encyclical

St. John Mary Vianney is a person who attracts and practically pushes all of us to these heights of the priestly life. And so We are pleased to add Our own exhortations to the others, in the hope that the priests of Our day may exert every possible effort in this direction. We are well aware of their devoted care and interest, and well acquainted with the difficulties they face each day in their apostolic activity. And even though We regret the fact that the surging currents of this world overwhelm the spirit and courage of some and make them grow tired and inactive, We also know from experience how many more stand firm in their faith despite many hardships, and how many constantly strive to stir up an ardent zeal for the very highest ideals in their own souls. And yet, when they became priests, Christ the Lord spoke these words so full of consolation to all of them: "I no longer call you servants but friends."[8] May this encyclical of Ours help the whole clergy to foster this divine friendship and grow in it, for it is the main source of the joy and the fruitfulness of any priestly work.

We have no intention, venerable brethren, of taking up each and every matter that has any reference to the life of a priest in the present day; as a matter of fact, following closely in the footsteps of St. Pius X, "We will not say anything that you have not already heard before, nor anything that will be completely new to anyone, but rather We will concentrate on recalling things that everyone ought to remember."[9] For a mere sketch of the qualities of this heavenly soul, if done properly, is enough to lead us readily to a serious consideration of certain things that are, it is true, necessary in every age, but which now seem to be so important that Our Apostolic office and duty force Us to put special emphasis on them on the occasion of this centenary.

---

[7] Cf. *AAS* 50 (1958) 966-967.   [8] *Pontificale Rom.*; cf. *John* 15, 15.
[9] Exhortation *"Haerent Animo," Acta Pii X*, p. 238.

72 POPE JOHN XXIII

A model for the clergy

The Catholic Church, which elevated this man in sacred orders, who was "wonderful in his pastoral zeal, in his devotion to prayer and in the ardor of his penance,"[10] to the honors of the saints of heaven, now, one hundred years after his death, offers him with maternal joy to all the clergy as an outstanding model of priestly asceticism, of piety, especially in the form of devotion to the Eucharist, and, finally, of pastoral zeal.

I

You cannot begin to speak of St. John Mary Vianney without automatically calling to mind the picture of a priest who was outstanding in a unique way in voluntary affliction of his body; his only motives were the love of God and the desire for the salvation of the souls of his neighbors, and this led him to abstain almost completely from food and from sleep, to carry out the harshest kinds of penances, and to deny himself with great strength of soul. Of course, not all of the faithful are expected to adopt this kind of life; and yet divine providence has seen to it that there has never been a time when the Church did not have some pastors of souls of this kind who, under the inspiration of the Holy Spirit, did not hesitate for a moment to enter on this path, most of all because this way of life is particularly successful in bringing many men who have been drawn away by the allurement of error and vice back to the path of good living.

The evangelical counsels

The wonderful devotion in this regard of St. John Vianney—a man who was "hard on himself, and gentle with others"[11]—was so outstanding that it should serve as a clear and timely reminder of the important role that priests should attribute to the virtue of penance in striving for perfection in their own lives. Our predecessor of happy memory, Pius XII, in order to give a clear picture of this

[10] Prayer of the Mass on the feast of St. John Mary Vianney.
[11] Cf. *Archiv. Secr. Vat.*, C.SS.Rituum, *Processus*, v. 227, p. 196.

doctrine and to clear up the doubts and errors that bothered some people, denied that "the clerical state—as such, and on the basis of divine law—requires, of its very nature or at least as a result of some demand arising from its nature, that those enrolled in it observe the evangelical counsels,"[12] and justly concluded with these words: "Hence a cleric is not bound by virtue of divine law to the evangelical counsels of poverty, chastity, obedience."[13]

And yet it would undoubtedly be both a distortion of the real mind of this same Supreme Pontiff (who was so interested in the sanctity of the clergy) and a contradiction of the perpetual teaching of the Church in this matter, if anyone should dare to infer from this that clerics were any less bound by their office than religious to strive for evangelical perfection of life. The truth is just the opposite; for the proper exercise of the priestly functions "requires a greater interior holiness than is demanded by the religious state."[14] And even if churchmen are not commanded to embrace these evangelical counsels by virtue of their clerical state, it still remains true that in their efforts to achieve holiness, these counsels offer them and all of the faithful the surest road to the desired goal of Christian perfection. What a great consolation it is to Us that at the present time many generous-hearted priests are showing that they realize this; even though they belong to the diocesan clergy, they have sought the help and aid of certain pious societies approved by Church authorities in order to find a quicker and easier way to move along the road to perfection.

Fully convinced as they are that the "highest dignity of the priesthood consists in the imitation of Christ,"[15] churchmen must pay special attention to this warning of their Divine Master: "If anyone wishes to come after me, let him deny himself, and take up his cross and follow me."[16] It is recorded that "the holy parish priest of Ars often thought these words of the Lord over carefully, and determined to apply them to his own actions."[17] He made the resolution readily, and with the help of God's grace and by constant effort, he

---

[12] Allocution *"Annus Sacer," AAS* 43 (1951) 29. [13] *Ibid.*
[14] St. Thomas, *Summa Theologica* II-II, q. 184, a. 8, in c.
[15] Cf. Pius XII, allocution, 16 April 1953: *AAS* 45 (1953) 288.
[16] *Matt.* 16, 24.   [17] Cf. *Archiv. Secret. Vat.*, v. 227, p. 42.

kept it to a wonderful extent; his example in the various works of priestly asceticism still points out the safest path to follow, and in the midst of this example, his poverty, chastity and obedience stand forth in a brilliant light.

The poverty of St. John Vianney

First of all, you have clear testimony of his poverty. The humble Curé of Ars was careful to imitate the Patriarch of Assisi in this regard, for he had accepted his rule in the Third Order of St. Francis and he carefully observed it.[18] He was rich in his generosity toward others but the poorest of men in dealing with himself; he passed a life that was almost completely detached from the changeable, perishable goods of this world, and his spirit was free and unencumbered by impediments of this kind, so that it could always lie open to those who suffered from any kind of misery; and they flocked from everywhere to seek his consolation. "My secret"—he said—"is easy to learn. It can be summed up in these few words: give everything away and keep nothing for yourself."[19]

This detachment from external goods enabled him to offer the most devoted and touching care to the poor, especially those in his own parish. He was very kind and gentle toward them and embraced them "with a sincere love, with the greatest of kindness, indeed with reverence."[20] He warned that the needy were never to be spurned since a disregard for them would reach in turn to God. When beggars knocked at his door, he received them with love and was very happy to be able to say to them: "I am living in need myself; I am one of you."[21] And toward the end of his life, he used to enjoy saying things like this: "I will be happy when I go; for now I no longer have any possessions; and so when God in his goodness sees fit to call me, I will be ready and willing to go."[22]

All of this will give you a clear idea of what We have in mind, venerable brethren, when We exhort all of Our beloved sons who share in the priesthood to give careful thought to this example of

---

[18] Cf. *ibid.*, v. 227, p. 137.
[19] Cf. *ibid.*, v. 227, p. 92.
[20] Cf. *ibid.*, v. 3897, p. 510.
[21] Cf. *ibid.*, v. 227, p. 334.
[22] Cf. *ibid.*, v. 227, p. 305.

poverty and charity. "Daily experience shows"—wrote Pius XI, with St. John Mary Vianney specifically in mind—"that priests who live modestly and follow the teaching of the gospel by paying little attention to their own interests, always confer wonderful benefits on the Christian people."[23] And the same Supreme Pontiff issued this serious warning to priests as well as to others in the course of a discussion of the current problems of society: "When they look around and see men ready to sell anything for money and to strike a bargain for anything at all, let them pass right through the midst of these attractions of vice without a thought or care for their own desires; and let them in their holiness spurn this base pursuit of wealth, and look for the riches of souls rather than for money, and let them long for and seek God's glory rather than their own."[24]

The use of possessions

It is very important for these words to sink deep into the mind of every priest. If someone owns things that are rightfully his, let him be careful not to hang on to them greedily. Instead he should remember that the prescriptions of the Code of Canon Law dealing with church benefices make it clear that he has a serious obligation "to use superfluous income for the poor or for pious causes."[25] May God grant that no one of Us ever lets that terrible sentence that the parish priest of Ars once used in rebuking his flock fall on him: "There are many people keeping their money hidden away while many others are dying of hunger."[26]

We know very well that at the present time there are many priests living in great need themselves. When they stop to realize that heavenly honors have been paid to one of their own who voluntarily gave up all he had and asked for nothing more than to be the poorest of all in his parish,[27] they have a wonderful source of inspiration for devoting themselves carefully and constantly to fostering evangelical poverty. And if Our paternal interest can offer

[23] Encyclical "*Divini Redemptoris,*" *AAS* 29 (1937) 99.
[24] Encyclical "*Ad catholici sacerdotii,*" *AAS* 28 (1936) 28.
[25] *C.J.C.*, can. 1473.
[26] Cf. *Sermons du B. Jean B.M. Vianney,* 1909, v. 1, p. 364.
[27] Cf. *Archiv. Secret. Vat.,* v. 227, p. 91.

any consolation, We want them to know that We are very happy that they are serving Christ and the Church so generously with no thought of their own interests.

Unbecoming indigence

However, even though We praise and extol this wonderful virtue of poverty so much, no one should conclude that We have any intention of giving Our approval to the unbecoming indigence and misery in which the ministers of the Lord are sometimes forced to live, both in cities and in remote rural areas. In this regard, when St. Bede the Venerable explained and commented on the words of the Lord on detachment from earthly things, he excluded possible incorrect interpretations of this passage with these words: "You must not think that this command was given with the intention of having the saints keep no money at all for their own use or for that of the poor (for we read that the Lord himself . . . had money-boxes in forming his Church . . .) but rather the idea was that this should not be the motive for serving God nor should justice be abandoned out of fear of suffering want."[28] Besides, the laborer is worthy of his hire,[29] and We share the feelings of Our immediate predecessor in urging the faithful to respond quickly and generously to the appeals of their pastors; We also join him in praising these shepherds for their efforts to see to it that those who help them in the sacred ministry do not lack the necessities of life.[30]

Model of chastity

John M. Vianney was an outstanding model of voluntary mortification of the body as well as of detachment from external things. "There is only one way"—he used to say—"for anyone to devote himself to God as he should through self-denial and the practice of penance: that is by devoting himself to it completely."[31] Throughout his whole life, the holy Curé of Ars carried this principle into practice energetically in the matter of chastity.

[28] *In Lucae Evangelium Expositio,* IV, in c. 12: Migne, PL 92, col. 494-5.
[29] Cf. *Luke* 10, 7.
[30] Cf. apostolic exhortation *"Menti Nostrae," AAS* 42 (1950) 697-699.
[31] Cf. *Archiv. Secret. Vat.,* v. 227, p. 91.

This wonderful example of chastity seems to have special application to the priests of our time who—as is unfortunately the case in many regions—are often forced by the office they have assumed to live in the midst of a human society that is infected by a general looseness in morals and a spirit of unbridled lust. How often this phrase of St. Thomas Aquinas is proved true: "It is harder to lead a good life in the work of caring for souls, because of the external dangers involved."[32] To this We might add the fact that they often feel themselves cut off from the society of others and that even the faithful to whose salvation they are dedicated do not understand them and offer them little help or support in their undertakings.

We want to use this letter, venerable brethren, to exhort, again and again, all of them, and especially those who are working alone and in the midst of very serious dangers of this kind, to let their whole life, so to say, resound with the splendor of holy chastity; St. Pius X had good reason to call this virtue the "choicest adornment of our order."[33]

Venerable brethren, do all you can and spare no effort to see to it that the clergy entrusted to your care may enjoy living and working conditions that will best foster and be of service to their ardent zeal. This means that every effort should be exerted to eliminate the dangers that arise from too great an isolation, to issue timely warnings against unwise or imprudent actions, and last of all to check the dangers of idleness or of too much external activity. In this regard, you should recall the wise directives issued by Our immediate predecessor in the encyclical *Sacra Virginitas*.[34]

St. John Vianney on chastity

It is said that the face of the Pastor of Ars shone with an angelic purity.[35] And even now anyone who turns toward him in mind and spirit cannot help being struck, not merely by the great strength of soul with which this athlete of Christ reduced his body to slavery,[36]

---

[32] *Summa Theologica* II-II, q. 184, a. 8, in c.
[33] Exhortation "*Haerent animo,*" *Acta Pii X*, IV, p. 260.
[34] *AAS* 46 (1954) 161-191; *TPS* I, 101-123.
[35] Cf. *Archiv. Secret. Vat.*, v. 3897, p. 536.
[36] Cf. *1 Cor.* 9, 27.

but also by the great persuasive powers he exercised over the pious crowds of pilgrims who came to him and were drawn by his heavenly meekness to follow in his footsteps. From his daily experiences in the Sacrament of Penance he got an unmistakable picture of the terrible havoc that is wrought by impure desire. This was what brought cries like these bursting from his breast: "If there were not very innocent souls to please God and make up for our offenses, how many terrible punishments we would have to suffer!" His own observations in this regard led him to offer this encouragement and advice to his hearers: "The works of penance abound in such delights and joys that once they have been tasted, nothing will ever again root them out of the soul. . . . Only the first steps are difficult for those who eagerly choose this path."[37]

Priest's chastity as help to others

The ascetic way of life, by which priestly chastity is preserved, does not enclose the priest's soul within the sterile confines of his own interests, but rather it makes him more eager and ready to relieve the needs of his brethren. St. John Mary Vianney has this pertinent comment to make in this regard: "A soul adorned with the virtue of chastity cannot help loving others; for it has discovered the source and font of love—God."

What great benefits are conferred on human society by men like this who are free of the cares of the world and totally dedicated to the divine ministry so that they can employ their lives, thoughts, powers in the interest of their brethren! How valuable to the Church are priests who are anxious to preserve perfect chastity! For We agree with Our predecessor of happy memory, Pius XI, in regarding this as the outstanding adornment of the Catholic priesthood and as something "that seems to Us to correspond better to the counsels and wishes of the Most Sacred Heart of Jesus, so far as the souls of priests are concerned."[38] Was not the mind of John Mary Vianney soaring to reach the counsels of this same divine charity when he wrote this lofty sentence: "Is the priesthood love of the Most Sacred Heart of Jesus?"[39]

[37] Cf. *Archiv. Secret. Vat.*, v. 3897, p. 304.
[38] Encyclical "*Ad catholici sacerdotii,*" *AAS* 28 (1936) 28.
[39] Cf. *Archiv. Secret. Vat.*, v. 227, p. 29.

The obedience of St. John Vianney

There are many pieces of evidence of how this man was also outstanding in the virtue of obedience. It would be true to say that the fidelity toward his superiors in the Church which he pledged at the time he became a priest and which he preserved unshaken throughout his life drove him to an uninterrupted immolation of his will for forty years.

All his life he longed to lead a quiet and retired life in the background, and he regarded pastoral duties as a very heavy burden laid on his shoulders and more than once he tried to free himself of it. His obedience to his bishop was admirable; We would like to mention a few instances of it in this encyclical, venerable brethren: "From the age of fifteen on, he ardently desired a solitary life, and as long as this wish was not fulfilled, he felt cut off from every advantage and every consolation that his state of life might have offered";[40] but "God never allowed this aim to be achieved. Undoubtedly, this was God's way of bending St. John Mary Vianney's will to obedience and of teaching him to put the duties of his office before his own desires; and so there was never a time when his devotion to self-denial did not shine forth";[41] "out of complete obedience to his superiors, John M. Vianney carried out his tasks as pastor of Ars, and remained in that office till the end of his mortal life."[42]

It should be noted, however, that this full obedience of his to the commands of his superiors rested on supernatural principles; in acknowledging and duly obeying ecclesiastical authority, he was paying the homage of faith to the words of Christ the Lord as He told His Apostles "He who hears you, hears me."[43] To conform himself faithfully to the will of his superiors he habitually restrained his own will, whether in accepting the holy burdens of hearing confessions, or in performing zealously for his colleagues in the apostolate such work as would produce richer and more saving fruits.

The importance of obedience

We are offering clerics this total obedience as a model, with full

---

[40] Cf. *ibid.*, v. 227, p. 74.
[42] Cf. *ibid.*, v. 3895, p. 153.
[41] Cf. *ibid.*, v. 227, p. 39.
[43] *Luke* 10, 16.

confidence that its force and beauty will lead them to strive for it more ardently. And if there should be someone who dares to cast doubt on the supreme importance of this virtue—as sometimes happens at the present time—let him take to heart these words of Our predecessor of happy memory, Pius XII, which everyone should keep firmly in mind: "The holiness of any life and the effectiveness of any apostolate has constant and faithful obedience to the hierarchy as its solid foundation, basis and support."[44]

For, as you well know, venerable brethren, Our most recent predecessors have often issued serious warnings to priests about the extent of the dangers that are arising among the clergy from a growing carelessness about obedience with regard to the teaching authority of the Church, to the various ways and means of undertaking the apostolate, and to ecclesiastical discipline.

An exhortation to obedience

We do not want to spend a lot of time on this, but We think it timely to exhort all of Our sons who share in the Catholic priesthood to foster a love in their souls that will make them feel attached to Mother Church by ever closer bonds, and then to make that love grow.

It is said that St. John M. Vianney lived in the Church in such a way that he worked for it alone, and burned himself up like a piece of straw being consumed on fiery coals. May that flame which comes from the Holy Spirit reach those of Us who have been raised to the priesthood of Jesus Christ and consume us too.

We owe ourselves and all we have to the Church; may we work each day only in her name and by her authority and may we properly carry out the duties committed to us, and may we be joined together in fraternal unity and thus strive to serve her in that perfect way in which she ought to be served.[45]

II

St. John M. Vianney, who, as We have said, was so devoted to the virtue of penance, was just as sure that "a priest must be spe-

[44] Exhortation *"In auspicando," AAS* 40 (1948) 375.
[45] Cf. *Archiv. Secret. Vat.*, v. 227, p. 136.

cially devoted to constant prayer."⁴⁶ In this regard, We know that shortly after he was made pastor of a village where Christian life had been languishing for a long time, he began to spend long and happy hours at night (when he might have been resting) in adoration of Jesus in the Sacrament of His love. The sacred tabernacle seemed to be the spring from which he constantly drew the powers that nourished his own piety and gave new life to it and promoted the effectiveness of his apostolic labor to such an extent that the wonderful words that Our predecessor of happy memory, Pius XII, used to describe the ideal Christian parish, might well have been applied to the town of Ars in the time of this holy man: "In the middle stands the temple; in the middle of the temple the sacred tabernacle, and on either side the confessionals where supernatural life and health are restored to the Christian people."⁴⁷

Prayer in the life of St. John Vianney

How timely and how profitable this example of constant prayer on the part of a man completely dedicated to caring for the needs of souls is for priests in Our own day, who are likely to attribute too much to the effectiveness of external activity and stand ready and eager to immerse themselves in the hustle and bustle of the ministry, to their own spiritual detriment!

"The thing that keeps us priests from gaining sanctity"—the Curé of Ars used to say—"is thoughtlessness. It annoys us to turn our minds away from external affairs; we don't know what we really *ought* to do. What we need is deep reflection, together with prayer and an intimate union with God." The testimony of his life makes it clear that he always remained devoted to his prayers and that not even the duty of hearing confessions or any other pastoral office could cause him to neglect them. "Even in the midst of tremendous labors, he never let up on his conversation with God."⁴⁸

But listen to his own words; for he seemed to have an inexhaustible supply of them whenever he talked about the happiness or the advantages that he found in prayer: "We are beggars who must ask

⁴⁶ Cf. *ibid.*, v. 227, p. 33.
⁴⁷ Cf. *Discorsi e Radiomessaggi di S.S. Pio XII*, v. 14, p. 452.
⁴⁸ Cf. *Archiv. Secret. Vat.*, v. 227, p. 131.

God for everything";[49] "How many people we can call back to God by our prayers!"[50] And he used to say over and over again: "Ardent prayer addressed to God: this is man's greatest happiness on earth!"[51]

And he enjoyed this happiness abundantly when his mind rose with the help of heavenly light to contemplate the things of heaven and his pure and simple soul rose with all its deepest love from the mystery of the Incarnation to the heights of the Most Holy Trinity. And the crowds of pilgrims who surrounded him in the temple could feel something coming forth from the depths of the inner life of this humble priest when words like these burst forth from his inflamed breast, as they often did: "To be loved by God, to be joined to God, to walk before God, to live for God: O blessed life, O blessed death!"[52]

Necessity of prayer life

We sincerely hope, venerable brethren, that these lessons from the life of St. John M. Vianney may make all of the sacred ministers committed to your care feel sure that they must exert every effort to be outstanding in their devotion to prayer; this can really be done, even if they are very busy with apostolic labors.

But if they are to do this, their lives must conform to the norms of faith that so imbued John Mary Vianney and enabled him to perform such wonderful works. "Oh the wonderful faith of this priest" —one of his colleagues in the sacred ministry remarked—"It is great enough to enrich all the souls of the diocese!"[53]

This constant union with God is best achieved and preserved through the various practices of priestly piety; many of the more important of them, such as daily meditation, visits to the Blessed Sacrament, recitation of the rosary, careful examination of conscience, the Church, in her wise and provident regulations, has made obligatory for priests.[54] As for the hours of the Office, priests have undertaken a serious obligation to the Church to recite them.[55]

The neglect of some of these rules may often be the reason why

---

[49] Cf. *ibid.*, v. 227, p. 1100.
[51] Cf. *ibid.*, v. 227, p. 45.
[53] Cf. *ibid.*, v. 227, p. 976.
[55] *Ibid.*, canon 135.
[50] Cf. *ibid.*, v. 227, p. 54.
[52] Cf. *ibid.*, v. 227, p. 29.
[54] *C.J.C.*, canon 125.

certain churchmen are caught up in the whirl of external affairs, gradually lose their feeling for sacred things and finally fall into serious difficulties when they are shorn of all spiritual protection and enticed by the attractions of this earthly life. John Mary Vianney on the contrary "never neglected his own salvation, no matter how busy he may have been with that of others."[56]

To use the words of St. Pius X: "We are sure of this much . . . that a priest must be deeply devoted to the practice of prayer if he is to live up to his rank and fulfill his duties properly. . . . For a priest must be much more careful than others to obey the command of Christ: You must always pray. Paul was only reaffirming this when he advised, as he did so often: Be constant in prayer, ever on the watch to give thanks; pray without ceasing."[57] And We are more than happy to adopt as Our own the words that Our immediate predecessor offered priests as their password at the very beginning of his pontificate: "Pray, more and more, and pray more intensely."[58]

St. John Vianney's devotion to the Eucharist

The devotion to prayer of St. John M. Vianney, who was to spend almost the whole of the last thirty years of his life in Church caring for the crowds of penitents who flocked to him, had one special characteristic—it was specially directed toward the Eucharist.

It is almost unbelievable how ardent his devotion to Christ hidden beneath the veils of the Eucharist really was. "He is the one"—he said—"who has loved us so much; why shouldn't we love Him in return?"[59] He was devoted to the adorable Sacrament of the altar with a burning charity and his soul was drawn to the sacred tabernacle by a heavenly force that could not be resisted.

This is how he taught his faithful to pray: "You do not need many words when you pray. We believe on faith that the good and gracious God is there in the tabernacle; we open our souls to Him;

[56] Cf. *Archiv. Secret. Vat.*, v. 227, p. 36.
[57] Exhortation *"Haerent animo," Acta Pii X*, IV, pp. 248-249.
[58] Discourse of June 24, 1939: *AAS* 31 (1939) 249.
[59] Cf. *Archiv. Secret. Vat.*, v. 227, p. 1103.

and feel happy that He allows us to come before Him; this is the best way to pray."[60] He did everything that there was to be done to stir up the reverence and love of the faithful for Christ hidden in the Sacrament of the Eucharist and to bring them to share in the riches of the divine Synaxis; the example of his devotion was ever before them. "To be convinced of this—witnesses tell us—all that was necessary was to see him carrying out the sacred ceremonies or simply to see him genuflect when he passed the tabernacle."[61]

Benefits from Eucharistic prayer

As Our predecessor of immortal memory, Pius XII, has said— "The wonderful example of St. John Mary Vianney retains all of its force for our times."[62] For the lengthy prayer of a priest before the adorable Sacrament of the Altar has a dignity and an effectiveness that cannot be found elsewhere nor be replaced. And so when the priest adores Christ Our Lord and gives thanks to Him, or offers satisfaction for his own sins and those of others, or finally when he prays constantly that God keep special watch over the causes committed to his care, he is inflamed with a more ardent love for the divine Redeemer to whom he has sworn allegiance and for those to whom he is devoting his pastoral care. And a devotion to the Eucharist that is ardent, constant and that carries over into works also has the effect of nourishing and fostering the inner perfection of his soul and assuring him, as he carries out his apostolic duties, of an abundance of the supernatural powers that the strongest workers for Christ must have.

We do not want to skip over the benefits that accrue to the faithful themselves in this way, as they see the piety of their priests and are drawn by their example. For, as Our predecessor of happy memory, Pius XII, pointed out in a talk to the clergy of this dear city: "If you want the faithful who are entrusted to your care to pray willingly and well, you must give them an example and let them see you praying in church. A priest kneeling devoutly and reverently before the tabernacle, and pouring forth prayers to God

---

[60] Cf. *ibid.*, v. 227, p. 45.   [61] Cf. *ibid.*, v. 227, p. 459.
[62] Cf. message of June 25, 1956: *AAS* 48 (1956) 579.

with all his heart, is a wonderful example to the Christian people and serves as an inspiration."[63] The saintly Curé of Ars used all of these helps in carrying out his apostolic office, and without a doubt they are suitable to all times and places.

The Mass and the priesthood

But never forget that the principal form of Eucharistic prayer is contained in the holy Sacrifice of the Altar. It is Our opinion that this point ought to be considered more carefully, venerable brethren, for it touches on a particularly important aspect of priestly life.

It is not Our intention at this time to enter upon a lengthy treatment of the Church's teaching on the priesthood and on the Eucharistic Sacrifice as it has been handed down from antiquity. Our predecessors Pius XI and Pius XII have done this in clear and important documents and We urge you to take pains to see to it that the priests and faithful entrusted to your care are very familiar with them. This will clear up the doubts of some; and correct the more daring statements that have sometimes been made in discussing these matters.

But We too hope to say something worthwhile in this matter by showing the principal reason why the holy Curé of Ars, who, as befits a hero, was most careful in fulfilling his priestly duties, really deserves to be proposed to those who have the care of souls as a model of outstanding virtue and to be honored by them as their heavenly patron. If it is obviously true that a priest receives his priesthood so as to serve at the altar and that he enters upon this office by offering the Eucharistic Sacrifice, then it is equally true that for as long as he lives as God's minister, the Eucharistic Sacrifice will be the source and origin of the holiness that he attains and of the apostolic activity to which he devotes himself. All of these things came to pass in the fullest possible way in the case of St. John Vianney.

For, if you give careful consideration to all of the activity of a priest, what is the main point of his apostolate if not seeing to it that wherever the Church lives, a people who are joined by the

---

[63] Cf. discourse of March 13, 1943: *AAS* 35 (1943) 114-115.

bonds of faith, regenerated by holy Baptism and cleansed of their faults will be gathered together around the sacred altar? It is then that the priest, using the sacred power he has received, offers the divine Sacrifice in which Jesus Christ renews the unique immolation which He completed on Calvary for the redemption of mankind and for the glory of His heavenly Father. It is then that the Christians who have gathered together, acting through the ministry of the priest, present the divine Victim and offer themselves to the supreme and eternal God as a "sacrifice, living, holy, pleasing to God."[64] There it is that the people of God are taught the doctrines and precepts of faith and are nourished with the Body of Christ, and there it is that they find a means to gain supernatural life, to grow in it, and if need be, to regain unity. And there besides, the Mystical Body of Christ, which is the Church, grows with spiritual increase throughout the world down to the end of time.

It is only right and fitting to call the life of St. John Vianney a priestly and pastoral one in an outstanding way, because he spent more and more time in preaching the truths of religion and cleansing souls of the stain of sin as the years went by, and because he was mindful of the altar of God in each and every act of his sacred ministry!

It is true of course that the holy Curé's fame made great crowds of sinners flock to Ars, while many priests experience great difficulty in getting the people committed to their care to come to them at all, and then find that they have to teach them the most elementary truths of Christian doctrine just as if they were working in a missionary land. But as important and sometimes as trying as these apostolic labors may be, they should never be permitted to make men of God forget the great importance of the goal which they must always keep in view and which St. John Vianney attained through dedicating himself completely to the main works of the apostolic life in a tiny country church.

Personal holiness and the Mass

This should be kept in mind, in particular: whatever a priest may plan, resolve, or do to become holy, he will have to draw, for

[64] *Rom.* 12, 1.

example and for heavenly strength, upon the Eucharistic Sacrifice which he offers, just as the Roman Pontifical urges: "Be aware of what you are doing; imitate what you hold in your hands."

In this regard, We are pleased to repeat the words used by Our immediate predecessor of happy memory in the apostolic exhortation entitled *Menti Nostrae:* "Just as the whole life of Our Savior was pointed toward His sacrifice of Himself, so too the life of the priest, who must reproduce the image of Christ in himself, must become a pleasing sacrifice with Him and through Him and in Him. . . . And so it is not enough for him to celebrate the Eucharistic Sacrifice, but in a very deep sense, he must live it; for in this way, he can draw from it the heavenly strength that will enable him to be profoundly transformed and to share in the expiatory life of the divine Redeemer himself. . . ."[65] And again: "The soul of the priest must refer what takes place on the sacrificial altar to himself; for just as Jesus Christ immolates Himself, his minister must immolate himself along with Him; just as Jesus expiates the sins of men, so too the priest must tread the lofty path of Christian asceticism to bring about his own purification and that of his neighbors."[66]

Safeguarding holiness

This lofty aspect of doctrine is what the Church has in mind when, with maternal care, she invites her sacred ministers to devote themselves to asceticism and urges them to celebrate the Eucharistic Sacrifice with the greatest possible interior and exterior devotion. May not the fact that some priests fail to keep in mind the close connection that ought to exist between the offering of the Sacrifice and their own self-dedication be the reason why they gradually fall off from that first fervor they had at the time of their ordination? St. John Vianney learned this from experience and expressed it this way: "The reason why priests are remiss in their personal lives is that they do not offer the Sacrifice with attention and piety." And he, who in his lofty virtue, was in the habit of "offering himself as an expiation for sinners"[67] used to weep "when he thought of the

---

[65] Apostolic exhortation *"Menti Nostrae," AAS* 42 (1950) 666-667.
[66] Cf. *ibid.*, 667-668.
[67] Cf. *Archiv. Secret. Vat.*, v. 227, p. 319.

unhappy priests who did not measure up to the holiness demanded by their office."[68]

Speaking as a Father, We urge Our beloved priests to set aside a time to examine themselves on how they celebrate the divine mysteries, what their dispositions of soul and external attitude are as they ascend the altar and what fruit they are trying to gain from it. They should be spurred to do this by the centenary celebrations that are being held in honor of this outstanding and wonderful priest, who drew such great strength and such great desire to dedicate himself "from the consolation and happiness of offering the divine victim."[69] May his prayers, which We feel sure they will have, bring a fullness of light and strength down upon Our beloved priests.

III

The wonderful examples of priestly asceticism and prayer that We have proposed for your consideration up to now, venerable brethren, also point clearly to the source of the pastoral skill and of the truly remarkable heavenly effectiveness of the sacred ministry of St. John M. Vianney. In this regard, Our predecessor of happy memory, Pius XII, gave a wise warning: "The priest should realize that the important ministry entrusted to him will be more fruitfully carried out, the more intimately he is united with Christ and led on by His spirit."[70] As a matter of fact, the life of the Curé of Ars offers one more outstanding argument in support of the supreme rule for apostolic labor that was laid down by Jesus Christ Himself: "Without me, you can do nothing."[71]

The Good Shepherd

We have no intention of trying to make a list of all the wonderful things done by this humble curé of a country parish, who drew such immense crowds to the tribunal of Penance that some people, out of contempt, called him "a kind of nineteenth-century rabble-rouser";[72] nor do We see any need of going into all of the particular

---

[68] Cf. *ibid.*, v. 227, p. 47.   [69] Cf. *ibid.*, pp. 667-668.
[70] Apostolic exhortation *"Menti Nostrae," AAS* 42 (1950) 676.
[71] *John* 15, 5.   [72] Cf. *Archiv. Secret. Vat.*, v. 227, p. 629.

ways in which he carried out his duties, some of which, perhaps, could not be accommodated to our times.

But We do want to recall this one fact—that this saint was in his own times a model of pastoral devotion in a tiny community that was still suffering from the loss of Christian faith and morals that occurred while the French Revolution was raging. This was the mission and command received just before taking over his pastoral office: "You will find little love of God in that parish; stir it up yourself."[73]

He proved to be a tireless worker for God, one who was wise and devoted in winning over young people and bringing families back to the standards of Christian morality, a worker who was never too tired to show an interest in the human needs of his flock, one whose own way of life was very close to theirs and who was prepared to exert every effort and make any sacrifice to establish Christian schools and to make missions available to the people: and all of these things show that St. John M. Vianney reproduced the true image of the good shepherd in himself as he dealt with the flock entrusted to his care, for he knew his sheep, protected them from dangers, and gently but firmly looked after them.

Without realizing it, he was sounding his own praises in the words he once addressed to his people: "Good shepherd! O shepherd who lives up to the commands and desires of Jesus Christ completely! This is the greatest blessing that a kind and gracious God can send to a parish."[74]

But there are three things in particular of lasting value and importance that the example of this holy man brings home to us and it is to these in particular that We would like to direct your attention, venerable brethren.

His esteem for the pastoral office

The first thing that strikes Us is the very high esteem in which he held his pastoral office. He was so humble by disposition and so much aware through faith of the importance of the salvation

---

[73] Cf. *ibid.*, v. 227, p. 15.   [74] Cf. *Sermons*, l. c., v. 2, p. 86.

of a human soul that he could never undertake his parish duties without a feeling of fear.

"My friend"—these are the words he used to open his heart to a fellow-priest—"you have no idea of how fearful a thing it is for a priest to be snatched away from the care of souls to appear before the judgment seat of God."[75]

Everyone knows—as We have already pointed out—how much he yearned and how long he prayed to be allowed to go off by himself to weep and to make proper expiation for what he called his miserable life; and We also know that only obedience and his zeal for the salvation of others got him to return to the field of the apostolate when he had abandoned it.

Sufferings for his sheep

But if he felt the great weight of this burden to be so heavy that it sometimes seemed to be crushing him, this was also the reason why he conceived his office and its duties in so lofty a fashion that carrying them out called for great strength of soul. These are the prayers he addressed to heaven as he began his parochial ministry: "My God, make the sheep entrusted to me come back to a good way of life. For all my life I am prepared to endure anything that pleases you."[76]

And God heard these fervent prayers, for later our saint had to confess: "If I had known when I came to the parish of Ars what I would have to suffer, the fear of it would certainly have killed me."[77]

Following in the footsteps of the great apostles of all ages, he knew that the best and most effective way for him to contribute to the salvation of those who would be entrusted to his care was through the cross. It was for them that he put up with all sorts of calumnies, prejudices and opposition, without complaint; for them that he willingly endured the sharp discomforts and annoyances of mind and body that were forced upon him by his daily administration of the Sacrament of Penance for thirty years with almost no

---

[75] Cf. *Archiv. Secret. Vat.*, v. 227, p. 1210.
[76] Cf. *Archiv. Secret. Vat.*, v. 227, p. 53.   [77] Cf. *ibid.*, v. 227, p. 991.

interruption; for them that this athlete of Christ fought off the powers of hell; for them, last of all, that he brought his body into subjection through voluntary mortification.

Almost everyone knows his answer to the priest who complained to him that his apostolic zeal was bearing no fruit: "You have offered humble prayers to God, you have wept, you have groaned, you have sighed. Have you added fasts, vigils, sleeping on the floor, castigation of your body? Until you have done all of these, do not think that you have tried everything."[78]

Need for comparison

Once again Our mind turns to sacred ministers who have the care of souls, and We urgently beg them to realize the importance of these words. Let each one think over his own life, in the light of the supernatural prudence that should govern all of our actions, and ask himself if it is really all that the pastoral care of the people entrusted to him requires.

With firm confidence that the merciful God will never fail to offer the help that human weakness calls for, let sacred ministers think over the offices and burdens they have assumed by looking at St. John M. Vianney as if he were a mirror. "A terrible disaster strikes us curés"—the holy man complained—"when our spirit grows lazy and careless"; he was referring to the harmful attitude of those pastors who are not disturbed by the fact that many sheep committed to them are growing filthy in the slavery of sin. If they want to imitate the Curé of Ars more closely, who was so "convinced that men should be loved, so that we can do good to them,"[79] then let these priests ask themselves what kind of love they have for those whom God has entrusted to their care and for whom Christ has died!

Because of human liberty and of events beyond all human control, the efforts of even the holiest of men will sometimes fail. But a priest ought to remember that in the mysterious counsels of divine Providence, the eternal fate of many men is bound up with his pastoral interest and care and the example of his priestly life. Is not

[78] Cf. *ibid.*, v. 227, p. 53.   [79] Cf. *Archiv. Secret. Vat.*, v. 227, p. 1002.

this thought powerful enough both to stir up the lackadaisical in an effective way and to urge on to greater efforts those who are already zealous in the work of Christ?

Preacher and catechist

Because, as is recorded, "he was always ready to care for the needs of souls,"[80] St. John M. Vianney, good shepherd that he was, was also outstanding in offering his sheep an abundant supply of the food of Christian truth. Throughout his life, he preached and taught catechism.

The Council of Trent pronounced this to be a parish priest's first and greatest duty and everyone knows what immense and constant labor John Vianney expended in order to be equal to carrying out this task. For he began his course of studies when he was already along in years, and he had great difficulty with it; and his first sermons to the people kept him up for whole nights on end. How much the ministers of the word of God can find here to imitate! For there are some who give up all effort at further study and then point too readily to his small fund of learning as an adequate excuse for themselves. They would be much better off if they would imitate the great perseverance of soul with which the Curé of Ars prepared himself to carry out this great ministry to the best of his abilities: which, as a matter of fact, were not quite as limited as is sometimes believed, for he had a clear mind and sound judgment.[81]

Obligation to learn

Men in Sacred Orders should gain an adequate knowledge of human affairs and a thorough knowledge of sacred doctrine that is in keeping with their respective positions and their abilities. Would that all pastors of souls would exert as much effort as the Curé of Ars did to overcome difficulties and obstacles in learning, to strengthen memory through practice, and especially to draw knowledge from the Cross of Our Lord, which is the greatest of all books. This is why his bishop made this reply to some of his critics: "I do

---

[80] Cf. *ibid.*, v. 227, p. 580.   [81] Cf. *ibid.*, v. 3897, p. 444.

not know whether he is learned; but a heavenly light shines in him."[82]

Model for preachers

This is why Our predecessor of happy memory, Pius XII, was perfectly right in not hesitating to offer this country curé as a model for the preachers of the Holy City: "The holy Curé of Ars had none of the natural gifts of a speaker that stand out in men like P. Segneri or B. Bossuet. But the clear, lofty, living thoughts of his mind were reflected in the sound of his voice and shone forth from his glance, and they came out in the form of ideas and images that were so apt and so well fitted to the thoughts and feelings of his listeners and so full of wit and charm that even St. Francis de Sales would have been struck with admiration. This is the kind of speaker who wins the souls of the faithful. A man who is filled with Christ will not find it hard to discover ways and means of bringing others to Christ."[83]

These words give a wonderful picture of the Curé of Ars as a catechism teacher and as a preacher. And when, towards the end of his life on earth, his voice was too weak to carry to his listeners, the sparkle and gleam of his eyes, his tears, his sighs of divine love, the bitter sorrow he evidenced when the mere concept of sin came to his mind, were enough to convert to a better way of life the faithful who surrounded his pulpit. How could anyone help being moved deeply with a life so completely dedicated to Christ shining so clearly there before him?

Up to the time of his blessed death, St. John M. Vianney held on tenaciously to his office of teaching the faithful committed to his care and the pious pilgrims who crowded the church, by denouncing evil of every kind, in whatever guise it might appear, "in season, out of season"[84] and, even more, by sublimely raising souls to God; for "he preferred to show the beauties of virtue rather than the ugliness of vice."[85] For this humble priest understood perfectly how great the dignity and sublimity of teaching the word of God really is.

[82] Cf. *ibid.*, v. 3897, p. 272.
[83] Cf. discourse of March 16, 1946: *AAS* 38 (1946) 186.   [84] *2 Tim.* 4, 2.
[85] Cf. *Archiv. Secret. Vat.*, v. 227, p. 185.

"Our Lord"—he said—"who Himself is truth, has as much regard for His word as for His Body."

The obligation to teach

So it is easy to realize what great joy it brought Our predecessors to point out an example like this to be imitated by those who guide the Christian people; for the proper and careful exercise of the teaching office by the clergy is of great importance. In speaking of this, St. Pius X had this to say: "We want especially to pursue this one point and to urge strongly that no priest has any more important duty or is bound by any stricter obligation."[86]

And so once again We take this warning which Our predecessors have repeated over and over again and which has been inserted in the Code of Canon Law as well,[87] and We issue it to you, venerable brethren, on the occasion of the solemn celebration of the centenary of the holy catechist and preacher of Ars.

In this regard We wish to offer Our praise and encouragement to the studies that have been carefully and prudently carried on in many areas under your leadership and auspices, to improve the religious training of both youngsters and adults by presenting it in a variety of forms that are especially adapted to local circumstances and needs. All of these efforts are useful; but on the occasion of this centenary, God wants to cast new light on the wonderful power of the apostolic spirit, that sweeps all in its path, as it is exemplified in this priest who throughout his life was a witness in word and deed for Christ nailed to the cross "not in the persuasive language devised by human wisdom, but in a manifestation of spiritual power."[88]

His ministry in the confessional

All that remains for Us to do is to recall at a little greater length the pastoral ministry of St. John M. Vianney, which was a kind of steady martyrdom for a long period of his life, and especially his administration of the sacrament of Penance, which calls for special praise for it brought forth richest and most salutary fruits.

---

[86] Encyclical letter "*Acerbo nimis*," *Acta Pii X*, II, p. 75.
[87] *C.J.C.*, canons 1330-1332.   [88] *1 Cor.* 2, 4.

"For almost fifteen hours each day, he lent a patient ear to penitents. This work began early in the morning and continued well on into the night."[89] And when he was completely worn out and broken five days before his death and had no strength left, the final penitents came to his bed. Toward the end of his life, the number of those who came to see him each year reached eighty thousand according to the accounts.[90]

His anguish over sins

It is hard to imagine what pain and discomfort and bodily sufferings this man underwent as he sat to hear confessions in the tribunal of Penance for what seemed like endless periods of time, especially if you recall how weakened he was by his fasts, mortifications, sicknesses, vigils and lack of sleep.

But he was bothered even more by a spiritual anguish that took complete possession of him. Listen to his mournful cries: "So many crimes against God are committed"—he said—"that they sometimes incline us to ask God to end this world! . . . You have to come to the town of Ars if you really want to learn what an infinite multitude of serious sins there are. . . . Alas, we do not know what to do, we think that there is nothing else to do than weep and pray to God."

And this holy man could have added that he had taken on himself more than his share of the expiation of these sins. For he told those who asked his advice in this regard: "I impose only a small penance on those who confess their sins properly; the rest I perform in their place."[91]

His concern for sinners

St. John M. Vianney always had "poor sinners," as he called them, in his mind and before his eyes, with the constant hope of seeing them turn back to God and weep for the sins they had committed. This was the object of all his thoughts and cares, and of the work that took up almost all his time and efforts.[92]

[89] Cf. *Archiv. Secret. Vat.*, v. 227, p. 18.
[90] Cf. *ibid.*
[91] Cf. *Archiv. Secret. Vat.*, v. 227, p. 1018.
[92] Cf. *ibid.*, v. 227, p. 18.

From his experience in the tribunal of Penance, in which he loosed the bonds of sin, he understood just how much malice there is in sin and what terrible devastation it wreaks in the souls of men. He used to paint it in hideous colors: "If we"—he asserted—"had the faith to see a soul in mortal sin, we would die of fright."[93]

But the sufferings of souls who have remained attached to their sins in hell did not add to the strength and vigor of his own sorrow and words as much as did the anguish he felt at the fact that divine love had been carelessly neglected or violated by some offense. This stubbornness in sin and ungrateful disregard for God's great goodness made rivers of tears flow from his eyes. "My friend"—he said—"I am weeping because you are not."[94]

And yet, what great kindness he displayed in devoting himself to restoring hope to the souls of repentant sinners! He spared no effort to become a minister of divine mercy to them; and he described it as "like an overflowing river that carries all souls along with it"[95] and throbs with a love greater than that of a mother, "for God is quicker to forgive than a mother to snatch her child from the fire."[96]

The seriousness of confession

Let the example of the Curé of Ars stir up those who are in charge of souls to be eager and well-prepared in devoting themselves to this very serious work, for it is here most of all that divine mercy finally triumphs over human malice and that men have their sins wiped away and are reconciled to God.

And let them also remember that Our predecessor of happy memory, Pius XII, expressed disapproval "in the strongest terms" of the opinion of those who have little use for frequent confession, where it is a matter of venial sins; the Supreme Pontiff said: "We particularly recommend the pious practice of frequent confession, which the Church has introduced, under the influence of the Holy Spirit, as a means of swifter daily progress along the road of virtue."[97]

[93] Cf. *ibid.*, v. 227, p. 290.
[94] Cf. *ibid.*, v. 227, p. 999.
[95] Cf. *ibid.*, v. 227, p. 978.
[96] Cf. *ibid.*, v. 3900, p. 1554.
[97] Encyclical letter *"Mystici Corporis," AAS* 35 (1943) 235.

Again, We have complete confidence that sacred ministers will be even more careful than others in faithfully observing the prescriptions of Canon Law,[98] which make the pious use of the Sacrament of Penance, which is so necessary for the attainment of sanctity, obligatory at certain specified times; and that they will treat those urgent exhortations which this same predecessor of Ours made "with a sorrowful soul" on several occasions[99] with the supreme veneration and obedience they deserve.

Necessity of personal holiness

As this encyclical of Ours draws to a close, We want to assure you, venerable brethren, of the high hopes We have that these centenary celebrations will, with the help of God, lead to a deeper desire and more intensive efforts on the part of all priests to carry out their sacred ministry with more ardent zeal and especially to work to fulfill "the first duty of priests, that is, the duty of becoming holy themselves."[100]

When We gaze from this height of the supreme pontificate to which We have been raised by the secret counsels of divine Providence and turn Our mind to what souls are hoping for and expecting, or to the many areas of the earth that have not yet been brightened by the light of the Gospel, or last of all to the many needs of the Christian people, the figure of the priest is always before Our eyes.

If there were no priests or if they were not doing their daily work, what use would all these apostolic undertakings be, even those which seem best suited to the present age? Of what use would be the laymen who work so zealously and generously to help in the activities of the apostolate?

And so We do not hesitate to speak to all of these sacred ministers, whom We love so much and in whom the Church rests such great hopes—these priests—and urge them in the name of Jesus

---

[98] *C.J.C.* canon 125, section 1.
[99] Cf. encyclical letter *"Mystici Corporis," AAS* 35 (1943) 235; encyclical letter *"Mediator Dei," AAS* 39 (1947) 585; apostolic exhortation *"Menti Nostrae," AAS* 42 (1950) 674.
[100] Apostolic exhortation *"Menti Nostrae," AAS* 42 (1950) 677.

Christ from the depths of a father's heart to be faithful in doing and giving all that the seriousness of their ecclesiastical dignity requires of them.

This appeal of Ours draws added force from the wise and prudent words of St. Pius X: "Nothing is needed more to promote the kingdom of Jesus Christ in the world than the holiness of churchmen, who should stand out above the faithful by their example, their words and their teaching."[101]

And this fits in perfectly with the words that St. John M. Vianney addressed to his bishop: "If you want the whole diocese to be converted to God, then all of the curés must become holy."

Help from bishops

And We especially want to commend these most beloved sons to you, venerable brethren, who bear the chief responsibility for the holiness of your clergy, so that you will be careful to go to them and help them in the difficulties—sometimes serious ones—that they face in their own lives or in carrying out their duties.

What is there that cannot be accomplished by a bishop who loves the clergy entrusted to his direction, who is close to them, really knows them, takes great care of them and directs them in a firm but fatherly way?

It is true that your pastoral care is supposed to extend to the whole diocese, but you should still take very special care of those who are in sacred orders, for they are your closest helpers in your work and are bound to you by many sacred ties.

Help from the faithful

On the occasion of this centenary celebration, We would also like to exhort paternally all of the faithful to offer constant prayers to God for their priests, so that each in his own way may help them attain holiness.

Those who are more fervent and devout are turning their eyes and their minds to the priest with a great deal of hope and expectation. For, at a time when you find flourishing everywhere the power

---

[101] Cf. epistle *"La ristorazione," Acta Pii X,* I, p. 257.

of money, the allure of pleasures of the senses, and too great an esteem for technical achievements, they want to see in him a man who speaks in the name of God, who is animated by a firm faith, and who gives no thought to himself, but burns with intense charity.

So let them all realize that they can help sacred ministers a great deal to achieve this lofty goal, if only they will show due respect for priestly dignity, and have proper esteem for their pastoral office and its difficulties, and finally be even more zealous and active in offering to help them.

A call for vocations

We cannot help turning our paternal spirit in a special way to young people; We embrace them with a warm love and remind them that, in them, the Church rests great hopes for the years to come.

The harvest indeed is great, but the laborers are few.[102] How many areas there are where the heralds of the Gospel truth are worn out by their labors and waiting eagerly and longingly for those to come who will take their place! There are peoples who are languishing in a miserable hunger for heavenly food more than for earthly nourishment. Who will bring the heavenly banquet of life and truth to them?

We have complete confidence that the youngsters of our time will be as quick as those of times past to give a generous answer to the invitation of the divine Master to provide for this vital need.

Priests often find themselves in difficult circumstances. This is not surprising; for those who hate the Church always show their hostility by trying to harm and deceive her sacred ministers; as the Curé of Ars himself admitted, those who want to overthrow religion always try in their hatred to strike at priests first of all.

But even in the face of these serious difficulties, priests who are ardent in their devotion to God enjoy a real, sublime happiness from an awareness of their own position, for they know that they have been called by the divine Savior to offer their help in a most holy work, which will have an effect on the redemption of the souls

[102] Cf. *Matt.* 9, 37.

of men and on the growth of the Mystical Body of Christ. So let Christian families consider it one of their most sublime privileges to give priests to the Church; and so let them offer their sons to the sacred ministry with joy and gratitude.

Lourdes and Ars

There is no need to dwell on this point, venerable brothers, since what We are urging is very close to your own hearts. For We are sure that you understand perfectly Our interest in these things and the forceful expression We are giving to it, and that you share it. For the present, We commit this matter of immense importance, closely bound up with the salvation of many souls, to the intercession of St. John M. Vianney.

We also turn Our eyes to the Mother of God, immaculate from the very beginning. Shortly before the Curé of Ars, filled with heavenly merits, completed his long life, she appeared in another part of France to an innocent and humble girl, and through her, invited men with a mother's insistence to devote themselves to prayers and Christian penance; this majestic voice is still striking home to souls a century later, and echoing far and wide almost endlessly.

The things that were done and said by this holy priest, who was raised to the honors of the heavenly saints and whose 100th anniversary We are commemorating, cast a kind of heavenly light beforehand over the supernatural truths which were made known to the innocent girl at the grotto of Lourdes. For this man had such great devotion to the Immaculate Conception of the Virgin Mother of God that in 1836 he dedicated his parish church to Mary Conceived Without Sin and greeted the infallible definition of this truth as Catholic dogma in 1854 with the greatest joy and reverence.[103]

So there is good reason for Us to link together this double centenary, of Lourdes and of Ars, as We give proper thanks to the most high God: each supplements the other, and each does honor to a nation We love very much and which can boast of having both of these most holy places in its bosom.

[103] Cf. *Archiv. Secret. Vat.*, v. 227, p. 90.

St. John Vianney, Model for Priests 101

Mindful of the many benefits that have been received, and trusting confidently that still more will come to Us and to the whole Church, We borrow the prayer that sounded so often on the lips of the Curé of Ars: "Blessed be the most holy and immaculate conception of the Blessed Virgin Mary, Mother of God. May all nations praise, all lands invoke and preach your Immaculate Heart!"[104]

Confident that this centennial celebration of St. John M. Vianney throughout the world will stir up the pious zeal of priests and of those whom God is calling to take up the priesthood, and will make all the faithful even more active and interested in supplying the things that are needed for priests' life and work, with all Our heart We impart the Apostolic Blessing to each and every one of them, and especially to you, venerable brethren, as a consoling pledge of heavenly graces and of Our good will.

Given at Rome, at St. Peter's, on August 1, 1959, the first year of Our Pontificate.

JOHN PP. XXIII

[104] Cf. *ibid.*, v. 227, p. 1021.

COUNSELS FOR SEMINARIANS

An Address of Pope John XXIII
to Seminarians in Rome

- *Memories of his own seminary years*
- *The personal sanctification of priests*
- *The value of reading Scripture*

BELOVED SONS! Our heart prompted Us to meet with you here, in order to confide to you some thoughts which were suggested to Us by the solemn festivities of the Synod.[1]

You make up a numerous and happy group in the diversity of your national origins, and in the glowing charm of your youth: your presence here is the beautiful and ready answer which divine Providence gives to the cares and anxieties of Holy Church, as to the quality, quantity, and apostolic zeal of the future members of her clergy. Your youthful group adorns the Roman Synod, as it were, with a bright promise of future blossoms, and the reflected light of its beauty shines over all the dioceses of the world from which you came.

Inspiring circumstances

Our meeting is enhanced and given a deeper meaning by the celebration of an event of the greatest importance in the religious life of the City, and by its surroundings—this church of St. Ignatius, which jealously guards its glorious memories and attests to the services rendered by the adjacent Roman College in the cause of sacred scholarship and the apostolate. Especially worthy of respect

[1] The third and final session of the Roman Synod had taken place on the day before this talk to the seminarians.—Ed.

is the mausoleum of Pope Gregory XV—Alexander Ludovisi—for whom a short pontificate (1621-1623) sufficed to achieve great merits for the role he played in the glorification of St. Ignatius and St. Francis Xavier, and in the establishment of world-wide missionary cooperation. Let Us confide to you in a whisper, as it were, that during Our seminary years in Rome We often repaired to this church to the altar of St. Louis and St. John Berchmans to ask for their intercession that the grace of chastity might be preserved in Us forever without any diminution of its delicate splendor.

In those youthful years, Our soul found happiness in seeking the presence and blessing of two saintly popes, first the great Leo XIII, and later St. Pius X, always fatherly and kind.

The Book of Judges

We will again seek inspiration in the sacred scriptures for Our conversation with you, who are Our youngest sons, just as We did in the last three days, when We addressed the solemn gathering of the priests of Our diocese. We find this inspiration in the Book of Judges, which as you well know, records the deeds of the men who accepted the inheritance of Moses and set the chosen people on the difficult course they were to steer in their life and history.

The chosen few

Gedeon, who had under his command an enormous multitude of soldiers, obviously ready and willing to face any risk and any obstacle, is told by the Lord that in great undertakings you must count, not on the many, but on the chosen few. Selection is the law of life, progress, and perfection.

Beloved sons! We like to imagine you, after all the years of preparation in your native lands, as regiments of soldiers who have been chosen and set aside, in obedience to the call of the Lord, for the future conquests by the Kingdom of God. We find this fact admirably described in chapter seven of Judges as follows: "The Lord said to Gedeon: You have too many soldiers with you for me to deliver Madian into their power, lest Israel vaunt itself against me and say: 'My own power brought me the victory.' Now proclaim to all the soldiers: 'If anyone is afraid or fearful, let him leave.' "[2] This is as much as to say: Whoever does not possess the necessary courage, and is fearful, let him turn back.

After these words were spoken, the multitude was reduced to twenty thousand: and these twenty thousand were further reduced to three hundred, according to the precise instructions of the Lord: "Lead them down to the water, and I will test them . . . there."[3] And here is the ordeal which tests the strength, dedication, and spirit of sacrifice of the individual soldiers: "You shall set to one side everyone who laps up the water . . ., to the other, everyone who kneels down to drink."[4]

The implications of this passage are clear: those who hesitate, those who are too mindful of their own comfort, and those who crave to satisfy their thirst at all the sources of human knowledge and experience, are not, and cannot be, soldiers of God's Kingdom.

Three thoughts

Beloved sons! The secret of fruitfulness and success in your future activity lies in this spirit of detachment. New soldiers of the modern age, you are going to undertake very worthy enterprises, which will bear no resemblance to earthly conquest or dominion. Rather, you will seek new conditions that will make possible a more orderly life together for people; you will, with ardent desire and action, devote yourselves to the unification of all humanity in Christ. Allow Us, then, to entrust to you three thoughts which are very dear to Us.

We did not receive them by heavenly revelation, as was the case with Gedeon, but they are the fruit of long hours of meditation and prayer. Here they are: Walk worthily; accept the Book and read it eagerly; sing the Psalms with understanding and frequently.[5]

[2] "Dixitque Dominus ad Gedeon: Multus tecum est populus, nec tradetur Madian in manus eius, ne glorietur contra me Israel et dicat: Meis viribus liberatus sum. Loquere ad populum, et cunctis audientibus praedica. Qui formidolosus et timidus est revertatur." (Judges 7, 2-3)
[3] "Duc eos ad aquas, et ibi probabo illos." (Judges 7, 4)
[4] "Qui lingua lambuerint aquas . . . separabis eos seorsum; qui autem curvatis genibus biberint, in altera parte erunt . . ." (Judges 7, 5-6)
[5] "Digne ambulate; accipite librum et devorate illum; psallite sapienter et frequenter."

Walking worthily

1. We say to you, first of all: Walk worthily. These words outline for you the necessity of leading a worthy life, harboring high ideals and purposes, and preserving a spotless priestly character.

Brothers

Although you came to Rome from different parts of the world, in your daily encounters you are like brothers unto one another. Basically, you are not in any way different from each other, since you share a common inheritance and a common goal in the service of God and souls. When you came to the center of the Catholic world, each of you carried with him from his native land treasures of ancient wisdom and of sound, noble, glorious tradition. Here you learn to know and, consequently, to appreciate one another better, and to share with each other the gifts of nature and grace which every one of you possesses.

Your young hearts, eagerly waiting to reap the future harvests of souls, well know that you are not here in Rome to prepare for positions of privilege; on the contrary, you are here to become the most willing, skilled, humble, and generous assistants of your bishops and of your brother priests, who are counting so much on you. This is, therefore, the most fruitful period of your formation.

True progress

This is why We say to you with an anxious heart: Walk worthily! That is tantamount to repeating God's invitation to faithful Abraham: "Walk in My presence and be perfect."[6]

This means, first and foremost, proceed with dignity; that is, you must progress in enriching your minds, which must open up to all things beautiful and sacred in the light of God; progress in purifying your heart, and freeing it from bondage to any one individual creature, thereby giving it the power to embrace all creatures, in their joys and sorrows; progress in strengthening and maturing your experience with a view to your future responsibility; progress con-

---

[6] *"Ambula coram me et esto perfectus."* (*Gen.* 17, 1)

stantly in developing an amiable and attractive disposition. In other words, you must move in the direction of "whatever things are true, whatever things are honorable, whatever things are just, whatever things are holy, and whatever things make you lovable and of good repute."[7] From Rome, this city of apostles and martyrs, of monks and missionaries, advance toward new conquests. For, whenever you stop to settle down in comfort and listen to the blandishments of the flesh, you run the risk of becoming like stagnant waters. Advance, then, but advance with dignity.

Clarity and watchfulness

All the elements of your formation should have splendor; you must look with clear eyes at whatever is before you, not only anticipating the chaste joy of celebrating the Mass in holiness, but also contemplating unflinchingly the difficulties you will meet, and the uncertainties and doubts which will threaten to cloud and paralyze your judgment.

Walk worthily! Be on your guard against the snares of your heart, your senses, your relations with others, and your reactions. A priest is not a man of impulse, nor is he a sentimentalist, or a partial, aloof, shy, and moody man. A priest is not satisfied with mediocrity. From the first precious years of his formation, he strives to attain self-knowledge, in order to overcome his failings, and approach the ideal perfection which God demands. And be thou perfect.

Sacred Scripture

2. The second thought is an invitation to enjoy the substantial pleasures afforded by sacred scripture: "Take the scroll and eat it up."[8]

Always keep the prophetic symbols of the Apocalypse before your eyes: it is the angel standing on the sea and the earth who, obeying the command uttered by the voice from heaven, offers the Sacred Book to you, just as he offered it to John the Apostle. What

---

[7] See *Phil.* 4, 8.
[8] "*Accipite librum, et devorate illum.*" (*Apoc.* 10, 9)

a meaningful symbol this is for the Church, who reaches across continents and hands you her precious treasure!

The Book indicates the will of God for each one of us: it points to the right conduct of life and to the secret of success in any effective form of the apostolate; in other words, the kind of apostolate which does not crave human results—indeed, such may not be forthcoming. You see how the Church operates: she sows in one century and reaps in subsequent ones by means of her councils, her synods, and her canonical rulings.

Nourishment from Scripture

Let the Sacred Book, then, guide you toward a firmer and more solid piety, and to a more glowing priestly life. At one time, We found in the writings of the Protopatriarch of Venice, St. Lawrence Justinian, a wonderful consonance of words on the subject of the benefits offered by the divine Book. We are now happy to quote from his work *"De Casto Connubio Verbi Dei,"* in which We found these profound and beautiful expressions: "The Sacred Book is indeed the mirror in which is reflected the knowledge of the Word; it is the holy tabernacle of the Godhead.[9] No one who approaches it in a spirit of purity, prudence, and humility will depart from it empty-handed. The Book teaches the ways of righteous living; under the surface of its words, what a current of lofty truths and of mysterious sacraments! In the Book are the wonders of the divine Omnipotence which created the world; in it is the cooperative role of the angels, as well as the instrumental function of man. Those holy pages exalt, first and foremost, the supreme goodness of the Creator, who by them wished to enlighten human ignorance, lead man to faith, sustain his hopes, and wean his spirit away from visible things, while nourishing it with things invisible and eternal."[10]

This is the substantial nourishment which the Divine Book alone can give you. This is the reason for the exhortation: "Take the

---

[9] *"Divinitatis armarium."*
[10] St. Lawrence Justinian, *Opera Omnia,* Venice, 1721, p. 157; see A. G. Cardinal Roncalli, "La Sacra Scrittura e San Lorenzo Giustiniani," *Rivista Biblica,* 1958, pp. 291-2.

scroll and eat it up." As a starting point for more specific manifestations of piety, and for the performance of your priestly mission, the Divine Book can open up before you the horizons of a profound and generous spiritual life, and show you the devotions which have always been the mark of a good priest, anytime and anywhere: the Eucharist, the Sacred Heart, the Most Precious Blood, the Blessed Virgin, and, lastly, the saints of the Old and New Testaments. The sacred scriptures form an orderly and admirable unit, which must be first absorbed by your minds, to enable you to educate God's people for the heights of piety, and the Christian conduct of life.

The Psalms

3. One last thought, beloved sons. "Sing the Psalms with understanding and frequently." Jesus' invitation to this effect is clear and imperative. "They must always pray and not lose heart."[11] Let your prayer, then, be incessant, meditative, and wise. Let it be your food and the very air you breathe, which keeps you spiritually alive by protecting you against the poisonous vapors of a worldly mentality that might even seriously jeopardize your vocation. Respond, then, to the joyous exhortation of the Apostle: "Let the word of Christ dwell in you abundantly: in all wisdom teach and admonish one another by psalms, hymns, and spiritual songs, singing in your hearts to God by his grace."[12]

Study of the Psalter

The Psalter is an invaluable source of prayer; in the near future you will have to become familiar with it, and make it the thought of your thoughts, and the living substance of your consecrated life. We want you to be conversant with the Psalter right now: you must, therefore, study it and know it both as a whole and in its individual parts. Meditate upon different psalms, in order to discover the hidden beauty of each, and thus acquire a real *"sensus Dei"* and

---

[11] *"Oportet semper orare, et non deficere."* (*Luke* 18, 1)
[12] *"Verbum Christi habitet in vobis abundanter in omni sapientia docentes et commonentes vosmetipsos psalmis, hymnis et canticis spiritualibus, in gratia cantantes in cordibus vestris Deo."* (*Col.* 3, 16)

"sensus Ecclesiae." Rest in the psalms, and rise from them to the contemplation of heavenly things, and learn from them to appreciate the things of the world, such as culture, history, and the daily occurrences of your personal life, with moderation and perspective.

The habit of prayer

It has been said that a priest must always have a prayer on his lips. This habit of prayer, however, like all the things of the spirit, cannot be stored away for future use and aired after ordination, because even then, unless the habit of prayer was formed long ago, there will be no dearth of motives or excuses, under the guise of other occupations and work, for letting the practice die out. Now is the time for you to become men of prayer: how much light, sweetness, spiritual balance, and even influence over souls, you will acquire from your familiarity with the Psalter, the substantial nourishment of your piety!

Papal affection

Beloved sons! We confided to you these three thoughts, and now We trust that they will germinate and blossom into a revival of devotion, both in your hearts and in the hearts of your brother seminarians all over the world.

The Pope loves you in a very special way, and prays for you many times a day, especially in the morning during Holy Mass, and in the evening at the rosary.

The Pope loves you. When, during audiences and gatherings, Our eyes turn to young seminarians, We feel their hearts close to Ours, in joyous and perfect harmony.

You embody the hope and certainty of the future. The Church loves you, and to you who know neither fatigue nor old age she entrusts the anxieties and preoccupations of her future. You are the flower-scented spring of tomorrow, which, with confident heart, We visualize as rich in holy affirmations for the Church of God, while Our hands are raised in a gesture of encouragement and benediction.

An exhortation

Continue, then, to walk worthily on the path you have chosen: draw from the sacred scriptures, the Old and New Testaments, the strength of your piety, the willingness of your obedience to the voice of the Church, the splendor of your chastity, and the generosity of your apostolate. May you be the consolation of your bishops, and the purest glory of your native lands. Humbly aware of your frailty, always place your trust in the strength of Jesus Christ, who summoned you to continue the work of the Redemption.

A heavenly vision

A priest may walk on earth, but his thoughts, his heart, and his eyes are turned toward heaven. "And they shall see his face and his name shall be on their foreheads. And night shall be no more, and they shall have no need of light of lamps, or light of sun, for the Lord God will shed light upon them, and they shall reign forever and ever."[13]

Our eyes contemplate this moving vision, while a choir of well-modulated voices begins and continues the exaltation of three canticles: *Benedictus, Magnificat,* and *Nunc Dimittis,* which, in the first pages of the Gospel, proclaim the realization of the ancient prophecies and the dawning of a new era, the era of the eternal Gospel, the Gospel of freedom, peace, and unity for the human family.

The Church, always courageous and progressive, entrusts this Gospel to you. Beloved sons, always keep it the way you receive it: "in your hearts and on your lips, to proclaim it worthily."[14]

We leave this heavenly vision with you, while We entreat God to continue lavishing his heavenly favors upon you; and We impart to you an affectionate and fatherly Apostolic Benediction, which We also wish to extend to your superiors, to your parents, who understood the inestimable gift of your priestly vocation, and to all

---

[13] "*Et videbunt faciem eius, et nomen eius in frontibus eorum. Et nox ultra non erit, e non egebant lumine lucernae, neque lumine solis, quoniam Dominus Deus illuminabit illos, et regnabunt in saecula saeculorum.*" (*Apoc.* 22, 4-5)

[14] "*in corde et in labiis vestris ut digne illud annuntietis!*"

the people who have a place in your thoughts, and to whom you are already devoting the best of your apostolate of prayer and sacrifice.

—January 28, 1960

THE ROMAN SYNOD AND THE PRIEST

An Address of Pope John XXIII
to the Clergy of Rome

- *Shunning excesses in religious devotions*
- *Means to an immaculate life*
- *Detachment from the world*
- *The letters of St. Peter*

BELOVED SONS! On the feast of St. Peter We met with you in the Vatican Basilica for the promulgation of the Synod. Earlier still, in the latter part of January, we shared days of spiritual intimacy and pastoral solicitude while celebrating that event, which quickly took its place in the annals of the diocese of Rome. Ever since, the heart of your bishop has maintained quiet but close, special contact with the mind and heart of every member of the secular and religious clergy of the City.

And from time to time, as We gave thanks to God, We have enjoyed recalling with a smile some of the good-humored remarks that had reached Our ears, declaring in prophetic tones that the escapade We were planning—an undertaking like that of a synod in Rome—was imprudent from the very first announcement. And later on, there were indications that some would still not be completely convinced until it was actually promulgated. Heavenly grace was not invoked in vain. From the very first meeting on January 24th in Our sacred Lateran Basilica to the more solemn one on June 29th close by the Tomb of St. Peter, We were able, with the help of the Lord, to celebrate what was certainly an *opus bonum*,[1] even if not, in some respects, an *opus perfectum*.[2]

[1] A good work.
[2] A completed work.

An Apostolic Meeting

We were all at the apostolic meeting. If a respectful comparison may be permitted Us, all of the twelve were there in full agreement. Even Thomas was there—that is, even those who had been timid and uncertain in the beginning. All were equally impressed by the Lord's goodness toward those who invoke Him and serve Him trustingly. *Umbram fugat veritas, noctem lux eliminat.*[3]

Since the actual promulgation, or more precisely, since November 1st, the Roman Synod has had the force of diocesan law. Through the words of the apostolic constitution *"Sollicitudo omnium Ecclesiarum,"* today every priest of the Roman clergy knows better than ever how he is supposed to act in all matters proper to him and his office. As the pages of the Synod become familiar to his mind, they repeat each day *"Hoc fac et vives."*[4]

Words of encouragement

Well, then, beloved sons of Ours, in this matter of your wonderful dispositions and your determination to translate these synodal regulations into practice, We thought that it would not displease you if We added a few more words to what We had the consolation of saying to you in Our talks during those blessed days last January: and We do so as new encouragement to all of you to act with honor before God, before Holy Church, and before men.

The sacred volume of the Roman Synod is circulating—do not be surprised at that—in the world, and it has been well received and appreciated by venerable pastors; in the last few days, they have told Us so personally and have written to let Us know how pleased they are. Right now We are preparing a translation of it into Italian and other languages for laymen, so that it may serve to put them too on the road toward knowledge of the clear and shining principles that support the wisest and most divine of establishments—the Church of Jesus, still militant here on earth, yet always assured of triumph in the never-ending life to come.

[3] Truth puts shadow to flight; light does away with the night. (From the Liturgy: Sequence *Lauda Sion*)
[4] "Do this and thou shalt live." (*Luke* 10, 28)

Frequent and Steady Reading of the Synod

Here is the first thing that We have to say to you.

Before all else, beloved sons, please accept Our invitation to get used to reading the Synod, for day by day it will reveal to you hidden beauties of thought and of wisdom. Make it a regular habit to go back over those pages and get their full flavor; this is of greater value—do not be displeased at hearing Us say this with complete frankness right here at the beginning, since the occasion for doing so presents itself—of greater value than taking special care to cultivate particular practices or devotions, which may be excessive in their veneration of Our Lady, the dear mother of Jesus and our mother—who will not be offended by these words of Ours—and of certain saints, for sometimes, as a result of these, the whole picture of the religious devotion of our good people is tarnished and impoverished.

We hope you understand what We mean. The priest has the duty of being on guard himself and of putting the people on their guard. Some pious practices merely satisfy the emotions; by themselves, they do not amount to fulfillment of religious obligations and so they are not even in full agreement with the first three commandments of the Decalogue, which are serious and obligatory.

Guidance from the Bible

With regard to reading the new code of diocesan life the Old and the New Testaments supply us with some valuable directions drawn from the prophets and from the evangelists. Ezechiel, for example, in the second chapter of his prophetic poem, reveals to us his vision of the scroll that a mysterious hand extended to him, with writing on the outside and the inside containing lamentations, songs, and woes. He too was invited to read and to devour the precious book and in his turn, he never stops inviting others to do so, as he feels in his loins its fullness and richness of life and in his mouth a sweetness like that of honey.[5]

St. John, too, along with the other Evangelists—just on the basis

[5] Cf. *Ezech.* 2, 8 to 3, 3.

of some indications in the biblical concordances that We have at hand—pays continuous homage to and constantly invites us to the same kind of reading, especially of the books that contain the words God addresses to our hearts, and that serve as a lamp lit to guide our steps along our path. *Vox Domini: divina lex: liber vitae.*[6]

Help from a psalm

Beloved sons, have you ever reflected on that sacred didactic poem, Psalm 118, that begins with *Beati immaculati in via,* or, as the latest translation goes: *Beati quorum immaculata est via,*[7] and that takes a turn toward the end with *Principes persequuntur me sine causa,*[8] and then finishes off with those very touching words: *vivat anima mea et laudet te: et decreta tua adjuvent me: Oberro ut ovis quae periit: quaere servum tuum, quia mandata tua non sum oblitus?*[9]

Please accept one more repetition—this is a habit of Ours—of an appeal to search into the depths of that collection of invitations and recommendations that stretches through the whole psalm as it is recited in the Sunday office, for you will find directions and comparisons that are more than just lofty poetry; you will find the spirit and substance of the synodal regulations.

We would enjoy offering you a number of examples. But you yourselves can easily discover some that are to your own taste. When We were young and assigned to humbler but still precious and meritorious tasks in the priestly ministry and in teaching, what a delightful lift it gave Our spirit to become the companion of St. Ambrose in his wonderful *Expositio in Psalmum centesimum decimum octavum*[10]—this very *Beati immaculati in via* that was just cited; in tome XV of Migne, it goes on for 342 pages, divided up into 22 sermons that offer rich food for a pious soul.

As for this invitation of Ours for you to put some very useful

---

[6] Voice of the Lord: divine law: book of life.
[7] Blessed are they whose way of life is spotless. (*Ps.* 118, 1)
[8] Princes persecute me without cause. (*Ps.* 118, 161)
[9] Let my soul live and praise thee, and let thy decrees help me. I go astray like a lost sheep; seek thy servant, for I have not forgotten thy commandments. (*Ps.* 118, 175-6)
[10] Explanation of Psalm 118.

variety into the ascetical practices of your daily life, which is so taken up with directly ministering to souls or with the service of the Holy Apostolic See, this passing mention is enough.

Three thoughts

With regard to the synod that has just been promulgated, We would rather speak to you of something that is very close to the heart of the lowly but official Shepherd of the whole flock of Christ (and in a special way of this holy and blessed portion—Rome, the first diocese of the world). Please lend an ear to three thoughts that We would like to pass on to you and to recommend to your pious attention.

Splendor of the Priest's Mission

1. The first is drawn from Psalm 14 of David: *Domine quis commorabitur in tabernaculo tuo, quis habitabit in monte sancto tuo.*[11] It has to do with the perfection that is a mark of our mission as priests, and it is the first light streaming from the Synod.

An immaculate life

Before all else: *ambulare sine macula.*[12] This means an immaculate life, personal conduct worthy of the gaze and admiration of the angels of the Lord, good enough to edify the faithful and to attract the attention and thoughtful consideration of the non-believers who happen to meet us. Any other praise, whether of personal characteristics or talent, of know-how or external success, is foolish and misleading. The priest reveals himself first of all at the altar in his observance and respect for liturgical laws. He reveals himself in his attention to promptness and simplicity, without any foolish sophistication that would weaken both himself and those who approach him; in a constant communication with blessed Jesus in words and thoughts and feelings; in the shining conformity of his external life with his conscience; and in his close familiarity with a personal con-

---
[11] O Lord, who shall dwell in thy tabernacle, who shall live on thy holy mountain? (*Ps.* 14, 1)
[12] To walk without stain.

fessor in order to insure good ascetical direction and effective self-discipline.

The altar

The altar, the altar, beloved sons, is the focal point for eyes and heart. It evokes the picture that characterizes our life, and it is the starting point for the full unfolding of the chief labors of a priest: confessions, spiritual direction, teaching catechism, caring for the sick, prompt and prudent and patient contact with the faithful of all ages and every social status in their doubts, their sorrows, their public calamities, their poverty.

A kindly attitude

Then: *facere justitiam et cogitare recta in corde suo*.[13] The habit of thinking ill of everything and everybody is an obstacle for you and for everyone around you. A moderate outlook towards all, but with eyes open and alive to the realities that are facing us and those who live with us; an habitual disposition to *nosce teipsum*,[14] in order to sympathize with others and to soften everything a little and turn it all to good, while finding motives for zeal in the example of others.

Above all, attention to governing your own tongue: *non calumniare; non facere malum proximo suo; non opprobrium inferre vicino suo*.[15] What a horrible thing these would be in the life of a priest!

Attitude toward the world

The fact that we must learn to control and discipline ourselves in this regard as we strive for perfection does not excuse us from passing stern judgment and condemning the things that are wrong in the world. It does not excuse us from trying to protect ourselves against such things or from refusing to let ourselves be deceived, or above

---

[13] To do justice and think right things in his heart.
[14] Know thyself.
[15] Not to slander; not to do evil to his neighbor; not to bring disgrace upon those close to him.

all from avoiding compromises with the world for the sake of some monetary advantage or material interest of ours that might be served, especially—and this is the worst and most damnable thing of all—if it is served at the expense of innocent persons.

Here, we are still on the level of the natural law. Woe to the priest who goes to the very limits of reprobation by daring to take false refuge behind the cloak of the mere appearances of canon law and of customs that are distorted or non-existent.

Serenity

A great blessing and motive for interior delight is to be found in this *commoratio*[16] of the priest in the tabernacle of the Lord: this dwelling *in monte sancto suo,*[17] despite his contact with the baseness of the world.

In order to add strength to our efforts to remain aloof and stay well above the seductions and enchantments of the present life, the 14th psalm is followed by psalms 15 and 16 which are also of David: *Conserva me, Deus, quoniam confugio in Te,*[18] and the prayer: *Audi, Domine, justam causam, attende clamorem meum.*[19]

Oh! what serene peace there is in this priestly life of ours that is sustained by the song. How it permits us to look at this magnificent volume of ours, *Prima Romana Synodus,*[20] and repeat the words of Psalm 16—with an attitude of respect for it and a clear conscience that we have respected it at all cost: *Si scrutaris cor meum, si visitas nocte, si igne me probas, non invenies in me iniquitatem. Non est transgressum os meum hominum more: secundum verba labiorum tuorum ego custodivi vias legis.*[21]

Notice that the old reading was actually *vias duras.*[22] Modern biblical scholars have made it clearer by having it read: *vias legis,*[23] thus showing a greater sense of trust in the Lord, who in imposing

[16] Lingering.   [17] In his holy mountain.
[18] Preserve me, O God, for I flee unto thee. (*Ps.* 15, 1)
[19] Hear, O Lord, a just cause, attend to my cry. (*Ps.* 16, 1)
[20] *The First Roman Synod.* (A copy of the Latin text of this work can be obtained by writing to Libreria Editrice Vaticana, Vatican City.—Ed.)
[21] If thou searchest my heart, if thou visitest me in the night, if thou triest me by fire, thou wilt not find iniquity in me. My mouth has not transgressed in the manner of men; I have kept the ways of the law according to the words of thy lips. (*Ps.* 16, 3-4)
[22] Hard ways.   [23] Ways of the law.

The Roman Synod and the Priest

His will offers the gentle comfort of His aid and the encouraging promise of sure reward on earth and in heaven.

TRUE DETACHMENT FROM THE WORLD

2. And now, beloved sons, here is a second thought for you, that We have plucked, not from the psalmist and prophet David, but from two great Doctors of the Church, Jerome and Augustine.

The Breviary, with which we are all familiar, reveals it in two simple but moving pages.

Our volume of the Synod, which is the code for priestly life, marks out the full extent of our detachment from the world, and indicates what kind of spirit should inspire our priestly labor for the souls that we priests are called upon—*vocati estis*[24]—to save and to sanctify.

A commentary of St. Jerome

What tones and accents you can find in the language of St. Jerome in his commentary on St. Matthew! *Grandis fiducia. Petrus piscator erat.*[25] (We know this St. Peter of ours very well *a juventute nostra et sua.*[26]) *Dives non fuerat: cibos manu et arte quaerebat: et tamen loquitur confidenter: reliquimus omnia: et quia non sufficit tantum relinquere jungit quod perfectum est: Et secuti sumus te: fecimus quod jussisti: quid igitur nobis dabis praemii?*[27]

The spirit of the world

Let us concentrate our attention on this: *relinquere omnia, Christum sequi.*[28] The two expressions suppose that a line of contact remains between, on the one hand, the boat and its oars, and on the other, Christ Jesus, whom we must serve and bring to others. You don't go on living and you don't exercise the priestly ministry

---

[24] You have been called.
[25] Great trust. Peter was a fisherman.
[26] From his youth and our own.
[27] He was not a rich man. He had to earn his food with his sweat and his skill. And still he speaks confidently: we have given up everything. And since giving up everything is not enough, he adds the thing that makes it perfect: and we have followed you; we have done what you commanded us to do. Therefore what reward are you going to give us? (Book III on *Matt.* 19)
[28] Give up everything; follow Christ.

and you don't serve the Church in the various offices of its central and world-wide administration without coming into contact with what the world and the spirit of the world represent. This spirit in itself is neither enough nor necessary for doing honor to the other element, that is, to service of the Lord in the priestly work par excellence—proclaiming the Gospel, administering sacramental grace, exercising charity in its various forms. Instead, it can be, and actually becomes, a daily temptation and enticement to be cold or superficial in carrying out the tasks that have to do with the priest's office and the responsibility he has assumed. A fancy for riches, distinction, honors and personal interests—and the pursuit of all these things—fits in very poorly with the *Christum sequi*[29] and is in flagrant contradiction to the *reliquimus omnia*,[30] which is the point of departure for any journey toward what has constituted the greatness and the true glory of Christianity, of the Church, and of the Catholic priesthood in all ages.

In this regard, please permit your Bishop and Father to express a regret that he feels very keenly in his heart and often sighs over in his prayers.

Sources of danger

The modern manifestations of technology and the extra comforts supplied by modern life represent a double source of danger: first, the fact of crafty reproduction and malicious diffusion of subtle intellectual and moral aberrations, repugnant to good sense, human and Christian; second and more concrete, the fact of error and of evil—this part has been going on *ab initio saeculorum*[31]—along with their imitation and visual reproduction in the press and films, which succeed in multiplying the copies, and thus the temptations, indefinitely.

A sad comparison

We want to seize this opportunity to pay tribute and offer encouragement to continued production and development of literary, scientific, moral, and religious works of a high calibre, at every level

---

[29] Follow Christ. [30] We have given up all things.
[31] From the beginning of time.

and in every form of the apostolate. We know this is being done in noteworthy fashion especially in certain regions both far from here and close by, and all of them are very worthy and very dear to Us. But oh! how little this contribution still is, compared to the immense and slimy flood of material in print and on film around the world that does not elevate individual souls and peoples to the knowledge, love, and worship of God, of truth, of goodness, of pure beauty, of justice, of brotherhood, and of peace, but rather ends up corrupting and poisoning their healthy outlook and sowing the vicious seeds of dissolution and ruin.

Beloved sons: you understand just what pangs of anguish your Father and Pastor is suffering as he approaches the conscience of each of you to tell you these things.

Care in reading

Ecce nos reliquimus omnia et secuti sumus Te.[32] This *omnia*[33] that we have left behind for the sake of Christ Jesus takes in, among other things, our reading or looking at newspapers, magazines, books, or entertainments that are in any way opposed to truth and the spirit of Christ, or to the teachings of the Holy Church, or to the prescriptions and counsels of the volume of our blessed Synod.

We beg all Our dear priests to put their hands over their hearts and examine their consciences well on this point, for We consider it most serious and important.

St. Augustine

This teaching is suggested to us by St. Jerome in the *"de Communi Abbatum"*[34] of the Breviary; and along with it, We have the work of another Doctor, whose heavenly knowledge and enlightenment far surpasses that of many other Fathers of the Church.

This time, St. Augustine is the one speaking, in his tenth sermon *De verbis Domini,*[35] and his words are also recorded in the Breviary in the Common of Abbots. They are not the words: *Reliquimus omnia et secuti sumus Te*[36] that the Apostles addressed to Jesus, but rather the loving and gentle words of Jesus Himself to His closest

---

[32] Behold, we have left all and followed thee.
[33] Everything. [34] On the Common of Abbots.
[35] On the words of the Lord. [36] We have left all and followed thee.

disciples, and to all who joined with them: *Venite ad me, omnes qui laboratis et onerati estis, et ego reficiam vos. Tollite jugum meum super vos, et discite a me quia mitis sum et humilis corde, et invenietis requiem animabus vestris. Jugum enim meum suave est, et onus meum leve.*[37]

The yoke of the Lord

What great praise and exaltation there are in these very words of the Lord Himself for all the tiring—even physically tiring—work, the great efforts, the pain and the suffering that go with the life of a priest! How well they apply to the good priests of every age! The special vocation they have received has made them the specially privileged ones of the Lord: but in their bodies, they remain mortal men, frail and weak and often vessels of clay. Yet a great reward has been set aside for them. Jesus, the first priest, is the one who guarantees it: *Ego reficiam vos.*[38]

It is interesting to note that while giving this assurance, Jesus extends an invitation to those closest to Him to fear nothing and take His yoke upon their shoulders: *"Jugum meum super vos"*; and he encourages them to learn from Him to imitate His meekness and His humble heart, as a guarantee of peace for their souls.

Oh! what horizons are unveiled to the zeal of every fervent priest in these few short gentle words.

Activism

As you read through the individual articles of the Roman Synod, the fact that there are so many of them may create the impression that it is favoring a full display of the kind of activism into which noble and fervent souls throw themselves with keen enthusiasm in their less mature years.

But St. Augustine, taking his inspiration from the words of Jesus, warns us to proceed calmly in governing our energies. *Si angustiantur vasa carnis, dilatentur spatia caritatis.*[39] Here he strikes a remark-

---

[37] Come to me, all you who labor and are burdened, and I will give you rest. Take my yoke upon you, and learn from me, for I am meek and humble of heart; and you will find rest for your souls. For my yoke is easy, and my burden light. (*Matt.* 11, 28-30)   [38] I will give you rest.
[39] If the vessels of flesh are constrained, the room for charity grows.

able note, in perfect harmony with the sublime hymn to charity in one of the wonderful pages composed by St. Paul (*1 Cor.* 13, 1-13), in which he succeeded in striking a balance between the feverish drive *quae urget*[40] and the careful measurement of how he spent himself, for the glory of Christ and of His Gospel and for the salvation of souls.

And so it is the same St. Augustine who steps in to correct and temper the excesses of activism, by explaining to us that the *jugum Domini super nos*[41] does not mean remaking the world, creating things visible and invisible, performing miracles even to the raising of the dead, but rather means remaining faithful to meekness and humility of heart, for this is the great secret of success at all times and in all circumstances.

The Letters of the First Pope

3. There is a third thought that comes to encourage all of us to pay honor to our Synod, beloved sons, and it comes from the familiar words of St. Peter, the first Bishop of Rome, humble, blessed, most holy, established by Jesus as the foundation stone of the one, holy, catholic, and apostolic Church, which, in the plans of Providence, exercises from Rome, its center, its primacy of honor and of jurisdiction over all the Churches throughout the world.

His voice comes down to us from far-off centuries, just as it sounded on the two occasions when he spoke from Rome to the Christians who made up the first communities in the East. It still expresses the same heavenly doctrine, the same spiritual direction, the same sound discipline that our Synod is proposing; the external circumstances have changed, but the provisions of the latter are just as wise and are well-adapted to the circumstances of present-day life.

Nourishment from St. Peter

These apostolic letters of St. Peter—like those of St. Paul, for that matter, and like all Sacred Scripture—ought to furnish spiritual nourishment for all the Catholics in the world. We welcome this

---

[40] That urges on.   [41] Yoke of the Lord upon us.

opportunity to invite the faithful to answer the challenge and live up to the Roman Synod's directions to everyone to read the Sacred Book; for nowadays ignorance of it on the part of any Catholic with self-respect is truly unforgivable.

Peter says that "our most dear brother Paul, according to the wisdom given him,"[42] in dealing with the patient suffering of Our Lord and its reference to universal salvation, touches upon some difficult points that the weak and the ignorant distort, as they do the rest of the Scriptures, to their own destruction.

But this warning was not directed at us priests. Indeed, the reading of Holy Scripture can bring to us so many advantages of every spiritual and pastoral kind, for our sanctification.

And so the priests of Rome and even the faithful should go back over the two letters of St. Peter with calm and with their usual careful preparation, for they really deserve to be studied and to become something that is very familiar and practically, you might say, known by heart.

Sublime practicality

It would go beyond the bounds of this meeting to go into citations and specific passages but We hope that Our invitation to you to meditate on these two encyclicals of the first Pope may do some good. Most substantial food in the form of doctrine that is both sublime and practical; true spiritual rapture that comes as a surprise for most and is very sweet for all those who become familiar with it. In his letter to the Romans, St. Paul set down astounding truths bearing on quite lofty matters that were of universal interest. St. Peter, on the other hand, wrote from Rome to encourage all of the priests and faithful, and he dealt for the most part with practical problems that have to do with the life of the Church and life in the Church in all times and ages. Let us priests of the diocese of Rome make it our treasure. Just a small taste of it will be enough to exhilarate us.

Consider the first chapter in the first letter, for example: the dignity of the Christian and the holiness of his life; then the duties, that shine brilliantly with grace in every way in the chosen race, the

---

[42] *2 Peter* 3, 15-16.

royal priesthood, the holy nation, the purchased people; the duty of obedience, the joys of the family, and of charity; the counsels given, in expectation of the end; the special recommendations for the old and the young.

A treasure for priests

Last of all, for priests, what a treasure of heavenly doctrine and advice! St. Peter himself, the *consenior et testis Christi passionum, qui et ejus, quae in futuro revelanda est, gloriae communicator,*[43] as he goes on speaking to priests: *Pascite qui in vobis est gregem Dei, providentes non coacte, sed spontanee secundum Deum, neque turpis lucri gratia, sed voluntarie; neque ut dominantes in cleris, sed forma facti gregis ex animo.*[44]

SHINING LIGHTS OF THE DIOCESE OF ROME

The second letter is less vivid and colorful than the first, dealing as it does with matters in dispute, with errors that are to be corrected, and with false teachers who are to be avoided.

But there is a touch of human emotion where Peter says *quod velox est depositio tabernaculi mei*[45] and promises to remember his faithful afterwards, too. *Dabo operam et frequenter habere vos post obitum meum, ut horum memoriam faciatis.*[46]

Venerable brethren and beloved sons!

St. Peter has this to say, among other things, in chapter three, verse eight of this second letter of his: there is one thing that you must not forget, my dear ones—a single day with the Lord is as a thousand years and a thousand years as a single day.

This idea comes suddenly to mind here at the end of this talk; it has given Us so much pleasure to be able to deliver it, just as was

---

[43] Fellow-presbyter and witness of the sufferings of Christ, the partaker also of the glory that is to be revealed in time to come. (*1 Peter* 5, 1)
[44] Tend the flock of God which is among you, governing not under constraint, but willingly, according to God; nor yet for the sake of base gain, but eagerly; nor yet as lording it over your charges, but becoming from the heart a pattern to the flock. (*1 Peter* 5, 2-3)
[45] That the putting off of my tabernacle is at hand. (*2 Peter* 1, 14)
[46] Moreover I will endeavor that even after my death you may often have occasion to call these things to mind. (*2 Peter* 1, 15)

true of all the cares—none of them, to be frank, very upsetting ones—that the preparing and celebrating of the Roman Synod imposed upon Us.

A blessed project

The conscience of St. Peter's lowly successor as Bishop of Rome is always kept open and attentive to the Lord in its intention of serving Him well, especially in his own diocese—*servus servorum Dei*[47]—while taking full advantage of the help offered by many, many souls who are also acting under the inspiration of heavenly doctrine and grace; and he can safely say in the light of what has been accomplished that the whole project of the Roman Synod was truly blessed. This is the idea suggested to Us by today's gathering, and it makes Our spirit expand with gratitude: *Divi et liberavi animam meam.*[48]

The synod that has just been celebrated implies and calls for a good deal of further effort to complete and carry out its work, and We will follow up on this little by little, without impatience, and with care to seize every opportunity that Providence may choose to offer Us for corresponding with the good will shown by everyone, with the desires of more tender souls, and with the present needs of our diocese. At the same time We will try to avoid any of the resentment that may be occasioned by hasty words, which can at times cause confusion and uncertainty in the hearts of those who are weak and timid.

Carrying out the decrees

Beloved sons, the Synod is over, celebrated and promulgated. Our feeling now—as is only natural—is that carrying it into practice does not depend so much on superintending committees—although these do have their proper place and deserve respect—as on the conscience of each and every priest.

As for Us—and We enjoy repeating it—We have now turned Our attention to the great undertaking of the Council, with serene confidence of complete success, and We pray God to grant you the

---

[47] Servant of the servants of God.   [48] I have spoken and set my soul free.

same kind of trust. And you will have it, beloved sons, to the extent that you learn to prize the tremendously powerful aid that practice of the synodal decrees can bring to individual members of the clergy, to religious communities, to institutions of higher learning and of ecclesiastical training, and to parishes.

The dioceses of the world are looking to Rome, to the Pope, to his fellow workers from the highest to the lowest, to his diocese. Let us not disappoint the hopes of the pilgrim who directs his steps toward this blessed city. Let us not refuse the role that is being offered us of being, in a sense, the heralds of the Second Vatican Council: heralds of the spirit of faith, of sincere piety, of order, and of peace.

RELATED EVIDENCE FROM PIUS IX

Beloved sons! Yes, for some months now, the Pope has been giving some of his *subsecivae*[49] hours to the history of the last few councils, with special attention to the First Vatican. Today, as We hear so many kind words echoing around Our humble person, wishing a continuation of the long life that the Lord has granted Us, Our thoughts go back to Our venerable predecessor Pius IX of most glorious and holy memory. Precisely at our age, at the completion of his 79th year and the beginning of his 80th—as is true of Us at this hour—he was getting ready for the imminent opening of the Vatican Council, which was to bring, and actually did bring so many benefits in the spiritual and the pastoral order to the Catholic Church throughout the world.

The shadow of Pius IX

Beloved sons! For some time We have enjoyed applying to Ourself what Cardinal Federigo Borromeo said of himself: "God knows my deficiencies, and the ones that I know too are enough to embarrass me."[50] And that is why on this occasion of Our 80th birthday We beg you to leave Us, in a sense, in the shadow of Our great predecessor Pius IX; We would like to read you a comment about him that We have in Our personal notes.

---

[49] Spare, leisure.   [50] Manzoni, *I promessi sposi*, chap. 26.

"His health is perfect," wrote Louis Veuillot. "His conversation is as keen and pointed as it is kind and good. His eye can always pick out his friends in a crowd, and he likes to say that he has seen them here and there. His hand, which is holding up so great a portion of the weight of the world, doesn't tremble at all. His ear hears even those who speak to him softly and fully grasps how filled their hearts are with love and respect. He keeps everything in mind, and remembers everything, except injuries."[51]

With these memories and with this encouragement to perfection in the priestly life that comes to Us and to all of you from so far off and yet remains so up-to-date, We put an end to Our talk; please accept for yourselves and for the souls entrusted to your care Our full Apostolic Blessing and Our fatherly best wishes that you may always respond fittingly to the grace of the Lord.

—November 24, 1960

[51] Louis Veuillot, *Rome pendant le Concile*, (ed. Lethielleux, Paris, 1927) II, 366.

THE ART OF SPIRITUAL DIRECTION

An Address of Pope John XXIII to Spiritual Directors of Seminaries

- *Need for bringing seminary training up to date*
- *The importance of obedience*
- *Implementation of the Council's decisions*

BELOVED SONS. This meeting comes just before the week of spiritual exercises with which We want to prepare for the opening of the Ecumenical Council. And so you can imagine what is in Our thoughts as We greet you who have been chosen for one of the loftiest and most vital services in the Church.

As you may know, We Ourself carried out this kind of ministry in the seminary of Bergamo at the end of the First World War. That invaluable priestly experience makes it easier for Us to understand what you feel within your souls, and makes Our conversation with you a little more intimate and to the point.

In the depths of consciences

First of all, We want to thank you, beloved sons, for the unseen yet valuable work that you are performing in an area of such promise for the apostolate. The dioceses are counting on you. The future of the Church, it might be said, rests greatly in your hands. It is true that the training of seminarians requires harmonious cooperation and effort on the part of all the faculty members of the seminary, under the wise and kind direction of the rector. But the most important role is yours, for your action is carried on in the inner depths of consciences, where deep convictions take root and where the real transformation of the young man called to the priesthood takes place. The breath of the Spirit of the Lord initiates and sets a crown on this [transformation]. But in the ordinary course of events, it will be hard for the young man to know how to follow His inspirations without the expert guidance of the spiritual director.

We can imagine your daily sacrifice, your anxieties, your silent sufferings. And God knows how many prayers, what great efforts, and at times what anguish you are offering each day for the graces of light and of perseverance for your spiritual children. In expressing Our gratitude to you, We feel that Our sentiments are those of Jesus Himself, who, in entrusting to you His most precious treasures, has called you to collaborate with Him in this sublime work of His grace.

A Difficult and Delicate Mission

We would also like to express Our pleasure and satisfaction with your congress, which promises wonderful results.

The art of arts

The training of young people—it can bear repeating—is a mission that is anything but easy. It is rightly called the art of arts. And this is more true when dealing with young people who are turning with an open and generous mind toward the priesthood. The man who is training seminarians realizes that his own personal preparation for this most lofty ministry must continue throughout the length of his service. He must study the psychology of students for the priesthood; he must live with his eyes open to the world around him; he must learn from life. But he must learn from books too: from study, from the experiences of his confreres and from the progress made in the pedagogical sciences, and especially from those texts and authors recommended by the Congregation of Seminaries.

We cannot hide the fact that mistakes have been committed—and are still being committed—in the educational field, with the ready excuse that the only requirements for the recognition and proper development of vocations are common sense, a clinical eye, and, above all, experience. It gives Us the greatest of pain to say this. More enlightened spiritual direction would have spared the Church various priests who are not altogether equal to the loftiness of their office, at the same time that it would have brought her a greater number of holy priests.

Contemporary difficulties

Besides, you know well that every age presents its own special difficulties to be met in the training of young people. In your case, you cannot forget that the seminarians belong to a generation that has been through the tragedy of two gigantic wars, and that they come from a world that is changing and developing with surprising swiftness. As a result, you may well feel at times a little perplexed in the face of certain expressions of an immature personality, in the face of aspirations and needs and demands that seem far removed from the mentality current only twenty years ago.

At times this may make you think that the traditional training has seen its day, and that new ways have to be tried out.

In this regard, We would like to openly express Our thoughts to you.

While it will not help you in training seminarians to adhere rigidly to plans and methods which are no longer useful, nevertheless you must be firmly convinced that the basic principles, without which the whole edifice would crumble and fall into ruins, retain their full force. You must also avoid carefully the danger of allowing marginal reforms, no matter how important and at times opportune they may be, to distract attention from the central problem in all seminary training.

The main object toward which you must direct your efforts is the creation in the young men of a complete and well-rounded idea of the priesthood based on the Gospel model, and an acute and vital awareness of the duty of tending toward holiness.

UNCHANGING VALIDITY OF BASIC PRINCIPLES

The problem of personal sanctification was the point of honor and of joy of your youthful years and of Ours, beloved sons.

Those called to the priesthood in this second half of the twentieth century can have nothing more at heart than this, both prior to ordination and during their growth in the priesthood; they must be firmly convinced of the emptiness of any apostolic effort that is not informed by a soul in the state of grace and tending toward sanctity.

A need for mortification

You must also take care that these young men begin to know and understand the world in which they are called to live and to work, and you must teach them to sanctify anything good and healthy and holy that progress may offer. But this does not mean accepting compromises with the spirit of the world, nor, even less, devaluing the importance of mortification and of self-denial. An ill-conceived up-to-date approach concerned only with making seminary life more pleasant, or appeasing nature too much, would create a personality that would be the very opposite to that of Jesus the Priest and Victim. On the contrary, a modern measuring up to the demands of the times will have to be achieved through a more profound assimilation of the personality of Jesus and of Jesus crucified. Seminarians must be made to love the self-denial of the Cross, so that they may learn to love the conditions of poverty in which the clergy often must live, and learn to face with courage the renunciations and the tiring labors of the apostolate.

Firm Discipline: Cheerful Devotion to Sacrifice

You sometimes hear people talk of self-formation, of self-mastery. Of course, no man is well trained if he does not know how to be a rule unto himself. Educators are correct in being concerned with granting the youngster a useful and progressive exercise of freedom that will prepare him to govern himself by himself in definite circumstances and better prepare him for the life of the ministry. But this should not be separated from a firm discipline. The young man will never learn to exercise self-mastery, if he has not learned to observe with love a strong rule that gives him practice in mortification and in the mastery of his will. Otherwise, in the full exercise of the ministry, he will not be ready for full and cheerful obedience to his bishop; and he may be tempted to attitudes of independence that may not sound like open rebellion, but that will find expression nevertheless in a personal course of action not in keeping with the plan for pastoral action being promoted and proposed by his superior.

Example—a most persuasive language

Finally, we will never be able to stress enough the importance of example. And this is what you give, beloved sons; this is what older priests give; oh, if only we could say that this is what all priests give! This is the eloquent language which is most persuasive for young people. And, while it is drawing down an abundance of the Lord's fruitful graces, the students will be learning from it almost spontaneously the things often so hard to explain in words.

LOFTY ZEAL FOR EXECUTING COUNCIL DECISIONS

Precisely because of his frequent and intimate contacts with seminarians, the figure of the spiritual director is one of those carved into memory, constituting—if they are truly edifying—one of the most effective supports for perseverance in the future. How many times a surprising renaissance of Christian life in a diocese will find its real explanation in the silent work of a holy spiritual director, who has known how to train generations of holy priests through his teachings and his example.

As We draw to a close Our carefully considered words on these grave and lofty matters concerning the training of seminarians—to whose good will, with heavenly grace and with the application of conciliar legislation, will be entrusted the restoration of fervor in the Church throughout the Catholic world—We would like to pay tribute, on this very solemn occasion, to the sacred memory of those priests who are now at rest in the eternal light and peace of the Lord, to whose ministry, as confessors and spiritual guides, you and We entrusted the depths of our consciences at various periods in our lives. They are more than worthy of our devoted commemoration.

Chosen souls that have entered eternity, and are enjoying its highest end or are in the course of reaching it—in any case, holy and blessed souls, every one of them—they are sharers, according to the teaching of the Catholic faith, in the affairs of the Church militant, and offer it aid, especially in its more solemn moments, like that of the Ecumenical Council. And so, may the grace of the Lord that made them deserving of honor for their sanctification of the clergy on earth in the past, obtain a breadth and sweep of fervor for the new generation that the Council intends to consecrate to the triumph of the Kingdom of Christ the Lord: *"in sanctitate et justitia coram ipso, omnibus diebus nostris."*[1]

A Shining Example: Vincenzo Pallotti

Beloved sons! The office of spiritual director is beset with difficulties and responsibilities. It is concerned with forming souls in the image of Jesus the priest. It is a divine work, not a human one. But, far from discouraging you, this serves as the basis for your confidence. It gives you one reason more for abandoning yourselves to the almighty mercy of the divine Artisan who wants to make use of you.

In the midst of the delight born of the new fervor accompanying the celebration of the Council, a deep pleasure and satisfaction for Us is the hope that, along with the honors of the altar being prepared for a number of venerable servants of God and Blessed from the Church's universal constellation of holiness, there will come the canonization of Blessed Vincenzo Pallotti. A most edifying priest, he was able to combine the spiritual direction of the young seminarians of the Pontifical Roman Seminary and of the students of the Urban College of Propaganda with the foundation of the Pious Society of the Catholic Apostolate. It was this that gave the first impulse in Rome to that appropriately-named Catholic Action which we now admire, as, in its flourishing state, it is applied to the great and true tasks of spreading the Gospel in modern society.

Spiritual director and apostle

All of the activity of this outstanding priest was directed toward the sanctification of the clergy and, as he left in writing, to the

---

[1] "in holiness and justice before him all our days." *Luke* 1, 75.

defense and conservation of the faith, and to the spread of charity among Catholics. His intention was that through the spread of faith and charity in the whole world, there would soon be but one flock and one shepherd.

He was the apostle of a many-faceted liturgical celebration that remains an outstanding reminder of his far-sighted apostolic devotion—We mean the Octave of the Epiphany that is celebrated in the church of Sant'Andrea della Valle,[2] as a powerful reminder of the development of a missionary consciousness in the Christian world and as an invocation of the unity of the Church among all the peoples of the earth.

A great work

Beloved sons. Here you have it: *verba et exempla*,[3] to carry on, under the guidance and inspiration of divine grace, the *opus magnum*[4] of modelling the hearts of future priests on the Heart of Christ.

With a serene trust that Jesus, the high priest, will make these words of Ours fruitful, We impart Our Apostolic Blessing to you and to all the seminarians entrusted to your care, as a pledge of heavenly blessings.

—September 9, 1962

[2] During the Octave of the Epiphany, Mass is celebrated in this church in many languages and many rites, with people from all parts of the world participating. The church is located in downtown Rome.—Trans.
[3] words and examples.
[4] great work.

III

On Church Unity

Good shepherd that he was, John XXIII wanted the entire world to be gathered together into one flock, the Catholic Church, the Mystical Body of Christ. Any disunity within that body, any isolation from it, grieved him deeply.

This concern runs throughout his pontificate, touching a great number of his letters and addresses; so many, indeed, that what we have printed here comprises only a tiny fraction of his thousands of words on the immense problem of unity.

His years in the East brought him into daily contact with the non-Latin rites of the Church and gave him great personal awareness of the diversity of liturgies and attitudes that the unity of the Church was capable of containing. He saw from close up that the Church was not to be exclusively identified with Western culture. If we are to judge from his numerous references to those years in the East, they made a deep, lasting impression on him. His awareness of the diversity possible within the Church manifests itself in the encyclical on the missions, in which he stresses the need for adaptation to local cultures and for the development of a native clergy.

From the very first week of his reign he extended a welcome to "separated brethren," his felicitous phrase for those Christians who were not within the Catholic Church. Other pontiffs and churchmen before him had been deeply concerned over the split in Christianity, of course, but none seems to have elicited so extensive and so worldwide a response. Certainly John had a remarkable ability to attract and win men's hearts. "I am Joseph, your brother," he exclaimed to separated Christians.

The Council, culmination of his dynamic pontificate, he viewed as aimed primarily at a renewal of the Catholic Church, but a renewal that would make the Church irresistibly attractive to non-Catholics. The documents in this section, then, are in a sense preparatory reading for the messages on the Council in part VI of the book.—Ed.

ONE FOLD, ONE SHEPHERD

An Excerpt from the 1958 Christmas Message of Pope John XXIII

- *The broken unity of Christians*
- *A resolve to pursue unity*

... THE VEXING PROBLEM of the broken unity of the heritage of Christ still remains; obstacles still hinder its solution; it portends a long road of serious difficulties and uncertainties.

The sadness of this sorrowful observation does not arrest—nor will it arrest, We pray God—the effort of Our soul to continue the loving invitation to Our dear separated brothers, who also carry on their forehead the name of Christ and who read His holy and blessed Gospel, and who are not insensible to the inspirations of religious piety, of beneficent and blessed charity.

... We intend to pursue humbly but fervently the duty urged upon Us by the words and example of Jesus, the divine Good Shepherd, which He continues to speak to Us as He views the harvests which whiten the vast missionary fields: "Them also I must bring ... and there shall be one fold and one shepherd"[1]; and which He speaks to Us in the prayer raised to His Father in His last hours on earth, when the supreme sacrifice was imminent: "That all may be one, even as thou, Father, in me and I in thee; that they also may be one in us that the world may believe that thou hast sent me."[2] ...

—December 23, 1958

[1] *John* 10, 16. [2] *John* 17, 21.

ST. LEO THE GREAT AND CHURCH UNITY

The Encyclical "Aeterna Dei Sapientia" of
Pope John XXIII to Catholic Bishops

- *The achievements of St. Leo as pope*
- *His contribution to unity*
- *A call for unity today*

GOD'S ETERNAL WISDOM "reacheth from end to end mightily and ordereth all things sweetly."[1] Its light shone with exceptional brilliance in the soul of Pope St. Leo I, for it would seem to have burned into it the very image of itself; so fearless the moral courage displayed by this Pope—"the greatest among the great," as Our late predecessor Pius XII rightly called him[2]—yet so gentle his fatherly concern.

The wisdom of his government, the wealth and scope of his teaching, the loftiness of his mind, his unfailing charity—these are the things which St. Leo the Great brought to enhance the fame of Peter's See, to which Almighty God in His providence has also raised Us. And now, on this fifteenth centenary of his death, We feel it incumbent upon Us to highlight his virtues and his immortal merits, confident that these can be of great spiritual value to us all, and increase the prestige and promote the spread of the Catholic Faith.

Life-long brilliance

Wherein, then, lies the true greatness of this Pope? In moral courage?—in that moral courage which he showed when, at the

[1] *Wisd.* 8, 1.
[2] Sermon, 12 Oct., 1952, in *Discorsi e Radiomessaggi*, xiv, p. 358.

River Mincius in 452, with no other armor to protect him than his high-priestly majesty, he boldly confronted the barbarous king of the Huns, Attila, and persuaded him to retreat with his armies across the Danube? That was certainly an heroic act and one which accorded well with the Roman pontificate's mission of peace. Yet we must think of it as but one isolated instance of a life-long activity of remarkable brilliance devoted to the religious and social welfare, not merely of Rome and of Italy, but of the whole Church throughout the world.

"The path of the just . . ."

"The path of the just, as a shining light, goeth forwards and increaseth even to perfect day."[3] These words of Holy Scripture may well be applied to the life and activity of St. Leo. To be convinced of this we have but to consider St. Leo in his three main characteristic roles: (1) as a man singularly dedicated to the service of the Apostolic See, (2) as Christ's chief Vicar on earth, and (3) as Doctor of the Universal Church.

FAITHFUL SERVANT OF THE APOSTOLIC SEE

Praise for a deacon

Leo was born towards the end of the fourth century. The *Liber Pontificalis* informs us that he was "of Tuscan nationality from his father Quintian."[4] Since, however, he spent his early years in Rome, he not unnaturally called this city his *patria* [homeland].[5] While still a young man he joined the ranks of the Roman clergy and in due course was ordained deacon. In this capacity he rendered signal service to Pope Sixtus III between the years 430 and 439, and played a considerable part in the conduct of Church affairs. Among the many friends he made at this time were St. Prosper, bishop of Aquitania, and Cassian, founder of the celebrated Abbey of St. Victor in Marseilles. Cassian, whom he persuaded to write *De Incarnatione Domini*[6] against the Nestorians, proclaimed him "the

[3] *Prov.* 4, 18.   [4] Cf. Ed. Duchesne, I, 238.   [5] Cf. Ep. 31, 4, Migne, *PL* 54, 794.
[6] Migne, *PL* 59, 9-272.

glory of the Church and the sacred ministry"[7]—praise indeed for a simple deacon!

Theologian and diplomat

At the request of the court of Ravenna the Pope sent St. Leo to Gaul to settle a dispute between the patrician Aetius and the prefect Albinus. It was while Leo was engaged on this mission that Sixtus III died. Recognizing Leo's unrivalled theological learning and practical wisdom in diplomacy and the conduct of affairs, the Roman Church could think of no more worthy candidate for Christ's vicarious power on earth than this deacon.

A most illustrious pope

Hence on September 29th, 440, he was consecrated bishop and entered upon his sovereign pontificate. He discharged this office with such masterly ability that he must be reckoned among the most illustrious of the early popes, few of whom reigned longer than he. He died in November, 461, and was buried in the porch of the Vatican Church. In 688, by order of Pope St. Sergius I, his body was removed to "Peter's Citadel" and later, on the building of the new basilica, found a resting-place in the altar dedicated to his name.

Christ's Vicar on Earth

What then were the more notable achievements of his life? To this question We would reply that rarely in her history has Christ's Church won such victories over her foes as in the pontificate of Leo the Great. He shone in the middle of the fifth century like a brilliant star in the Christian firmament.

The Pelagian and Nestorian heresies

To be convinced of this we have but to consider the way in which he discharged his office as teacher of the Catholic Faith. In this

---

[7] *De Incarn. Domini, contra Nestorium,* lib. vii, prol. *PL* 50, 9.

field he won for himself a name equal to that of St. Augustine of Hippo and St. Cyril of Alexandria. St. Augustine, as we know, in defending the Faith against the Pelagians, insisted on the absolute necessity of divine grace for right living and the attainment of eternal salvation. St. Cyril, faced with the errors of Nestorius, upheld Christ's divinity and the fact that the Virgin Mary is truly the Mother of God. These truths lie at the very heart of our Catholic faith, and St. Leo, who entered into the doctrinal inheritance of both these men of learning, the brightest luminaries of the Eastern and Western Church, was among all his contemporaries by far the most fearless protagonist of them.

Defender of Church unity

St. Augustine, then, is celebrated in the universal Church as "Doctor of divine grace," and St. Cyril as "Doctor of the Incarnate Word." By the same token St. Leo is universally proclaimed as "Doctor of the Church's unity."

For the integrity of doctrine was not his only concern. We have but to cast a cursory glance over the great volume of evidence of his amazing industry as pastor and writer to realize that he was equally concerned with the upholding of moral standards and the defense of the Church's unity.

Consider, too, the field of liturgical composition and the due regard which this religious and saintly Pope had for the unity of worship. Many of the principal prayers contained in the *Leonine Sacramentary*[8] were either written by him or modelled on his compositions.

On the Incarnation: his letter to Flavian

Most noteworthy, perhaps, is his timely and authoritative intervention in the controversy as to whether there was in Jesus Christ a human nature in addition to the divine nature. His efforts were responsible for the magnificent triumph of the true doctrine concerning the incarnation of the Word of God. This fact alone would assure him his place in history.

[8] Migne, *PL* 55, 21-156.

Our principal evidence for it is his Epistle to Flavian, Bishop of Constantinople, in which he expounds the dogma of the Incarnation with remarkable clarity and precision, showing how it accords with the teaching of the Prophets, the Gospel, the apostolic writings, and the Creed.[9]

Let Us quote a significant passage from this epistle: "Without detriment, therefore, to the properties of either of the two natures and substances which are joined in the one person, majesty took on humility; strength, weakness; eternity, mortality; and, in order to pay off the debt which attached to our condition, inviolable nature was united with passible nature, so that, as suited the cure of our ills, one and the same Mediator between God and men, the Man Jesus Christ, could die with the one nature and not die with the other. Thus true God was born in the whole and perfect nature of true man; complete in what was His own, complete in what was ours."[10]

Condemnation of Ephesine Council

Not content with this, St. Leo, having made perfectly clear "what the Catholic Church universally believes and teaches concerning the mystery of the Lord's incarnation,"[11] followed up this epistle to Flavian with a condemnation of the Ephesine Council of 449. At this council the supporters of Eutyches had, by violent and unconstitutional means, done all they could to impose the groundless dogmatic assertions of this "very foolish and exceedingly ignorant man,"[12] who obstinately maintained that there was only one nature in Christ, the divine nature.

The Pope, with evident justification, branded this "a robber council."[13] In violation of the express commands of the Apostolic See, it had presumed by every means at its disposal to arrogate to itself no less a task than "the breaking down of the Catholic Faith"[14] and "the strengthening of execrable heresy."[15]

[9] Cf. *ibid.*, 54, 757.   [10] *Ibid.*, col. 759.
[11] Ep. 29 *to the Emperor Theodosius, PL* 54, 783.   [12] Cf. Ep. 28, *PL* 54, 756.
[13] Cf. Ep. 95, 2, *to the Empress Pulcheria, PL* 54, 943.
[14] Cf. *ibid.*   [15] Cf. *ibid.*

The Council of Chalcedon

But St. Leo's principal title to fame is the Council of Chalcedon, held in 451. In spite of pressure from the Emperor Marcian, the Pope refused to allow it to be summoned except on condition that his own legates should preside over it.[16] It proved, venerable brethren, to be one of the greatest events in the history of the Church, renowned alike for its solemn definition of the doctrine of the two natures in God's Incarnate Word, and its recognition of the magisterial primacy of the Roman Pontiff. We need not, however, enter into any more detailed discussion of it here, for Our predecessor Pius XII has already dealt with it in an important encyclical addressed to the entire Catholic world on the fifteenth centenary of its convocation.[17]

The twenty-eighth canon

St. Leo's delay in ratifying the acts of this council is further proof of his genuine concern for the Church's unity and peace. We cannot attribute this delay to any remissness on his part, or to any cause of a doctrinal character. Obviously his intention—as he himself explains—was to thwart the twenty-eighth canon, which voiced the agreement of the Fathers of the council to the primacy of the See of Constantinople over all the churches of the East.

Whether or not this canon was inserted in defiance of the protests of the papal legates, or to win the favor of the Byzantine Emperor, is not clear. To St. Leo, it appeared to undermine the prerogatives of other more ancient and more illustrious churches, prerogatives which had been recognized by the Fathers of the Council of Nicea. He also saw it as detracting somewhat from the authority of the Apostolic See itself. His misgivings were occasioned not so much by the wording of the twenty-eighth canon as by the policies of those who framed it.

Two letters illustrate this point: one sent by the bishops of the

---

[16] Cf. Ep. 89, 2, *to the Emperor Marcian, PL* 54, 931; Ep. 103 *to the Gallic Bishops, PL* 54, 988-991.
[17] Encycl. *"Sempiternus Rex,"* 8th Sept. 1951, *AAS* 43 (1951) 625-44.

council,[18] and the other written by Leo himself in refutation of their arguments and sent to the Emperor Marcian. This letter contains the following admonition:—

"Things secular stand on a different basis from things divine, and there can be no sure building save on that rock which the Lord has set as the foundation (*Matt.* 16, 18). He who covets what is not his due, loses what is rightfully his."[19]

The sad history of the schism that was later to separate so many illustrious Eastern churches from the church of Rome bears striking testimony to the accuracy of St. Leo's prophetic vision, here expressed, and to his presentiment of the future disruption of Christian unity.

Toward full Catholic unity

To complete this account We would mention in passing two further instances of St. Leo's unfailing solicitude for the defense of the Catholic Church's unity: his intervention in the dispute concerning the date of Easter, and his great efforts to create an atmosphere of mutual respect, trust and cordiality in the Holy See's public relations with Christian princes. To see the Church at peace was the dearest desire of his heart. He frequently prevailed upon these princes to join forces with the bishops and lend them the support of their counsels "for the concord of Catholic unity,"[20] so as to win from Almighty God "a priestly palm, besides a kingly crown."[21]

DOCTOR OF THE CHURCH

Besides being a watchful shepherd of Christ's flock and a stouthearted defender of the true faith, St. Leo is honored also as a Doctor of the Church, one, that is, who excelled in expounding and sponsoring those divine truths which every Roman pontiff safeguards and proclaims.

---

[18] Cf. C. Kirch, *Enchir. fontium hist. eccl. antiquae*, Freiburg im Br., edn. 4, 1923, n. 943.
[19] Ep. 104, 3 *to the Emperor Marcian*, PL 54, 995; cf. Ep. 106, *to Anatolius, bishop of Constantinople*, PL 54, 995.
[20] Ep. 114, 3 *to the Emperor Marcian*, PL 54, 1022.
[21] *Ibid.*

Pope Benedict's eulogy

In support of this We quote that magnificent eulogy of St. Leo written by Pope Benedict XIV in his apostolic constitution *Militantis Ecclesiae,* October 12, 1754, when he made him a Doctor of the Church:—

"It was due to his excelling virtue, his teaching, and his most vigilant zeal as shepherd of his people, that he won from our forefathers the title 'Great.' In expounding the deeper mysteries of our faith and vindicating it against the errors that assail it, in imparting disciplinary rules and moral precepts, the excellence of his teaching is so radiant with the majestic richness of priestly eloquence and has so won the admiration of the world and the enthusiasm alike of councils, Fathers and writers of the Church, that the fame and reputation of this wisest of popes can hardly be rivalled by any other of the Church's holy doctors."[22]

The Sermons

It is through his many extant sermons and epistles that he principally lays claim to the title of Doctor. The *Sermons* cover a great variety of subjects, nearly all of which have some connection with the liturgical cycle. In all these writings he is not just the exegete elucidating a book of sacred scripture, not just the theologian at pains to investigate some divinely revealed truth. He is the saintly exponent of the Christian mysteries. He explains them with clarity and with a wealth of detail, in accordance with the faith of the councils, the Fathers, and the popes who preceded him.

His style is simple, majestic, lofty, persuasive, a model of classic eloquence. But in declaring the truth he never sacrificed precision to mere rhetoric. He did not speak or write to be admired, but to enlighten the minds of his hearers, and to awaken in them the desire to live lives in conformity with the truths they professed.

The Epistles

The *Epistles* are the letters he wrote as Sovereign Pontiff to the

[22] Benedict XIV Pont. Max. opera omnia, vol. 18, *Bullarium,* tom. III, part II, Prati 1847, p. 205.

princes, priests, deacons and religious *of the universal Church*. They display his exceptional qualities of leadership. They show him as a man of keen intellect, yet full of practical good sense; a man of character who kept to his decisions, yet a father most ready to forgive; on fire with the charity which St. Paul indicated to all Christians as "a more excellent way."[23]

For that blend of justice and mercy, of strength and gentleness, which we observe in his character is surely attributable to that same charity which Jesus Christ demanded of Peter when He made him a shepherd to feed His lambs and His sheep.[24]

In very truth St. Leo's life-long endeavor was to appear before the world in the character of Christ, the Good Shepherd. In evidence of this, We may quote the following passage from the *Epistles*:—

"We are encompassed by both the gentleness of mercy and the strictness of justice. And because 'all the ways of the Lord are mercy and truth' (*Ps.* 24, 10), We are forced according to Our loyalty to the Apostolic See so to moderate Our opinions as to weigh men's misdeeds in the balance (for, of course, they are not all of one measure), and to reckon some as to a certain degree pardonable, but others as altogether reprehensible."[25]

Devotion to truth, harmony, peace

All in all, these epistles and sermons are an eloquent testimony to St. Leo's passionate devotion, in thought and feeling, word and action, to the welfare of the Catholic Church and the cause of truth, harmony and peace.

THE FIFTEENTH LEONINE CENTENARY AND THE SECOND VATICAN COUNCIL

Venerable brethren, the time is drawing near for the Second Ecumenical Council of the Vatican. Surrounding the Roman Pontiff and in close communion with him, you, the bishops, will present to the world a wonderful spectacle of Catholic unity. Meanwhile

---

[23] *1 Cor.* 12, 31. [24] Cf. *John* 21, 15-17.
[25] *Ep.* 12, 5 *to the African Bishops, PL* 54, 652.

We, for Our part, will seek to give instruction and comfort by briefly recalling to mind St. Leo's high ideals regarding the Church's unity. Our intention in so doing is indeed to honor the memory of a most wise pope, but at the same time to give the faithful profitable food for thought on the eve of this great event.

Church unity in the thought of Leo

First, St. Leo teaches that the Church must be one because Jesus Christ, her Bridegroom, is one. "For the Church is that virgin, the spouse of one husband, Christ, who does not allow herself to be corrupted by any error. Thus throughout the whole world we are to have one entire and pure communion."[26]

In St. Leo's view, this remarkable unity of the Church has its well-spring in the birth of God's Incarnate Word. "For Christ's birth is the source of life for Christian people; the birthday of the Head is the birthday of the Body. Although every individual is called in his own turn, and all the Church's sons are separated from one another by intervals of time, yet the entire body of the faithful, born in the baptismal font, is born with Christ in His nativity, just as all are crucified with Him in His passion, raised again in His resurrection, and set at the Father's right hand in His ascension."[27]

It was Mary who participated most intimately in this secret birth "of the body, the Church,"[28] because the Holy Spirit gave fruitfulness to her virginity. St. Leo praises Mary as "the Lord's virgin, handmaid and mother,"[29] "she who gave God birth" [*Dei genitrix*],[30] "a virgin for ever."[31]

Furthermore, the sacrament of baptism—as St. Leo rightly claims —makes those who are washed in the sacred font not only members of Christ, but also sharers in His kingship and His priesthood. "All those who are reborn in Christ, the sign of the cross makes kings; the Holy Spirit's anointing consecrates them priests."[32] Confirma-

---

[26] Ep. 80, 1 *to Anatolius, Bishop of Constantinople, PL* 54, 913.
[27] Sermon 26, 2 *on the Feast of the Nativity, PL* 54, 213.   [28] *Col.* 1, 18.
[29] Cf. Ep. 165, 2 *to the Emperor Leo, PL* 54, 1157.   [30] Cf. *ibid.*
[31] Cf. Serm. 22, 2 *on the Feast of the Nativity, PL* 54, 195.
[32] Serm. 4, 1 *on the Feast of the Nativity, PL* 54, 149; cf. Serm. 64, 6 *on the Passion, PL* 54, 357; Ep. 69, 4, *PL* 54, 870.

tion, called by St. Leo "sanctification by chrism,"[33] strengthens their assimilation to Jesus Christ, the Head of His body, the Church, and the sacrament of the Eucharist perfects this union. "For," as St. Leo says, "the reception of Christ's body and blood does nothing less than transform us into that which we consume, and henceforth we bear in soul and body Him in whose fellowship we died, were buried, and are risen again."[34]

But mark this well: unless the faithful remain bound together by the same ties of virtue, worship and sacrament, and all hold fast to the same belief, they cannot be perfectly united with the divine Redeemer, the universal Head, so as to form with Him one visible and living body. "A whole faith," says St. Leo, "a true faith, is a mighty bulwark. No one can add anything to it, no one can take anything away from it; for unless it is one, it is no faith at all."[35]

To preserve this unity of faith, all teachers of divine truths—all bishops, that is—must necessarily speak with one mind and one voice, in communion with the Roman pontiff. "It is the union of members in the body as a whole which makes all alike healthy, all alike beautiful, and this union of the whole body requires unanimity. It calls especially for harmony among the priests. They have a common dignity, yet they have not uniform rank, for there was a distinction of power even among the blessed apostles, notwithstanding the similarity of their honorable state, and while the election of them all was equal, yet it was given to one to take the lead over the rest."[36]

The Bishop of Rome, center of visible unity

St. Leo, therefore, maintained that the Bishop of Rome, as Peter's successor and Christ's Vicar on earth, is the focal center of the entire visible unity of the Catholic Church. And St. Leo's opinion is clearly supported by the evidence of the Gospels and by ancient Catholic tradition, as these words show: "Out of the whole world one man is chosen, Peter. He is set before all the elect of every

---

[33] Serm. 66, 2 *on the Passion, PL* 54, 365-6.
[34] Serm. 64, 7 *on the Passion, PL* 54, 357.
[35] Serm. 24, 6 *on the Feast of the Nativity, PL* 54, 207.
[36] Ep. 14, 11 *to Anastasius, bishop of Thessalonica, PL* 54, 676.

nation, before all the apostles and all the Fathers of the Church; so that although there are among God's people many priests and many pastors, Peter governs by personal commission all whom Christ rules by His supreme authority. Great and wonderful, beloved, is the share in its own power which the Divine Condescension assigned to this man. And if it desired other princes to share anything in common with him, never except through him did it accord what it did not deny to others."[37]

And since St. Leo regarded this indissoluble bond between Peter's divinely-given authority and that of the other apostles as fundamental to Catholic unity, he was never tired of insisting that "this authority [to bind and to loose] was also passed on to the other apostles, and what was established by this decree found its way to all the princes of the Church. But there was good reason for committing what was intended for all to the care of one in particular. And so it was entrusted to Peter individually because the figure of Peter was to be put ahead of all those in charge of the Church."[38]

The magisterial prerogative of St. Peter and his successors

There is, moreover, another essential safeguard of the Church's visible unity which did not escape the notice of this saintly Pope: that supreme authority to teach infallibly, which Christ gave personally to Peter, the prince of the apostles, and to his successors. Leo's words are quite unequivocal: "The Lord takes special care of Peter; He prays especially for Peter's faith, for the state of the rest will be more secure if the mind of their chief be not overthrown. Hence the strength of all the rest is made stronger in Peter, and the assistance of divine grace is so ordained that the stability which through Christ is given to Peter, should through Peter be transmitted to the other apostles."[39]

Applied to St. Peter this pronouncement is clear and emphatic enough; yet unhesitatingly St. Leo claims the same prerogative for himself. Not that he wanted worldly honor, but he had no doubt

---

[37] Serm. 4, 2 *on the Anniversary of his Elevation, PL* 54, 149-150.
[38] *Ibid.* col. 151; cf. Serm. 83, 2 *on the Feast of the Apostle Peter, PL* 54, 430.
[39] Serm. 4, 3, *PL* 54, 151-2; cf. Serm. 83, 2, *PL* 54, 451.

whatever that he was just as much Christ's vicar as was the Prince of the Apostles. Consider, for example, this passage from his sermons:—

"Mindful, then, of Our God-given responsibility, We find no reason for pride in solemnly celebrating the anniversary of Our priesthood, for we acknowledge with all sincerity and truth that it is Christ who does the work of Our ministry in all that We do rightly. We do not glory in Ourselves, for without Him We can do nothing. We glory in Him who is all Our power."[40]

By that he did not mean that St. Peter had no further influence on the government of Christ's Church. While he trusted in the continued activity of the Church's divine Founder, he trusted too in the protection of the Apostle Peter whose heir and successor he claimed to be, and whose office of authority "he in his turn discharged."[41] He attributed the success of his universal ministry more to the merits of the Apostle than to his own industry. Many passages from his writings might be quoted in support of this statement. We choose the following:—

"And so if anything is rightly done and rightly decreed by Us, if anything is won from the mercy of God by Our daily supplications, it is due to his [Peter's] works and merits, whose power lives and whose authority prevails in his See."[42]

Nor must we think that St. Leo was preaching a doctrine that had never before been taught. For, that his supreme office as universal pastor came from Christ Himself was also the teaching of his predecessors St. Innocent I[43] and St. Boniface I,[44] and was in full accord with those passages of the Gospels which he so often expounded (*Matt.* 16, 17-18; *Luke* 22, 31-32; *John* 21, 15-17). He frequently referred to "the care which, principally by divine mandate, We must have for all the churches."[45]

---

[40] Serm. 5, 4 *on the Anniversary of his Ordination, PL* 54, 154.
[41] Cf. Serm. 3, 4 *on the Anniversary of his Elevation, PL* 54, 147.
[42] Serm. 3, 3 *on the Anniversary of his Elevation, PL* 54, 146; cf. Serm. 83, 3 *on the Feast of the Apostle Peter, PL* 54, 432.
[43] Ep. 30 *ad Concil. Milev., PL* 20, 590.
[44] Ep. 13 *to Rufus, bishop of Thessaly,* 11 Mar., 422, in C. Silva-Tarouca S. I. *Epistolarum Romanorum Pontificum collect. Thessal.,* Rome 1937, p. 27.
[45] Ep. 14, 1 *to Anastasius, bishop of Thessalonica, PL* 54, 668.

The spiritual greatness of Rome

Small wonder then that St. Leo habitually combines the praises of Rome with those of the Prince of the Apostles. He begins one of his sermons on the apostles Peter and Paul by apostrophizing the City in these words:—

"It was through these men, O Rome, that the light of Christ's Gospel shone upon you. . . . It was they who promoted you to such glory, making you a holy nation, a chosen people, a priestly and royal state, the capital of the world through Peter's holy See. By the worship of God you gained a wider empire than you did by earthly government. For although your boundaries were extended by your many victories and you stretched your rule over land and ocean, yet your labors in war gained you less subjects than have been won for you by the peace of Christ."[46]

Recalling St. Paul's magnificent testimony to the faith of the first Christians in Rome, this great Pope bids the Romans preserve the faith whole and entire and without flaw. These are the words of fatherly encouragement he uses:—

"You, therefore, beloved of God and honored by apostolic approval—for it is to you that the teacher of the Gentiles, the blessed Apostle Paul, says: 'Your faith is spoken of in the whole world' (*Rom.* 1, 8)—preserve in yourselves that which you know to have been the cause of this great preacher's good opinion of you. Let not a man of you make himself undeserving of this praise, or allow so much as a taint of Eutyches' impious doctrine to infect a people that has remained for so long untouched by heresy, taught by the Holy Spirit."[47]

The vast influence of St. Leo's work

St. Leo's heroic efforts to safeguard the authority of the Church of Rome were not in vain. It was principally due to his personal prestige that "the citadel of the apostolic rock" was extolled and venerated not only by the Western bishops who took part in the councils held at Rome, but by more than five hundred Eastern

---

[46] Serm. 82, 1 *on the Feast of the Apostles Peter and Paul, PL* 54, 422-3.
[47] Serm. 86, 3 *against the heresy of Eutyches, PL* 54, 468.

bishops assembled at Chalcedon,[48] and even by the Byzantine emperors.[49]

We might also quote that magnificent tribute paid by Theodoret, Bishop of Cyrus, to the Roman Bishop and his privileged flock. Writing in 449, before the famous Council of Chalcedon, Theodoret says:—

"It is fitting that you should in all things have the pre-eminence, in view of the many peculiar privileges possessed by your See. Other cities are distinguished for their size or beauty or population . . . but your city has the greatest abundance of good things from the Giver of all good. It is of all cities the greatest and most famous, the mistress of the world and teeming with population. . . . It has, too, the tombs of our common fathers and teachers of the Truth, Peter and Paul, to illumine the souls of the faithful. These two saintly men did indeed have their rising in the East, but they shed their light in all directions, and voluntarily underwent the sunset of life in the West, from whence now they illumine the whole world. It is they who have made your See so glorious. This is the foremost of all your goods. Their See is still blessed by the light of God's presence, for He has placed Your Holiness in it to shed abroad the rays of the one true Faith."[50]

Nor did these great honors paid to Leo by the official representatives of the Eastern Churches terminate with his death. The Byzantine liturgy keeps the 18th of February as his feast day, and most truly proclaims him as "leader of orthodoxy, teacher renowned for his holiness and majesty, star of the world, glory and light of Christians, lyre of the Holy Spirit."[51]

The Gelasian Menology re-echoes these praises: "As bishop of great Rome, this father of ours, Leo, whom we admire for his self-mastery and purity and his many other virtues, gained by these virtues many notable achievements, but his most brilliant achievements are those which concern the true Faith."[52]

---

[48] Mansi, *Concil. ampliss, collect.* VI, p. 913.
[49] Ep. 100, 3 *from the Emperor Marcian, PL* 54, 972; Ep. 77, 1 *from the Empress Pulcheria, PL* 54, 907.
[50] Ep. 52, 1 *from Theodoret, Bishop of Cyrus, PL* 54, 847.
[51] *Menaia tou holou eniautou* III, Rome 1896, p. 612.
[52] Migne *PG* 117, 319.

A Call to Unity

East and West

Our purpose, venerable brethren, in focusing attention on these facts has been to establish beyond doubt that in ancient times East and West alike were united in the generosity of their tribute to the holiness of St. Leo the Great. Would that it were so today; that those who are separated from the Church of Rome, yet still have the welfare of the Church at heart, might bear witness once more to that ancient, universal esteem for St. Leo.

For if only they will settle their differences—those lamentable differences concerning the teaching and pastoral activity of this great pope—then the faith in which they believe will shine forth with renewed splendor; namely, that "there is one God, and one mediator of God and men, the man Christ Jesus."[53]

Universality of Christ's command

We are St. Leo's successor in Peter's See of Rome. We share his firm belief in the divine origin of that command which Jesus Christ gave to the Apostles and their successors to preach the gospel and bring eternal salvation to the whole world. We cherish, therefore, St. Leo's desire to see all men enter the way of truth, charity and peace.

The Council

It is to render the Church better able to fulfill this high mission of hers that We have resolved to summon the Second Ecumenical Council of the Vatican. We are fully confident that this solemn assembly of the Catholic hierarchy will not only reinforce that unity in faith, worship and discipline which is a distinguishing mark of Christ's true Church,[54] but will also attract the gaze of the great majority of Christians of every denomination, and induce them to gather around "the great Pastor of the sheep"[55] who entrusted His flock to the unfailing guardianship of Peter and his successors.[56]

---

[53] *1 Tim.* 2, 5.
[54] Cf. Conc. Vat. I, Sess. III, cap. 3 *de fide*.
[55] *Heb.* 13, 20.
[56] Cf. *John* 21, 15-17.

St. Irenaeus

Our fervent appeal for unity is intended, therefore, to be the echo of that which was made many times by St. Leo in the fifth century. We wish, too, to make Our own those words which St. Irenaeus addressed to the faithful of all the churches, when God's Providence called him from Asia to rule the See of Lyons and confer on it the fame of his martyrdom. Recognizing that the Bishops of Rome were heirs to that power which had been handed down in uninterrupted succession from the two Princes of the Apostles,[57] he went on to address the following appeal to all Christians:—

"For with this church, by reason of its pre-eminent superiority, all the churches—that is, all Christians everywhere—must be united; and it is through communion with it that all these faithful (*or* those who preside over the churches) have preserved the apostolic tradition."[58]

That all may be one

But our greatest desire is that this Our call to unity shall re-echo the Saviour's prayer to His Father at the Last Supper: "That they all may be one, as thou, Father, in me, and I in thee; that they also may be one in us."[59]

Are we to say that this prayer went unheeded by the heavenly Father, who yet accepted the sacrifice of Christ's blood on the Cross? Did not Christ say that His Father never failed to hear Him?[60] He prayed for the Church; He sacrificed Himself on the Cross for it, and promised it His unfailing presence. Assuredly, then, we must believe that this Church has always been, and still is, *one, holy, catholic and apostolic*; for thus was it founded.

Some hopeful signs

Unfortunately, however, the sort of unity whereby all believers in Christ profess the same faith, practise the same worship and obey the same supreme authority, is no more evident among the

---

[57] *Adv. Haer.* l. III, c. 2, *PG* 7, 848.
[58] *Ibid.*
[59] *John* 17, 21.
[60] Cf. *John* 11, 42.

Christians of today than it was in bygone ages. We do, however, see more and more men of good will in various parts of the world earnestly striving to bring about this visible unity among Christians, a unity which truly accords with the divine Saviour's intentions, commands and desires; and this to Us is a source of joyous consolation and ineffable hope. This desire for unity, We know, is fostered in them by the Holy Spirit, and it can only be realized in the way in which Jesus Christ has prophesied it: "There will be one fold and one shepherd."[61]

Day of peace and reconciliation

We therefore beg and implore Christ our mediator and advocate with the Father[62] to give all Christians the grace to recognize those marks by which His true Church is distinguished from all others, and to become its devoted sons. May God in His infinite kindness hasten the dawn of that long-awaited day of joyful, universal reconciliation. Then will all Christ's redeemed, united in a single family, join in praising the divine mercy, singing in joyous harmony those words of the psalmist of old: "Behold, how good and how pleasant it is for brethren to dwell together in unity."[63]

That day of peace and reconciliation between sons of the same heavenly Father and co-heirs of the same eternal happiness, will indeed be a day of triumph for the Mystical Body of Jesus Christ.

CONCLUSION

Storms continue

Venerable brethren, the fifteenth centenary of the death of St. Leo the Great finds the Catholic Church in much the same plight as she was at the turn of the fifth century. The same waves of bitter hostility break upon her. How many violent storms does she not encounter in these days of ours—storms which trouble Our fatherly heart, even though our divine Redeemer clearly forewarned us of them!

On every side We see "the faith of the gospel"[64] imperilled. In

[61] *John* 10, 16.   [62] Cf. *1 Tim.* 2, 5; *1 John* 2, 1.   [63] *Ps.* 132, 1.
[64] Cf. *Phil.* 1, 27.

some quarters an attempt is being made—usually to no avail—to induce bishops, priests and faithful to withdraw their allegiance from this See of Rome, the stronghold of Catholic unity.

Leo's patronage invoked

To rid the Church of these dangers We confidently invoke the patronage of that most vigilant of popes who labored and wrote and suffered so much for the cause of Catholic unity.

To those of you who suffer patiently in the cause of truth and justice, We speak the consoling words which St. Leo once addressed to the clergy, public officials and people of Constantinople: "Be steadfast, therefore, in the spirit of Catholic truth, and receive apostolic exhortation through Our ministry. 'For unto you it is given for Christ, not only to believe in him, but also to suffer for him' (*Phil.* 1, 29)."[65]

We pray, too, for those of you who have the security and stability of Catholic unity. Unworthy as We are, We are nonetheless the divine Redeemer's vicar, and Our prayer for you is the same as that which Christ prayed to the heavenly Father for His own beloved disciples and for those who would believe in Him: "Holy Father . . . I pray . . . that they may be made perfect in one."[66]

Charity, the bond

That perfection and consummation of unity which We most earnestly beg God to grant to all the Church's sons, can be achieved only through charity. For charity is "the bond of perfection."[67] It is charity alone that makes it possible for us to love God above all else, and makes us ready and glad to do all the good we can to others in a spirit of generosity. It is charity alone which makes "the temple of the living God,"[68] the holy Church, and all her sons throughout the world, radiant with supernatural beauty.

Perfect in the whole, perfect in the individual

These sons of the Church, therefore, We counsel once more in the words of St. Leo: "The faithful, wholly and singly, are God's

---

[65] *Ep. 50, 2 to the people of Constantinople, PL 54, 843.*
[66] *John* 17:11, 20, 23.   [67] *Col.* 3, 14.   [68] Cf. *2 Cor.* 6, 16.

temple; and just as His temple is perfect in the whole, so must it be perfect in the individual. For although all the members are not equally beautiful, nor can there be parity of merits in so great a variety of parts, nevertherless the bond of charity makes them all alike sharers in the beauty of the whole. For they are all united in the fellowship of holy love, and though they do not all make use of the same gifts of grace, they nevertheless rejoice with one another in the good things which are theirs. Nor can the object of their love be anything which bears no relation to themselves, for in the very fact of rejoicing in another's progress they are enriched by their own growth."[69]

Around a single standard

We cannot end this encyclical, venerable brethren, without referring once more to Our own and St. Leo's most ardent longing: to see the whole company of the redeemed in Jesus Christ's precious blood reunited around the single standard of the militant Church. Then let the battle commence in earnest, as we strive with might and main to resist the adversary's assaults who in so many parts of the world is threatening to annihilate our Christian faith.

"Then are God's people strongest," said St. Leo, "when the hearts of all the faithful unite in one common act of holy obedience; when in the camp of the Christian army the same preparation is made on all sides for the fight and for defence."[70]

For in the Church of Christ, if love is queen, no prince of darkness can prevail. "The devil's works are then most effectually destroyed, when men's hearts are reunited in the love of God and the love of one another."[71]

In furtherance of this expectation, venerable brethren, We lovingly impart to each and every one of you, and to the flocks committed to your watchful care, that earnest of the blessings of heaven, Our Apostolic Benediction.

Given at Rome, at St. Peter's, on the eleventh day of November in the year 1961, the fourth of Our Pontificate.

JOHN PP. XXIII

[69] Serm. 48, 1, *on Lent, PL* 54, 298-99.
[70] Ep. 88, 2, *PL* 54, 441-2.
[71] Ep. 95, 2 *to the Empress Pulcheria, PL* 54, 943.

ONE, HOLY, CATHOLIC, APOSTOLIC

An Address of Pope John XXIII after a
Mass in the Byzantine-Slav Rite

- *Personal memories of the East*
- *Aims of the Ecumenical Council*
- *Unity in diversity*
- *Holiness in relation to the Council*
- *Catholicity of the Church*

VENERABLE BRETHREN, beloved sons! The beauty and harmony of the Byzantine-Slav Rite that has just been celebrated, so touching in its appeal to the salient points of revealed doctrine and of religious devotion, would be enough to excuse Us from giving the usual homily; but Our heart insists on pouring forth an expression of the fatherly pleasure and satisfaction We feel, in repayment both for the reflections of heavenly visions that have made such a deep impression on Our soul and for the excitement stirred up in all of us by this peaceful, fraternal gathering of the representatives of all the rites of the Catholic Church around the Bishop of Rome.

Memories

The lowly successor of Peter who is speaking to you followed the various parts of the liturgical celebration and took part in it with his whole being: mind, heart, eyes, words. From the depths of distant memories—you can just imagine it—the resounding tone of the prayers and the swinging, smoking censers brought back to him the faces of the dear people of Bulgaria, of Constantinople, and of Greece. He spent his first years as a bishop in their midst and what a pleasure and a joy it was for him to link the slow, melodious, and

One, Holy, Catholic, Apostolic 161

penetrating prayer of the *Góspodi pomílui*¹ with the *Kyrie eleison*. We find it hard to describe to you the tender feelings that always seize Us when Our mind's eye goes back nostalgically to days and peoples and places that are far away but dear to Us and blessed.

Brevis sermo,² then. Just a few words, venerable brethren, for We will save until tomorrow the longer and fuller expression of Our thoughts, Our aims, and Our hopes.³

Beginning of the Council

Today's ceremony marks the beginning of the more solid and substantial preparatory phase of the Second Ecumenical Council of the Vatican. It was only natural for it to take its beginning from the altar of the Lord and from the appeals raised up by Christian piety and devotion, for they will guarantee a proper spirit and eventual success to the great undertaking to which We have in a sense vowed Ourself.

Beloved sons! What difference does it make whether or not We see it unfold and reach a conclusion with Our own eyes? Our soul is trusting and serene, and is fully satisfied with having replied to this happy inspiration simply and directly and with keeping Ourself ready to do all and dare all to make it a success.

An expression of universality

On another occasion earlier this year, the Eastern liturgies in all their richness and beauty and colorful splendor were called upon to open a sacred and solemn public display of prayer and study under the arches of the Vatican basilica. The various ceremonies that take place here acquire new dignity and a crown of exultation and glory from the presence of representatives of the priesthood and the laity from all over the world.

This morning, have we not tasted the meaning of this gradual unveiling of lights, of hymns, of secret formulas and words and

---

¹ These words from the Byzantine-Slav Liturgy are the equivalent of the *"Kyrie eleison"* in the Roman liturgy.   ² A short talk.
³ The Holy Father is referring to his address to the preparatory commissions for the Second Vatican Council on November 14, 1960. An English translation is printed in *TPS*, VI, 376-85.

found it to be a kind of expression of the majesty and the face and figure of the Church of Christ, the universal mother, pitching her tents over the whole world, through the long and dangerous centuries that have passed since the beginning?

A restoration of splendor

Everything that the new Ecumenical Council is to do is really aimed at restoring to full splendor the simple and pure lines that the face of the Church of Jesus had at its birth, and at presenting it as its divine founder made it: *sine macula et sine ruga*.[4] Its journey through the centuries is still a long way from the point where it will be transported into an eternity of triumph. So the highest and noblest aim of the Ecumenical Council (whose preparation is just now beginning and for whose success the whole world is praying) is to pause a little in a loving study of the Church and try to rediscover the lines of her more fervent youth, and to reconstruct them in a way that will reveal their power over modern minds that are tempted and deceived by the false theories of the prince of this world, the open or hidden adversary of the Son of God, Redeemer and Savior.

The ceremony at which We have just assisted with so much joy shows Us the main outline of this venerable Mother of ours, whom we honor each day with the homage of faith in the Apostles' Creed, which salutes her as one, holy, catholic, and apostolic.

One Church

Bringing various rites with different languages and different histories together here in adoration of the Most Holy Trinity is a prime and solemn public display of our respect for the unity of this divine institution, the Church. There is no beauty to compare with the diversity in rites, language, imagery, and symbols, in which the liturgy is rich, for it expresses in different ways the intimate union of the faithful who make up the Mystical Body of Christ. It reasserts the deepest and most solid reason for the various races of men to be united, for they are all called on to pay honor to Christ, and through Him, to the Most Blessed Trinity.

[4] without blemish or wrinkle.

The will of the Lord

The symbol and the guarantee of this unity is the pontiff, who takes the place of Peter and stands at the peak of the sacred order: hierarchy, doctrine, worship, sacraments. Yes, *unus Dominus, una fides, unum baptisma!*[5] The thing that recurs most often in the talks of Jesus is His exaltation of the *sacramentum unitatis*,[6] which draws together in one single inspiration all peoples and all tongues with all their natural historical variations. It is sealed by the last prayer, the last sigh uttered by Jesus to His heavenly Father, at the tragic hour of His sacrifice: *"Pater sancte, serva eos in nomine tuo, quos dedisti mihi, ut sint unum sicut et nos."*[7]

Hence the Latin liturgy that is used and recognized by a great part of the world, by the group of the faithful that is numerically largest, is very deserving of esteem among the various forms of worship. But the unity appears in all its perfection and wonder and splendor when all the Eastern liturgies, in a sense, clear the path for it and join it in rousing chorus at the same altar.

HOLY CHURCH

For each of us who has taken part in it, today's ceremony will always remain a call to holiness.

If our correspondence to the grace of Christ, which is the font of all holiness, falls short of the affirmation of the *tu solus Dominus, tu solus sanctus, tu solus altissimus*[8] We have addressed to Him, then we run the risk of reducing these ceremonies to an empty form devoid of spiritual meaning and on a level with the various forms or distractions to be found in that human activity which is directed to material things and forgets about the eternal.

The basis of all effort

This is the reason behind a declaration that amounts to a commandment and a sacred duty: put the holiness of the clergy and

---

[5] one Lord, one faith, one baptism.
[6] sacrament of unity.
[7] "Holy Father, keep in thy name those whom thou hast given me, that they may be one even as we are." (*John* 17, 11)
[8] Thou alone art Lord, thou alone art holy, thou alone art most high.

the laity right at the very basis of every effort to develop the energies of the Church and make sure that everyone is careful to have a proper regard for it, in keeping with the teaching of the divine Master and the example of the saints.

Beloved sons! We do not hesitate to say that all of Our cares and efforts to make the Council a great success might well be in vain if this collective effort at sanctification were not whole-hearted and universal. Nothing can make as much of a contribution to it as the quest for and the achievement of holiness. The prayers and virtues of individuals, and their interior spirit become an instrument of immense good.

Holy men in Church history

Four great figures in history, who were outstanding teachers in the Church and who point up the differences in rites, stand here before us to represent the East and the West in the act of holding up the apostolic Chair,[9] as if they were proclaiming to the whole world and to all ages what it is that makes the Church—let us rather call it the Holy Church—truly great: that is, the holiness of its doctors, its bishops, and its pontiffs.

Just look at the glorious names of these men, giants in their holiness and in their service to the magisterium of the Church: Athanasius and John Chrysostom, Ambrose and Augustine. Their statues are ringed by a magnificent crown formed by the images of other pontiffs and the doctors from all times and from many different backgrounds whose sacred relics are treasured here or in the other basilicas and churches of Rome.

It gives Us particular pleasure to express Our devotion by recalling the name of St. Josaphat, Bishop and Martyr, the one to whom today's Eastern liturgy (itself associated with the name of Chrysostom) was dedicated and whose glorification was greeted with a wave of devotion and of religious exultation during the pontificate of Pius IX, almost at the very opening of the First Vatican Council.

---

[9] *Cathedra*—official teaching chair, symbol of authority. In the apse of the Basilica of St. Peter, four gigantic statues hold aloft the reliquary containing a chair identified by tradition as the throne St. Peter used at Rome.—Tr.

Holiness and the Council

So, if the Second Vatican is to be a success, effective cooperation is necessary, and the only form it can take consists in efforts to grow in holiness by each and every bishop and priest and the Christian people as well.

Let each and every one of us—Pope, Fathers of the Council, fellow workers—resolve that all through this year, starting today in a systematic manner, we will remain on duty, which will mean first of all sanctification and then study and hard work. It is up to the faithful to choose the particular way in which they can cooperate through prayer—constant prayer—and through the shining example of their Christian lives in the framework of the specific activities carried on by each of them.

CATHOLIC CHURCH

This is a distinctive mark of the last testament that the Lord entrusted to Peter and to his successors. It is like a deep root, that has spread through the bowels of the earth, until it now touches the most distant borders, far beyond Palestine where the command *"Euntes"*[10] was proclaimed, and beyond Rome and Greece, which, furnished Providence with the human elements that made it possible for the Gospel message to be preached swiftly everywhere, even though it did mean the sacrifice of countless martyrs.

Through God's grace, this catholicity has remained intact through the course of the centuries, just as Jesus had predicted and promised, despite variations in liturgy and different pastoral applications, which actually add to its beauty.

The heritage of Christ must not be understood and applied in terms of the needs or demands of any one country or another, or on the basis of the shifting events of its history, but rather with complete fidelity to the promises of Jesus, who has assured us that His assistance will go on till the end of time.

Catholicity is not weakened but rather is strengthened and enriched as the Church spreads and multiplies its activity. This per-

---

[10] "Going." Cf. *Matt.* 28, 19. "Going therefore, make disciples of all nations."

fect compatibility of catholicity with the other notes is basic and it is in accord with sound doctrine: *"quod unitatis simul, sanctitatis et apostolicae successionis praerogativa debeat effulgere."*[11] (Pius IX to the bishops of England, Sept. 16, 1864).

Apostolic Church

The apostolicity of the Church is the living flame through which Christ, the king of all peoples and all ages, reassumes and recapitulates all things in Himself, as St. Paul says so clearly in the words that our Pius X adopted as his own: *instaurare omnia in Christo!*[12]

When we say that Jesus extends His dominion over all the structures that make up society, we recall the biblical vision of the *Filii tui de latere surgent.*[13] From the open side of the divine Savior comes forth the power of virtue.

St. Paul could recognize that he was *minimus apostolorum,*[14] and yet still an apostle and, for that reason, sure of his calling and of the gifts of grace that would make his ministry fruitful.

The Catholic Church is not an archeological museum. It is the ancient village fountain that gives water to the generations of today, as it gave it to those of days gone by.

Dear young people, today you paid homage to the notes of the Church—one, holy, catholic, and apostolic—in the thought-provoking beauty of the chant and ceremonies; you are the heirs of a great tradition, and as you grow older, continue to try to do it honor.

Two prayers

Venerable brother Archbishop, who celebrated today's Mass, please be kind enough to permit Us to repeat the prayer with which you lifted up our souls in one last heavenly plea:

"Jesus Christ, risen from the dead, true God of ours, through the intercession of Thy holy and immaculate Mother, of the glorious leaders of the Apostles, Peter and Paul, of our father St. John

---

[11] "That the prerogatives of unity and at the same time of holiness and apostolic succession should shine forth." Pius IX to the bishops of England, September 16, 1864.   [12] to restore all things in Christ.
[13] Thy sons will arise from thy side.   [14] the least of the apostles.

Chrysostom, Archbishop of Constantinople, of Saints Joachim and Anne, of St. Josaphat, Archbishop and Martyr, and of all the saints, have mercy on us, and save us through Thy goodness and out of Thy love for men."

We would like to add to this the other prayer you uttered before the Ikon of the Savior:

"O Lord, Thou who dost bless those who bless Thee, and sanctify those who trust in Thee, save Thy people and bless Thy inheritance. Guard Thy whole Church, sanctify those who love the beauty of Thy house, grant them glory as their reward through Thy divine power and do not abandon us who hope in Thee. Give peace to the world, which is Thine, to Thy churches, to priests, to our rulers, and to all Thy people, so that every good grace and every perfect gift may come down from on high and descend from Thee, Father of lights; and to Thee we render glory, thanks, and adoration, to the Father, the Son and the Holy Spirit, now and forever world without end."

—November 13, 1960

THE MISSIONS

The Encyclical "Princeps Pastorum" of Pope John XXIII to Catholic Bishops

- *Need for a native clergy*
- *The primacy of priest formation*
- *Local cultural values in the universal Church*
- *The role of lay leaders*

ON THE DAY when "the Prince of the Shepherds"[1] entrusted to Us His lambs and sheep,[2] God's flock, which dwells all over the earth, We responded to the sweet invitation of His love with a sense of Our unworthiness but with trust in His all-powerful assistance. And the magnitude, the beauty, and the importance of the Catholic missions have been constantly on Our mind.[3] For this reason, We have never ceased to devote to them Our greatest solicitude and attention. And at the close of the first year marking the anniversary of Our reception of the triple tiara, in the sermon which We delivered on that solemn occasion We mentioned as among the happiest events of Our pontificate the day, October 10th, on which over four hundred missionaries gathered in the most holy Vatican Basilica to receive from Our hands the crucifix, image of Jesus Christ Crucified, before leaving for distant parts of the world to illumine them with the light of Christianity.

Early interest

The most provident Lord, in His secret and loving designs, willed that, in its very first years, Our priestly mission should be oriented toward the furthering of this cause; in fact, immediately after the

---

[1] *1 Peter* 5, 4.   [2] Cf. *John* 21, 15-17.
[3] Cf. *"Homilia in die Coronationis habita," AAS* 50 (1958) 886; p. 17 above.

conclusion of the first World War, Our predecessor Benedict XV called Us to Rome from Our diocese, so that We could devote Our zeal to the Pontifical Congregation for the Propagation of the Faith, a function which We most willingly performed during four years of Our priestly life. We happily recall Whitsunday in 1922, the third centenary of the foundation of the Congregation for the Propagation of the Faith, which is especially entrusted with the task of carrying the beneficial light of the Gospel, and heavenly grace, to the farthest reaches of the earth. It was with great joy that We participated in the Congregation's centennial festivities on that day.

Also at that time Our predecessor Pius XII by word and example incited Us to give Our warmest support to missionary activities and projects. Just before the College of Cardinals was convened for the conclave during which, by divine inspiration, he was chosen as the successor of St. Peter, he spoke the following words in Our presence: "We cannot expect anything greater or more beneficial from the new Vicar of Christ than these two most important things: that he will strive with all his might to propagate the doctrine of the Gospel among all men, and that he will bring peoples together in a spirit of true peace and strengthen them therein."[4]

Subject of this letter

With these and many other sweet memories in Our mind, and aware of the grave duties imposed upon the Supreme Shepherd of the flock of God, We would like, venerable brethren—seizing an occasion offered by that memorable apostolic letter, *Maximum illud*,[5] with which, forty years ago, Our predecessor Benedict XV furthered the cause of the Catholic missions by establishing new rules and enkindling the faithful with new zeal—We would like, We repeat, to speak to you with a fatherly heart, by means of this letter, on the necessity and hopes of extending God's kingdom to the many parts of the world where missionaries labor zealously, sparing no effort in order that new branches of the Church may grow and produce wholesome fruits.

---

[4] Cf. "*La propagazione della fede,*" *Scritti di A. G. Roncalli*, Rome, 1958, p. 103 ff.
[5] Cf. *AAS* 11 (1919) 440 ff.

Our predecessors Pius XI and Pius XII also issued decrees and exhortations to the furtherance of this cause,[6] which We confirmed with like authority and like charity when We issued Our first encyclical letter, "*Ad Petri Cathedram.*"[7] We think, however, and We feel sure that We will never do enough to carry out the wishes of the divine Redeemer in this matter until all sheep are happily gathered in one fold under the leadership of one shepherd.[8]

A cry for help

When We turn Our mind and Our heart to the supernatural blessings of the Church that are to be shared with those people whose souls have not yet been suffused with the light of the Gospel, there appear before Our eyes either regions of the world where bountiful crops grow, thrive, and ripen, or regions where the labors of the toilers in God's vineyard are very arduous, or regions where the enemies of God and Jesus Christ are harassing and threatening to destroy Christian communities by violence and persecutions, and are striving to smother and crush the seed of God's word.[9] We are everywhere confronted by appeals to Us to ensure the eternal salvation of souls in the best way We can, and a cry seems to reach Our ears: "Help us!"[10] Innumerable regions have already been made fruitful by the sweat and blood of messengers of the Gospel "from every nation under heaven,"[11] and native apostles, with the help of divine grace, are blossoming like new buds and are bringing forth saving fruits. We desire to reach those regions with Our words of praise and encouragement, and with Our affection. We also wish to give them Our instructions and admonitions, which are prompted by firm hope based on the infallible promise of Our divine Master, that is contained in these words: "Behold, I am with you all days, even unto the consummation of the world."[12] "Take courage, I have overcome the world."[13]

---

[6] Cf. Pius XI's encyclical "*Rerum Ecclesiae,*" *AAS* 18 (1926) 65 ff.; Pius XII's encyclicals "*Evangelii praecones,*" *AAS* 43 (1951) 497 ff., and "*Fidei donum,*" *AAS* 49 (1957) 225 ff. An English translation of the latter is in *TPS* IV, 295-312.
[7] Encyclical "*Ad Petri Cathedram,*" *AAS* 51 (1959) 497 ff.; p. 24 ff. above.
[8] Cf. *John* 10, 16. [9] Cf. *Matt.* 13, 19.
[10] *Acts* 16, 9. [11] *Acts* 2, 5.
[12] *Matt.* 28, 20. [13] *John* 16, 33.

I

The first World War involved many countries all over the world and caused grievous losses to many individuals and nations. When it finally ended, Benedict XV's apostolic letter[14] (which We mentioned above), like the exalted invitation of a fatherly voice, inflamed the souls of all Catholics to expand peacefully the Kingdom of God, the only one, We say, which can give and secure permanent peace and prosperity to all men, children of their heavenly Father. From that time, during forty very active years, the works and undertakings of the heralds of the Gospel have been flourishing and producing increasingly abundant fruits every day; and the most noteworthy result is the fact that a local hierarchy and clergy have been increasingly developed in the mission areas.

A local hierarchy

It is necessary that missionaries obey the words of Our immediate predecessor, Pius XII, to the effect that they "must constantly keep before their mind's eyes their ultimate goal, which is to establish the Church firmly in other countries, and subsequently to entrust it to a local hierarchy, chosen from their own people."[15] Therefore, this Apostolic See, abundantly and at the opportune time, has taken measures especially in recent times, to establish or re-establish a hierarchy in those areas in which local conditions favored the foundation of episcopal sees, and if possible, to place locally born prelates at their head. At any rate, it is well known that this has always been the principal and constant goal of the Sacred Congregation for the Propagation of the Faith. It was an apostolic letter, however, which highlighted the importance and immediacy of the matter as never before. In this letter Our predecessor Benedict XV urgently reminded the authorities in charge of the missions to nurture carefully the vocations of those who felt the divine call to the priesthood in mission territories and to contribute to the quantitative and qualitative growth of that clergy which was called native. (Neither slight nor discrimination was

[14] *AAS* 11 (1919) 440 ff.
[15] Encyclical *"Evangelii praecones," AAS* 43 (1951) 507.

intended by the word "native," or was ever expressed or implied by the language of the Roman pontiffs and ecclesiastical documents.)

Growth of native clergy

This exhortation of Benedict XV, which was repeated by Our predecessors Pius XI and Pius XII, with the help of God's divine Providence has had visible and copious results. We want you to join Us in rendering thanks to God for the fact that a numerous and elect legion of bishops and priests has arisen in the mission territories, Our brethren and beloved sons, who fill Our heart with great expectations. If We cast even a cursory glance on the ecclesiastical situation in the areas which are entrusted to the Sacred Congregation for the Propagation of the Faith, with the exception of those at present under persecution, We note that the first bishop of east Asian origins was consecrated in 1923, and the first vicars apostolic of African Negro descent were named in 1939. By 1959, We count 68 Asian and 25 African bishops. The remaining native clergy grew in number from 919 in 1918 to 5553 in 1957 in Asia, and during the same period in Africa from 90 in 1918 to 1811 in 1957. With such an admirable increase in the numbers of the clergy did the Lord of the harvest[16] desire to reward adequately the labors and merits of those who zealously did mission work, either individually or in co-operation with many others, responding with a generous heart to the repeated exhortations of this Apostolic See.

Mutual exchange

It was, therefore, with good reason that Our predecessor Pius XII was able to affirm with satisfaction: "Once upon a time it seemed as though the life of the Church used to prosper and blossom chiefly in the regions of ancient Europe, whence it would flow, like a majestic river, through the remaining areas which, to use the Greek term, were considered almost the periphery of the world; today, however, the life of the Church is shared, as though by a mutual irradiation of energies, among all individual members of

---

[16] Cf. *Matt.* 9, 38.

the Mystical Body of Christ. Not a few countries on other continents have long since outgrown the missionary stage, and are now governed by an ecclesiastical hierarchy of their own, have their own ecclesiastical organization, and are liberally offering to other Church communities those very gifts, spiritual and material, which they formerly used to receive."[17]

Encouraging vocations

We wish especially to exhort the bishops and clergy of the new Christian communities to pray to God, and to conduct themselves in such a way that the priestly gift they are enjoying may grow in spiritual fruitfulness; in their talks with the people, as often as feasible they should praise the dignity, the beauty, and the merits of the priesthood, and, by so doing, they will induce all those whom God has chosen for this exalted honor to respond to the call with an open and generous heart. They should also cause the faithful entrusted to their care to pray to God for this cause, in unity of spirit with the whole Church, which, in response to the divine Redeemer's exhortations, prays "the Lord of the harvest to send forth laborers into his harvest,"[18] especially at the present time, when "the harvest indeed is great, but the laborers are few."[19]

Place of foreign missionaries

However, Christian communities to which missionaries still devote their zeal, although already governed by their own hierarchy, are still in need of the work of missionaries from other countries, either because of the vastness of the territory, or the increasing number of converts, or the multitude of those who have not yet benefited from the doctrine of the Gospel. To such missionaries, no doubt, apply these words of Our immediate predecessor: "These cannot be considered foreigners, for all Catholic priests who truly answer their vocation feel themselves native sons wherever they work, in order that the Kingdom of God may flourish and de-

---

[17] Pius XII's Christmas broadcast, *AAS* 38 (1946) 20.
[18] *Luke* 10, 2.   [19] *Ibid.*

velop."[20] Let them therefore work united by the bond of that loving, brotherly, and sincere charity which mirrors the love they must feel toward the divine Redeemer and His Church; and, in prompt and filial obedience to their bishops, whom "the Holy Spirit placed ... to rule the Church of God,"[21] they must be "of one heart and one soul,"[22] grateful to each other for the mutual cooperation and help; indeed, if they act in this manner, it should be apparent to everyone's eyes that they are the disciples of Him who, in His own and most distinctive "new" commandment, exhorted all to a mutual and always increasing love.[23]

II

Our predecessor Benedict XV, in his apostolic letter *"Maximum illud,"* especially exhorted Catholic mission authorities to mold and shape the minds and souls of the clergy selected from the local population, and to do so in such a way that their formation and education would turn out "perfect and complete in every respect."[24] "In fact," he wrote, "a native priest, having a place of birth, character, mentality, and emotional make-up in common with his countrymen, is in a privileged position for sowing the seeds of the Faith in their hearts: indeed, he knows much better than a stranger the ways of persuasion with them."[25]

Personal sanctification

Regarding the requirements of a perfect priestly formation and education, it is necessary that seminarians be induced, tactfully but firmly, to espouse those virtues which are the prime qualification of the priestly calling, "that is, the duty to achieve personal sanctification."[26] The newly-ordained native clergy of those countries must enter into pious competition with the clergy of those older dioceses which have long been producing priests in their midst who were

---

[20] Letter of Pius XII to Cardinal Adeodatus Piazza, *AAS* 47 (1955) 542; *TPS* V, 253-4.
[21] *Acts* 20, 28.
[22] *Acts* 4, 32.
[23] Cf. *John* 13, 34 and 15, 12.
[24] *AAS* 11 (1919) 445.
[25] *Ibid.*
[26] Pius XII's apostolic letter *"Menti Nostrae,"* *AAS* 42 (1950) 477.

such mirrors of virtue that they are proposed as examples to the clergy of the whole Church. In fact, it is through sanctity that priests can and must be the light of the world and the salt of the earth.[27] In other words, they can, especially by their sanctity, show their own countrymen and the whole world the beauty and the supernatural power of the Gospel; they can teach all men that a perfect Christian life is a goal toward which all of God's children must strive, struggling and persevering with all their strength, regardless of their place of birth, their walk of life, or the degree of civilization they enjoy.

Native teachers in seminaries

Furthermore, Our fatherly soul harbors the happy hope that everywhere the local clergy will be able to select from among its ranks just and holy men capable of governing, forming, and educating their own seminarians. That is the reason why We are already instructing the bishops and the mission authorities to choose without hesitation from among the local clergy those priests who, for their exceptional virtue and wise actions, qualify as teachers in the local seminaries and are able to lead their students to sanctity.

Adaptation to locality

Furthermore, venerable brethren, as you well know, the Church has prescribed at all times that priests must prepare for their calling by means of a solid intellectual and spiritual education. Indeed, no one will doubt, especially in our time, that young people of all races and from all parts of the world are capable of absorbing such an education; this fact has already been clearly demonstrated. Without doubt, the formation to be given to this clergy must take into account the circumstances which obtain in different areas and nations. This extremely wise norm applies to all students for the priesthood; it is advisable that young seminarians never be "educated in places too far removed from human society,"[28] because "once they step out into the world, they will have problems in

---
[27] Cf. *Matt.* 5, 13-14.
[28] Pius XII's apostolic letter *"Menti Nostrae," AAS* 42 (1950) 686.

dealing both with simple people and with intellectuals; this will often cause them to assume the wrong attitude toward the Christian population, or to regard the formation they received as a bad one."[29] Indeed, it is necessary that youths not only conform to the ideal of priestly spiritual perfection in everything, but also that they "gradually and prudently penetrate the mentality and feelings of the people"[30]—of the people, We repeat, whom they must enlighten with the truth of the Gospel and lead to perfection of life, with the help of God's grace. Therefore, it is necessary that seminary superiors conform to this plan of training and education while yet welcoming those material and technical facilities which the genius of mankind has made the patrimony, as it were, of every civilization in order to insure an easier and better life and to preserve the bodily health and safety of mankind.

Training for responsibility

The formation of the local clergy, as Our same predecessor, Benedict XV, wrote, must enable them, in compliance with the first requirement of their divine calling, "to assume rightly the rule of their people"[31]—to lead their people, by the influence of their teaching and their ministry, along the path to eternal salvation. To this end, We highly recommend that everyone, whether local or foreign, who contributes to the formation in question, do his conscientious best to develop in these students a sense of the importance and difficulty of their mission, and a capability for wisely and discreetly using the freedom allowed to them. This should be done so that they may be in a position to assume, quickly and progressively, all the functions, even the most important ones, pertaining to their calling, not only in harmonious cooperation with the foreign clergy, but also on an equal footing with them.[32] Indeed, this is the touchstone of the effectiveness of their formation, and will be the best reward for the efforts of all those who contributed to it.

[29] *Ibid.*   [30] *Ibid.*, p. 687.
[31] Apostolic letter *"Maximum illud," AAS* 11 (1919) 445.
[32] Cf. Pius XII's apostolic letter *"Menti Nostrae," AAS* 42 (1950) 686.

Missiology

Indeed, in considering all the elements pertaining not only to the right intellectual and spiritual formation of the students for the priesthood but also to the needs and to the special mentality and emotional make-up of their own people, this Apostolic See has always recommended, both to the foreign and to the local clergy, that they should study the discipline of missiology. Our predecessor Benedict XV established chairs of this discipline in the Pontifical Urban Athanaeum of the Propagation of the Faith;[33] and Our immediate predecessor, Pius XII, remarked with satisfaction on the founding of the Institute of Missiology in the same university; "not a few faculties and chairs of missiology," he said, "have been established in Rome and in other places."[34] Therefore, in the curricula of the seminaries of mission countries, there will be no lack of studies pertaining to the various missiological disciplines, nor of technical training in all the practical skills which are considered useful for the future work of the clergy in those countries. Therefore it is absolutely necessary that their training not only conform to the best ecclesiastical traditions of a solid and undiluted education, but also that it open up and sharpen the minds of the seminarians in such a way as to enable each individual to evaluate correctly his own and his country's particular kind of culture, especially as it pertains to philosophical and theological teachings and their relation to the Christian religion.

The Church and cultures

"The Catholic Church," stated Our same predecessor, "has never fostered an attitude of contempt or outright rejection of pagan teachings but, rather, has completed and perfected them with Christian doctrine, after purifying them from all dross of errors. So, too, the Church, to a certain extent, consecrated native art and culture . . ., as well as the special customs and traditional institutions of the people . . .; she has even transformed their feast days,

[33] *Ibid.*, p. 448.
[34] Encyclical *"Evangelii praecones," AAS* 43 (1951) 500.

leaving unchanged their methods of computation and their form, but dedicating them to the memory of the martyrs and to the celebration of the sacred mysteries."[35] We Ourself have already expressed Our thoughts on this matter as follows: "Wherever artistic and philosophical values exist which are capable of enriching the culture of the human race, the Church fosters and supports these labors of the spirit. On the other hand, the Church, as you know, does not identify itself with any one culture, not even with European and Western civilization, although the history of the Church is closely intertwined with it; for the mission entrusted to the Church pertains chiefly to other matters, that is, to matters which are concerned with religion and the eternal salvation of men. The Church, however, which is so full of youthful vigor and is constantly renewed by the breath of the Holy Spirit, is willing, at all times, to recognize, welcome, and even assimilate anything that redounds to the honor of the human mind and heart, whether or not it originates in parts of the world washed by the Mediterranean Sea, which, from the beginning of time, had been destined by God's Providence to be the cradle of the Church."[36]

Conversion of the learned

If native priests are well instructed in these practical matters and serious disciplines, and if they overcome difficulties and are equipped to take the right course of action, they will be able, under guidance of their bishops, to make highly valuable contributions. In particular, they will find a more sympathetic audience among the educated citizens of their own countries and will be able to attract them to the Christian truth, in the manner of the famous missionary, Matthew Ricci. This will happen especially in those countries which possess an ancient and highly-developed civilization of their own. Indeed, local priests are entrusted with the mission of "bringing every mind into captivity to the obedience of Christ,"[37] as Paul, that incomparable missionary and apostle of the people, affirmed;

---
[35] *Ibid.*, p. 522.
[36] Cf. "Address to Participants in Second World Congress of Negro Writers and Artists," *Osservatore Romano*, April 3, 1959. Brief summary in *TPS* V, 290-1.
[37] *2 Cor.* 10, 5.

thus, they will also be "held in great honor by the members of the intellectual elite of their country."[38]

Study centers

Therefore, making use of their judgment and co-operation, bishops will take care to establish, at opportune moments, study centers to meet the needs of one or more regions in order to make basic doctrine known and understood. In these, both foreign and local priests can employ their learning and experience to benefit the particular countries in which they were born or in which they have chosen to spread the Christian truth. In this connection, We should also like to quote the teaching of Our immediate predecessor, Pius XII, expressed in these words: there must be promoted "the publication and dissemination of Catholic books of every description";[39] and care must be taken to advance "the use of modern means of communication in spreading Christian doctrine. No one can ignore the importance of gaining the good will of native peoples and making them favorable to Catholicism."[40] Certainly, all methods cannot be employed in all places; all opportunities must be taken, however, to fulfill different needs, whenever they arise, even though, sometimes, "one sows, another reaps."[41]

Social welfare work

To propagate the truth of Jesus Christ is the truest function of the Church. Indeed, "it is the solemn duty of the Church to impart to . . . peoples, so far as possible, the outstanding blessings of her life and her teaching, from which a new social order should be derived, based on Christian principles."[42] Therefore, in mission territories, the Church takes the most generous measures to encourage social welfare projects, to support welfare work for the poor, and to assist Christian communities and the peoples concerned. Care must be taken, however, not to clutter and obstruct the apostolic work of

---

[38] Pius XI's encyclical *"Rerum Ecclesiae," AAS* 18 (1926) 77.
[39] Encyclical *"Fidei donum," AAS* 49 (1957) 233; *TPS* IV, 301.
[40] *Ibid.*   [41] *John* 4, 37.
[42] Encyclical *"Fidei donum," AAS* 49 (1957) 231; *TPS* IV, 300.

the missions with an excessive quantity of secular projects. Economic assistance must be limited to necessary undertakings which can be easily maintained and utilized, and to projects whose organization and administration can be easily transferred to the lay men and women of the particular nation, thus allowing the missionaries to devote themselves to their task of propagating the faith, and to other pursuits aimed directly at personal sanctification and eternal salvation.

Universality

If it is true, as We said, that in order for the apostolate to bear abundant fruits, the most important requirement the native priests must meet is that they should know, and carefully evaluate, everything connected with the institutions peculiar to their countries, what Our predecessor said of the whole world will remain even truer: "the prospects and plans of the Church, which embrace the whole world, will be the prospects and plans of their daily Christian lives."[43] To this end, the native clergy not only will be bound to know the affairs and developments of the universal Church, but must also be guided by, and filled with, the charity which embraces all the faithful. This is the reason why St. John Chrysostom said of Christian liturgical celebrations: "When we approach the altar, we pray, above all, for the whole universe and the common good";[44] and St. Augustine uttered a beautiful sentence: "Extend your charity to the whole world, if you want to love Christ, because the members of Christ's body covered the whole world."[45]

Ultra-nationalism

Indeed, it was in this spirit that Our predecessor Benedict XV, in order to preserve the integrity of the concept of Catholic unity, which must inspire all missionary work, sternly warned of a danger which he did not hesitate to define in these words, and which must be avoided by missionaries in their thoughts, lest it jeopardize the

---

[43] *Ibid.*, p. 238; English translation *op. cit.*, p. 305.
[44] *Hom. II in 2 Cor.*, Migne, *PG* 61, 398.
[45] *In Ep. Ioan. ad Parthos*, Tr. X, c. 5, Migne, *PL* 35, 2060.

effectiveness of their actions: "It would be a sad thing if any missionary should appear to be so oblivious of his dignity as to think of his country on earth rather than of his fatherland in heaven, and be excessively concerned with increasing the power and the glory of his own nation above all other nations. Such conduct would greatly impair the cause of the apostolate, and would cut the sinews of charity in his heart, while lowering his prestige in the eyes of the public."[46]

This danger, in different ways and forms, could arise again in our time, especially since several countries already enlightened by the light of the Gospel have been aroused to seek freedom and self-government. The acquisition of political freedom can sometimes be accompanied by disorders and excesses which are detrimental to the common good and are the opposite of the spirit of Christian charity.

We feel perfectly confident, however, that the native clergy is animated by lofty purposes and sentiments which conform to the general principles of the Christian religion and entirely correspond with the teachings of the Catholic Church, which embraces all men with the same love; We are also certain that they contribute their share to the real interests of their own nations. In this connection, Our predecessor very aptly uttered the following words of warning: "The Catholic Church is not a stranger among any people or nation."[47] No Christian community anywhere will ever achieve unity with the Universal Church, from which emanates the supernatural life of Jesus Christ, if the local clergy and population succumb to the influence of a particularist spirit, if they arouse enmity in other nations, and if they are misled and perturbed by an ultranationalism which can destroy the spirit of universal charity—that charity upon which the Church of God is built and is called "Catholic."

III

Our predecessor Benedict XV, as We mentioned above, stressed particularly the necessity of a scholarly, intensive, and adequate

---

[46] Apostolic letter "*Maximum illud,*" *AAS* 11 (1919) 446.
[47] *Ibid.*, p. 445.

formation of the native clergy, which must be equal to current circumstances. Undoubtedly he was aware of another need, equally important: the need to educate and indoctrinate the laity of each nation in such a way that they will not only be worthy of their Christian calling in their private lives, but will also engage in active apostolic work. Our immediate predecessor Pius XII dealt with the subject well and significantly,[48] and recommended again and again that today this cause be attended to with great fervor and be carried out to the greatest degree and as soon as possible.

Need for lay help

Our predecessor Pius XII—and this redounds to his special credit and praise—exhorted the laity, with eloquent and abundant doctrine and repeated admonitions, willingly and zealously to enter the apostolic field and give their active co-operation to the ecclesiastical hierarchy, in the same way in which, since the times of the early Church, and throughout the centuries, the faithful have co-operated with their bishops and their clergy, to enable them to carry out their tasks more easily and with greater efficacy, in religious and social fields. Our times require this effort, not less, nay, even more, since requirements of this kind have grown, and the greatly increased multitudes are hungry for the spiritual food of true doctrine. Indeed, their circumstances have become more difficult and complex. And, wherever the Church fights her peaceful battles, she must be able to count on a complete organization, including not only the different grades of the hierarchy, but also the ranks of the laity proper. It is also necessary that her work of salvation be carried out equally by all.[49]

Numbers not enough

In order to achieve this purpose, it is hardly sufficient for new Christian communities to convert men to the Catholic religion and, after purifying them with the water of Baptism, to number them

---

[48] Encyclical *"Evangelii praecones," AAS* 43 (1951) 510 ff.
[49] Pius XII's encyclical *"Mystici Corporis," AAS* 35 (1943) 200-01; Pius XI's encyclical *"Rerum Ecclesiae," AAS* 18 (1926) 78.

among the members of the Church; it is altogether necessary, after giving the individual a Christian education suitable to his circumstances and times, to make him capable of promoting, as much as he can, the present and future good and growth of the Church. The sheer number of Christians means little if they lack virtue; that is, if, while enjoying the name of Catholic, they do not stand firm in their determination; if their spiritual life does not flourish and fails to produce wholesome fruits; if, after being reborn to divine grace, they do not excel in that spirit of vigorous and sensible youthfulness which is always ready to perform generous and useful deeds. Their profession of faith must not only be a statistic in a census, but must create a new man,[50] and give all his actions a supernatural strength, inspiring, guiding, and controlling them.

Need for planning

Nevertheless, men recruited from the ranks of the laity will find it difficult fully to achieve their goal, if the clergy, either foreign or local, will not plan, at the right time, the program which We mentioned above, and which the first Vicar of Jesus already outlined in the following words: "You, however, are a chosen race, a royal priesthood, a holy nation, a purchased people; that you may proclaim the perfection of him who has called you out of darkness into his marvelous light."[51]

Education for the apostolate

Indeed, a Christian formation and education which would only consider teaching the faithful the formulas of the catechism and inculcating in their minds the principal precepts of moral theology, with a brief list of possible cases, without inspiring their souls and wills to act according to the instructions received, would run the serious risk of acquiring for the Church a passive flock. On the contrary, it is necessary that the sheep of the Christian flock not only listen to their Shepherd, but also know his voice,[52] and that the faithful willingly follow him to the pastures of eternal life,[53] so that

[50] Cf. *Eph.* 4, 24.
[51] *1 Peter* 2, 9.
[52] Cf. *John* 10, 4 and 14.
[53] Cf. *John* 10, 9-10.

one day they may receive from the Prince of Shepherds the "unfading crown of glory."[54] These sheep as We said, recognizing and following the Shepherd, who lays down his life for his sheep,[55] will give themselves entirely to him, and, obeying the divine Will with the most ardent zeal, will lovingly and actively strive to bring into the one and only true fold all the other sheep, who not only are not following him, but have long been straying away from him, who is "the way, and the truth, and the life."[56]

Profession of the Christian faith is not intelligible without strong, lively apostolic fervor; in fact, "everyone is bound to proclaim his faith to others, either to give good example and encouragement to the rest of the faithful, or to check the attacks of unbelievers,"[57] especially in our time, when the Universal Church and human society are beset by many difficulties.

Arousing zeal

To make a full and effective Christian education possible, it is absolutely necessary that administrators and teachers find ways and means by which they will be able to understand and approach the minds of others and their characteristic temperaments, their inclinations and their intentions. This should be done so that the new followers of Jesus Christ will assimilate the precepts of the truth of the Gospel, together with its norms and requirements and will be wholly formed by them. Our Redeemer did, in fact, entrust each one of us with compliance with this great commandment: "Thou shalt love the Lord thy God with thy whole heart, and with thy whole soul, and with thy whole mind."[58] Indeed, the sublimity of the Christian calling should shine in all its splendor before the eyes of those who embrace the Catholic religion, so that their hearts will be fired with the desire, the strong resolution to lead a life adorned with all the Christian virtues and distinguished by apostolic activity: a life, We say, modeled on the luminous example of Jesus Christ, who, taking upon Himself our nature, commanded us to follow in His footsteps.[59]

[54] *1 Peter* 5, 4.
[55] Cf. *John* 10, 11.
[56] *John* 14, 6.
[57] St. Thomas Aquinas, *Summa Theologica* II-II, q. 3, a. 2, ad 2.
[58] *Matt.* 22, 37.
[59] Cf. *1 Peter* 2, 21; *Matt.* 11, 29; *John* 13, 15.

Witnesses to the truth

Anyone who deems himself a Christian must know that he is bound by his conscience to the basic, imperative duty of bearing witness to the truth in which he believes and to the grace which has transformed his soul. A great Father of the Church has said: "He (Christ) left us on earth in order that we should become like beacons of light and teachers unto others; that we might act like leaven, move among men like angels, be like men unto children, and like spiritual men unto animal men, in order to win them over, and that we may be like seed, and bear abundant fruits. There would be no need for sermons, if our lives were shining; there would be no need for words, if we bore witness with our deeds. There would be no more pagans, if we were true Christians."[60]

All Christians all over the world must fulfill this obligation; yet it is easy to see that if it were carried out in the mission territories, it would bear special and abundant fruits, particularly valuable for extending the Kingdom of God among those who do not know the wonderful gift of our Faith and the supernatural power of grace. Thus Jesus Christ admonishes us: "Even so let your light shine before men, in order that they may see your good works and give glory to your Father in heaven";[61] and St. Peter exhorts the faithful to "abstain from carnal desires which war against the soul. Behave yourselves honorably among the pagans, that, whereas they slander you as evildoers, they may, through observing you by reason of your good works, glorify God in the day of visitation."[62]

Union in charity

The testimony rendered by individuals must be confirmed and enlarged by the testimony of the whole Christian community, in the same way in which the newly established Church enjoyed the unanimous backing and close-knit support of all the faithful, who "continued steadfastly in the teaching of the Apostles, and in the communion of the breaking of the bread and in the prayers."[63]

---

[60] St. John Chrysostom, *Hom. X in I Tim.*, Migne, *PG* 62, 551.
[61] *Matt.* 5, 16.   [62] *1 Peter* 2, 12.   [63] *Acts* 2, 42.

Their unity in the practice of the most generous charity gave them profound joy and mutual edification; in fact, they were "praising God and being in favor with all the people. And day by day the Lord added to their company such as were to be saved."[64]

Union in prayer and in active participation in the mysteries of the sacred liturgy enormously enriches and completes the Christian life of individuals and of the whole community, and it greatly helps educate the soul to charity, which is the distinguishing mark of the true Christian; a charity, We say, which overcomes all differences between languages and nationalities, and amicably embraces all men, whether brothers or enemies. In this connection, We like to repeat the words of Our predecessor Pope Clement: "When they (the pagans) hear from us that God says, 'You have no merit if you love those who love you, but you have merit if you love your enemies and those who hate you'[65]—when they hear this, they admire the grace of your charity; but when they see that we not only do not love those who hate us, but do not even reciprocate the love of those who love us, they will mock us and God's name will be blasphemed."[66] The greatest missionary of all, St. Paul the Apostle, at the time when he was on the point of bringing the message of God's word to the people, as far as the farthest reaches of the western world, wrote to the Romans and exhorted them to practice "love without pretense."[67] Earlier, with sublime expression, he had praised that virtue—without which a Christian is nothing.[68]

Material help

Charity also becomes visible through material help; as Our predecessor Pius XII stated: "The body also requires a multitude of members, which are joined together for the purpose of helping one another. If in our mortal organism one member ails, all the other members suffer with it; and those members which are sound, come to the help of the sick one; by the same token, in the Church, the

---

[64] *Acts* 2, 47. [65] Cf. *Luke* 6, 32-35.
[66] F. X. Funk, *Patres Apostolici*, v. I, p. 201.
[67] *Rom.* 12, 9 ff. [68] *1 Cor.* 13, 2.

individual members do not live only for themselves, but also to help the others, and all of them help one another for their mutual comfort, as well as for a better development of the Mystical Body."[69]

The material necessities which affect the faithful also affect the life and structure of the Church. It is therefore necessary that native Christians become accustomed to supporting, spontaneously and within the limits of their means, their churches, institutions, and clergy, who are entirely devoting themselves to them. It does not matter whether they can give much, but it is of the greatest importance that what is contributed is proof of a conscience that is practicing Christian discipline.

IV

The Christian faithful, members of a living organism, cannot remain aloof and think that they have done their duty when they have satisfied their own spiritual needs; every individual must give his assistance to those who are working for the increase and propagation of God's kingdom. Our predecessor Pius XII reminded all of their common duty in these words: "A principal note of the Church is catholicity; consequently, a man is no true member of the Church unless he is likewise a true member of the entire body of Christian believers and is filled with an ardent desire to see her take root and flourish in every land."[70]

The duty of teaching the Faith

In this matter, therefore, all Christians must compete in pious rivalry, and give constant proof of their concern for the spiritual well-being of other people by defending their Faith and teaching it to those who either do not know it at all, or do not know it well enough and therefore misjudge it. It is necessary that priests, families, and local apostolic organizations instill this religious duty in the young, from early childhood and adolescence, even in newly

---

[69] Pius XII's encyclical *"Mystici Corporis," AAS* 35 (1943) 200.
[70] Pius XII's encyclical *"Fidei donum," AAS* 49 (1957) 237; *TPS* IV, 304.

established Christian communities. Nor is there a dearth of favorable opportunities for stressing, in a suitable and effective manner, this duty of an apostolate: as for example, the preparation of children or newly baptized adults for the sacrament of Confirmation, through which "new strength is granted to the faithful courageously to guard and defend their Mother Church and the Faith they received from her."[71] This preparation is especially suited for populations who have in their local customs special initiation rites, through which adolescents are officially received into their tribal groups.

Catechists

We cannot neglect here to give credit to the work of catechetical organizations, which, in the course of the long history of the Catholic missions, have always given them special, necessary help. There was never a time when catechists were not excellent assistants to missionaries, sharing their labors and relieving them. Our predecessors have openly affirmed that "for the propagation of the Gospel, it is important that their numbers be multiplied,"[72] and have stated that their function was "perhaps the most shining example of the apostolate to be carried out by the laity."[73] We, too, while again giving catechists Our warmest praise, exhort them to meditate even more attentively on the happiness of soul which this work brings, and never to cease from making the greatest efforts, under the guidance of the ecclesiastical hierarchy, to cultivate better the study of religion and their own spiritual formation. Catechists must learn from the hierarchy not only the rudimentary elements of the Faith, but also the practice of virtue and a fervent, sincere love for Christ. Instrumental in the establishment and subsequent abundant growth of new Christian communities is the care devoted to increasing the numbers of those who effectively help the ecclesi-

---

[71] Pius XII's encyclical *"Mystici Corporis," AAS* 35 (1943) 201.
[72] Pius XI's encyclical *"Rerum Ecclesiae," AAS* 18 (1926) 78.
[73] Sermon by Pius XII to participants in the World Congress for the Lay Apostolate, *AAS* 49 (1957) 937; *TPS* IV, 132.

astical hierarchy, and to perfecting their formation for any other labors they may have to perform in order to carry out their task in the most effective and perfect manner.

Catholic Action

In Our first encyclical letter, We already recalled various important reasons which make it imperative, in our time, to recruit in all parts of the world "the laity to the ranks of a peaceful militia, Catholic Action, so that the laity should co-operate in the apostolate of the hierarchy."[74] We commented on this with the following words: "It gives Us great comfort that, over the years, in lands that are still mission territories, these valuable aides to bishops and priests have worked so hard for the success of their projects."[75] And now, impelled "by the love of Christ,"[76] We wish to renew urgently the exhortations and appeals of Our predecessor Pius XII: "It is necessary that laymen give their generous, zealous, and active cooperation, joining the clergy in their apostolic work and swelling to large numbers the ranks of Catholic Action."[77] The bishops of mission countries endeavored to do their best to carry out the directives of the Supreme Pontiff, together with the regular and religious clergy, and the most generous and well-trained laymen; We can state that splendid successes in this field are being achieved all over the earth.

Adaptation to local conditions

However, it is necessary—and We can never warn sufficiently of this—that this form of apostolate be carefully adapted to local conditions and needs. What has been done in one country cannot be carried over indiscriminately to another. The people concerned, submitting in all things to the directives of the ecclesiastical hierarchy and willingly obeying their pastors, must beware of defeating

[74] Encyclical *"Ad Petri Cathedram," AAS* 51 (1959) 523; p. 48 above.
[75] *Ibid.*
[76] *2 Cor.* 5, 14.
[77] Pius XII's encyclical *"Evangelii praecones," AAS* 43 (1951) 513.

the purposes of the apostolate by carrying the burden of an excessive number of activities. For thus they thwart valuable efforts and dissipate valuable energy through compartmentalized and overly specialized projects, which, while satisfactory elsewhere, may be less useful where different conditions and needs prevail. In Our first encyclical, We also promised to deal with the subject of Catholic Action in more detail and at greater length; when We do, We trust that the mission territories will receive additional support and a new incentive. In the meantime, let everyone work in perfect harmony and with supernatural inspiration, in the certainty that only thus will they be able to say that they are serving the divine cause and the common good of their people.

Training for leadership

Catholic Action is an association of laymen "who are entrusted with certain duties, which involve executive responsibilities, to be carried out in submission to the hierarchy";[78] thus laymen do hold executive offices therein. For this reason it is necessary to train men who are capable of enkindling different organizations with apostolic zeal and insuring their most efficient operation; men and women, We say, who in order to be worthy of managerial and executive roles in these organizations, entrusted to them by the ecclesiastical hierarchy, must furnish convincing proof that they possess a solid Christian formation, both intellectual and moral, in order that "they may impart to others what, with the help of God's grace, they have won for themselves."[79]

The Christian school

It can rightly be said that the natural seat and, as it were, the training ground, where these lay executives of Catholic Action are prepared for their functions, is the Christian school; and this school will achieve its purposes, and fulfill its task, only insofar as its

---

[78] Cf. Pius XII's *"Epistola de Actione Catholica,"* October 11, 1946, *Discorsi e Radiomessaggi di S.S. Pio XII*, v. VIII, p. 468.
[79] Encyclical *"Ad Petri Cathedram," AAS* 51 (1959) 524. Cf. p. 49 above.

teachers, whether priests, religious, or laymen, educate and turn out true Christians.

Schools of the apostolate

Everyone is aware of the great importance, present and future, of the mission country schools, and of how much effort and work the Church has devoted to establishing schools of every description and level and to defending their existence and well-being. It is obviously difficult to add to school curricula a program of formation for Catholic Action executives, and therefore it will often be necessary to resort to extracurricular methods to bring together the most promising youths, and train them in the theory and practice of the apostolate. The local ordinaries must, therefore, use their prudent judgment in assessing the best ways and means for opening schools of the apostolate, in which, obviously, the type of instruction will be different from that in ordinary schools. Sometimes the task will be to preserve from false doctrine children and adolescents who must attend non-Catholic schools; in any event, it will always be necessary to balance the humanistic and technological education offered by the public schools with a formation based on spiritual values, so that the schools may not turn out falsely educated men, swollen with arrogance, who can hurt the Church and their own people instead of helping them. Their spiritual education must always be commensurate with their intellectual development, and must be planned to make them lead a life inspired by Catholic principles in their particular social and professional environments; in time, they must be able to take their places in Catholic organizations. To this end, if Catholic youths should be forced to leave their communities and attend public schools in other towns and cities, it will be expedient to open social centers and boarding houses, in which Christian life and morals are safely preserved, and the talents and energies of the young people are directed toward lofty apostolic ideals.

By thus entrusting to the schools the special and highly useful tasks of preparing Catholic Action executives, We do not, however, intend to exempt families from their responsibilities, or to minimize in any way their influence, which at times equips them even better for nurturing apostolic fervor in the souls of their children, for instructing them in Christian precepts, and for preparing them for action. The home is, in fact, an excellent and irreplaceable school.

Problems in public life

The "good fight"[80] in the cause of the Faith is fought not only in the secrecy of the individual conscience or in the privacy of the home, but also in public life in all of its forms. In all the different parts of the world there exist nowadays problems of various kinds. There is no solution to these problems in exclusively human advice nor in principles which are often in contrast with the precepts of Christian law. Several mission countries are now "undergoing such speedy changes in social, economic, and political life that their entire future appears to depend on the outcome of those changes."[81] Indeed, problems which some countries have already solved or are solving with the help of their experience and traditions, are urgently in need of solution in other countries. There the problems are beset by serious dangers, inasmuch as they could be approached with deplorable levity, by resorting to certain doctrines which disregard, or even oppose, the religious values of individuals and nations. In order to safeguard both their private interests and those of the Church, Catholics must not ignore such problems, or wait until they are given the wrong solutions, which would thereafter require a much greater expenditure of energy in order to correct them and would place further obstacles in the path of the propagation of the Christian religion in the world.

Christians in public life

The laymen of mission countries exert their most direct and effective influence in the field of public activity, and it is necessary that Christian communities take urgent, timely measures to bring laymen into the public life of their countries for the common good—

---

[80] *2 Tim.* 4, 7.
[81] Pius XII's encyclical "Fidei donum," *AAS* 49 (1957) 229; *TPS* IV, 298.

men who not only acquit themselves creditably in their professions and trades, but are also an asset to the Church which re-created them in her grace. Thus may their pastors praise them with the words which we read in the writings of St. Basil: "I thanked the Most Holy God for the fact that, even though busily attending to public affairs, you did not neglect the interests of the Church: on the contrary, each one of you has been solicitous of her affairs just as though they had been your own private affairs, and, indeed, as though your life depended on it."[82]

Particularly in the field of education, in organized public welfare, in trade unions, and in public administration, will the talents of local Catholic experts play a paramount role, if they, following the duty imposed by their consciences—a duty whose neglect would be traitorous—base their thinking and action on Christian principles. These, as we learn from experience acquired in the course of many centuries, possess the highest power and influence for the pursuit of the common good.

Aid to missions from Catholic groups

Everybody knows how the mutual assistance which is exchanged among Catholic organizations established all over the world can be —as Our predecessor Pius XII has pointed out—of great use and much value to the apostolate of the laity in mission territories. On the educational plane, these organizations can help by devising Christian solutions to current problems, especially social problems, in the newly established nations; on the apostolic plane, they can help by recruiting and organizing a body of laymen, willing to serve under Christ's banner. We know that this has been done, and is being done, by lay missionaries who chose to leave their countries, either temporarily or for life, in order to contribute, by manifold activities, to the social and religious welfare of mission countries. Let us pray fervently to God that the numbers of these generous Christians be multiplied, and that God's support will never be absent in their difficulties and labors, which they are meeting with truly apostolic spirit. The secular institutes will be able to give the

---

[82] *Ep. 288*, Migne, *PG* 32, 855.

local laity in mission territories generous and loyal help, if, by their example, they attract imitators, and if they place their talents and work, promptly and willingly, at the disposal of the local ordinaries, in order to speed the growing-up process of the new Christian communities.

Lay help from afar

We appeal especially to all Catholic laymen everywhere who are distinguishing themselves in their professions and in public life to consider seriously how they can help their newly acquired brethren in the Faith, even without leaving their countries. They can do this by giving them the benefit of their advice, their experience, and their technical assistance; they can, without too much labor or grave inconvenience, sometimes give them help that will be decisive. Good men will surely find a way to fulfill this fatherly desire of Ours. They will make Our wish known to those whom they find favorably disposed, in order first to arouse good will, and then to channel it into the most suitable work.

Students from abroad

Our immediate predecessor exhorted the bishops "with the same affectionate interest that shares work with others in fraternal harmony and excludes all selfish considerations" to provide for the spiritual assistance of young Catholics who come to their dioceses from mission countries to study and to acquire the necessary experience for assuming leadership in their own nations.[83] All of you, venerable brethren, are aware of the intellectual and moral dangers to which they will be exposed in a society which is not only different from their own but also, alas, may be unfavorable ground for the growth of their Faith, and not capable of attracting them to the practice of Christian virtue. Each one of you, moved by the missionary spirit which is a conscientious duty of all pastors, will meet this situation with the greatest charity and zeal, using the most suitable means. It will not be difficult for you to find these students

[83] Encyclical *"Fidei donum,"* *AAS* 49 (1957) 245; *TPS* IV, 310.

and entrust them to the care of priests and laymen who are equipped for this task. It should not be difficult to assuage their spiritual needs, and, last but not least, to have them experience the sweet consolations of Christian charity in which we are all brothers, ministering to one another's welfare. Therefore, to the many kinds of help which you are now giving the missions, add this particular one, which brings close to your hearts those regions of the world which, although far away, are entrusted to your care.

To these students We would like not only to reveal the affection We feel for them, but also to exhort them, urgently and lovingly, to carry their heads high and proud, marked with the sign of Jesus' blood and with the sacred chrism; We would like to exhort them during their stay abroad never to bypass an opportunity not only to acquire the right professional training but also to achieve perfection in their religious education. Although they will be exposed to dangers and evils, they will nevertheless have a wonderful opportunity to share in many spiritual advantages while living in Catholic countries, if all the faithful remember that, whoever and wherever they are, they must be a good example to others and bring mutual edification to one another.

V

After conversing with you, venerable brethren, on the most important and typical needs of the Church in mission countries, We cannot fail to express Our heartfelt gratitude to all those who are toiling for the propagation of the Faith in the farthest reaches of the earth, without sparing any efforts. For the missionaries from both the religious and the regular clergy; for the holy virgins who are fruitfully and actively helping in the missions; and for the lay missionaries, precious allies of the clergy, who have been diligent in helping to advance the cause of religion—for all of them, We offer Our daily and special prayers, and every kind of help that lies within Our power. The success of their work, which is apparent in the spiritual vigor of newly established Christian communities, is an indication of God's favor and a proof of the solicitude and wisdom with which the Sacred Congregation for the Propagation of the Faith and the Congregation of the Oriental Church are carrying out their work.

A call for help

We exhort all the bishops, the clergy, and the faithful of the dioceses of the whole world, who are contributing to relieve the spiritual and material necessities of the missions by their prayers and offerings, to increase voluntarily their badly needed contributions. Despite the scarcity of priests which besets even the pastors of the oldest dioceses, there should be no hesitation in encouraging missionary vocations and in releasing the very best and most useful laymen, that they may be placed at the disposal of the new dioceses; heavenly consolations will soon be derived from this sacrifice, made for the furtherance of God's cause.

Indeed, just as such needs constantly increase, so in equal measure increases the generous effort in which the faithful of the whole world are engaging to co-operate with missionary organizations which, under the guidance of the Sacred Congregation for the Propagation of the Faith, are channeling contributions received from every source toward the most suitable and urgent destinations. Willing help and material contributions readily and copiously offered by their brethren will encourage the members of newly established Christian communities to live in the service of their religion, and will bring them the warmth of supernatural affection, which is nourished in the human heart by grace.

Perseverance

Many dioceses and Christian communities in mission territories are being harassed by difficulties and sometimes even by active persecution. We therefore exhort everyone to persevere courageously in the battle which he is fighting for God's cause: the pastors who are giving their children in God the example of a faith which does not falter even in mortal danger; and the faithful who are being so grievously tried by adversity and are therefore so dear to the Sacred Heart of Jesus, who promised beatitude and abundant rewards to those who suffer persecution for justice's sake.[84] God, in His inscrutable but always merciful designs, will sustain them with heavenly favors, consolations, and joy. The whole Church is united with the persecuted in a communion of prayer and sorrow, with the certainty that final victory will be hers.

From the bottom of Our heart, We call down upon the missions the worthy protection of their patrons and martyrs, and, first and foremost, the intercession of Mary, Mother and Queen of the Missions. With the greatest affection We impart to each one of you, venerable brethren, and to all those who in any way contribute to the propagation of God's kingdom, Our Apostolic Blessing. May it be a token and a pledge of the supernatural favors of the Eternal Father, who appeared to the world through His Son, the savior of mankind, and may it kindle and multiply missionary zeal in the hearts of all.

Given at Rome, at St. Peter's, on November 28, 1959, the second year of Our Pontificate.

JOHN PP. XXIII

[84] Cf. *Matt.* 5, 10-12.

IV

On Peace

The Roman Pontiffs have long been the world's leading spokesmen for peace. And Pope John certainly continued this tradition, injecting a sense of personal anguish into all his appeals for the end of hostility and armed conflict. His great encyclical "Pacem in terris" was, of course, his climactic statement on this problem but his concern was evident throughout his pontificate. We have space here for only a sampling of his many letters and addresses on peace.

He appealed to the consciences of world leaders both in customary annual talks, such as the Christmas messages, and in special pleas inspired by the threat or presence of specific armed conflicts, as, for example, in Algeria, the Congo, and Cuba—particularly in the latter when a confrontation of the Soviet Union and the United States made nuclear war seem imminent. While usually no specific mention was made of the country in question, the timing and language of such messages clearly indicated their objective.

Pope John's natural revulsion for war was undoubtedly strengthened by his own experience of the battlefield in the First World War, when he did military service both as an ordinary soldier in the medical corps and as a chaplain to the troops. And, as he did in all his messages, when he spoke of peace he succeeded in making each listener feel personally involved, this time by his repeated insistence that peace between nations requires first of all that there be peace within individual hearts.—Ed.

True Christian Peace

The 1959 Christmas Broadcast of Pope John XXIII

- *Inadequacy of merely human efforts*
- *Primacy of peace of heart*
- *Social peace and the dignity of man*
- *Causes of unrest*
- *The special duty of Catholics*

VENERABLE BRETHREN, dear children! Christmas is with us, the second Christmas of Our pontificate. Gazing at the scene from afar, united in spirit with Mary and Joseph on the road to Bethlehem, we taste, a few days in advance, the sweetness which comes to us from the angelic hymn announcing the heavenly peace offered to all men of good will. And thus, from day to day, We reflect that the road to Bethlehem truly marks the path for the right approach to that peace which is on the lips, in the eager desires, and in the hearts, of all.

An invitation

The liturgy has reminded and exhorted us with a joyful invitation; in the words of Pope Leo the Great, "Exult in the Lord, dear people; lift up your hearts in spiritual joy, for the day of redemption is being renewed, the day of age-long expectation, of the announcement of the happiness that has no end."[1] And at the same time—as if in chorus with that solemn and touching voice which comes to us from the fifth century—we hear rising in unison, as it were, the imploring voices of the supreme pontiffs who ruled the

---

[1] *Serm. XX in Nativitate Domini, PL* 54, 193.

Church both before and after the two wars that tore humanity apart in our generation. We hear the very recent words of the nineteen Christmas messages of our Holy Father, Pius XII of ever dear and happy memory.

We hear an unending invitation, then, to hasten our steps along the road to Bethlehem, which is the road of peace for us.

Human efforts

In the world of today, how many roads to peace have been proposed and imposed? And how many roads have been suggested even to Us, who rejoice indeed, with Mary and Joseph, in the sure knowledge of Our path and have no fear of the possibility of going astray?

From World War II right up to the present time, what a variety of utterances, what an abuse of this sacred word, "peace, peace."[2]

We pay homage to the good will of the many guides and proclaimers of peace in the world: statesmen, experienced diplomats and influential writers.

But human efforts in the matter of universal peacemaking are still far from the point where heaven and earth meet.

The fact is that true peace cannot come save from God. It has only one name: the peace of Christ. It has one aspect, that impressed on it by Christ who, as if to anticipate the counterfeits of man, emphasized: "Peace I leave with you, my peace I give to you."[3]

CHRISTIAN PEACE

The appearance of true peace is threefold:

Peace of heart

Peace of heart: peace is before all else an interior thing, belonging to the spirit, and its fundamental condition is a loving and filial dependence on the will of God. "Thou hast made us for Thyself, O Lord, and our heart is restless till it rests in Thee."[4]

---

[2] *Jer.* 6, 14. [3] *John* 14, 27.
[4] St. Augustine, *Confessions* 1, I, 1, 1; *PL* 32, 661.

All that weakens, that breaks, that destroys this conformity and union of wills is opposed to peace. Chief among such disrupters is wrongdoing, sin. "Who hath resisted him, and hath had peace?"[5] Peace is the happy legacy of those who keep the divine law. "Much peace have they who love thy law."[6]

For its part, good will is simply the sincere determination to respect the eternal laws of God, to conform oneself to His commandments and to follow His paths—in a word, to abide in truth. This is the glory which God expects to receive from man. "Peace among men of good will."[7]

Social peace

Social peace: this is solidly based on mutual and reciprocal respect for the personal dignity of man. The Son of God was made man, and His redeeming act concerns not only mankind as a whole, but also the individual man.

He "loved me and gave himself up for me." Thus spoke St. Paul to the Galatians.[8] And if God has loved man to such a degree, that indicates that man belongs to Him and that the human person has an absolute right to be respected.

Such is the teaching of the Church, which, for the solution of these social questions, has always fixed her gaze on the human person and has taught that things and institutions—goods, the economy, the state—are primarily for man, not man for them.

The disturbances which unsettle the internal peace of nations trace their origins chiefly to this source: that man has been treated almost exclusively as a machine, a piece of merchandise, a worthless cog in some great machine or a mere productive unit.

It is only when the dignity of the person comes to be taken as the standard of value for man and his activities that the means will exist to settle civil discord and the often profound divisions between, for example, employers and the employed. Above all, it is only then that the means will exist to secure for the family those conditions of life, work and assistance which can make it better directed to its

[5] *Job* 9, 4.
[6] *Ps.* 118, 165.
[7] *Luke* 2, 14.
[8] *Gal.* 2, 30.

function as a cell of society and the primary community instituted by God Himself for the development of the human person.

No peace will have solid foundations unless hearts nourish the sentiment of brotherhood which ought to exist among all who have a common origin and are called to the same destiny. The knowledge that they belong to the same family extinguishes lust, greed, pride and the instinct to dominate others, which are the roots of dissensions and wars. It binds all in a single bond of higher and more fruitful solidarity.

International peace

International peace: the basis of international peace is, above all, truth. For in international relations, too, the Christian saying is valid: "The truth shall make you free."[9]

It is necessary, then, to overcome certain erroneous ideas: the myths of force, of nationalism, or of other things that have poisoned fraternal life among peoples. And it is necessary that peaceful "living-together" be based on moral principles and be in accord with the teaching of right reason and of Christian doctrine.

Along with and enlightened by truth, should come justice. This removes the causes of quarrels and wars, solves the disputes, fixes the tasks, defines the duties and gives the answer to the claims of each party.

Justice in its turn must be integrated and sustained by Christian charity. That is, love should be for one's neighbor and one's own people, not concentrated on one's self in an exclusive egotism which is suspicious of another's good. But it ought to expand and reach out spontaneously toward the community of interests, to embrace all peoples and to interweave common human relations. Thus it will be possible to speak of *living together,* and not of mere *coexistence* which, precisely because it is deprived of this inspiration of mutual dependence, raises barriers behind which are harbored mutual suspicion, fear and terror.

---

[9] *John* 8, 32.

Errors of Man In His Search for Peace

Peace is a gift of God beyond compare. Likewise, it is the object of man's highest desire. It is, moreover, indivisible. None of the lineaments which make up its unmistakable appearance can be ignored or excluded.

In addition, since the men of our time have not completely carried into effect the conditions of peace, the result has been that God's paths toward peace have no meeting point with those of man. Hence there is the abnormal situation of this postwar period which has created, as it were, two blocs, with all their uneasiness. There is not a state of war, but neither is there peace, the thing which nations ardently desire.

Need for good will

At all times, because true peace is indivisible in its various aspects, it will not succeed in establishing itself on the social and international planes unless it is also, and in the first place, an interior fact. This requires then before all else—it is necessary to repeat—"men of good will." It is precisely to them that the angels of Bethlehem announced peace: "Peace among men of good will."[10] Indeed they alone can give reality to the conditions contained in the definition of peace given by St. Thomas—the orderly harmony of citizens—and therefore order and harmony.[11]

But how will true peace be able to put forth the twofold blossom of order and harmony if the persons who hold positions of public responsibility, before pondering the advantages and risks of their decisions, fail to recognize themselves as persons subject to the eternal moral laws?

It will be necessary again and again to remove the obstacles erected by the malice of man. And the presence of these obstacles is noted in the propaganda of immorality, in social injustice, in involuntary unemployment, in poverty contrasted with the luxury of those who can indulge in dissipation, in the dreadful lack of pro-

---

[10] *Luke* 2, 14.   [11] *Contra Gentiles* 3, c. 146.

portion between the technical and moral progress of nations, and in the unchecked armaments race, where there has yet to be a glimpse of a serious possibility of solving the problem of disarmament.

The Work of the Church

Very recent events have created an atmosphere of so-called relaxation, which has caused hopes to blossom anew in many minds after life has been lived for so long in a state of fictitious peace, in a situation of very great instability that more than once has been threatened with complete rupture.

All of that makes obvious how rooted in the souls of all is the craving for peace.

Prayer of the Church

In order that this common desire may be promptly fulfilled, the Church prays confidently to Him who rules the destinies of nations and can direct the hearts of rulers to good. No daughter of the world, but living and working in the world, the Church, as it has from the dawn of Christianity, offers "prayers, intercessions and thanksgivings . . . for all men; for kings, and for all in high positions, that we may live a quiet and peaceful life in all piety and worthy behavior," as St. Paul wrote to Timothy.[12] So also today the Church accompanies with prayer whatever in international relations contributes to the tranquility of meetings, the peaceful resolution of controversies, the rapprochement of peoples, and mutual cooperation.

Besides prayer, the Church makes available its maternal offices, points to the incomparable treasure of its doctrine and urges its children to lend their active cooperation for peace, recalling St. Augustine's famous invitation: "It is more glorious to slay war with words than men with steel; and it is true glory to secure peace by peaceful means."[13]

It is a function and office proper to the Church that it should devote itself to peace. And the Church is aware of having omitted

[12] *1 Tim.* 2, 1-2.
[13] St. Augustine, *Epistle 229*, II; *PL* 33, 1019.

nothing that was within its capacities to obtain peace for nations and individuals. The Church looks with favor on every initiative which can help to spare humanity new conflicts, new massacres and incalculable new destruction.

Unfortunately, the causes which have disturbed, and now disturb, international order have not yet been removed. It is therefore necessary to dry up the sources of evil. Otherwise the dangers to peace will remain a constant threat.

Causes of uneasiness

The causes of international uneasiness were clearly proclaimed by Our predecessor, Pius XII of immortal memory, especially in his Christmas messages of 1942 and 1943. It is well to repeat them.

These causes are: the violation of the rights and dignity of the human person and interference with the rights of the family and of employment; the overthrow of the juridical order and of the sound concept of the state that is in keeping with the Christian spirit; any impairment of the liberty, integrity and security of other nations; the systematic oppression of the cultural and linguistic characteristics of national minorities; the egotistical calculations of all who strive to seize control of the economic sources of widely used materials, to the detriment of other peoples; and, in particular, the persecution of religion and of the Church.

False notions

It needs still to be noted that the peace which the Church prays for cannot possibly be achieved if it is mistaken for a yielding or a relaxation of its firmness in the face of ideologies and systems of life which are in open and irreconcilable opposition to Catholic teaching. Nor does peace denote indifference to the laments which come to Us even now from the unhappy lands where the rights of man are ignored and falsehood is adopted as a system.

Still less can one forget the sorrowful Calvary of the Church of Silence, where the confessors of the Faith, rivaling the early Christian martyrs, are endlessly exposed to sufferings and torments for the cause of Christ. These established facts put one on guard against excessive optimism. But they render all the more earnest Our prayers for a truly universal return to respect for human and Christian liberty.

Oh! May all men of good will return to Christ and listen to His divine teaching, which is the teaching of His vicar on earth and of His lawful pastors, the bishops. They shall find the truth which frees from error, falsehood and deceit, and which will hasten the attainment of the peace of Bethlehem, that peace which was announced by the angels to men of good will.

Exhortation and Paternal Wishes

With such a wish and with such a prayer, behold, we have arrived, all of us, like Mary and Joseph, like the humble shepherds from the hills around Bethlehem and like the Wise Men from the East, before the crib of our newborn Saviour. O Jesus, how tenderly we approach the simple crib! How sweet and devout are our hearts and feelings! How eager is our desire to unite all our labors in the great work of universal peace in Thy presence, divine Author and Prince of Peace!

Duty of Catholics

At Bethlehem all men must find their place. In the first rank should be Catholics. Today especially the Church wishes to see them pledged to an effort to make His message of peace a part of themselves. And the message is an invitation to orient every act in accordance with the dictates of divine law, which demands the unflinching adherence of all, despite sacrifice. Along with such a deepened understanding must go action. It is utterly intolerable for Catholics to restrict themselves to the position of mere observers. They should feel clothed, as it were, with a mandate from on high.

The effort, no doubt, is long and arduous. But the mystery of Christmas gives to all the certainty that nothing of men's good will is lost, nothing, that is, of any act performed in good will (perhaps without being entirely aware of it) for the coming of God's kingdom on earth and in order that the city of man may be modeled after the city of God. Ah, the city—the "city of God"—which St. Augustine hailed as resplendent with the truth that saves, with the charity that gives life and with the eternity that reassures![14]

The hand of God

Venerable brethren and dear children, scattered throughout the whole world, the final sentiments expressed in this second Christmas message recall to Us the first one which We addressed to the world on December 23, 1958. A year ago the new successor of St. Peter, still trembling under the first emotions of the lofty mission conferred on him as pastor of the Universal Church, somewhat shy about the name of John which he had chosen for himself in token of a good will that was at once anxious yet firm with regard to the program for preparing the ways of the Lord, suddenly thought of the valleys to be filled and the mountains to be brought low, and he began to advance on his way. And then, day by day, he was to recognize in great humility of spirit that truly the hand of the Most High was with him. The spectacle of religious and devout throngs, who from every part of the world gathered here in Rome or at Castelgandolfo to greet him, to hear him, and to beg his blessing, was constant and touching, often giving cause for surprise and wonder.

A sacred conversation

We have also been offered gifts which We treasure with lively feelings of gratitude. Among the most pleasing and significant of these gifts is a genuine old Venetian painting, the subject of which is a sacred conversation: Mary and Joseph with Jesus, and an attractive little St. John offering a ripe fruit to Jesus who, in the act of accepting the fruit with a tender smile, diffuses a celestial sweetness over the whole painting. The picture now occupies a place of honor and has become familiar to Us during Our daily prayer in Our private oratory.

Allow Us, venerable brethren and dear children, to draw from this painting a most happy inspiration for Our Christmas greeting

[14] St. Augustine, *Epistle 138*, III; *PL* 33, 533.

which We are pleased to extend, with sincere and friendly regard, to all members of the Holy Church and to the whole world.

Preoccupation with the peace of Bethlehem occupies first place among Our concerns. But that sacred conversation widens in scope before Our eyes, until around Jesus, Mary, Joseph, and John are gathered all those who are with Us and with you in the spirit of the universal mission entrusted to Our humble person, and who are particularly dear to Us, "in the heart of Christ."

We mean those who suffer from the anxieties and miseries of life and to whom Christmas brings a sweet ray of comfort and hope: the sick and the infirm, who are the object of assiduous and watchful attention and very special affection; those who are suffering in spirit or in their hearts because of the uncertainties of the future, or because of economic hardships or the humiliation imposed upon them through some fault committed or presumed; little children, especially dear to Jesus, who through their very weakness and fragility exact a more inviolable respect and require more delicate attention; and the aged, often tempted by moments of melancholy or by the thought that they are useless.

A pledge of prayer

Confronted by this picture, the Church pledges her prayer and her attention, as well as the solicitude of her apostolate, to all of them, because they are particularly dear to her, and not to them alone but also to the humble, to the poor, to workers, to employers, and to those who are vested with public and civil power.

And how could We omit remembrance on this day before Christmas Eve of Our venerable bishops, both of the Latin and Oriental Rites, the sweetness of whose fervor for personal sanctification and dedication to souls We have frequently tasted in our fraternal meetings? How could We omit the generous and heroic bands of missionary men and women and of catechists, the compact and noble army of the diocesan and religious clergy, the religious women belonging to innumerable and praiseworthy institutes, and the Catholic laity, all on fire with zeal for works of Christian piety, of manifold types of assistance, of charity and education? Nor do We wish to forget Our separated brethren for whom Our prayers rise unceasingly to heaven so that the promise of Christ may be fulfilled: one shepherd and one flock.

The Pope's task

The task of humble Pope John is to "prepare for the Lord a perfect people,"[15] which is exactly like the task of the Baptist, who is his patron and from whom he takes his name. And it is not possible to imagine a higher and more precious perfection than that of the triumph of Christian peace, which is peace of heart, peace in the social order, in life, in well-being, in mutual respect and in the brotherhood of all nations.

Venerable brethren, dear children, for this *pax Christi*, the abundant and enlightening peace of Christmas, it is Our delight once more to express Our wishes and to impart Our blessing.

—December 23, 1959

---

[15] *Luke* 1, 17.

THE WAY TO PEACE

A Radio Address of Pope John XXIII

- *A grave warning to world rulers*
- *Attitude of the true Christian*
- *Need for prayer*

VENERABLE BRETHREN, beloved sons!
The Apostle Peter in his speech to those who were come together in the house of the Roman centurion Cornelius declared that all the nations of the earth without distinction were henceforth invited to pay heed to the universal Fatherhood of God. And he summed up this heavenly doctrine in words of peace: *annuntians pacem per Iesum Christum.*[1]

This same message is the very beat of Our heart, the heart of a father and of a bishop of the Holy Church. It comes more anxiously to Our lips whenever clouds seem to be gathering darkly on the horizon.

Other popes and peace

We have before Us the memory of the popes who most closely preceded Us and their outspoken manifestations of solicitude and anxious appeals, which have become part of history.

From the exhortation of Pius X a few days before his saintly death,[2] when the first European conflagration was imminent, to the encyclical of Benedict XV, "*Pacem, Dei munus pulcherrimum,*"[3] "Peace, the most beautiful gift of God,"; from the warning call of Pius XI, which looked to true peace "*non tam tabulis inscriptam,*

---

[1] "preaching peace through Jesus Christ." (*Acts* 10, 36.)
[2] Cf. *AAS* 6 (1914) 373.
[3] *AAS* 12 (1920) 209 ff.

quam in animis consignatam,"[4] to that fervent last appeal of Pius XII on August 24, 1939: "It is by the power of sound reason, not by force of arms, that justice makes its way,"[5]—we have a whole series of pleas, sometimes deeply sorrowful and moving, always paternal, calling upon the whole world to guard against the danger while there is yet time, and assuring the nations that whereas everything is lost, and lost to everyone, through war, nothing will be lost through peace.

The responsibility of rulers

We make this appeal Our own, extending it once more to those who bear on their consciences the gravest weight of public, recognized responsibility. The Church by her very nature cannot remain indifferent to human suffering, even were it no more than anxiety and worry. And this is why We call upon the rulers of nations to face squarely the tremendous responsibilities they bear before the tribunal of history, and, what is more, before the judgment seat of God; this is why We entreat them not to fall victims to false, deceptive pressures.

It is indeed upon wise men that the issue depends: that force shall not prevail, but right, through free and sincere negotiations; that truth and justice shall be affirmed through the safeguarding of the essential liberties and invincible values of every nation and every human person.

A sacred warning

Without exaggerating the importance of what has so far had only the appearance—though We must say the very irresponsible and tragically deplorable appearance—of a threat of war, as reported in the sources of daily public information, it is quite natural that We should make Our own the anxious solicitude of Our predecessors and express it through a sacred warning to all Our children, as We feel it Our right and duty to name them, believers in God and in His

---

[4] "not as written into treaties but rather as sealed in the hearts of men." Cf. the papal bull *"Infinita Dei,"* May 29, 1924: *AAS* 16 (1924) 213.
[5] Pius XII, *Discorsi e Radiomessaggi,* I (1939), 306.

Christ, and unbelievers as well, for all men belong to God and to Christ by right of origin and of redemption.

Warnings from Saints Peter and Paul

Those two pillars of the Church, Saint Peter and Saint Paul, give us the warning. The former gives it in his repeated affirmation of peace in Christ, the Son of God; the latter, the Doctor of the Gentiles, gives it in a very detailed statement of counsels and instructions which are timely and appropriate for all who now hold or will hold any post of responsibility in the history of the human race.

The words of St. Paul

"Brethren, draw your strength from the Lord, from that mastery which His power supplies . . . it is not against flesh and blood that we enter the lists. We have to do with princedoms and powers, with those who have mastery of the world in these dark days, with malign influences in an order higher than ours."[6]

As one with the wisdom and the fullness of fatherhood of the humble successor of St. Peter and as custodian of the deposit of doctrine—which remains forever the great divine Book, open to all men of all nations—and consequently as the keeper of Christ's Gospel, We deem it opportune to offer some personal, concrete reflections on those matters in today's world which are causing uncertainty and fear.

Following the counsel of St. Paul in regard to the attitude to be taken towards the evil spirits in an order higher than ours, we should note his interesting description of the good fighter poised to meet the assault of his adversary: *"In omnibus perfecti stare*[7]: your loins girt with truth, the breastplate of justice fitted on, and your feet shod in readiness to publish the gospel of peace, *evangelium pacis*. With all this, take up the shield of faith, with which you will be able to quench all the fire-tipped arrows of your wicked enemy; make the helmet of salvation your own, and the sword of the spirit, God's word."[8]

[6] *Eph.* 6, 10 and 12.   [7] "Stand in all things perfect."   [8] *Eph.* 6, 14-17.

The Christian attitude

All these are spiritual weapons described in figures of speech by means of which, beloved brethren and children, you can see what can and ought to be the attitude of a good Christian in the face of any event, at any time and under any circumstances. What comes from the evil one and from unbridled natural inclinations is a war of the spirit; but always war; and always the hideous fire that can penetrate and overcome everything.

Thus, through the guidance of the Apostle of the Gentiles, we are led to the clearest and most solid foundation upon which must be based the attitude of the Christian spirit in the face of anything providence may dispose or permit. Between two words, war or peace, are entwined the anguish and the hopes of the world, the anxieties and the joy of individuals and of society.

The horrors of war

Anyone who remembers the history of the not too distant past, a past recorded in books as an epoch of misfortune, and who still has a vivid recollection of the bloodstained half-century between 1914 and the present, and who remembers the sufferings of our peoples and our lands—although there were peaceful interludes between one tribulation and the next—trembles at the thought of what can happen to each one of us and to the whole world. Every war brings upheaval and destruction to individuals, to peoples, to entire regions. What could happen today—considering the frightful effects of new weapons of destruction and ruin which human ingenuity continues to multiply, to everyone's loss?

In Our youth We were always deeply moved by the ancient cry of despair of Desiderius, the King of the Lombards, which he uttered when the army of Charlemagne first appeared on the Alps: he tore his hair and cried out, *"O ferrum, heu ferrum."*[9] What then should be said of the modern instruments of war derived from the secrets of nature and capable of unleashing unheard-of energy to wreak havoc and destruction?

[9] "The sword, alas, the sword." Monachi San Gallensis, Gesta Karoli, Lib. II, par. 17. (Monumenta Germaniae Historica, Scriptores, t. 2, Hannoverae 1829, p. 760, line 3.)

Thanks be to God, We are persuaded that up to now there is no serious threat of war, immediate or remote. In making this reference of Our own to a subject that the press of all nations is discussing, We mean nothing more than to seize yet another opportunity of appealing with confidence to the calm, sure wisdom of the statesmen and men of government in every country who preside over the direction of public affairs.

The weapon of prayer

It is true that at the end of his letter to the Ephesians, written in a prison in Rome where he was chained to a Roman soldier guarding him, the Apostle Paul took his inspiration from military weapons to teach Christians the arms necessary to defend against and overcome spiritual enemies; not surprisingly, at the end of the list of weapons he stresses prayer as the most effective of them all.

Listen to his words: *"Galeam salutis adsumite et gladium spiritus, quod est verbum Dei; per omnem orationem et obsecrationem orantes omni tempore in spiritu et in ipso vigilantes in omni instantia et obsecratione pro omnibus sanctis."*[10] "Use every kind of prayer and supplication, pray at all times in the Holy Spirit; keep awake to that end with all perseverance; offer your supplication for all the saints."

With this earnest invitation the Doctor of the Gentiles brings us to the particular reason why we are united here today in spirit in a gathering that a mere hint has been sufficient to bring about and that has resulted in a great uplifting of spirit towards order and peace. The children of the Catholic Church well know this aspiration and this invocation.

In days of sorrow universal prayer to Almighty God, Creator of the universe, to His Son Jesus Christ, made man for man's salvation, and to the Holy Spirit, Lord and lifegiver, has brought from heaven and upon earth wonderful answers, which are recorded as happy and glorious pages in the history of mankind and of indi-

---

[10] "Make the helmet of salvation your own, and the sword of the spirit, God's word. Use every kind of prayer and supplication; pray at all times in the spirit; keep awake to that end with all perseverance; offer your supplication for all the saints." (*Eph.* 6, 17-18)

vidual nations. We must open our hearts and empty them of the malice with which at times the spirit of error and evil seeks to infect them, and thus purified, we must lift them up confident of receiving heaven's blessing as also prosperity in the things of this earth.

Assemblies for peace

Venerable brothers and beloved children, our simple and spontaneous meeting together in spirit today could well be—who knows?—the first of a series of assemblies of peace, not marred by pointless clamoring but gladdened by a heartfelt sentiment of elevation and peace, an assurance of the tranquillity and nobility of life in the happiness of Christian society, which is, in Christ, divine brotherhood and a foretaste of the joys of heaven.

Reflect that the Catholic Church, scattered throughout a world that is today, alas, troubled and divided, is preparing for a universal gathering—the ecumenical council—which is aimed at the promotion of that true brotherhood of nations which exalts Christ Jesus, the glorious and immortal King of ages and of peoples, light of the world, and the way, the truth, and the life.[11]

An invitation to prayer

This afternoon, during the Holy Sacrifice of the Mass, the blood of Jesus Christ has come down upon us, upon our lives, upon our souls. By it we are sanctified and redeemed and lifted up with joy.

We have prayed together and in so doing we have felt great joy in our hearts. Let us continue to pray in this way, as St. Paul invites us to do at the end of his touching letter. Let us pray with one another and for one another, and for all the scattered creatures of God who make up the Holy Church and the human family, which is also all His own.

We would extend our most urgent invitation to prayer to priests, to consecrated souls, to young children, and to the suffering. Let us all together beg the Father of Light and of Grace to enlighten the minds and move the wills of those who hold the chief responsibility for the life or death of peoples. Let us pray for the peoples them-

[11] Cf. *1 Tim.* 1, 17; *John* 8, 12; 14, 6.

selves that they may not allow themselves to be dazzled by exacerbated nationalism and destructive rivalry, and that, as We so earnestly exhorted in our encyclical *"Mater et Magistra,"* the relationships in the life of human society may be reintegrated in truth, in justice and in love. Let us all pray that by means of the penetration of the Christian spirit morality may prevail: the vigorous strength of Christian families, the source of noble power and dignity and of blessed and joyful well-being.

Ever and always let us pray for the peace of Christ here below, among all men of good will: *ut cunctae familiae gentium, peccati vulnere disgregatae, suavissimo subdantur Christi imperio.*[12]

An appeal to Mary

And finally we turn to you, O Blessed Virgin Mary, mother of Jesus and our mother also. How can we, with trembling hearts, apply ourselves to this greatest problem of life or death, which overshadows all mankind, without confiding ourselves to your intercession to preserve us *a periculis cunctis?*[13]

This is your hour, O Mary! Blessed Jesus entrusted us to you in the supreme moment of His bloody sacrifice. We are certain of your intervention.

On September 8th the Church celebrated the anniversary of your most happy birth, saluting you as the beginning of the salvation of the world and the heavenly promise of an increase of peace.

Yes, yes, for this we supplicate you, O our most sweet mother, O Queen of the World! Of victorious war or of a conquered people there is no need, but of a renewed and more robust state of safety, of fruitful and serene peace. Of this there is need, and for this we cry out in a loud voice: *salutis exordium et pacis incrementum. Amen. Amen.*[14]

—September 10, 1961

---

[12] "that all the families of the nations, rent asunder by the wound of sin, may be subjected to the most gentle rule of Christ."
[13] "from every evil."
[14] "beginning of salvation and increase of peace. Amen. Amen."

THE FIFTH COMMANDMENT

An Address of Pope John XXIII at a Time of International Strife

- *The divine command*
- *Troubles in North Africa*
- *Recognition of rights of others*

BELOVED SONS, your joyous presence here, like that of others who have preceded you, is a reason for edification and joy for the whole Catholic Church. How could the Pope fail to derive from it satisfaction and encouragement, even for himself? Indeed, he more than anyone rejoices in it.

But, in this vale of tears—*in hac lacrymarum valle*—the joy of spirit that comes from so many displays of religious piety and charity is often accompanied by notes of profound sorrow.

Today We wish to open Our heart to you and confide to you what most pains and afflicts it. You will be able thus to join more closely in the prayer We raise to Almighty God, master of wills, beseeching Him to direct them toward an absolute respect for His holy law, which is the same for everyone.

With the utmost seriousness, and with Our eyes fixed on those of the leaders who have the power of decision and on those of their assistants who can influence the decisions, We wish this supplication to ring out to the four corners of the earth.

The divine command

Our anxiety is great at the sight of blood drenching the earth, wherever it may happen, and whether it is according to or contrary to the rules of armed conflict. But what can be said when it is a question of human victims being sacrificed in contempt of agreements that are being worked out or sought after, victims who are sacrificed at random, as an erroneous affirmation of rights?

The divine command rings out, firm and grave: *Non occides.* Thou shalt not kill. It is a definite command, given by the Author of life; a command established for the protection and defense of a right which is the same for all, and the transgression of which brings fatal consequences and disastrous repercussions in the area of international relations.

Trouble in North Africa

Oh! the Mediterranean shores of Africa, where, twelve years ago, We traversed the vast semicircle from Tunisia to Morocco, lands which work and concord could have, and still can, quicken with life for the benefit of the inhabitants and to the triumph of justice. May the day soon dawn that will see peace reign over all those regions, the peace of brotherhood that is so much desired and invoked; peace, the bearer of well-being for all families!

We renew, as on other occasions, Our heartfelt appeal: may no one assume to himself the right of destroying human lives! May all see, instead, in every man the image of God the Creator, Father of us all, and may the hands of those who are brothers in Christ the Redeemer be joined together.

Do not kill! Neither by the sword nor by the spoken word or the press, neither by acquiescence nor by an aggravating nationalism.

The earth and all it contains belongs to God. *Domini est terra et plenitudo ejus.* God is the Master, we the inhabitants of earth. It is our duty on this earth to favor that peaceful evolution of peoples which recognizes the rights of one's neighbors, even when this involves personal limitations or renunciation.

A unanimous impulse

Thus, men of different origins, but respectful of each other, will offer to the world a display of honest collaboration, of a complementary exchange of energies and interest, in a unanimous impulse for the common good and for the betterment of all peoples.

May God grant Our wishes and Our prayers! And may you,

beloved sons and daughters, support the arms upraised in prayer by the common Father of Christianity and echo His words.

May men listen to the tremulous but strong voice which rises from this glorious tomb of the Apostle Peter.

With the abandonment of all obstinacy and all violence, may the dominion of law and mutual charity prevail and may the authors and builders of peace be blessed on the blood-drenched soil of Africa.

—June 3, 1962

A CALL FOR NEGOTIATIONS

A Broadcast of Pope John XXIII
to World Leaders

- *The Church and peace*
- *The wisdom of negotiating*
- *An appeal for prayer*

"I BESEECH THEE, O Lord, let thy ear be attentive to the prayer of thy servant, and to the prayer of thy servants who desire to fear thy name."[1]

This ancient biblical prayer rises to Our trembling lips today from the depths of a heart that is greatly moved and afflicted.

While the Second Vatican Ecumenical Council has just been opened amidst the joy and hopes of all men of good will, threatening clouds now come to darken once again the international horizon and to sow fear in millions of families.

As We stressed when welcoming the 86 extraordinary missions present at the opening of the Council,[2] the Church has nothing nearer to her heart than peace and brotherhood among all men, and she strives tirelessly to achieve this.

We recalled in this regard the grave duties of those who bear the responsibility of power, and We added: "In all conscience let them give ear to the anguished cry of 'peace! peace!' which rises up to heaven from every part of the world, from innocent children and those grown old, from individuals and from communities."[3]

The value of negotiating

Today We repeat that solemn warning. We beseech all rulers not to remain deaf to the cry of mankind. Let them do everything in

[1] *2 Esd.* 1, 11.
[2] Cf. *TPS*, VIII, 268-71.
[3] *Ibid.*, 270.

their power to save peace. By so doing, they will spare the world the horrors of a war that would have disastrous consequences such as no one can foresee.

Let them continue to negotiate, because this sincere and open attitude is of great value as a witness for the conscience of each one and in the face of history. To promote, favor and accept negotiations, at all levels and at all times, is a rule of wisdom and prudence which calls down the blessing of heaven and earth.

A world-wide prayer for peace

May all Our children, may all those who have been marked with the seal of Baptism and nourished by Christian hope, may all those, finally, who are united to Us by faith in God, join their prayers to Ours to obtain from heaven the gift of peace: a peace which will be true and lasting only if it is based on justice and equity.

And upon all those who contribute to this peace, upon all those who work with a sincere heart for the true welfare of men, may there descend the special blessing which We lovingly bestow in the name of Him who wished to be called the "Prince of Peace."[4]

—October 25, 1962

[4] *Is.* 9, 6.

V

Two Great Encyclicals

Certainly among the high points of Pope John's pontificate was the release of his two great social encyclicals, "Mater et Magistra" and "Pacem in Terris." Both received world-wide acclaim, not only from those within the Church itself but from non-Catholics and non-Christians alike.

Nor was the praise confined to any particular economic or intellectual sector of the community. Thus "Mater et Magistra" had wide appeal to scholars as well as to the world of labor; yet it was a document which the most hard-headed, practical business manager could enthusiastically welcome. It restated certain basic principles: that the goods of this world belong to all, not just a privileged few; that all men are equal in natural dignity; that there is a social obligation inherent in the right of private property; that there is an obligation on the wealthy, both individuals and nations, to help the less fortunate. At the same time it proclaimed in equally forceful language the other side of the coin, so to speak. Thus it emphasized that the primary responsibility rests on each individual to provide for his own livelihood and development—and similarly with nations; that wages and other compensation for work done should be based at least in part on the value of the contribution made to the enterprise and to the economy. Similarly "Pacem in Terris" was hailed by people from every walk of life and every nation.

These documents presented the truth, whole, entire, and nonpartisan; and although not basically different from similar pronouncements over the centuries from the Chair of Peter, they caught the public imagination to a greater degree than ever before—possibly because of the overwhelming personality of this great man.

We are presenting here the TPS translations of these two encyclicals, together with special commentaries on each by the Rev. John F. Cronin, S.S. In addition we are presenting some of the comments Pope John himself made before and after issuing these great documents.—Ed.

A PREVIEW OF MATER ET MAGISTRA

An Address of Pope John XXIII
to an Audience of Workers

- *Earlier social encyclicals*
- *New problems*
- *Source of encouragement*

VENERABLE BRETHREN, beloved sons.
Your very solemn, respectful, yet vibrant and surging presence here close by the sacred memorials to St. Peter, the Prince of the Apostles, fills Our heart and yours with an extraordinary joy.

What was it that brought you here in such great numbers—people from every country, of every age group, every social class, every language?

A great pope and a letter

You came together here in tribute to the memory of a great pope and a letter—a letter he wrote for his own times and sent to the whole world. It was one that did not deal with any of the usual subjects for a pope; he was not trying to stir up Christian devotion and piety. Rather, it was a doctrinal and practical treatment of the work that goes on in factories and fields, the work of all the people who use their human energies—arms and head and heart, body and mind—to earn a living, to find a little prosperity, to add to the wealth of the whole world.

His lowly successor, the pope now speaking to you, was a little boy ten years old in 1891; but he can still recall very well what happened in his own parish and all around him: how the opening words of that document, *"Rerum novarum"* (We were just starting in on Latin then), were repeated in the churches and in meetings as the title of a teaching that was not really new but as old as the Gospel of Jesus the Savior, but that had, in that May of 1891, been cast in a new light that was better adapted to the conditions of the modern world. It dealt with contemporary situations and issues, matters about which everyone wanted to have his own say—and many were doing so, but rashly, thus creating the danger of confusion and stirring up temptation to social disorder.

The Age-old Teaching of the Living Peter

Pope Leo, a wonderful pontiff, wanted to dig into the treasures of the age-old teaching of the Church and bring forth the just and holy doctrine, the enlightening truth that would supply direction to the social order according to the needs of his time.

Principles recalled

That encyclical, *"Rerum novarum,"* took a clear, decisive, and courageous stand, especially on the relationships between farmers and working-men (who were commonly referred to as the proletariat) on the one hand, and land-owners and businessmen on the other. It pointed out how vitally necessary it was to work out an arrangement that would be just and equitable, and thus beneficial to both sides, by making use of both the intervention of the State and the sincere and honest efforts of those who were involved, the workers and employers.

So *"Rerum novarum"* served as a first great and solemn reminder of principles in this area and it stirred up everybody to some extent. Even though it limited itself to the special problems of the worker that had to do with the relationships We have just mentioned, it had the great merit of revealing a horizon that was all the brighter because it drew its light and warmth from the Holy Catholic Church and from the inexhaustible fonts of the Old and the New Testaments.

Troubled years

The forty years that followed upon the first publication of this doctrine and upon the first impression made by it—that is, the years from 1891 to 1931—were marked by events that were vital, complex, and sometimes violent. The fluctuations in the development of, and in the recurring strife between, various classes and peoples, which were brought on by the first war, became so dark and threatening that they suggested to the ample mind, clear vision, and warm heart of Pope Pius XI the idea of resuming the Holy See's conversation with the world of labor and giving it a better idea of the social teaching of the Church and her attitude toward new situations. The latter had gradually arisen from the new achievements of human ingenuity and from progress in new techniques, which were resulting in the abandonment of traditional methods that had become burdensome for the masses of people laboring in the factories and fields.

FROM LEO XIII TO PIUS XI AND PIUS XII

And so we saw a new papal document called *"Quadragesimo anno"* appear as a reminder and a fuller development of the foundations for the social economy that had been laid down by *"Rerum novarum"*; it marked out the steps to be taken—in the light of Christian principles, of course—toward new experiences, new relationships of world-wide cooperation between workingmen, between families, and between nations; yes, it marked out the path, but it also offered encouragement and correctives for a happy and gainful progress.

This teaching of Pius XI in *"Quadragesimo anno"* was also met with great joy and exultation.

New problems, old principles

It contained a detailed study of the great new problems that had arisen in the area of industry and offered a solution for them; and at the same time it broadened and brightened the horizon of the social question. This was especially true in the case of the clear portrayal and the new and penetrating picture that it gave of labor, property, salary, their relationships to the demands of the common good, and hence their over-all social aspects. Right at the top he placed the supreme principle that always has to rule over any relationship of this kind: not unrestrained free competition, not economic domination, both of which are blind forces: but the eternal and sacred notions of justice and charity.

The demands of justice cannot be satisfied unless society is organically rearranged through the reconstitution of intermediate bodies toward a socio-economic end.

A powerful and important conclusion brought out in *"Quadragesimo anno"* was the need of steady, patient effort for cooperation between great and small nations.

The words of Pius XII

At this point, beloved sons, having paid tribute to Popes Leo and Pius XI, We would like to render homage to the sacred and blessed memory of the Holy Father, Pius XII, who followed along in the furrow opened up by *"Quadragesimo anno"* and scattered his lofty teaching over the various sectors of sociology that he had occasion to deal with when he took up the internal structure of individual political communities, as well as the relations between them on the world plane.

His words, both spoken and written, were often intended for particular occasions or problems, but they were still characterized by the broad sweep of the horizons touched upon and revealed. What riches there are in those volumes he left behind for our admiration and veneration: they are like a collection that is always worth going back to for the precious treasures that abound there!

A third document

Venerable brethren and beloved sons, We want you to realize that everything We have said up to now is just an introduction to the luminous point We have been leading up to—beyond *"Rerum novarum,"* beyond *"Quadragesimo anno,"* to a third document that will first commemorate both of them and then enrich them with the new experiences gained from the social activities that have been growing and multiplying beyond all measure these last thirty years. Finally, it will add a kind of crown in the form of a fuller, richer, more complete explanation of Christian doctrine, which the one, holy, catholic, apostolic, and Roman Church in its everlasting and fruitful youthfulness is always ready to offer for the light and guidance of all ages and peoples.

THE NEW ENCYCLICAL THAT IS COMING

We have to admit that Our original plan was to offer it to you and to the whole Catholic Church on the very day of the joyful commemoration of the seventieth anniversary of *"Rerum novarum"* (1891—May 15th—1961). This third document was to be of general interest and in the form of an encyclical that would be both ample and solemn.

Reason for delay

We are happy to assure you that Our promise has been kept: the encyclical is ready. However, since We want it to reach all those who believe in Christ and all good souls scattered throughout the world at the very same time in its official Latin text and in the various languages currently in use, We have decided to delay publication of the text for a while.

A worthy gathering

And so, beloved sons, permit Us to tell you once again: having you here in Rome at this time means a very great deal to Us.

This week brings us close to Pentecost and prepares the way for it; it reminds us once again of those who gathered together on Sion: *"viri religiosi ex omni natione quae sub caelo est."*[1]

Beloved sons, descendants of those wonderful Catholics who first greeted the great Pope Leo's proclamation of Catholic social doctrine seventy years ago and paid it great honor, you have gathered here as the representatives of all the Christian workers of the earth.

And so you deserve to have Peter's humble successor do as Peter did on Sion and let you in on a secret and reveal in brief form the contents of this third papal document, which will soon offer salutary food and delicious nourishment to your souls and, We hope,

[1] "devout men from every country under heaven." (*Acts* 2, 5)

to all those who trust in the holy and blessed Church of Christ Jesus: *Magister et Salvator mundi.*²

As We priests read the Breviary each day, We pray: *Spiritus Sancti gratia illuminet sensus et corda nostra.*³ So, too, may the grace of the Holy Spirit be with you as you listen to Us, to enlighten your intellect and your hearts.

PROSPECTUS OF THE SOLEMN DOCUMENT

The solemn document that will, within a few weeks—We would like to repeat it—become the joy of your eyes and healthy and substantial nourishment for your minds, is made up of four distinct sections.

Its four parts

First: a synthesis of the teaching of three popes, Leo and the two Piuses, XI and XII.

Second: the presentation of an initial group of problems involving social action that are still urgent and pressing, even after seventy years.

Third: a statement of new, serious, and sometimes dangerous problems that have arisen during this recent period of our own.

Fourth and finally: a new synthesis of social relationships, in the light of the teaching of Holy Church.

The first part

The first section is one with which you are already familiar from what We have said up to now as an introduction to this talk of Ours. It reflects the general lines and principles of the wise path that papal teaching pointed out in the *"Rerum novarum"* of Leo XIII and later pursued in the *"Quadragesimo anno"* of Pius XI and the notes of a social nature scattered through the various writings and talks of Pius XII.

Profound changes have taken place in these last few years, both

---

² Teacher and Savior of the world. (Cf. *John* 4, 42)
³ May the grace of the Holy Spirit enlighten our hearts and minds.

in the internal structure of individual political communities and in their relations to each other: changes and problems that demand clearer definitions and fuller development of the teachings traced in outline form in *"Rerum novarum,"* as they apply—We have already said this—to the new conditions of the present day.

The second part

Turning to the second section, we find ourselves face to face with these new problems. First of all the ones that have to do with the relationships between private initiative and the role of public authority in the economic field; next, the ever increasing number of associations in various areas of life; then, remuneration for labor; the demands of justice and their relation to the means and methods of production; and the very serious matter of private property.

It is not a waste of time to repeat that in taking up these problems and offering a solution to them, the coming encyclical takes into account and follows the developments that have taken place from the teaching of Leo XIII through that of Pius XI to the wise and enlightened messages of Pius XII; but this teaching is always dominated by one basic theme—an unshakeable affirmation and vigorous defense of the dignity and rights of the human person.

The third part

The third section of the encyclical takes up the most obvious and urgent problems of the present moment. They lend a characteristic tone and color to this particular papal document.

FOR SOLIDARITY, HUMAN AND CHRISTIAN

The first of them to come to the fore is the problem of farming. Agriculture once was—what are We saying, it *once* was?—it was for thousands of years, from the first pages of the holy Bible onwards, the treasure and the perennial springtime that was renewed each year on earth, the poetry and enchantment of life: and now many, many human communities have been reduced, or are on the point of being reduced, to a state that is usually described as one of depression. One of the greatest demands of justice is precisely this justice of restoring economic and social balance between the two sectors of human society.

Our coming document will propose the principal rules and directives, based on solidarity as Christians and human beings, that will, We believe, make an effective contribution toward the achievement of this great and noble aim.

The problem of poverty

Another problem of world-wide proportions that is an object of Our concern and that claims Our anguished attention in the apostolic ministry that We carry on, with the help and cooperation of all those who believe and live in Christ and His Church, is the state of dire need and misery and hunger in which millions and millions of human beings find themselves forced to struggle. This is the basis for the uneasiness that is at times a cruel reality in the relationships between political communities that are economically developed and those that are economically under-developed.

This is properly called the problem of the modern era, although, to be entirely truthful, in a study of the history of peoples that includes the age-old vicissitudes of all the masses of mankind spread throughout the world, it was possible in the past to consider it as inexorable, in view of the ancient and continuous causes for the backwardness of economic systems in relation to the unfortunate conditions of a number of regions.

Obligation to help

Beloved sons, it is both right and holy for Us to issue a new warning and to exalt the principle of the solidarity of all human beings and for Us to remind people and to preach in a loud voice about the duty that communities and individuals with abundant means of support at their disposal have, to go to the aid of those who find themselves in conditions of need and want.

Unfortunately, the help that has appeared up to now does not get at the roots of what is causing these conditions of want and misery. For this reason, efforts at cooperation on a world level are necessary, efforts of many kinds that will be disinterested and will aim at putting extensive capital as well as intelligent and competent technical assistance at the disposal of countries that are economically underdeveloped so that steps may be taken toward achieving economic development and social progress at one and the same time. Care must be taken to supply the information and advice that will interest those most directly concerned in human labor—the workers themselves—in striving toward an improvement in their own conditions, on the individual, family, and social levels.

FIRST LIGHT AND STRENGTH: THE PRECEPT OF THE LORD

This is a great undertaking, a noble objective and one that is vital to the very peace of the world. If it is to be achieved with unremitting vigor, sincere understanding and active cooperation between peoples are absolutely necessary.

Respect for a moral order

All of this supposes—and We would like to say it once again here beneath this kindly sky and in front of the greatest temple in all Christendom—it supposes, We repeat—the *praeceptum Domini*[4] that affirms and proclaims recognition of and respect for a moral order that applies to everyone and everything and that recognizes its basis in God, our instructor and judge, the bestower of all good things, of wealth and of mercy, and the terrible avenger of justice and fairness, whom none can escape.

This is the basic reason for permitting and praising intervention by religion and by the Holy Church in the economic and social field. Always the Ten Commandments, beloved sons; always the Gospel. From blessed Jesus, "the way, the truth, the light of the world," the wonder-worker who placed Himself at the service of human needs and weaknesses, the divine martyr for human expiation, and the victorious and triumphant king of all ages and peoples—it is from Him that the effort in search of justice takes its inspiration and grows in strength. May the work of defending the weak and the needy and

[4] precept of the Lord.

improving their lot lead to a new display of the wonders of charity that will ensure the salvation and the resurrection of men and of ethnic groups, the transformation of backward zones and depressed areas.

A great responsibility

This is the great responsibility resting on everyone and no one has a right to shirk it. The final judgment passed on the universe when it has fulfilled its destiny is this: *Venite benedicti, discedite maledicti.*[5] These words are both conclusion and summary of the history of the world, consummated and resolved in an enumeration of all the various kinds and instances of social help that have been granted or denied, by man to man, by family to family, by people to people.

The fourth part

The fourth section of the new encyclical will present you with an enchanting picture of the way in which human society is to be reorganized. Studying the nature of man and the doctrine of the Church in the light of Revelation is the surest way to achieve a human life in society that will be dignified, peaceful, and fruitful. It is only natural for us to hope that this doctrine, which has truth as its foundation, justice as its goal, and love as its dynamic element, will be not only learned but assimilated, spread, and translated into action.

The vast and interesting document closes with some valuable suggestions that will be of great help and assistance in developing an awareness of his social duties in each and every person and in bringing it more and more into play in his activities.

A little picture

Beloved sons, please look forward to the encyclical with joy and study it well.

We have had a good deal to say to you in this long talk and We have spoken as a shepherd to his flock with his heart open to the

---

[5] Come ye blessed, depart ye cursed. (*Matt.* 25, 34 and 41)

interests of the spirit but not unmindful of the goods of the earth; now as We go back over all of this, We would like to offer you a little picture that you will find both pleasant and instructive.

The feeling that stirred within all the faithful in the Holy Church when the encyclical *"Rerum novarum"* of Pope Leo XIII was announced in 1891 was surprise at hearing the sound of a new bell coming from the old tower of the parish church, from every parish in the world, whether in cities or villages; it chimed in with the concert of the other great church bells that were already familiar to the good faithful from the old, established customs of religious piety. That sound in 1891 did not turn out to be discordant with the ring of the other bells; instead it was completely harmonious, vibrant, joyous.

Forty years later

Forty years later, in 1931, not one, but several new bells were added to the parish tower. The encyclical *"Quadragesimo anno"* was the great feat of Pope Pius XI, who gave the signal for the sounding of a whole broad and wonderful harmony of invitations and warnings on the social question and on the many new problems that were facing men who were sincere and upright and who looked to the perennial fonts of the Gospel teachings, intended for all men, as the source of their inspiration.

The yearly commemoration of *"Rerum novarum"* has been going on for exactly seventy years; this year's celebration is reason enough for special joy and exultation and for cheerful, heartfelt encouragement, for it is taking place in times when the fervent cooperation of sacred pastors and of many, many lay people in carrying out the maternal interest and cares of the Church has developed to a much greater extent, and has been directed toward spreading sound doctrine and seeing to its direct application on a vast scale.

ENTHUSIASTIC AND FERVENT SOCIAL APOSTOLATE

The exultation comes from realizing that the zeal that was first aroused by Pope Leo's deed and later on by his successors' is still carrying on, still stirring up enthusiasm, still strengthening interest and sympathy for a fine social apostolate and the determination to carry it through.

Now it is not just the shrill cry of one or a few bells that we hear from the old tower and from the new ones that are appearing in ever greater numbers on the plain, on the hills, everywhere that nature exerts its attraction and offers its fruitful gifts. Rather, it is a veritable deluge, a festival of bronze harmoniously pealing forth to spread the glory of Christ, the Son of God, our brother, teacher, redeemer, and the savior of the human race, always reaching out with the mysterious streams of His grace to touch human beings, not just to prepare them for heavenly goods and set them on the way to them, but reaching out to their bodies as well and to all that is truly good in life here below in the civic and social order.

The words of St. John

It is good and helpful for us to draw encouragement from this commemoration and from the other celebrations, large and small, that will take place after this throughout the world; but this encouragement ought to be inspired by the words that the Evangelist St. John, Our Lord's favorite, wrote in the first of his three letters (some moving passages from which We enjoyed in the Breviary this very morning).

It is a teaching handed down by the apostle of Jesus: "God is light and no darkness can find any place in Him."[6] We should live in this light in a mutual communion with Him. If we have sinned, the blood of Jesus, His son, purifies us, as Jesus is the one who makes up for the sins of the whole world. Here are some other moving words: "You must learn to live and to walk with Christ." *"Qui dicit se in ipso manere, debet sicut ille ambulavit, et ipse ambulare."*[7]

A magnificent program

What a magnificent program this is for Christian life and for apostolic social activity! To live in Christ who is divine light, uni-

---

[6] *1 John* 1, 5.
[7] "He who says that he abides in him, ought himself also to walk just as he walked." (*1 John* 2, 6)

versal charity; to move in His footsteps and His company: *in ipso manere: cum ipso ambulare,* which means an activity that is dynamic yet calm, orderly, and peaceful, in praise of God, and in the service of justice, of fairness, of brotherhood as Christians and human beings.

If we act in this way and move in this direction, then we are in the truth—let us say it humbly in the words of our St. John—We are in the Truth, that is to say, in God: in His son Jesus Christ, to whom be glory and benediction through all ages. Amen, Amen.[8]

—May 14, 1961

[8] Cf. *1 John* 5, 20.

A Commentary on

MATER ET MAGISTRA

by Rev. John F. Cronin, S.S.

THE SPIRIT OF THE ENCYCLICAL

POPE JOHN XXIII issued his first great social encyclical letter less than two years before his death. The appearance of this document was the first clear sign of a major change in the character of his pontificate. During the first half of his brief reign few persons had understood the greatness of this humble and kindly pontiff. True, he had surprised the world by his calling of an ecumenical council, but in mid-1961 this was still very much in the preparatory stage. At this time nearly everyone recognized the goodness of Pope John, but there were not many who perceived his greatness.

Mater et Magistra showed the true character of this beloved Pope. As a literary and scholarly document, it is not the equal of *Pacem in Terris*. There are obvious indications that ideas were sought from many sources, and the resulting synthesis lacks the unity and clarity of the peace encyclical. There are important omissions, notably the absence of any direct treatment of land reform in developing nations. Some vital problems, such as the population explosion, are treated hesitantly and indecisively in spots.

These imperfections do not detract from the enduring value of *Mater et Magistra*, or Christianity and Social Progress as it is generally called in English. As the Pontiff was to note later, lasting reform is evolutionary, not revolutionary. It is difficult to ask the Church to accept, in a short space of time, extensive changes in its approach to the modern world. Here we have the beginning of the *aggiornamento*, not its flowering. But it was a strong and decisive beginning.

Historical circumstances often compelled earlier popes to take somewhat negative roles in relation to modern progress. Many times they were reacting to events, rather than leading mankind to new and more progressive goals. Pope Pius IX was progressive by inclination, but the bloody revolutions of the mid-nineteenth century caused him to react in a cautious manner. The great encyclicals of Pope Leo XIII did much to apply Church thinking to current social and political problems. But in these documents there are condemnations that are misunderstood when read out of historical context. The same mixture of progressivism and caution is found in the major writings and addresses of Popes Pius XI and Pius XII. To the modern world they spoke lofty and enduring truths. But at times they did not speak in the language of the world, so that their wisdom was not always fully appreciated.

By contrast, *Mater et Magistra* is a completely modern document. It addresses itself to current problems in a language and tone that can be understood and appreciated by everyone. The treatment of agriculture, for example, is meaningful to farmers throughout the world. Developing nations everywhere can recognize the delicate and perceptive insight into their problems. Organized labor and the working man must welcome the strong endorsement of workers' aims and aspirations.

Modernity, however, is not important if the message expressed lacks real significance. The greatness of the encyclical stems from its central theme, not its mode of presentation. This theme may be described as the confrontation of modern problems in a spirit of Christian optimism. More than any other modern pontiff, Pope John asked the Christian to become a part of the world, so that he might humanize and Christianize it. Earlier papal social writings seemed to embody detached, aloof, and impartial judgments passed upon the problems of the day. This encyclical is a fatherly letter of encouragement written by one who in spirit is a participant in the struggle for justice and love, and not merely a spectator or judge.

In the past, Christian social thinkers have often been accused of being romanticists in their thinking. There was a tendency in some of their writings to look backward to some supposedly ideal time of history. Reform to them was a revival of this period, with suitable modifications for contemporary needs. They found it difficult to separate enduring principles of sound social conduct from the accidental trappings of a given period of time, such as the age of the guilds or the characteristics of feudal society. As a consequence, even critics endowed with good will often found elements which caused them to criticize these thinkers as reactionary or impractical.

Pope John takes as his starting point the atomic and electronic era. This is the real world that will be with us for decades to come. It is a world characterized by drastic social, political, technical, and scientific changes. There is much that is good in these developments, but there are also grave potentialities for evil. In one of the few critical passages in the encyclical, the Pope notes: "This era in which we live is in the grip of deadly errors; it is torn by deep disorders." But at once he counters this judgment with characteristic optimism: "But it is also an era which offers to those who work with the Church immense possibilities in the field of the apostolate. And therein lies our hope." (No. 260)

Behind this optimism there are both natural and supernatural reasons. In the natural sphere, there has been considerable social and political progress in recent decades. The encyclical notes the decline of colonialism and the generous aid programs sponsored by wealthy nations and by international bodies. It welcomes the aid given to families by social-insurance systems. The efforts of modern governments to stabilize the business cycle, to insure a steady price level, and to prevent unemployment are mentioned with approval. The extension of the protective power of the state did not lead to the evils predicted by the prophets of gloom.

A secular historian could have developed these points just as well as did the Pope. His unique contribution is his supernatural outlook upon human nature. In the midst of all the fears and evils in the world, this gentle pontiff saw the guiding hand of God. Like the prophets of Israel, he could see war and fear of war as a scourge and a warning to sinful mankind, yet these punishments were visited by a loving Father. They were meant to heal, not to destroy. The duty of the Christian is to participate in this process of healing. He is to seek the good in persons, in organizations, and in movements of modern society. He is to encourage and develop this good, and not merely content himself with denouncing evil.

Viewed in this light, the encyclical is an integral part of the pattern that includes the Vatican Council, *Pacem in Terris*, the new attitude toward "separated brethren" and non-Christians, and the tentative openings to the Communist world. It is a pattern of courage, humility, and optimism. The Church is sure enough of her enduring strength that she can confess human errors of the past, see the truth and goodness in those who differ from her, and begin to lay the foundations of mutual trust even in quarters that seem least likely to accept her mission. If this optimism seems impractical or excessive to some, they might note the unbelievable changes in interreligious relationships in the past few years.

We would not be faithful to the revered memory of Pope John if we were to begin within the Church a "cult of personality" and ascribe all these changes exclusively to the person of this great pontiff. His social teaching builds upon the work of his predecessors. Thus the inner renewal in the Church can be traced to many actions of St. Pius X, and was deeply stimulated by decisions taken by Pope Pius XII, especially his Scripture encyclical, *Divino Afflante Spiritu*. The Ecumenical Council revealed that pressures for modernization and reform were much more widespread than was generally realized. The genius of Pope John was his intuitive sense, not uncommon in those who live saintly lives, that these movements should be fostered and encouraged.

The Social Problem Today

The encyclical sees as the chief social problem today the need for securing greater balance and perspective in economic life. This is a time of immense growth and rapid change. Scientific and technical changes are revolutionary, witness such developments as the release of nuclear energy, advances in synthetic chemistry, automation, television, jet aircraft, and the initial conquest of interplanetary space. Social changes are equally extensive. Among the items noted are growth in social security systems, a more responsible attitude in labor unions, improvement in basic education, the breaking down of class barriers, and widespread interest in world affairs.

Unfortunately, progress has been uneven in many sectors of the world economy. Agriculture, for example, has tended to lag behind the industrial and service sectors. Within individual nations there are depressed areas. Among the nations of the world, there is a marked disparity in the economic wealth possessed by different countries. Because of this, many workers and their families are condemned to live in utterly subhuman conditions. In some areas, the enormous wealth and privilege of the few "stands in violent, offensive contrast to the utter poverty of the vast majority." (No. 69) There are other parts of the world in which the privations of workers are deliberately planned as means for an inhumanly rapid economic development. Even in prosperous areas, the rate of pay does not always correspond to the real contribution of workers. At the same time, some persons are paid well for services of doubtful value or for relatively unimportant activities.

These problems are summarized toward the end of Part I of the encyclical, and also early in Part II. Pope John responds to the issues posed by modern trends in three stages: Part II updates the teachings of his predecessors, particularly in regard to the function of the state, the complexity of modern society, the role of labor, and the position to be accorded to private property. Part III discusses problems not considered at length by his predecessors, namely, agriculture, population growth, and the needs of developing nations. Part IV is pastoral, dealing primarily with the engagement of the Christian in the modern world.

The most difficult and controversial aspect of Part II is its treatment of the relationships of the individual, society, and the state under present-day conditions. Catholic teaching in regard to the functions of government and the social aspects of property and business involves complex and delicate questions, even when studied in terms of abstract principles. Its presentation in this encyclical is complicated by the effort to include the immense ramifications of social relationships that have developed in modern society. Nor was understanding of the Pope's teaching made easier by the controversies over the welfare state, "socialization," and the alleged leftward leanings of the present document.

To clarify these difficult issues, we must first note that Catholic social teaching has emphasized equally the rights and the social responsibilities of the individual and the family. Individuals have certain basic rights, such as the right to live, to own property, and to have the opportunity to work for a living. They have the right to marry, to rear their children in decent comfort, and to provide with reasonable security for the hazards of the future. But individuals and families do not live in isolation. They are part of a broader society composed of others with equal rights and privileges. Hence it is not sufficient for each individual to assert his rights, he must also respect the rights of others. This fact is one basis of his social reponsibilities.

Individuals living in organized fashion with others constitute a society. The term society may be used to characterize the common life of any group of people. We can speak of world society, national society, or a parish society. One of the most powerful and necessary expressions of organized society is civil government, or the state. While the state is the supreme secular society in a nation, it should never be considered as identical with organized society. The right to associate for lawful and morally proper purposes is natural to man and need not be conferred by the state. Nor may the state withhold or limit such rights, except when the common good of all demands certain regulations. Such regulations should be designed to secure the orderly exercise of the right of association, not to suppress or inhibit this right.

Society exists to secure the welfare of its members. It should promote their material and spiritual development, to the degree possible. While the civil state is supreme in its proper sphere of operations, its broad powers should be used for the welfare of individuals and families. It should enhance their rights and opportunities, not diminish them. Power in society should be decentralized so far as possible. Higher and more powerful groups should not assume functions that can and will be carried out adequately by lesser groups.

It is a difficult and delicate task to apply these principles to the detailed problems of modern economic and political life. A proper balance must be struck between the rights of the individual, his duties to society, and the functions of the state in maintaining the conditions that promote the common good of the community. Under certain circumstances (for example, when confronted with a totalitarian state) our emphasis will rest heavily upon the rights of individuals and of private associations. At the other extreme, when economic power and privilege run rampant, we must stress the power and duty of the state to intervene to protect the weak and defenseless.

Few persons would question the asserting of individual rights against a Communist state, or the duty of government to protect women and children against economic exploitation all too common during the nineteenth century. Here we face clear extremes and the application of principles are self-evident. The critical problems of today, in terms of correct balancing of individual rights and the powers of society, are found in the much more complex situations, such as those prevailing in North America and Western Europe.

In these areas society has assumed a far greater role in individual lives than was common in the nineteenth century or earlier. We read of the organization man, the individual whose life is dominated by the company for which he works. Books are written about image makers and status seekers, indicating that society influences our deepest thoughts and aspirations. We are lost in the lonely crowd, and ruled by public opinion. As part of this phenomenon, the state is assuming a wide variety of regulatory and welfare functions that were unheard-of a century ago. Can these trends be harmonized with individual rights, or is the individual becoming a mere automaton?

Pope John confronts this tendency with cautious optimism. He notes that the increasing complexity of modern life stems largely from progress in science, technology, and communications. These make possible the easier fulfillment of man's natural urge to form associations. As society becomes richer and more complex, the duties of the state increase accordingly, as it carries out its power of co-ordination and regulation as demanded by the common good. But all these developments are the "creation of men who are free and autonomous by nature." (No. 63) What man creates, man can guide and direct in accord with the moral law.

The Pope would have us avoid two extremes. One is the negative reaction of merely decrying modern society as destructive of individual rights and freedoms. The other extreme involves a fatalistic acceptance of every new development as inevitable and irreversible. We will be free men by acting as free men, accepting or rejecting, questioning, modifying, experimenting, debating, proving what is good, remedying what is evil, and generally being masters of our own destiny. Our task is to humanize and Christianize this modern world, and not sigh for some ideal out of the remote past or the far distant future.

Mastering the Modern World

In performing the task of making modern society responsive to the true demands of human nature, special consideration must be given to the role of work, the structure of industry, and the function of private property.

The wage of the worker must be determined in accordance with justice and equity, and not merely left to the play of the marketplace. But economic factors must also be considered in determining what is a just wage. Thus, the contribution of the worker and the quantity and quality of available resources will affect the amount available for wages.

For a truly humanized economy, more is needed than justice in salaries. The worker should be given an opportunity to participate intelligently in the process of production. He should be consulted and given some voice in day-by-day problems that he confronts at work. Even more, his representatives should participate as a matter of right in national and international economic bodies, whose decisions vitally affect the interest of workers.

A humanized economy will also favor owners of small business enterprises and craftsmen who are independent contractors. Public policy will assist them in securing the necessary technical skills for competition in the modern world. Indeed, in every area it is essential that the state seek to balance economic development with social progress. Inequalities among classes, regions, and nations should be lessened by wise social policy. The goods of this world should be distributed in an equitable fashion, not concentrated in the hands of a few persons or a few nations.

To achieve these results, it is not necessary to re-examine the traditional Catholic teaching on the nature and role of private property. It is true that the separation of ownership and control in the large corporation does not readily conform to textbook descriptions of private property. Likewise, the encyclical notes that, in recent years, workers have found economic security by means other than ownership. Social security, pension systems, and the possession of needed work skills are often vital elements in protecting the worker and his family. Nevertheless, private ownership is still basic in safeguarding individual freedoms. Its value should not be downgraded in modern society. It is essential, however, that goods be properly distributed and that owners recognize their social obligations.

New Aspects of the Social Question

Under this heading, Pope John treats of three rather closely related modern problems: agriculture, population growth, and the needs of developing nations. They are related problems since most developing nations are primarily rural, and many of them are faced with strong population pressures upon available food resources.

The papal treatment of agriculture reflects the background of the Pope. He was always proud of his peasant origins and he could write with lyric beauty about the spiritual and cultural values of rural living. But he was realist enough to emphasize that farmers also need material incentives to keep them from migrating to the cities. In some parts of the world, this calls for technical assistance to increase productivity. There are other areas where the greater need is price control to secure adequate incomes. Certainly the disparity, in most parts of the world, between agriculture, industry, and service occupations calls for a strong social policy aimed at correcting such inequalities. Farmers, through their own co-operative associations and with state help, should receive incomes sufficient to give them living standards comparable to those enjoyed in the cities.

Likewise, inequalities among nations should be reduced. This is a moral obligation incumbent upon wealthy nations. They should give, in addition to emergency aid for those in dire need, loans, grants, and technical assistance to enable developing nations to care for themselves. This help should be genuinely disinterested and not tainted with political or cultural imperialism. By implication, the Pope praises, not only wealthy nations that have shared with those in need, but also private business firms who have invested in these areas, and the United Nations and its related bodies.

In regard to population problems, the encyclical does not go as far as some Catholic thinkers would have preferred. While the Pope does not contradict the arguments of demographers relating to a probable population explosion, he obviously prefers to wait for better evidence before facing the possible need for population control. He stresses the overall abundance of the wealth given us by the Creator, the need for political and social reforms to make this wealth available in nations now suffering from great poverty, and the principle that births must not be restricted by means contrary to the natural law.

The caution of the Holy Father reflects a fear that demographers tend to consider population control as the sole weapon to be used against poverty in Asia and Latin America. If this attitude prevails, there is not only the danger that immoral methods will be used—witness the prevalence of abortions in Japan—but also the possibility that needed social reforms may be deferred. In the absence of social and political changes, a stable population level in Asia and Latin America would only perpetuate poverty, exploitation, and discrimination.

Pastoral Thoughts

In stressing the duty of the Christian to master and practice the social teaching of the Church, Pope John notes two points in particular: one must learn by doing; and there is no conflict between a true spiritual life and apostolic engagement in the world.

This emphasis upon learning through action is particularly valuable in correcting romanticist and doctrinaire tendencies among Catholic social actionists. One is to observe, judge, and act in the concrete circumstances of modern life. The Christian reformer observes the existential needs in his trade union, in housing, in land reform, or in racial tensions. Then, using his background of Catholic social teaching, he devises a program of action that is both practical and morally sound. He should be expert both in social ethics and in his chosen field of action.

A commitment of this nature need in no way endanger the spiritual life of the Christian. Of course, he avoids the heresy of activism and does not let his apostolate so absorb his energies that he fails to pray. But his prayer in turn is not self-centered; it opens immense reservoirs of energy which he devotes to love of neighbor. Such a person has a sure grasp of the demands of justice. "Animated, too, by the charity of

Christ, he finds it impossible not to love his fellow men." (No. 257) As a child of the Church, he helps it with its "immense task, to humanize and to Christianize this modern civilization of ours." (No. 256)

This modern civilization of ours—here once again the basic theme of the encyclical shows through. This modern civilization of ours. We are part of it, not outsiders. But from the inside, our lifelong task is to make it more human, and more Christian. This is the message of the Church, mother and teacher of nations.

MATER ET MAGISTRA

An Encyclical of Pope John XXIII
on Christianity and Social Progress

- *The earlier social encyclicals*
- *New problems to be faced*
- *Sources of encouragement*

MOTHER AND TEACHER of all nations—such is the Catholic Church in the mind of her Founder, Jesus Christ; to hold the world in an embrace of love, that men, in every age, should find in her their own completeness in a higher order of living, and their ultimate salvation. She is "the pillar and ground of the truth."[1] To her was entrusted by her holy Founder the twofold task of giving life to her children and of teaching them and guiding them—both as individuals and as nations—with maternal care. Great is their dignity, a dignity which she has always guarded most zealously and held in the highest esteem.

2. Christianity is the meeting-point of earth and heaven. It lays claim to the whole man, body and soul, intellect and will, inducing him to raise his mind above the changing conditions of this earthly existence and reach upwards for the eternal life of heaven, where one day he will find his unfailing happiness and peace.

Temporal and eternal

3. Hence, though the Church's first care must be for souls, how she can sanctify them and make them share in the gifts of heaven, she concerns herself too with the exigencies of man's daily life, with

[1] Cf. *1 Tim.* 3, 15.

his livelihood and education, and his general, temporal welfare and prosperity.

4. In all this she is but giving effect to those principles which Christ Himself established in the Church He founded. When He said "I am the way, and the truth, and the life,"[2] "I am the light of the world,"[3] it was doubtless man's eternal salvation that was uppermost in His mind, but He showed His concern for the material welfare of His people when, seeing the hungry crowd of His followers, He was moved to exclaim: "I have compassion on the multitude."[4] And these were no empty words of our divine Redeemer. Time and again He proved them by His actions, as when He miraculously multiplied bread to alleviate the hunger of the crowds.

5. Bread it was for the body, but it was intended also to foreshadow that other bread, that heavenly food of the soul, which He was to give them on "the night before He suffered."

Teaching and example

6. Small wonder, then, that the Catholic Church, in imitation of Christ and in fulfillment of His commandment, relies not merely upon her teaching to hold aloft the torch of charity, but also upon her own widespread example. This has been her course now for nigh on two thousand years, from the early ministrations of her deacons right down to the present time. It is a charity which combines the precepts and practice of mutual love. It holds fast to the twofold aspect of Christ's command to *give*, and summarizes the whole of the Church's social teaching and activity.

The impact of Rerum novarum

7. An outstanding instance of this social teaching and action carried on by the Church throughout the ages is undoubtedly that magnificent encyclical on the christianizing of the conditions of the working classes, *Rerum novarum*, published seventy years ago by Our predecessor Leo XIII.[5]

---

[2] *John* 14, 6.   [3] *John* 8, 12.   [4] *Mark* 8, 2.
[5] *Acta Leonis XIII*, xi, 1891, pp. 97-144.

8. Seldom have the words of a pontiff met with such universal acclaim. In the weight and scope of his arguments, and in the forcefulness of their expression, Pope Leo XIII can have but few rivals. Beyond any shadow of doubt, his directives and appeals have established for themselves a position of such high importance that they will never, surely, sink into oblivion. They opened out new horizons for the activity of the universal Church, and the Supreme Shepherd, by giving expression to the hardships and sufferings and aspirations of the lowly and oppressed, made himself the champion and restorer of their rights.

9. The impact of this remarkable encyclical is still with us even today, so many years after it was written. It is discernible in the writings of the popes who succeeded Pope Leo. In their social and economic teaching they have frequent recourse to the Leonine encyclical, either to draw inspiration from it and clarify its application, or to find in it a stimulus to Catholic action. It is discernible too in the subsequent legislation of a number of states. What further proof need we of the permanent validity of the solidly grounded principles, practical directives and fatherly appeals contained in this masterly encyclical? It also suggests new and vital criteria by which men can judge the magnitude of the social question as it presents itself today, and decide on the course of action they must take.

Part I

RERUM NOVARUM AND AFTERWARDS

Social Conditions at the Time of Rerum Novarum

10. Leo XIII spoke in a time of social and economic upheaval, of heightening tensions and actual revolt. Against this dark background, the brilliance of his teaching stands out in clear relief.

A purely naturalistic economics in vogue

11. As is well known, the outlook that prevailed on economic matters was for the most part a purely naturalistic one, which de-

nied any correlation between economics and morality. Personal gain was considered the only valid motive for economic activity. In business the main operative principle was that of free and unrestricted competition. Interest on capital, prices—whether of goods or of services—profits and wages, were to be determined by the purely mechanical application of the laws of the market place. Every precaution was to be taken to prevent the civil authority from intervening in any way in economic matters. The status of trade unions varied in different countries. They were either forbidden, tolerated, or recognized as having private legal personality only.

12. In an economic world of this character, it was the might of the strongest which not only arrogated to itself the force of law, but also dominated the ordinary business relationships between individuals, and thereby undermined the whole economic structure.

Deplorable working conditions

13. Enormous riches accumulated in the hands of a few, while large numbers of workingmen found themselves in conditions of ever increasing hardship. Wages were insufficient even to the point of reaching starvation level, and working conditions were often of such a nature as to be injurious alike to health, morality and religious faith. Especially inhuman were the working conditions to which women and children were sometimes subjected. There was also the constant spectre of unemployment and the progressive disruption of family life.

14. The natural consequence of all this was a spirit of indignation and open protest on the part of the workingman, and a widespread tendency to subscribe to extremist theories far worse in their effects than the evils they purported to remedy.

PREPARING THE WAY FOR A NEW ORDER

15. It was at such a time and under pressure of such circumstances as these that Leo XIII wrote his social encyclical, *Rerum novarum*, based on the needs of human nature itself and animated by the principles and spirit of the Gospel. His message, not unnatu-

rally, aroused opposition in some quarters, but was recieved by the majority of people with the greatest admiration and enthusiasm.

A complete synthesis

It was not, of course, the first occasion on which the Apostolic See had come out strongly in defense of the earthly interests of the poor; indeed, Leo himself had made other pronouncements which in a sense had prepared the way for his encyclical. But here for the first time was a complete synthesis of social principles, formulated with such historical insight as to be of permanent value to Christendom. It is rightly regarded as a compendium of Catholic social and economic teaching.[5a]

No solution apart from religion and Church

16. In this Leo XIII showed his complete mastery of the situation. There were those who presumed to accuse the Church of taking no interest in social matters other than to preach resignation to the poor and generosity to the rich, but Leo XIII had no hesitation in proclaiming and defending the legitimate rights of the workers. As he said at the beginning of his exposition of the principles and precepts of the Church in social matters: "We approach the subject with confidence, and in the exercise of the rights which manifestly appertain to Us, for no practical solution of this question will be found apart from the counsel of religion and of the Church."[6]

17. You know well enough, venerable brethren, the basic economic and social principles for the reconstruction of human society enunciated so clearly and authoritatively by this great Pope.

Work—a specifically human activity

18. They concern first of all the question of work, which must be regarded not merely as a commodity, but as a specifically human

---

[5a] In the Latin text this paragraph is part of the preceding one, hence we have not assigned it a number. For format reasons we have broken paragraphs down in a few places but have kept our numbering system keyed to the Latin paragraphs.—Ed.
[6] *Ibid.*, p. 107.

activity. In the majority of cases a man's work is his sole means of livelihood. Its remuneration, therefore, cannot be made to depend on the state of the market. It must be determined by the laws of justice and equity. Any other procedure would be a clear violation of justice, even supposing the contract of work to have been freely entered into by both parties.

Private property and its social aspect

19. Secondly, private ownership of property, including that of productive goods, is a natural right which the State cannot suppress. But it naturally entails a social obligation as well. It is a right which must be exercised not only for one's own personal benefit but also for the benefit of others.

The State's role

20. As for the State, its whole *raison d'être* is the realization of the common good in the temporal order. It cannot, therefore, hold aloof from economic matters. On the contrary, it must do all in its power to promote the production of a sufficient supply of material goods, "the use of which is necessary for the practice of virtue."[7] It has also the duty to protect the rights of all its people, and particularly of its weaker members, the workers, women and children. It can never be right for the State to shirk its obligation of working actively for the betterment of the condition of the workingman.

21. It is furthermore the duty of the State to ensure that terms of employment are regulated in accordance with justice and equity, and to safeguard the human dignity of workers by making sure that they are not required to work in an environment which may prove harmful to their material and spiritual interests. It was for this reason that the Leonine encyclical enunciated those general principles of rightness and equity which have been assimilated into the social legislation of many a modern state, and which, as Pope Pius XI declared in the encyclical *Quadragesimo anno*,[8] have made no small contribution to the rise and development of that new branch of jurisprudence called labor law.

---

[7] St. Thomas, *De regimine principum*, I, 15.   [8] Cf. *AAS* 23 (1931) 185.

Right to enter into associations

22. Pope Leo XIII also defended the worker's natural right to enter into association with his fellows. Such associations may consist either of workers alone or of workers and employers, and should be structured in a way best calculated to safeguard the workers' legitimate professional interests. And it is the natural right of the workers to work without hindrance, freely, and on their own initiative within these associations for the achievement of these ends.

Human solidarity and Christian brotherhood

23. Finally, both workers and employers should regulate their mutual relations in accordance with the principle of human solidarity and Christian brotherhood. Unrestricted competition in the *liberal* sense, and in the Marxist creed of class warfare, are clearly contrary to Christian teaching and the nature of man.

24. These, venerable brethren, are the basic principles upon which a genuine social and economic order must be built.

25. The response of good Catholics to this appeal and the enterprise they showed in reducing these principles into practice is hardly surprising. But others too, men of good will from every nation in the world, were impelled, under pressure of human necessity, to pursue the same course.

26. Hence, the Leonine encyclical is rightly regarded, even today, as the *Magna Charta*[9] of social and economic reconstruction.

THE ENCYCLICAL QUADRAGESIMO ANNO

Confirmation, clarification, re-application

27. Forty years after the appearance of this magnificent summary of Christian social principles, Our predecessor Pius XI published his own encyclical, *Quadragesimo anno*.[10]

28. In it the Supreme Pontiff confirmed the right and duty of the Catholic Church to work for an equitable solution of the many

---

[9] Cf. *ibid.*, p. 189.   [10] *Ibid.*, pp. 177-228.

pressing problems weighing upon human society and calling for a joint effort by all the people. He reiterated the principles of the Leonine encyclical and stressed those directives which were applicable to modern conditions. In addition, he took the opportunity not only to clarify certain points of this teaching which had given rise to difficulties even in the minds of Catholics, but also to reformulate Christian social thought in the light of changed conditions.

29. The difficulties referred to principally concerned the Catholic's attitude to private property, the wage system, and moderate socialism.

Private property; the wage system

30. With regard to private property, Our predecessor reaffirmed its origin in natural law, and enlarged upon its social aspect and the obligations of ownership.

31. As for the wage system, while rejecting the view that it is unjust of its very nature, he condemned the inhuman and unjust way in which it is so often implemented, and specified the terms and conditions to be observed if justice and equity are not to be violated.

32. In this connection, as Our predecessor clearly points out, it is advisable in the present circumstances that the wage-contract be somewhat modified by applying to it elements taken from the contract of partnership, so that "wage-earners and other employees participate in the ownership or the management, or in some way share in the profits."[11]

33. Of special doctrinal and practical importance is his affirmation that "if the social and individual character of work be overlooked, it can be neither justly valued nor equitably recompensed."[12] In determining wages, therefore, justice demands that account be taken not only of the needs of the individual workers and their families, but also of the financial state of the business concern for which they work and of "the economic welfare of the whole people."[13]

[11] Cf. *ibid.*, p. 199.   [12] Cf. *ibid.*, p. 200.   [13] Cf. *ibid.*, p. 201.

On socialism

34. Pope Pius XI further emphasized the fundamental opposition between Communism and Christianity, and made it clear that no Catholic could subscribe even to moderate socialism. The reason is that socialism is founded on a doctrine of human society which is bounded by time and takes no account of any objective other than that of material well-being. Since, therefore, it proposes a form of social organization which aims solely at production, it places too severe a restraint on human liberty, at the same time flouting the true notion of social authority.

Other problems of the day

35. Pius XI was not unaware of the fact that in the forty years that had supervened since the publication of the Leonine encyclical the historical scene had altered considerably. It was clear, for example, that unregulated competition had succumbed to its own inherent tendencies to the point of practically destroying itself. It had given rise to a great accumulation of wealth, and, in the process, concentrated a despotic economic power in the hands of a few "who for the most part are not the owners, but only the trustees and directors of invested funds, which they administer at their own good pleasure."[14]

36. Hence, as the Pope remarked so discerningly, "economic domination has taken the place of the open market. Unbridled ambition for domination has succeeded the desire for gain; the whole economic regime has become hard, cruel and relentless in frightful measure."[15] As a consequence, even the public authority was becoming the tool of plutocracy, which was thus gaining a stranglehold on the entire world.

The remedy

37. Pius XI saw the re-establishment of the economic world within the framework of the moral order and the subordination of individual and group interests to the interests of the common good

[14] Cf. *ibid.*, p. 210 *et seq.*   [15] Cf. *ibid.*, p. 211.

as the principal remedies for these evils. This, he taught, necessitated an orderly reconstruction of society, with the establishment of economic and vocational bodies which would be autonomous and independent of the State. Public authority should resume its duty of promoting the common good of all. Finally, there should be cooperation on a world scale for the economic welfare of all nations.

38. Thus Pius XI's teaching in this encyclical can be summed up under two heads. First he taught what the supreme criterion in economic matters ought *not* to be. It must not be the special interests of individuals or groups, nor unregulated competition, economic despotism, national prestige or imperialism, nor any other aim of this sort.

39. On the contrary, all forms of economic enterprise must be governed by the principles of social justice and charity.

40. The second point which We consider basic in the encyclical is his teaching that man's aim must be to achieve in social justice a national and international juridical order, with its network of public and private institutions, in which all economic activity can be conducted not merely for private gain but also in the interests of the common good.

Pius XII's Broadcast Message, Pentecost Sunday, 1941

Toward greater precision

41. For all that he did to render more precise the Christian definition of social rights and duties, no small recognition is due to Our late predecessor Pius XII. On Pentecost Sunday, June 1st, 1941, he broadcast his message "to call to the attention of the Catholic world a memory worthy of being written in letters of gold on the Church's calendar: the fiftieth anniversary of the publication of the epoch-making social encyclical of Leo XIII, *Rerum novarum*,"[16] and "to render to Almighty God from the bottom of Our heart, Our humble thanks for the gift, which . . . He bestowed on the Church in that encyclical of His vicar on earth, and to praise Him for the life-giving breath of the Spirit which through it, in ever-growing measure from that time on, has blown on all mankind."[17]

[16] Cf. *AAS* 33 (1941) 196.   [17] Cf. *ibid.*, p. 197.

The Church's competence

42. In that broadcast message the great Pontiff claimed for the Church "the indisputable competence" to "decide whether the bases of a given social system are in accord with the unchangeable order which God our Creator and Redeemer has shown us through the Natural Law and Revelation."[18] He confirmed the perennial validity and inexhaustible worth of the teaching of *Rerum novarum*, and took occasion "to give some further directive moral principles on three fundamental values of social and economic life. These three fundamental values, which are closely connected one with the other, mutually complementary and dependent, are: the use of material goods, work, and the family."[19]

The use of material goods

43. Concerning the use of material goods, Our predecessor declared that the right of every man to use these for his own sustenance is prior to every other economic right, even that of private property. The right to the private possession of material goods is admittedly a natural one; nevertheless, in the objective order established by God, the right to property cannot stand in the way of the axiomatic principle that "the goods which were created by God for all men should flow to all alike, according to the principles of justice and charity."[20]

Work

44. On the subject of work, Pius XII repeated the teaching of the Leonine encyclical, maintaining that a man's work is at once his duty and his right. It is for individuals, therefore, to regulate their mutual relations where their work is concerned. If they cannot do so, or will not do so, then, and only then, does "it fall back on the State to intervene in the division and distribution of work, and this must be according to the form and measure that the common good properly understood demands."[21]

---

[18] Cf. *ibid.*, p. 196.
[19] Cf. *ibid.*, p. 198 *et seq.*
[20] Cf. *ibid.*, p. 199.
[21] Cf. *ibid.*, p. 201.

The family

45. In dealing with the family the Supreme Pontiff affirmed that the private ownership of material goods has a great part to play in promoting the welfare of family life. It "secures for the father of a family the healthy liberty he needs in order to fulfil the duties assigned him by the Creator regarding the physical, spiritual and religious welfare of the family."[22] It is in this that the right of families to migrate is rooted. And so Our predecessor, in speaking of migration, admonished both parties involved, namely the country of departure and the country receiving the newcomers, to seek always "to eliminate as far as possible all obstacles to the birth and growth of real confidence"[23] between the nations. In this way both will contribute to, and share in, the increased welfare of man and the progress of culture.

SUBSEQUENT CHANGES

46. But in the twenty years which have elapsed since the changing economic climate noted at that time by Pius XII the economic scene has undergone a radical transformation, both in the internal structure of the various states and in their relations with one another.

Science, technology, economics

47. In the field of science, technology and economics we have the discovery of nuclear energy, and its application first to the purposes of war and later, increasingly, to peaceful ends; the practically limitless possibilities of chemistry in the production of synthetic materials; the growth of automation in industry and public services; the modernization of agriculture; the easing of communications, especially by radio and television; faster transportation and the initial conquest of interplanetary space.

The social field

48. In the social field we have the development of social insurance and, in the more economically advanced communities, the

[22] Cf. *ibid.*, p. 202.   [23] Cf. *ibid.*, p. 203.

introduction of social security systems. Men in labor unions are showing a more responsible awareness of the major social and economic problems. There is a progressive improvement in basic education, a wider distribution of essential commodities, greater opportunities for advancement in industry and the consequent breaking down of class barriers, and a keener interest in world affairs shown by people of average education.

At the same time, however, this assessment of the increased efficiency of social and economic systems in a growing number of communities serves also to bring to light certain glaring discrepancies. There is, in the first place, a progressive lack of balance between agriculture on the one hand, and industry and public services on the other. Secondly, there are areas of varying economic prosperity within the same political communities. Finally—to take a world view—one observes a marked disparity in the economic wealth possessed by different countries.

The political field

49. To turn to the political field, We observe many changes. In a number of countries all classes of citizens are taking a part in public life, and public authorities are injecting themselves more each day into social and economic matters. We are witnessing the break-away from colonialism and the attainment of political independence by the peoples of Asia and Africa. Drawn together by their common needs nations are becoming daily more interdependent. There is, moreover, an ever-extending network of societies and organizations which set their sights beyond the aims and interests of individual countries and concentrate on the economic, social, cultural and political welfare of all nations throughout the world.

The Reasons for This New Encyclical

50. As We pass all this in review, We are aware of Our responsibility to take up this torch which Our great predecessors lighted, and hand it on with undiminished flame. It is a torch to lighten the pathways of all who would seek appropriate solutions to the many social problems of our times. Our purpose, therefore, is not merely

to commemorate in a fitting manner the Leonine encyclical, but also to confirm and make more specific the teaching of Our predecessors, and to determine clearly the mind of the Church on the new and important problems of the day.

Part II
EXPLANATION AND DEVELOPMENT OF THE TEACHING OF *RERUM NOVARUM*

Personal Initiative and State Intervention in the Economy

Two roles

51. It should be stated at the outset that in the economic order first place must be given to the personal initiative of private citizens working either as individuals or in association with each other in various ways for the furtherance of common interests.

52. But—for reasons explained by Our predecessors—the civil power must also have a hand in the economy. It has to promote production in a way best calculated to achieve social progress and the well-being of all citizens.

Principle of subsidiarity

53. And in this work of directing, stimulating, co-ordinating, supplying and integrating, its guiding principle must be the "principle of subsidiary function" formulated by Pius XI in *Quadragesimo anno*.[24] "This is a fundamental principle of social philosophy, unshaken and unchangeable. . . . Just as it is wrong to withdraw from the individual and commit to a community what private enterprise and industry can accomplish, so too it is an injustice, a grave evil and a disturbance of right order, for a larger and higher association to arrogate to itself functions which can be performed efficiently by smaller and lower societies. Of its very nature the true aim of all social activity should be to help members of the social body, but never to destroy or absorb them."[25]

[24] *AAS* 23 (1931) 203. [25] *Ibid.*, p. 203.

54. The present advance in scientific knowledge and productive technology clearly puts it within the power of the public authority to a much greater degree than ever before to reduce imbalances which may exist between different branches of the economy or between different regions within the same country or even between the different peoples of the world. It also puts into the hands of public authority a greater means for limiting fluctuations in the economy and for providing effective measures to prevent the recurrence of mass unemployment. Hence the insistent demands on those in authority—since they are responsible for the common good—to increase the degree and scope of their activities in the economic sphere, and to devise ways and means and set the necessary machinery in motion for the attainment of this end.

55. But however extensive and far-reaching the influence of the State on the economy may be, it must never be exerted to the extent of depriving the individual citizen of his freedom of action. It must rather augment his freedom while effectively guaranteeing the protection of his essential personal rights. Among these is a man's right and duty to be primarily responsible for his own upkeep and that of his family. Hence every economic system must permit and facilitate the free development of productive activity.

Co-operation essential

56. Moreover, as history itself testifies with ever-increasing clarity, there can be no such thing as a well-ordered and prosperous society unless individual citizens and the State co-operate in the economy. Both sides must work together in harmony, and their respective efforts must be proportioned to the needs of the common good in the prevailing circumstances and conditions of human life.

57. Experience has shown that where personal initiative is lacking, political tyranny ensues and, in addition, economic stagnation in the production of a wide range of consumer goods and of services of the material and spiritual order—those, namely, which are in a great measure dependent upon the exercise and stimulus of individual creative talent.

58. Where, on the other hand, the good offices of the State are

lacking or deficient, incurable disorder ensues: in particular, the unscrupulous exploitation of the weak by the strong. For men of this stamp are always in evidence, and, like cockle among the wheat, thrive in every land.

RAMIFICATIONS OF THE SOCIAL PROCESS

An increase in social relationships

59. Certainly one of the principal characteristics which seem to be typical of our age is an increase in social relationships, in those mutual ties, that is, which grow daily more numerous and which have led to the introduction of many and varied forms of associations in the lives and activities of citizens, and to their acceptance within our legal framework. Scientific and technical progress, greater productive efficiency and a higher standard of living are among the many present-day factors which would seem to have contributed to this trend.

60. This development in the social life of man is at once a symptom and a cause of the growing intervention of the State, even in matters which are of intimate concern to the individual, hence of great importance and not devoid of risk. We might cite as examples such matters as health and education, the choice of a career, and the care and rehabilitation of the physically and mentally handicapped.

It is also partly the result, partly the expression of a natural, well-nigh irresistible urge in man to combine with his fellows for the attainment of aims and objectives which are beyond the means or the capabilities of single individuals. In recent times this tendency has given rise to the formation everywhere of both national and international movements, associations and institutions with economic, cultural, social, sporting, recreational, professional and political ends.

Advantages and disadvantages

61. Clearly, this sort of development in social relationships brings many advantages in its train. It makes it possible for the

individual to exercise many of his personal rights, especially those which we call economic and social and which pertain to the necessities of life, health care, education on a more extensive and improved basis, a more thorough professional training, housing, work, and suitable leisure and recreation. Furthermore, the progressive perfection of modern methods of thought-diffusion—the press, cinema, radio, television—makes it possible for everyone to participate in human events the world over.

62. At the same time, however, this multiplication and daily extension of forms of association brings with it a multiplicity of restrictive laws and regulations in many departments of human life. As a consequence, it narrows the sphere of a person's freedom of action. The means often used, the methods followed, the atmosphere created, all conspire to make it difficult for a person to think independently of outside influences, to act on his own initiative, exercise his responsibility and express and fulfil his own personality. What then? Must we conclude that these increased social relationships necesarily reduce men to the condition of being mere automatons? By no means.

Creation of free men

63. For actually this growth in the social life of man is not a product of natural forces working, as it were, by blind impulse. It is, as we saw, the creation of men who are free and autonomous by nature—though they must, of course, recognize and, in a sense, obey the laws of economic development and social progress, and cannot altogether escape from the pressure of environment.

64. The development of these social relationships, therefore, can and ought to be realized in a way best calculated to promote its inherent advantages and to preclude, or at least diminish, its attendant disadvantages.

Proper balance necessary

65. To this end, a sane view of the common good must be present and operative in men invested with public authority. They must take account of all those social conditions which favor the full

development of human personality. Moreover, We consider it altogether vital that the numerous intermediary bodies and corporate enterprises—which are, so to say, the main vehicle of this social growth—be really autonomous, and loyally collaborate in pursuit of their own specific interests and those of the common good. For these groups must themselves necessarily present the form and substance of a true community, and this will only be the case if they treat their individual members as human persons and encourage them to take an active part in the ordering of their lives.

66. As these mutual ties binding the men of our age one to the other grow and develop, governments will the more easily achieve a right order the more they succeed in striking a balance between the autonomous and active collaboration of individuals and groups, and the timely co-ordination and encouragement by the State of these private undertakings.

67. So long as social relationships do in fact adhere to these principles within the framework of the moral order, their extension does not necessarily mean that individual citizens will be gravely discriminated against or excessively burdened. On the contrary, we can hope that they will help him to develop and perfect his own personal talents, and lead to that organic reconstruction of society which Our predecessor Pius XI advocated in his encyclical *Quadragesimo anno* as the indispensable prerequisite for the fulfilment of the rights and obligations of social life.[26]

THE REMUNERATION OF WORK

Millions in dire straits

68. We are filled with an overwhelming sadness when We contemplate the sorry spectacle of millions of workers in many lands and entire continents condemned through the inadequacy of their wages to live with their families in utterly sub-human conditions. This is probably due to the fact that the process of industrialization in these countries is only in its initial stages, or is still not sufficiently developed.

69. Nevertheless, in some of these lands the enormous wealth,

[26] Cf. *ibid.*, p. 222 *et seq.*

the unbridled luxury, of the privileged few stands in violent, offensive contrast to the utter poverty of the vast majority. In some parts of the world men are being subjected to inhuman privations so that the output of the national economy can be increased at a rate of acceleration beyond what would be possible if regard were had to social justice and equity. And in other countries a notable percentage of income is absorbed in building up an ill-conceived national prestige, and vast sums are spent on armaments.

70. In economically developed countries, relatively unimportant services, and services of doubtful value, frequently carry a disproportionately high rate of remuneration, while the diligent and profitable work of whole classes of honest, hard-working men gets scant reward. Their rate of pay is quite inadequate to meet the basic needs of life. It in no way corresponds to the contribution they make to the good of the community, to the profits of the company for which they work, and to the general national economy.

Factors determining just wage

71. We therefore consider it Our duty to reaffirm that the remuneration of work is not something that can be left to the laws of the marketplace; nor should it be a decision left to the will of the more powerful. It must be determined in accordance with justice and equity; which means that workers must be paid a wage which allows them to live a truly human life and to fulfill their family obligations in a worthy manner. Other factors too enter into the assessment of a just wage: namely, the effective contribution which each individual makes to the economic effort, the financial state of the company for which he works, the requirements of the general good of the particular country—having regard especially to the repercussions on the overall employment of the working force in the country as a whole—and finally the requirements of the common good of the universal family of nations of every kind, both large and small.

72. The above principles are valid always and everywhere. So much is clear. But their degree of applicability to concrete cases cannot be determined without reference to the quantity and quality

JOHN XXIII
SUPREME PONTIFF OF THE UNIVERSAL CHURCH
October 28, 1958 – June 3, 1963

During his coronation—"*We assert vigorously and sincerely that it is Our particular intention to be the shepherd, the pastor. . . .*"

Good Shepherd...

. . . **to the aged**—"*Long life is venerable in itself . . . but above all it is a great gift of God.*"

. . . **to the sick and suffering**—"*Let those who are afflicted know that the Pope is with his children especially at times that are sad and bitter.*"

... to the little ones—"*We would like to sweep all of you up in Our arms and offer you to the Lord.*"

"*There are some who . . . fail to mirror in themselves the image of Jesus Christ. We cannot find it in Us to threaten or abuse them, for the love We bear them is a father's love. Instead We appeal to them. . . .*"

Servant of the Servants of God

On his view of the papacy—"*Who I am as an individual means nothing. It is a brother who speaks to you, a brother who has become Father through Our Lord's will.*"

On the imitation of Christ—*"The Pope ... considers himself the servant of everyone, and tries to act accordingly."*

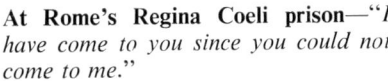

At Rome's Regina Coeli prison—*"I have come to you since you could not come to me."*

Witness

At the opening of the great "council of renewal"—"*A new day is dawning on the Church... It is yet the dawn, but the sun in its rising has already set our hearts aglow.*"

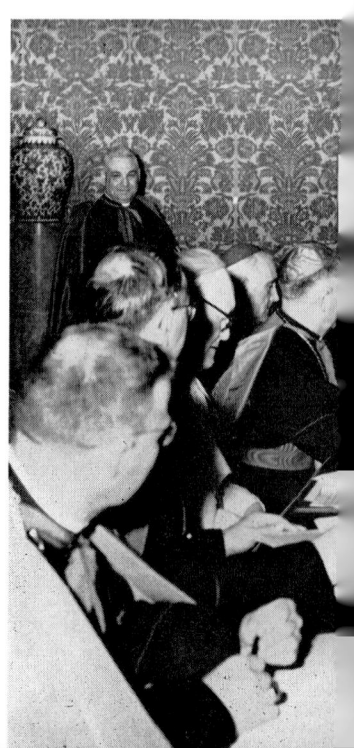

to Christ's Truth

On freedom—"*Only the truth of Christ makes us free. It supplies the answer that each man seeks but—because of the self-commitment demanded—sometimes fears to heed.*"

Reviewing the difference of opinion among Council Fathers during the first session—"*It was providential, for it served to clarify issues, and to demonstrate to the world the existence in the Church of the holy freedom of the sons of God.*"

On the Church and ecumenism—"*In my nightly meditations I have always had before me that crucified Jesus with His arms open to welcome all. For the duty of the Catholic and Apostolic Church is to work for the realization of the prayer of the Divine Master: that all may be one.*"

On the universal concern of the Council—"*If we confined ourselves exclusively to our own individual concerns and those of Catholics, entrenched behind the ramparts of the Catholic Church, we would surely be inadequate (or so it has always seemed to Us) to the demands of our divine Redeemer.*"

Recalling the Council's opening ceremonies with Protestant and Orthodox observers—*"When my glance rested upon your group, on each of you personally, I drew a special comfort from your presence."*

Apostle of Unity

A Priest forever...

...before

On his vocation—"*From Our childhood We had but one thought with regard to the direction Our life was to take, and that was to become a priest.*"

To his "parishioners"—"*The voice of the Church is like the voice of a mother: it may seem monotonous at times, but it has tones of tenderness and of strength that keep us from evil and save us.*"

God and before the people

On celebration of his Christmas Mass—"*We chose . . . the simplicity of Our private chapel . . . so that We might have surroundings similar to those of the humble churches of the countryside and mountains. . . .*"

To newly-consecrated bishops—"*The title which will henceforward accompany your family name—Humble Bishop of God's Church—equals the highest distinction you can possess in time and for eternity.*"

To a missionary bishop—"*The humble Vicar of Christ each morning gathers about his chalice the enormous garland of all his children in every part of the world. He turns with particular tenderness to the laborers of the Gospel....*"

First among Equals

Bishop of Rome

Recalling joyful encounters with his "dear sons of Rome"—"*The sight of so many hands reaching out to Us, of arms waving from so many buses, stores, and windows, made Us feel that all were saying as one: We love this man whom Providence has drawn from the holiness and nobility of the countryside and raised to the heights of the Roman Pontificate.*"

To throngs in St. Peter's Square—*"As you return home to your children, hug them and say: this is the embrace of the Pope."*

From a Father's heart—*"The Pope's thoughts go each morning and many times daily to the homes and buildings where Romans work and suffer."*

Welcoming diplomats from nations to the Council—" addition to its religious signi cance, the Council has also social aspect which concerns t life of peoples. Your presen here very plainly shows that

On the brotherhood of man—"*We still hope that . . . the richer peoples will help those who are suffering from need, the stronger ones will protect the weak, those who enjoy more in the way of comforts of civilization will help the nations that have not yet reached a proper level of prosperity.*"

To an international group of architects—"*The essential nature of a council surely has not escaped you. Perhaps your very profession enables you to understand it more than others do, for you have the task of building. . . .*"

Friend of All Nations

Paying tribute to the United States—*"America has continued . . . to render her legislation—which is derived from principles of Christian morality—ever more in keeping with the dignity of the human person."*

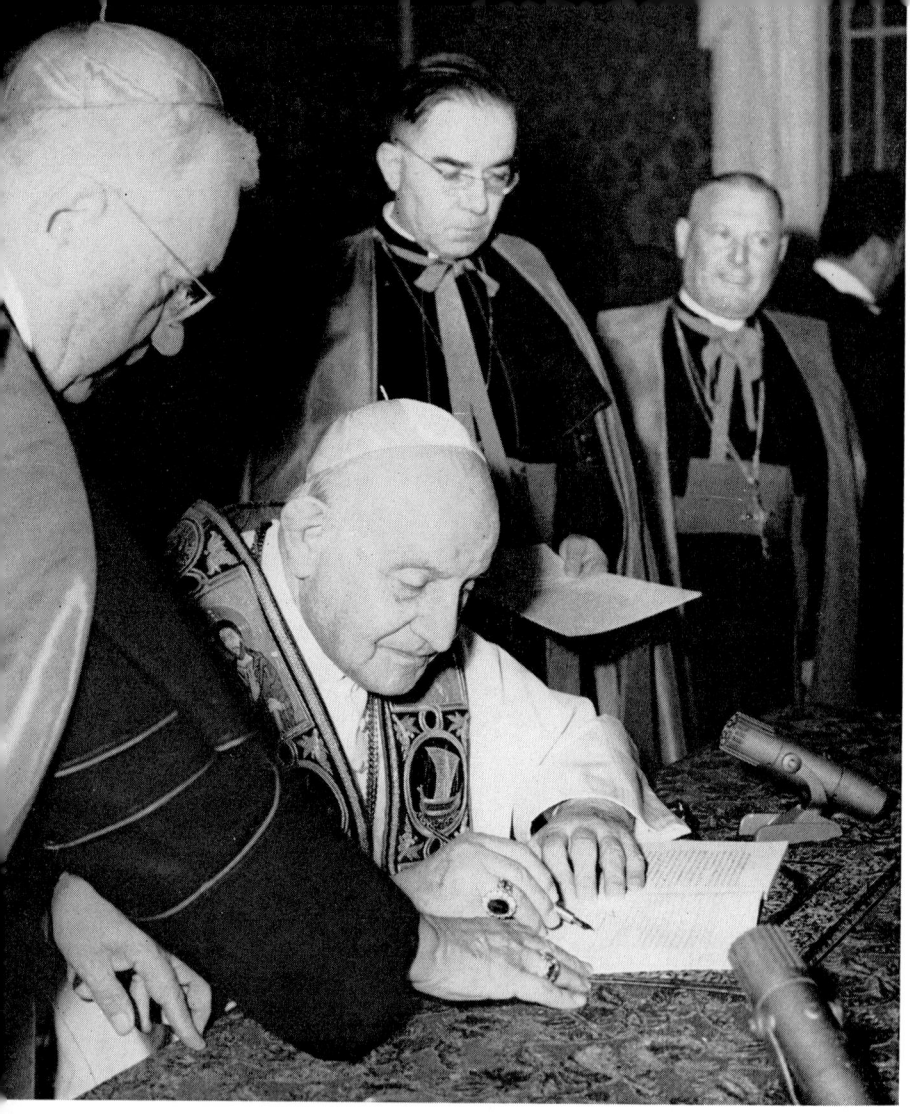

Signing "Pacem in Terris," his encyclical on peace—*"We have sought not only to illustrate the foundation of the structure of peace . . . but We have also indicated the different levels on which to build this structure and, almost, the very stones necessary for its construction."*

Artisan of Peace

"The world will never be the dwelling-place of peace, till peace has found a home in the heart of each and every man."

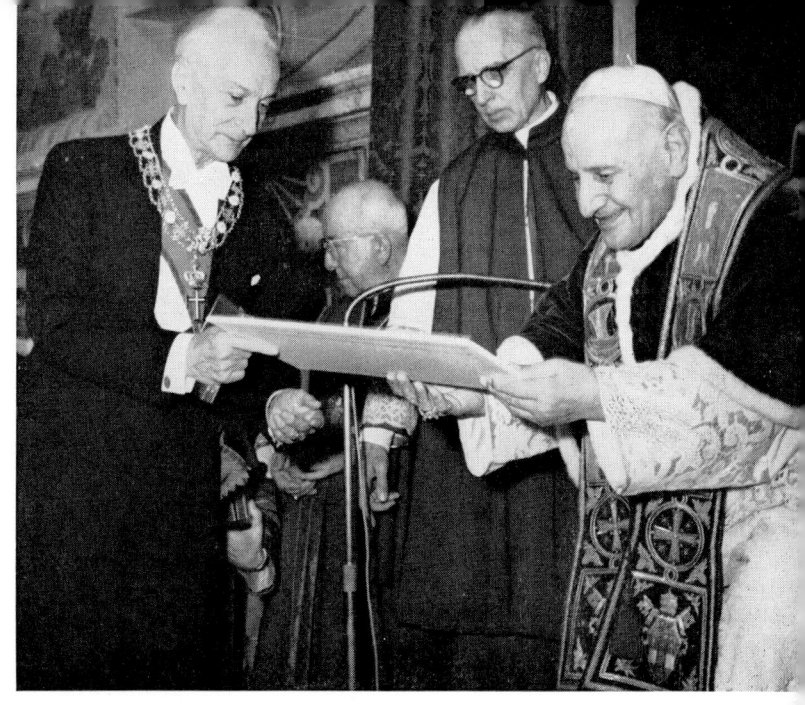

Accepting the 1962 Balzan peace prize—"*The peacemakers called blessed in the Gospel are not men who do nothing. They are, on the contrary, the active artisans of peace.*"

of available resources; and these can—and in fact do—vary from country to country, and even, from time to time, within the same country.

BALANCING ECONOMIC DEVELOPMENT AND SOCIAL PROGRESS

True purpose of the economy

73. In view of the rapid expansion of national economies, particularly since the war, there is one very important social principle to which We would draw your attention. It is this: Economic progress must be accompanied by a corresponding social progress, so that all classes of citizens can participate in the increased productivity. The utmost vigilance and effort is needed to ensure that social inequalities, so far from increasing, are reduced to a minimum.

74. As Our predecessor Pius XII observed with evident justification: "Likewise the national economy, as it is the product of the men who work together in the community of the State, has no other end than to secure without interruption the material conditions in which the individual life of the citizens may fully develop. Where this is secured in a permanent way, a people will be, in a true sense, economically rich, because the general well-being, and consequently the personal right of all to the use of worldly goods, is thus actuated in conformity with the purpose willed by the Creator."[27] From this it follows that the economic prosperity of a nation is not so much its total assets in terms of wealth and property, as the equitable division and distribution of this wealth. This it is which guarantees the personal development of the members of society, which is the true goal of a nation's economy.

Sharing ownership

75. We must notice in this connection the system of self-financing adopted in many countries by large, or comparatively large firms. Because these companies are financing replacement and plant expansion out of their own profits, they grow at a very rapid rate. In such cases We believe that the workers should be allocated

[27] Cf. *AAS* 33 (1941) 200.

shares in the firms for which they work, especially when they are paid no more than a minimum wage.

76. We should recall here the principle enunciated by Pius XI in *Quadragesimo anno*: "It is entirely false to ascribe to the property alone or to the work alone whatever has been obtained through the combined effort of both, and it is wholly unjust for either, denying the efficacy of the other, to arrogate to itself whatever has been produced."[28]

77. Experience suggests many ways in which the demands of justice can be satisfied. Not to mention other ways, it is especially desirable today that workers gradually come to share in the ownership of their company, by ways and in the manner that seem most suitable. For today, even more than in the time of Our predecessor, "every effort must be made that at least in future a just share only of the fruits of production be permitted to accumulate in the hands of the wealthy, and that an ample sufficiency be supplied to the workers."[29]

The demands of the common good

78. But a further point needs emphasizing: Any adjustment between wages and profits must take into account the demands of the common good of the particular country and of the whole human family.

79. What are these demands? On the national level they include: employment of the greatest possible number of workers; care lest privileged classes arise, even among the workers; maintenance of equilibrium between wages and prices; the need to make goods and services accessible to the greatest number; elimination, or at least the restriction, of inequalities in the various branches of the economy—that is, between agriculture, industry and services; creation of a proper balance between economic expansion and the development of social services, especially through the activity of public authorities; the best possible adjustment of the means of production to the progress of science and technology; seeing to it that the benefits which make possible a more human way of life will be

---

[28] *AAS* 23 (1931) 195.   [29] *Ibid.*, p. 198.

available not merely to the present generation but to the coming generations as well.

80. The demands of the common good on the international level include: the avoidance of all forms of unfair competition between the economies of different countries; the fostering of mutual collaboration and good will; and effective co-operation in the development of economically less advanced communities.

81. These demands of the common good, both on a national and a world level, must also be borne in mind when assessing the rate of return due as compensation to the company's management, and as interest or dividends to investors.

The Structure of Industry

The requirements of human dignity

82. Justice is to be observed not only in the distribution of wealth, but also in regard to the conditions in which men are engaged in producing this wealth. Every man has, of his very nature, a need to express himself in his work and thereby to perfect his own being.

83. Consequently, if the whole structure and organization of an economic system is such as to compromise human dignity, to lessen a man's sense of responsibility or rob him of opportunity for exercising personal initiative, then such a system, We maintain, is altogether unjust—no matter how much wealth it produces, or how justly and equitably such wealth is distributed.

Pius XII's directive

84. It is not possible to give a concise definition of the kind of economic structure which is most consonant with man's dignity and best calculated to develop in him a sense of responsibility. Pius XII, however, comes to our rescue with the following directive: "The small and average sized undertakings in agriculture, in the arts and crafts, in commerce and industry, should be safeguarded and fostered. Moreover, they should join together in co-operative associations to gain for themselves the benefits and advantages that

usually can be gained only from large organizations. In the large concerns themselves there should be the possibility of moderating the contract of work by one of partnership."[30]

Artisans and co-operative enterprises

85. Hence the craftsman's business and that of the family farm, as well as the co-operative enterprise which aims at the completion and perfection of both these concerns—all these are to be safeguarded and encouraged in harmony with the common good and technical progress.

86. We shall return shortly to the question of the family farm. Here We consider it appropriate to say something about artisan and co-operative enterprises.

87. First of all it is necessary to emphasize that if these two kinds of undertaking are to thrive and prosper they must be prepared constantly to adjust their productive equipment and their productive methods to meet new situations created by the advance of science and technology and the changing demands and preferences of the consumer. This adaptation must be effected principally by the workers themselves and the members of the co-operatives.

88. Both these groups, therefore, need a thoroughgoing technical and general education, and should have their own professional organizations. It is equally important that the government take the proper steps regarding their training, taxation, credit, social security and insurance.

89. Furthermore, these two categories of citizens—craftsmen and members of co-operatives—are fully entitled to these watchful measures of the State, for they are upholding true human values and contributing to the advance of civilization.

90. We therefore paternally invite Our beloved sons—craftsmen and members of co-operatives throughout the world—to realize the greatness of this task which is theirs in the State. By the force of their example they are helping to keep alive in their own community a true sense of responsibility, a spirit of co-operation, and the constant desire to create new and original work of outstanding merit.

---

[30] Broadcast message, 1 Sept. 1944: *AAS* 36 (1944) 254.

The Participation of Workers in Medium and Large Concerns

Active part essential

91. We, no less than Our predecessors, are convinced that employees are justified in wishing to participate in the activity of the industrial concern for which they work. It is not, of course, possible to lay down hard and fast rules regarding the manner of such participation, for this must depend upon prevailing conditions, which vary from firm to firm and are frequently subject to rapid and substantial alteration. But We have no doubt as to the need for giving workers an active part in the business of the company for which they work—be it a private or a public one. Every effort must be made to ensure that the enterprise is indeed a true human community, concerned about the needs, the activities and the standing of each of its members.

92. This demands that the relations between management and employees reflect understanding, appreciation and good will on both sides. It demands, too, that all parties co-operate actively and loyally in the common enterprise, not so much for what they can get out of it for themselves, but as discharging a duty and rendering a service to their fellow men.

Balancing unity of direction with role of individuals

All this implies that the workers have their say in, and make their own contribution to, the efficient running and development of the enterprise. As Pius XII remarked, "the economic and social function which every man aspires to fulfil, demands that the carrying on of the activity of each one not be completely subjected to the others."[31]

Obviously, any firm which is concerned for the human dignity of its workers must also maintain a necessary and efficient unity of direction. But it must not treat those employees who spend their days in service with the firm as though they were mere cogs in the machinery, denying them any opportunity of expressing their wishes or bringing their experience to bear on the work in hand, and

---

[31] Allocution, 8 Oct. 1956: *AAS* 48 (1956) 799-800. *TPS*, III, 405-09.

keeping them entirely passive in regard to decisions that regulate their activity.

93. We would observe, finally, that the present demand for workers to have a greater say in the conduct of the firm accords not only with man's nature, but also with recent progress in the economic, social and political spheres.

94. For although many unjust and inhuman economic and social imbalances still exist in our day, and there are still many errors affecting the activity, aims, structure and operation of economies the world over, it is an undeniable fact that, thanks to the driving impulse of scientific and technical advance, productive systems are today rapidly becoming more modernized and efficient—more so than ever before. Hence a greater technical skill is required of the workers, and more exacting professional qualifications. Which means that they must be given more assistance, and more free time in which to complete their vocational training as well as to carry out more fittingly their cultural, moral and religious education.

95. As a further consequence, the modern youth is enabled to devote a longer time to his basic schooling in the arts and sciences.

96. All this serves to create an environment in which workers are encouraged to assume greater responsibility in their own sphere of employment. In politics, too, it is of no small consequence that citizens are becoming daily more aware of their responsibility for furthering the common good in all spheres of life.

The Participation of Workers in the Economy as a Whole

97. In modern times we have seen an extensive increase in the number of workers' associations, and their general recognition in the juridical codes of single states and on the international level. Members are no longer recruited in order to agitate, but rather to co-operate, principally by the method of collective bargaining. But it is worthwhile stressing here how timely and imperative it is that workers be given the opportunity to exert their influence throughout the State, and not just within the limits of their own spheres of employment.

The more important decisions

98. The reason for this is that the individual productive concerns, regardless of their size, efficiency and importance in the State, form but a part—an integral part—of a nation's entire economic and social life, upon which their own prosperity must depend.

99. Hence it is not the decisions made within the individual productive units which have the greatest bearing on the economy, but those made by public authorities and by institutions which tackle the various economic problems on a national or international basis. It is therefore very appropriate, or even necessary, that these public authorities and institutions bring the workers into their discussions, and those who represent the rights, demands and aspirations of the workingmen; and not confine their deliberations to those who merely represent the interests of management.

Praise and appreciation

100. It is Our prerogative to be a Father, and there is a special place in Our thoughts and in Our heart for those professional groups and Christian associations of workers which exist and operate in so many parts of the world. We know the nature and extent of the difficulties under which these dearest sons of Ours are laboring, as they strive continually and effectually to promote in their own countries and throughout the world the material and moral interests of the working people.

101. They are fully deserving of Our praise. The importance of their work must be gauged not merely by its immediate and obvious results, but also by its effect on the working world as a whole, where it helps to spread sound principles of action and the wholesome influence of the Christian religion.

102. We wish further to praise those dear sons of Ours who in a true Christian spirit collaborate with other professional groups and workers' associations which respect the natural law and the freedom of conscience of their members.

103. We must also express here Our heartfelt appreciation of the work that is being done by the International Labor Organization —popularly known in various countries as the O.I.L. or I.L.O. or

O.I.T. For many years now it has been making an effective and valued contribution to the establishment in the world of an economic and social order marked by justice and humanity, an order which recognizes and safeguards the lawful rights of the workingman.

Private Property

Conditions changing

104. It is well-known that in recent years in the larger industrial concerns a distinction has been growing between the ownership of productive goods and the responsibility of company managers. This has created considerable problems for public authorities, whose duty it is to see that the aims pursued by the leaders of the principal organizations—especially those which have an important part to play in the national economy—do not conflict in any way with the interests of the common good. Experience shows that these problems arise whether the capital which makes possible these vast undertakings belongs to private citizens or to public corporations.

105. It is also true that more and more people today, through belonging to insurance groups and systems of social security, find that they can face the future with confidence—the sort of confidence which formerly resulted from their possession of a certain amount of property.

An advanced view of work

106. And another thing happening today is that people are aiming at proficiency in their trade or profession rather than the acquisition of private property. They think more highly of an income which derives from work and the rights consequent upon work, than of an income which derives from capital and the rights of capital.

107. And this is as it should be. Work, which is the immediate expression of a human personality, must always be rated higher than the possession of external goods which of their very nature are merely instrumental. This view of work is certainly an indication of an advance that has been made in our civilization.

Confirmation of the right of ownership

108. What, then, of that social and economic principle so vigorously asserted and defended by Our predecessors: man's natural right to own private property, including productive goods? Is this no longer operative today, or has it lost some of its validity in view of the economic conditions We have described above? This is the doubt that has arisen in many minds.

109. There is no reason for such a doubt to persist. The right of private ownership of goods, including productive goods, has permanent validity. It is part of the natural order, which teaches that the individual is prior to society and society must be ordered to the good of the individual.

Moreover, it would be quite useless to insist on free and personal initiative in the economic field, while at the same time withdrawing man's right to dispose freely of the means indispensable to the achievement of such initiative.

Further, history and experience testify that in those political regimes which do not recognize the rights of private ownership of goods, productive included, the exercise of freedom in almost every other direction is suppressed or stifled. This suggests, surely, that the exercise of freedom finds its guarantee and incentive in the right of ownership.

110. This explains why social and political movements for the harmonizing of justice and freedom in society, though until recently opposed to the private ownership of productive goods, are today reconsidering their position in the light of a clearer understanding of social history, and are in fact now declaring themselves in favor of this right.

Guarantee for both individual and society

111. Accordingly, We make Our own the directive of Our predecessor Pius XII: "In defending the principle of private ownership the Church is striving after an important ethico-social end. She does not intend merely to uphold the present condition of things as if it were an expression of the divine Will, or to protect on principle the rich and plutocrats against the poor and indigent. . . . The Church

aims rather at securing that the institution of private property be such as it should be according to the plan of the divine Wisdom and the dispositions of Nature."[32] Hence private ownership must be considered as a guarantee of the essential freedom of the individual, and at the same time an indispensable element in a true social order.

Wages and property

112. Moreover, in recent years, as we have seen, the productive efficiency of many national economies has been increasing rapidly. Justice and fairness demand, therefore, that, within the limits of the common good, wages too shall increase. This means that workers are able to save more and thus acquire a certain amount of property of their own. In view of this it is strange that the innate character of a right which derives its force and validity from the fruitfulness of work should ever be called in question—a right which constitutes so efficacious a means of asserting one's personality and exercising responsibility in every field, and an element of solidity and security for family life and of greater peace and prosperity in the State.

The effective distribution of property

113. But it is not enough to assert that the right to own private property and the means of production is inherent in human nature. We must also insist on the extension of this right in practice to all classes of citizens.

114. As Our predecessor Pius XII so rightly affirmed: The dignity of the human person "normally demands the right to the use of the goods of the earth, to which corresponds the fundamental obligation of granting an opportunity to possess property to all if possible."[33] This demand arises from the moral dignity of work. It also guarantees "the conservation and perfection of a social order which makes possible a secure, even if modest, property to all classes of people."[34]

[32] Broadcast message, 1 Sept. 1944: *AAS* 36 (1944) 253.
[33] Broadcast message, 24 Dec. 1942: *AAS* 35 (1943) 19.
[34] Cf. *ibid.*, p. 20.

115. Now, if ever, is the time to insist on a more widespread distribution of property, in view of the rapid economic development of an increasing number of states. It will not be difficult for the body politic, by the adoption of various techniques of proved efficiency, to pursue an economic and social policy which facilitates the widest possible distribution of private property in terms of durable consumer goods, houses, land, tools and equipment (in the case of craftsmen and owners of family farms), and shares in medium and large business concerns. This policy is in fact being pursued with considerable success by several of the socially and economically advanced nations.

Public Ownership

Its lawfulness

116. This, of course, is not to deny the lawfulness of State and public ownership of productive goods, especially those which "carry with them a power too great to be left to private individuals without injury to the community at large."[35]

Principle of subsidiarity

117. State and public ownership of property is very much on the increase today. This is explained by the exigencies of the common good, which demand that public authority broaden its sphere of activity. But here, too, the "principle of subsidiary function" must be observed. The State and other agencies of public law must not extend their ownership beyond what is clearly required by considerations of the common good properly understood, and even then there must be safeguards. Otherwise private ownership could be reduced beyond measure, or, even worse, completely destroyed.

Precautions

118. It is important, too, not to overlook the fact that the economic enterprises of the State and other agencies of public law must be entrusted to men of good reputation who have the necessary

[35] Encyclical *"Quadragesimo anno," AAS* 23 (1931) 214.

experience and ability and a keen sense of responsibility towards their country. Furthermore, a strict check should constantly be kept upon their activity, so as to avoid any possibility of the concentration of undue economic power in the hands of a few State officials, to the detriment of the best interests of the community.

The Social Function of Property

Goods meant for all

119. Our predecessors have insisted time and again on the social function inherent in the right of private ownership, for it cannot be denied that in the plan of the Creator all of this world's goods are primarily intended for the worthy support of the entire human race.

Hence, as Leo XIII so wisely taught in *Rerum novarum*: "whoever has received from the divine bounty a large share of temporal blessings, whether they be external and corporeal, or gifts of the mind, has received them for the purpose of using them for the perfecting of his own nature, and, at the same time, that he may employ them, as the steward of God's Providence, for the benefit of others. 'He that hath a talent,' says St. Gregory the Great, 'let him see that he hide it not; he that hath abundance, let him quicken himself to mercy and generosity; he that hath art and skill, let him do his best to share the use and the utility thereof with his neighbor.' "[36]

Always vast field for personal charity

120. In recent years the State and other agencies of public law have extended, and are continuing to extend, the sphere of their activity and initiative. But this does not mean that the doctrine of the social function of private ownership is out of date, as some would maintain. It is inherent in the very right of private ownership.

Then, too, a further consideration arises. Tragic situations and urgent problems of an intimate and personal nature are continually arising which the State with all its machinery is unable to remedy or assist. There will always remain, therefore, a vast field for the exercise of human sympathy and the Christian charity of individ-

[36] *Acta Leonis XIII*, xi, 1891, p. 114.

Mater et Magistra 281

uals. We would observe, finally, that the efforts of individuals, or of groups of private citizens, are definitely more effective in promoting spiritual values than is the activity of public authority.

The real treasure

121. We should notice at this point that the right of private ownership is clearly sanctioned by the Gospel. Yet at the same time, the divine Master frequently extends to the rich the insistent invitation to convert their material goods into spiritual ones by conferring them on the poor. "Lay not up to yourselves treasures on earth; where the rust and moth consume and where thieves break through and steal. But lay up to yourselves treasures in heaven; where neither the rust nor moth doth consume, and where thieves do not break through nor steal."[37] And the Lord will look upon the charity given to the poor as given to Himself. "Amen, I say to you, as long as you did it to one of these my least brethren, you did it to me."[38]

PART III
NEW ASPECTS OF THE SOCIAL QUESTION

OTHER AREAS IN NEED

122. History shows with ever-increasing clarity that it is not only the relations between workers and managers that need to be reestablished on the basis of justice and equity, but also those between the various branches of the economy, between areas of varying productivity within the same political community, and between countries with a different degree of social and economic development.

THE DEPRESSED STATE OF AGRICULTURE

A shifting population

123. First, with regard to agriculture, it would not appear that the rural population as a whole is decreasing, but it is an undeniable

---
[37] *Matt.* 6, 19-20.   [38] *Matt.* 25, 40.

fact that many people are moving away from their farms into more thickly populated areas as well as into the cities themselves. When we realize that this movement of population is going on in nearly every part of the world, often on a large scale, we begin to appreciate the complexity of the human problems involved and their difficulty of solution.

124. We know that as an economy develops, the number of people engaged in agriculture decreases, while the percentage employed in industry and the various services rises. Nevertheless, We believe that very often this movement of population from farming to industry has other causes besides those dependent upon economic expansion. Among these there is the desire to escape from confining surroundings which offer little prospect of a more comfortable way of life. There is the lure of novelty and adventure which has taken such a hold on the present generation, the attractive prospect of easy money, of greater freedom and the enjoyment of all the amenities of town and city life. But a contributory cause of this movement away from the country is doubtless the fact that farming has become a depressed occupation. It is inadequate both in productive efficiency and in the standard of living it provides.

A fundamental problem

125. Nearly every country, therefore, is faced with this fundamental problem: What can be done to reduce the disproportion in productive efficiency between agriculture on the one hand, and industry and services on the other; and to ensure that agricultural living standards approximate as closely as possible those enjoyed by city-dwellers who draw their resources either from industry or from the services in which they are engaged? What can be done to persuade agricultural workers that, far from being inferior to other people, they have every opportunity of developing their personality through their work, and can look forward to the future with confidence?

Contributing to the solution

126. It seems to Us opportune to indicate certain directives that can contribute to a solution of this problem: directives which We

believe have value whatever may be the historical environment in which one acts—on condition, obviously, that they be applied in the manner and to the degree allowed, suggested, or even demanded by the circumstances.

SOME REMEDIES

The extension of essential public services

127. In the first place, considerable thought must be given, especially by public authorities, to the suitable development of essential facilities in country areas—such as roads; transportation; means of communication; drinking water; housing; health services; elementary, technical and professional education; religious and recreational facilities; and the supply of modern installations and furnishings for the farm residence. Such services as these are necessary nowadays if a becoming standard of living is to be maintained. In those country areas where they are lacking, economic and social progress is either prevented or greatly impeded, with the result that nothing can be done to retard the drift of population away from the land, and it even becomes difficult to make a good appraisal of the numbers involved.

Importance of gradual, balanced development of the economy

128. If a country is to develop economically, it must do so gradually, maintaining an even balance between all sectors of the economy. Agriculture, therefore, must be allowed to make use of the same reforms in the method and type of production and in the conduct of the business side of the venture as are permitted or required in the economic system as a whole. All such reforms should correspond as nearly as possible with those introduced in industry and the various services.

129. In this way, agriculture will absorb a larger amount of industrial goods and require a better system of services. But at the same time it will provide both industry and the services and the country as a whole with the type of products which, in quantity and quality, best meet the needs of the consumer and contribute to the stability of the purchasing power of money—a major consideration in the orderly development of the entire economic system.

130. One advantage which would result from the adoption of this plan would be that it would be easier to keep track of the movement of the working force set free by the progressive modernization of agriculture. Facilities could then be provided for the training of such people for their new kind of work, and they would not be left without economic aid and the mental and spiritual assistance they need to ensure their proper integration in their new social milieu.

The need for a suitable economic policy

131. In addition, a sound agricultural program is needed if public authority is to maintain an evenly balanced progress in the various branches of the economy. This must take into account tax policies, credit, social insurance, prices, the fostering of ancillary industries and the adjustment of the structure of farming as a business enterprise.

Taxation

132. In a system of taxation based on justice and equity it is fundamental that the burdens be proportioned to the capacity of the people contributing.

133. But the common good also requires that public authorities, in assessing the amount of tax payable, take cognizance of the peculiar difficulties of farmers. They have to wait longer than most people for their returns, and these are exposed to greater hazards. Consequently, farmers find greater difficulty in obtaining the capital necessary to increase returns.

Credit banks

134. For this reason, too, investors are more inclined to put their money in industry rather than agriculture. Farmers are unable to pay high rates of interest. Indeed, they cannot as a rule make the trading profit necessary to furnish capital for the conduct and development of their own business. It is therefore necessary, for reasons of the common good, for public authorities to evolve a special credit policy and to form credit banks which will guarantee such capital to farmers at a moderate rate of interest.

Social insurance and social security

135. In agriculture the existence of two forms of insurance may be necessary: one concerned with agricultural produce, the other with the farm workers and their families. We realize that agricultural workers earn less per capita than workers in industry and the services, but that is no reason why it should be considered socially just and equitable to set up systems of social insurance in which the allowances granted to farm workers and their families are substantially lower than those payable to other classes of workers. Insurance programs that are established for the general public should not differ markedly whatever be the economic sector in which the individuals work or the source of their income.

136. Systems of social insurance and social security can make a most effective contribution to the overall distribution of national income in accordance with the principles of justice and equity. They can therefore be instrumental in reducing imbalances between the different classes of citizens.

Price protection

137. Given the special nature of agricultural produce, modern economists must devise a suitable means of price protection. Ideally, such price protection should be enforced by the interested parties themselves, though supervision by the public authority cannot be altogether dispensed with.

138. On this subject it must not be forgotten that the price of agricultural produce represents, for the most part, the reward of the farmer's labor rather than a return on invested capital.

139. Hence, in *Quadragesimo anno* Pope Pius XI rightly observed that "a proper proportion between different wages is also a matter of importance." He continued: "And intimately connected with this is a proper proportion between the prices charged for the products of the various economic groups, agricultural, industrial, and so forth."[39]

140. While it is true that farm produce is mainly intended for

---

[39] Cf. *AAS* 23 (1931) 202.

the satisfaction of man's primary needs, and the price should therefore be within the means of all consumers, this cannot be used as an argument for keeping a section of the population—farm workers—in a permanent state of economic and social inferiority, depriving them of the wherewithal for a decent standard of living. This would be diametrically opposed to the common good.

The promotion of ancillary industries

141. Moreover, the time has come to promote in agricultural regions the establishment of those industries and services which are concerned with the preservation, processing and transportation of farm products. Enterprises relating to other sectors of the economy might also be established there. In this case the rural population would have another means of income at their disposal, a means which they could exploit in the social milieu to which they are accustomed.

THE STRUCTURE OF THE FARM UNIT

142. It is not possible to determine *a priori* what the structure of farm life should be, since rural conditions vary so much from place to place and from country to country throughout the world. But if we hold to a human and Christian concept of man and the family, we are bound to consider as an ideal that form of enterprise which is modelled on the basis of a community of persons working together for the advancement of their mutual interests in accordance with the principles of justice and Christian teaching. We are bound above all to consider as an ideal the kind of farm which is owned and managed by the family. Every effort must be made in the prevailing circumstances to give effective encouragement to farming enterprises of this nature.

143. But if the family farm is not to go bankrupt it must make enough money to keep the family in reasonable comfort. To ensure this, farmers must be given up-to-date instruction on the latest methods of cultivation, and the assistance of experts must be put at their disposal. They should also form a flourishing system of co-operative undertakings, and organize themselves professionally to

take an effective part in public life, both on the administrative and the political level.

THE SELF-ADVANCEMENT OF THE FARMING COMMUNITY

Nobility of the work

144. We are convinced that the farming community must take an active part in its own economic advancement, social progress and cultural betterment. Those who live on the land can hardly fail to appreciate the nobility of the work they are called upon to do. They are living in close harmony with Nature—the majestic temple of Creation. Their work has to do with the life of plants and animals, a life that is inexhaustible in its expression, inflexible in its laws, rich in allusions to God the Creator and Provider. They produce food for the support of human life, and the raw materials of industry in ever richer supply.

145. Theirs is a work which carries with it a dignity all its own. It brings into its service many branches of engineering, chemistry and biology, and is itself a cause of the continued practical development of these sciences in view of the repercussions of scientific and technical progress on the business of farming. It is a work which demands a capacity for orientation and adaptation, patient waiting, a sense of responsibility, and a spirit of perseverance and enterprise.

Solidarity and co-operation

146. It is important also to bear in mind that in agriculture, as in other sectors of production, association is a vital need today—especially in the case of family farms. Rural workers should feel a sense of solidarity with one another, and should unite to form co-operatives and professional associations. These are very necessary if farm workers are to benefit from scientific and technical methods of production and protect the prices of their products. They are necessary, too, if they are to attain an equal footing with other professional classes who, in most cases, have joined together in associations. They are necessary, finally, if farm workers are to have their proper voice in political circles and in public administration.

The lone voice is not likely to command much of a hearing in times such as ours.

Social responsibility

147. In using their various organizations, agricultural workers —as indeed all other classes of workers—must always be guided by moral principles and respect for the civil law. They must try to reconcile their rights and interests with those of other classes of workers, and even subordinate the one to the other if the common good demands it. If they show themselves alive to the common good and contribute to its realization, they can legitimately demand that their efforts for the improvement of agricultural conditions be seconded and complemented by public authority.

148. We therefore desire here to express Our satisfaction with those sons of Ours the world over who are actively engaged in cooperatives, in professional groups and in worker movements intent on raising the economic and social standards of the agricultural community.

Vocation and mission

149. In the work on the farm the human personality finds every incentive for self-expression, self-development and spiritual growth. It is a work, therefore, which should be thought of as a vocation, a God-given mission, an answer to God's call to actuate His providential, saving plan in history. It should be thought of, finally, as a noble task, undertaken with a view to raising oneself and others to a higher degree of civilization.

Toward a Balanced Internal Economy

Helping the less developed

150. Among citizens of the same political community there is often a marked degree of economic and social inequality. The main reason for this is the fact that they are living and working in different areas, some of which are more economically developed than others.

Where this situation obtains, justice and equity demand that public authority try to eliminate or reduce such imbalances. It should ensure that the less developed areas receive such essential public services as their circumstances require, in order to bring the standard of living in these areas into line with the national average. Furthermore, a suitable economic and social policy must be devised which will take into account the supply of labor, the drift of population, wages, taxes, credit, and the investing of money, especially in expanding industries. In short, it should be a policy designed to promote useful employment, enterprising initiative, and the exploitation of local resources.

The common good

151. But the justification of all government action is the common good. Public authority, therefore, must bear in mind the interests of the state as a whole; which means that it must promote all three areas of production—agriculture, industry and services—simultaneously and evenly. Everything must be done to ensure that citizens of the less developed areas are treated as responsible human beings, and are allowed to play the major role in achieving their own economic, social and cultural advancement.

Contribution of private enterprise

152. Private enterprise too must contribute to an economic and social balance in the different areas of the same political community. Indeed, in accordance with "the principle of subsidiary function," public authority must encourage and assist private enterprise, entrusting to it, wherever possible, the continuation of economic development.

INTERNATIONAL DISPROPORTIONS

Land and population

153. It is not out of place to remark here on a problem which exists in quite a number of countries, namely, a gross disproportion between land and population. In some countries arable land

abounds, but there is a scarcity of population; whereas in other countries the position is reversed: the population is large, arable land scarce.

Surpluses and scarcities

154. Again, some countries use primitive methods of agriculture, with the result that, for all their abundance of natural resources, they are not able to produce enough food to feed their population; whereas other countries, using modern methods of agriculture, produce a surplus of food which has an adverse effect on the economy.

155. It is therefore obvious that the solidarity of the human race and Christian brotherhood demand the elimination as far as possible of these discrepancies. With this object in view, people all over the world must co-operate actively with one another in all sorts of ways, so as to facilitate the movement of goods, capital and men from one country to another. We shall have more to say on this point later on.

The F.A.O.

156. Here We would like to express Our sincere appreciation of the work which the F.A.O.[39a] has undertaken to establish effective collaboration among nations, to promote the modernization of agriculture especially in less developed countries, and to alleviate the suffering of hunger-stricken peoples.

Obligation of the wealthy nations

157. Probably the most difficult problem today concerns the relationship between political communities that are economically advanced and those in the process of development. Whereas the standard of living is high in the former, the latter are subject to extreme poverty. The solidarity which binds all men together as members of a common family makes it impossible for wealthy nations to look with indifference upon the hunger, misery and

[39a] The United Nations Food and Agricultural Organization.—Ed.

poverty of other nations whose citizens are unable to enjoy even elementary human rights. The nations of the world are becoming more and more dependent on one another and it will not be possible to preserve a lasting peace so long as glaring economic and social imbalances persist.

158. Mindful of Our position as the father of all peoples, We feel constrained to repeat here what We said on another occasion: "We are all equally responsible for the undernourished peoples.[40] [Hence], it is necessary to educate one's conscience to the sense of responsibility which weighs upon each and every one, especially upon those who are more blessed with this world's goods."[41]

The Mystical Body of Christ

159. The Church has always emphasized that this obligation of helping those who are in misery and want should be felt most strongly by Catholics, in view of the fact that they are members of the Mystical Body of Christ. "In this we have known the charity of God," says St. John, "because he has laid down his life for us; and we ought to lay down our lives for the brethren. He that hath the substance of this world and shall see his brother in need and shall shut up his bowels from him; how doth the charity of God abide in him?"[42]

160. It is therefore a great source of joy to Us to see those nations which enjoy a high degree of economic wealth helping the nations not so well provided, so that they may more effectively raise their standard of living.

INTERNATIONAL AID

Emergency aid

161. Justice and humanity demand that those countries which produce consumer goods, especially farm products, in excess of their own needs should come to the assistance of those other countries where large sections of the population are suffering from want

---
[40] Allocution, 3 May, 1960: *AAS* 52 (1960) 465. *TPS,* VI, 280.
[41] Cf. *ibid.*
[42] *1 John* 3, 16-17.

and hunger. It is nothing less than an outrage to justice and humanity to destroy or to squander goods that other people need for their very lives.

162. We are, of course, well aware that over-production, especially in agriculture, can cause economic harm to a certain section of the population. But it does not follow that one is thereby exonerated from extending emergency aid to those who need it. On the contrary, everything must be done to minimize the ill effects of overproduction, and to spread the burden equitably over the entire population.

Scientific, technical and financial co-operation

163. Of itself, however, emergency aid will not go far in relieving want and famine when these are caused—as they so often are—by the primitive state of a nation's economy. The only permanent remedy for this is to make use of every possible means of providing these citizens with the scientific, technical and professional training they need, and to put at their disposal the necessary capital for speeding up their economic development with the help of modern methods.

164. We are aware how deeply the public conscience has been affected in recent years by the urgent need of supporting the economic development and social progress of those countries which are still struggling against poverty and economic disabilities.

165. International and regional organizations, national and private societies, all are working towards this goal, increasing day by day the measure of their own technical co-operation in all productive spheres. By their combined efforts thousands of young people are being given facilities for attending the universities of the more advanced countries, and acquiring an up-to-date scientific, technical and professional training. World banking institutes, individual states and private persons are helping to furnish the capital for an ever richer network of economic enterprises in the less wealthy countries. It is a magnificent work that they are doing, and We are most happy to take this occasion of giving it the praise that it deserves. It is a work, however, which needs to be increased, and We hope that the

years ahead will see the wealthier nations making even greater efforts for the scientific, technical and economic advancement of those political communities whose development is still only in its initial stages.

SOME ADDITIONAL COUNSELS

166. We consider it Our duty to give further advice on this matter.

Learning from the past

167. In the first place, those nations which are still only at the beginning of their journey along the road to economic development would do well to consider carefully the experiences of the wealthier nations which have traversed this road before them.

Proper balance essential

168. Increase in production and productive efficiency is, of course, sound policy, and indeed a vital necessity. However, it is no less necessary—and justice itself demands—that the riches produced be distributed fairly among all members of the political community. This means that everything must be done to ensure that social progress keeps pace with economic progress. Again, every sector of the economy—agriculture, industry and the services—must progress evenly and simultaneously.

Respecting a nation's individuality

169. The developing nations, obviously, have certain unmistakable characteristics of their own, resulting from the nature of the particular region and the natural dispositions of their citizens, with their time-honored traditions and customs.

170. In helping these nations, therefore, the more advanced communities must recognize and respect this individuality. They must beware of making the assistance they give an excuse for forcing these people into their own national mold.

Offering disinterested aid

171. There is also a further temptation which the economically developed nations must resist: that of giving technical and financial aid with a view to gaining control over the political situation in the poorer countries, and furthering their own plans for world domination.

172. Let us be quite clear on this point. A nation that acted from these motives would in fact be introducing a new form of colonialism—cleverly disguised, no doubt, but actually reflecting that older, outdated type from which many nations have recently emerged. Such action would, moreover, have a harmful impact on international relations, and constitute a menace to world peace.

173. Necessity, therefore, and justice demand that all such technical and financial aid be given without thought of domination, but rather for the purpose of helping the less developed nations to achieve their own economic and social growth.

174. If this can be achieved, then a precious contribution will have been made to the formation of a world community, in which each individual nation, conscious of its rights and duties, can work on terms of equality with the rest for the attainment of universal prosperity.

Respecting the true hierarchy of values

175. Scientific and technical progress, economic development and the betterment of living conditions, are certainly valuable elements in a civilization. But we must realize that they are essentially instrumental in character. They are not supreme values in themselves.

176. It pains Us, therefore, to observe the complete indifference to the true hierarchy of values shown by so many people in the economically developed countries. Spiritual values are ignored, forgotten or denied, while the progress of science, technology and economics is pursued for its own sake, as though material well-being were the be-all and end-all of life. This attitude is contagious, especially when it infects the work that is being done for the less developed countries, which have often preserved in their ancient

traditions an acute and vital awareness of the more important human values, on which the moral order rests.

177. To attempt to undermine this national integrity is clearly immoral. It must be respected and as far as possible clarified and developed, so that it may remain what it is: a foundation of true civilization.

THE CHURCH'S CONTRIBUTION

Embracing all peoples

178. The Church is by divine right universal. History itself bears this out, for the Church is present everywhere on earth, doing all that she can to embrace all peoples.

179. Now, in bringing people to Christ, the Church has invariably—both now and in the past—brought them many social and economic advantages. For true Christians cannot help feeling obliged to improve their own temporal institutions and environment. They do all they can to prevent these institutions from doing violence to human dignity. They encourage whatever is conducive to honesty and virtue, and strive to eliminate every obstacle to the attainment of this aim.

Never an alien

180. Moreover, in becoming as it were the life-blood of these people, the Church is not, nor does she consider herself to be, a foreign body in their midst. Her presence brings about the rebirth, the resurrection, of each individual in Christ; and the man who is reborn and rises again in Christ never feels himself constrained from without. He feels himself free in the very depth of his being, and freely raised up to God. And thus he affirms and develops that side of his nature which is noblest and best.

Unity, not uniformity

181. "The Church of Jesus Christ," as Our predecessor Pius XII observed with such penetration, "is the repository of His wisdom; she is certainly too wise to discourage or belittle those peculiarities and differences which mark out one nation from another. It is quite

legitimate for nations to treat those differences as a sacred inheritance and guard them at all costs. The Church aims at unity, a unity determined and kept alive by that supernatural love which should be actuating everybody; she does not aim at a uniformity which would only be external in its effects and would cramp the natural tendencies of the nations concerned. Every nation has its own genius, its own qualities, springing from the hidden roots of its being. The wise development, the encouragement within limits, of that genius, those qualities, does no harm; and if a nation cares to take precautions, to lay down rules, for that end, it has the Church's approval. She is mother enough to befriend such projects with her prayers."[43]

Role of Catholic citizens

182. It is a source of profound satisfaction to Us to see the prominent part which is being played by Catholic citizens of the less wealthy countries in the economic and social development of their own state.

183. Then, too, the Catholics of the wealthier states are doing all they can to increase the effectiveness of the social and economic work that is being done for the poorer nations. We would give Our special approval to the increasing assistance they are giving, in all sorts of ways, to African and Asian students scattered throughout the universities of Europe and America; and to the care that is being devoted to the training of those persons who are prepared to go to the less wealthy areas in order to engage in work of a technical and professional nature.

184. To these Our beloved sons in every land who, in promoting genuine progress and civilization, are a living proof of the Church's perennial vitality, We wish to extend Our kind and fatherly word of appreciation and encouragement.

POPULATION INCREASE AND ECONOMIC DEVELOPMENT

A statement of the problem

185. How can economic development and the supply of food keep pace with the continual rise in population? This is a question

[43] Encyclical *"Summi Pontificatus," AAS* 31 (1939) 428-9.

which constantly obtrudes itself today—a world problem, as well as one for the poverty-stricken nations.

186. As a world problem, the case is put thus: According to sufficiently reliable statistics the next few decades will see a very great increase in human population, whereas economic development will proceed at a slower rate. Hence, we are told, if nothing is done to check this rise in population, the world will be faced in the not too distant future with an increasing shortage in the necessities of life.

187. As it affects the less developed countries, the problem is stated thus: The resources of modern hygiene and medicine will very shortly bring about a notable decrease in the mortality rate, especially among infants, while the birth rate—which in such countries is unusually high—will tend to remain more or less constant, at least for a considerable period. The excess of births over deaths will therefore show a steep rise, whereas there will be no corresponding increase in the productive efficiency of the economy. Accordingly, the standard of living in these poorer countries cannot possibly improve. It must surely worsen, even to the point of extreme hardship. Hence there are those who hold the opinion that, in order to prevent a serious crisis from developing, the conception and birth of children should be secretly avoided, or, in any event, curbed in some way.

The problem examined

188. Truth to tell, we do not seem to be faced with any immediate or imminent world problem arising from the disproportion between the increase of population and the supply of food. Arguments to this effect are based on such unreliable and controversial data that they can only be of very uncertain validity.

189. Besides, the resources which God in His goodness and wisdom has implanted in Nature are well-nigh inexhaustible, and He has at the same time given man the intelligence to discover ways and means of exploiting these resources for his own advantage and his own livelihood. Hence, the real solution of the problem is not to be found in expedients which offend against the divinely established moral order and which attack human life at its very source,

but in a renewed scientific and technical effort on man's part to deepen and extend his dominion over Nature. The progress of science and technology that has already been achieved opens up almost limitless horizons in this field.

190. As for the problems which face the poorer nations in various parts of the world, We realize, of course, that these are very real. They are caused, more often than not, by a deficient economic and social organization, which does not offer living conditions proportionate to the increase in population. They are caused, also, by the lack of effective solidarity among such peoples.

191. But granting this, We must nevertheless state most emphatically that no statement of the problem and no solution to it is acceptable which does violence to man's essential dignity; those who propose such solutions base them on an utterly materialistic conception of man himself and his life.

Only possible solution

192. The only possible solution to this question is one which envisages the social and economic progress both of individuals and of the whole of human society, and which respects and promotes true human values. First consideration must obviously be given to those values which concern man's dignity generally, and the immense worth of each individual human life. Attention must then be turned to the need for worldwide co-operation among men, with a view to a fruitful and well-regulated interchange of useful knowledge, capital and manpower.

Respect for the laws of life

193. We must solemnly proclaim that human life is transmitted by means of the family, and the family is based upon a marriage which is one and indissoluble and, with respect to Christians, raised to the dignity of a sacrament. The transmission of human life is the result of a personal and conscious act, and, as such, is subject to the all-holy, inviolable and immutable laws of God, which no man may ignore or disobey. He is not therefore permitted to use certain ways

and means which are allowable in the propagation of plant and animal life.

194. Human life is sacred—all men must recognize that fact. From its very inception it reveals the creating hand of God. Those who violate His laws not only offend the divine majesty and degrade themselves and humanity, they also sap the vitality of the political community of which they are members.

Education toward sense of responsibility

195. It is of the utmost importance that parents exercise their right and obligation toward the younger generation by securing for their children a sound cultural and religious formation. They must also educate them to a deep sense of responsibility in life, especially in such matters as concern the foundation of a family and the procreation and education of children. They must instill in them an unshakable confidence in divine Providence and a determination to accept the inescapable sacrifices and hardships involved in so noble and important a task as the co-operation with God in the transmitting of human life and the bringing up of children.

To the attaiment of this end nothing can be more effective than those principles and that supernatural aid which the Church supplies. On this score alone the right of the Church to full liberty in the exercise of her mission must be recognized.

Science in the service of life

196. Genesis relates how God gave two commandments to our first parents: to transmit human life—"Increase and multiply"[44]—and to bring nature into their service—"Fill the earth, and subdue it."[45] These two commandments are complementary.

197. Nothing is said in the second of these commandments about destroying nature. On the contrary, it must be brought into the service of human life.

198. We are sick at heart, therefore, when We observe the con-

[44] *Gen.* 1, 28.   [45] *Ibid.*

tradiction which has beguiled so much modern thinking. On the one hand we are shown the fearful specter of want and misery which threatens to extinguish human life, and on the other hand we find scientific discoveries, technical inventions and economic resources being used to provide terrible instruments of ruin and death.

199. A provident God grants sufficient means to the human race to find a dignified solution to the problems attendant upon the transmission of human life. But these problems can become difficult of solution, or even insoluble, if man, led astray in mind and perverted in will, turns to such means as are opposed to right reason, and seeks ends that are contrary to his social nature and the intentions of Providence.

WORLD-WIDE CO-OPERATION

Interdependence of nations

200. The progress of science and technology in every aspect of life has led, particularly today, to increased relationships between nations, and made the nations more and more dependent on one another.

201. As a rule no single commonwealth has sufficient resources at its command to solve the more important scientific, technical, economic, social, political and cultural problems which confront it at the present time. These problems are necessarily the concern of a whole group of nations, and possibly of the whole world.

202. Individual political communities may indeed enjoy a high degree of culture and civilization. They may have a large and industrious population, an advanced economic structure, great natural resources and extensive territories. Yet, even so, in isolation from the rest of the world they are quite incapable of finding an adequate solution to their major problems. The nations, therefore, must work with each other for their mutual development and perfection. They can help themselves only in so far as they succeed in helping one another. That is why international understanding and co-operation are so necessary.

The effects of mutual distrust

203. Yet although individuals and nations are becoming more and more convinced of this twofold necessity, it would seem that men in general, and particularly those with high responsibility in public life, are showing themselves quite incapable of achieving it. The root of such inability is not to be sought in scientific, technical or economic reasons, but in the absence of mutual trust. Men, and consequently states, are in mortal fear of each other. Each fears that the other harbors plans of conquest and is only waiting for a favorable moment to put these plans into effect. Hence each organizes its own defense and builds up munitions of war as a deterrent against the would-be aggressor.

204. The result is a vast expenditure of human energy and natural resources on projects which are disruptive of human society rather than beneficial to it; while a growing uneasiness gnaws at men's hearts and makes them less responsive to the call of nobler enterprises.

Failure to acknowledge the moral order

205. The root cause of so much mistrust is the presence of ideological differences between nations, and more especially between their rulers. There are some indeed who go so far as to deny the existence of a moral order which is transcendent, absolute, universal and equally binding upon all. And where the same law of justice is not adhered to by all, men cannot hope to come to open and full agreement on vital issues.

206. Yes, both sides speak of *justice* and *the demands of justice*, but these words frequently take on different or opposite meanings according to which side uses them. Hence, when rulers of nations appeal to *justice* and *the demands of justice,* they not only disagree on terms, but often increase the tension that exists between their states. And so the belief is engendered that if a nation is to assert its rights and pursue its own interests, there is only one way open to it: to have recourse to violence; ignoring the fact that violence is the source of the very greatest evils.

God, the foundation of the moral order

207. Mutual trust among rulers of states cannot begin nor increase except by recognition of, and respect for, the moral order.

208. But the moral order has no existence except in God; cut off from God it must necessarily disintegrate. Moreover, man is not just a material organism. He consists also of spirit; he is endowed with reason and freedom. He demands, therefore, a moral and religious order; and it is this order—and not considerations of a purely extraneous, material order—which has the greatest validity in the solution of problems relating to his life as an individual and as a member of society, and problems concerning individual states and their inter-relations.

209. It has been claimed that in an era of scientific and technical triumphs such as ours man can well afford to rely on his own powers, and construct a very good civilization without God. But the truth is that these very advances in science and technology frequently involve the whole human race in such difficulties as can only be solved in the light of a sincere faith in God, the Creator and Ruler of man and his world.

Supreme importance of spiritual and moral values

210. The almost limitless horizons opened up by scientific research only go to confirm this truth. More and more men are beginning to realize that science has so far done little more than scratch the surface of nature and reality. There are vast hidden depths still to be explored and adequately explained. Such men are appalled when they consider how these gigantic forces for good can be turned by science into engines of destruction. They realize then the supreme importance of spiritual and moral values, if scientific and technical progress is to be used in the service of civilization, and not involve the whole human race in irremediable disaster.

211. Furthermore, the increasing sense of dissatisfaction with worldly goods which is making itself felt among citizens of the wealthier nations, is rapidly destroying the treasured illusion of an earthly paradise. Men, too, are becoming more and more conscious

of their rights as human beings, rights which are universal and inviolable; and they are aspiring to more just and more human relations with their fellows. The effect of all this is to make the modern man more deeply aware of his own limitations, and to create in him a striving for spiritual values. All of which encourages Us in the hope that individuals and nations will one day learn to unite in a spirit of sincere understanding and profitable co-operation.

Part IV

THE REBUILDING OF A SOCIAL ORDER BASED ON TRUTH, JUSTICE AND LOVE

Incomplete and False Ideologies

The problem stated

212. After all this scientific and technical progress, and even because of it, the problem remains: how to build up a new order of society based on a more balanced human relationship between political communities on a national and international level?

The whole man

213. The attempt to find a solution to this problem has given birth to a number of theories. Some of these were little more than ephemeral; others have undergone, and are still undergoing, substantial change; others again are proving themselves less and less attractive to modern man.

Why is this? It is because these ideologies do not take account of the whole man, nor even of his most important part. In particular, they take little account of certain inevitable human weaknesses such as sickness and suffering, weaknesses which even the most advanced economic and social systems cannot completely eliminate. Finally, they fail to take account of that deep-rooted sense of religion which exists in all men everywhere, and which nothing, neither violence nor cunning, can eradicate.

214. The most fundamental modern error is that of imagining that man's natural sense of religion is nothing more than the out-

come of feeling or fantasy, to be eradicated from his soul as an anachronism and an obstacle to human progress. And yet this very need for religion reveals a man for what he is: a being created by God and tending always toward God. As we read in St. Augustine: "Lord, you have made us for yourself, and our hearts can find no rest until they rest in you."[46]

The real Source of justice, truth and love

215. Let men make all the technical and economic progress they can, there will be no peace nor justice in the world until they return to a sense of their dignity as creatures and sons of God, who is the first and final cause of all created being. Separated from God a man is but a monster, in himself and toward others; for the right ordering of human society presupposes the right ordering of man's conscience with God, who is Himself the source of all justice, truth and love.

216. Here is a spectacle for all the world to see: thousands of Our sons and brothers, whom We love so dearly, suffering years of bitter persecution in many lands, even those of an ancient Christian culture. And will not men who see clearly and compare the superior dignity of the persecuted with that refined barbarity of their oppressors, soon return to their senses, if indeed they have not already done so?

"Unless the Lord build the house . . ."

217. The most perniciously typical aspect of the modern era consists in the absurd attempt to reconstruct a solid and fruitful temporal order divorced from God, who is, in fact, the only foundation on which it can endure. In seeking to enhance man's greatness, men fondly imagine that they can do so by drying up the source from which that greatness springs and from which it is nourished. They want, that is, to restrain and, if possible, to eliminate the soul's upward surge toward God. But today's experience of so much disillusionment and bloodshed only goes to confirm those words of Scripture: "Unless the Lord build the house, they labor in vain that build it."[47]

[46] *Confessions* I, 1.   [47] *Ps.* 126, 1.

The Enduring Validity of the Church's Social Teaching

218. The permanent validity of the Catholic Church's social teaching admits of no doubt.

The fundamental principle

219. This teaching rests on one basic principle: individual human beings are the foundation, the cause and the end of every social institution. That is necessarily so, for men are by nature social beings. This fact must be recognized, as also the fact that they are raised in the plan of Providence to an order of reality which is above nature.

220. On this basic principle, which guarantees the sacred dignity of the individual, the Church constructs her social teaching. She has formulated, particularly over the past hundred years and through the efforts of a very well informed body of priests and laymen, a social doctrine which points out with clarity the sure way to social reconstruction. The principles she gives are of universal application, for they take human nature into account, and the varying conditions in which man's life is lived. They also take into account the principal characteristics of contemporary society, and are thus acceptable to all.

Must be studied, applied, taught

221. But today, more than ever, it is essential that this doctrine be known, assimilated, and put into effect in the form and manner that the different situations allow and demand. It is a difficult task indeed, yet a most noble one. To the performance of it We call, not only Our own sons and brothers scattered throughout the world, but also men of goodwill everywhere.

222. First, We must reaffirm most strongly that this Catholic social doctrine is an integral part of the Christian conception of life.

223. It is therefore Our urgent desire that this doctrine be studied more and more. First of all it should be taught as part of the daily curriculum in Catholic schools of every kind, particularly

seminaries, although We are not unaware that in some of these latter institutions this has been done for a long time now and in an outstanding way. We would also like to see it added to the religious instruction programs of parishes and of associations of the lay apostolate. It must be spread by every modern means at our disposal: daily newspapers, periodicals, popular and scientific publications, radio and television.

224. Our beloved sons, the laity, can do much to help this diffusion of Catholic social doctrine by studying it themselves and putting it into practice, and by zealously striving to make others understand it.

225. They should be convinced that the best way of demonstrating the truth and efficacy of this teaching is to show that it can provide the solution to present-day difficulties. They will thus win those people who are opposed to it through ignorance of it. Who knows, but a ray of its light may one day enter their minds.

Christian Education

226. It is not enough merely to formulate a social doctrine. It must be translated into reality. And this is particularly true of the Church's social doctrine, the light of which is truth, justice its objective, and love its driving force.

227. It is vitally important, therefore, that Our sons learn to understand this doctrine. They must be educated to it.

Theory and practice

228. No Christian education can be considered complete unless it covers every kind of obligation. It must therefore aim at implanting and fostering among the faithful an awareness of their duty to carry on their economic and social activities in a Christian manner.

229. The transition from theory to practice is of its very nature difficult; and it is especially so when one tries to reduce to concrete terms a social doctrine such as that of the Church. There are several reasons why this is so; among them We can mention man's deep-rooted selfishness, the materialism in which modern society is

steeped, and the difficulty of determining sometimes what precisely the demands of justice are in a given instance.

230. Consequently, a purely theoretical instruction in man's social and economic obligations is inadequate. People must also be shown ways in which they can properly fulfill these obligations.

231. In Our view, therefore, formal instruction, to be successful, must be supplemented by the students' active co-operation in their own training. They must gain an experimental knowledge of the subject, and that by their own positive action.

232. It is practice which makes perfect, even in such matters as the right use of liberty. Thus one learns Christian behavior in social and economic matters by actual Christian action in those fields.

Lay apostolate's role in social education

233. The lay apostolate, therefore, has an important role to play in social education—especially those associations and organizations which have as their specific objective the christianization of contemporary society. The members of these associations, besides profiting personally from their own day to day experience in this field, can also help in the social education of the rising generation by giving it the benefit of the experience they have gained.

Christian spirit—not hedonism

234. But We must remind you here of an important truth: the Christian conception of life demands of all—whether highborn or lowly—a spirit of moderation and sacrifice. That is what God calls us to by His grace.

235. There is, alas, a spirit of hedonism abroad today which beguiles men into thinking that life is nothing more than the quest for pleasure and the satisfaction of human passions. This attitude is disastrous. Its evil effects on soul and body are undeniable. Even on the natural level temperance and simplicity of life are the dictates of sound policy. On the supernatural level, the Gospels and the whole ascetic tradition of the Church require a sense of mortification and penance which assures the rule of the spirit over the flesh, and offers an efficacious means of expiating the punishment

due to sin, from which no one, except Jesus Christ and His Immaculate Mother, is exempt.

Practical Suggestions

Method of approach

236. There are three stages which should normally be followed in the reduction of social principles into practice. First, one reviews the concrete situation; secondly, one forms a judgment on it in the light of these same principles; thirdly, one decides what in the circumstances can and should be done to implement these principles. These are the three stages that are usually expressed in the three terms: *look, judge, act*.

237. It is important for our young people to grasp this method and to practice it. Knowledge acquired in this way does not remain merely abstract, but is seen as something that must be translated into action.

When differences arise . . .

238. Differences of opinion in the application of principles can sometimes arise even among sincere Catholics. When this happens, they should be careful not to lose their respect and esteem for each other. Instead, they should strive to find points of agreement for effective and suitable action, and not wear themselves out in interminable arguments, and, under pretext of the better or the best, omit to do the good that is possible and therefore obligatory.

239. In their economic and social activities, Catholics often come into contact with others who do not share their view of life. In such circumstances, they must, of course, bear themselves as Catholics and do nothing to compromise religion and morality. Yet at the same time they should show themselves animated by a spirit of understanding and unselfishness, ready to co-operate loyally in achieving objects which are good in themselves, or can be turned to good. Needless to say, when the hierarchy has made a decision on any point Catholics are bound to obey their directives. The Church has the right and obligation not merely to guard ethical and reli-

gious principles, but also to declare its authoritative judgment in the matter of putting these principles into practice.

The layman's responsibility

240. These, then, are the educational principles which must be put into effect. It is a task which belongs particularly to Our sons, the laity, for it is their lot to live an active life in the world and organize themselves for the attainment of temporal ends.

241. In performing this task, which is a noble one, they must not only be well qualified in their trade or profession and practice it in accordance with its own proper laws, they must also bring their professional activity into conformity with the Church's social teaching. Their attitude must be one of loyal trust and filial obedience to ecclesiastical authority.

They must remember, too, that if in the transaction of their temporal affairs they take no account of those social principles which the Church teaches, and which We now confirm, then they fail in their obligations and may easily violate the rights of others. They may even go so far as to bring discredit on the Church's teaching, lending substance to the opinion that, in spite of its intrinsic value, it is in fact powerless to direct men's lives.

MATTER AND SPIRIT

Immense progress, yet fearful decline

242. As We have noted already, modern man has greatly deepened and extended his knowledge of nature's laws, and has harnessed the forces of nature, making them subservient to his ends. The magnitude of his achievements deserves ungrudging admiration; nor is he yet at the end of his resources.

Nevertheless, in his striving to master and tranform the world around him he is in danger of forgetting and of destroying himself. As Our predecessor Pope Pius XI lamented in *Quadragesimo anno*: "And so bodily labor, which, even after original sin, was decreed by Providence for the good of man's body and soul, is in many instances changed into an instrument of perversion; for from the factory dead matter goes out improved, whereas men there are corrupted and degraded."[48]

243. Similarly, Our predecessor Pius XII rightly asserted that our age is marked by a clear contrast between the immense scientific and technical progress and the fearful human decline shown by "its monstrous masterpiece . . . transforming man into a giant of the physical world at the expense of his spirit, which is reduced to that of a pygmy in the supernatural and eternal world."[49]

244. And so the words of the Psalmist about the worshippers of false gods are strikingly verified today. Men are losing their own identity in their works, which they admire to the point of idolatry: "The idols of the Gentiles are silver and gold, the works of the hands of men."[50]

True hierarchy of values

245. In Our paternal care as universal Pastor of souls, We earnestly beg Our sons, immersed though they be in the business of this world, not to allow their consciences to sleep; not to lose sight of the true hierarchy of values.

246. Certainly, the Church teaches—and has always taught—that scientific and technical progress and the resultant material well-being are good things and mark an important phase in human civilization. But the Church teaches, too, that goods of this kind must be valued according to their true nature: as instruments used by man for the better attainment of his end. They help to make him a better man, both in the natural and the supernatural order.

247. May these warning words of the divine Master ever sound in men's ears: "For what doth it profit a man, if he gain the whole world and suffer the loss of his own soul? Or what exchange shall a man give for his soul?"[51]

Making Sunday holy

248. Allied to what We have said so far is the question of the Sunday rest.

---

[48] *AAS* 23 (1931) 221 *et seq.*
[49] Broadcast message, Christmas Eve, 1953: *AAS* 46 (1954) 10.
[50] *Ps.* 113, 4.   [51] *Matt.* 16, 26.

249. To safeguard man's dignity as a creature of God endowed with a soul in the image and likeness of God, the Church has always demanded a diligent observance of the third Commandment: "Remember that thou keep holy the sabbath day."[52] God certainly has the right and power to command man to devote one day a week to his duty of worshipping the eternal Majesty. Free from mundane cares, he should lift up his mind to the things of heaven, and look into the depths of his conscience, to see how he stands with God in respect of those necessary and inviolable relationships which must exist between the creature and his Creator.

250. In addition, man has a right to rest a while from work, and indeed a need to do so if he is to renew his bodily strength and to refresh his spirit by suitable recreation. He has also to think of his family, the unity of which depends so much on frequent contact and the peaceful living together of all its members.

251. Thus, religion and moral and physical well-being are one in demanding this periodic rest, and for many centuries now the Church has set aside Sunday as a special day of rest for the faithful, on which they participate in the Holy Sacrifice of the Mass, the memorial and application of Christ's redemptive work for souls.

252. Heavy in heart, We cannot but deplore the growing tendency in certain quarters to disregard this sacred law, if not to reject it outright. This attitude must inevitably impair the bodily and spiritual health of the workers, whose welfare We have so much at heart.

253. In the name of God, therefore, and for the sake of the material and spiritual interests of men, We call upon all, public authorities, employers and workers, to observe the precepts of God and His Church, and to remember their grave responsibilities before God and society.

The Christian's Work in the World

Not to lessen commitment

254. We have only been able to touch lightly upon this matter, but Our sons, the laity especially, must not suppose that they would

---

[52] *Exod.* 20, 8.

be acting prudently to lessen their personal Christian commitment in this passing world. On the contrary, We insist that they must intensify it and increase it continually.

255. In His solemn prayer for the Church's unity, Christ Our Lord did not ask His Father to remove His disciples from the world: "I pray not that thou shouldst take them out of the world, but that thou shouldst keep them from evil."[53] Let no man therefore imagine that a life of activity in the world is incompatible with spiritual perfection. The two can very well be harmonized. It is a gross error to suppose that a man cannot perfect himself except by putting aside all temporal activity, on the plea that such activity will inevitably lead him to compromise his personal dignity as a human being and as a Christian.

Perfection through daily work

256. That a man should develop and perfect himself through his daily work—which in most cases is of a temporal character—is perfectly in keeping with the plan of divine Providence. The Church today is faced with an immense task: to humanize and to Christianize this modern civilization of ours. The continued development of this civilization, indeed its very survival, demand and insist that the Church do her part in the world. That is why, as We said before, she claims the co-operation of her laity. In conducting their human affairs to the best of their ability, they must recognize that they are doing a service to humanity, in intimate union with God through Christ, and to God's greater glory. And St. Paul insisted: "Whether you eat or drink, or whatsoever else you do, do all to the glory of God."[54] "All whatsoever you do in word or in work, do all in the name of the Lord Jesus Christ, giving thanks to God and the Father by him."[55]

Greater efficiency in temporal affairs

257. To search for spiritual perfection and eternal salvation in the conduct of human affairs and institutions is not to rob these of

---

[53] *John* 17, 15.   [54] *1 Cor.* 10, 31.   [55] *Col.* 3, 17.

the power to achieve their immediate, specific ends, but to enhance this power.

The words of our divine Master are true for all time: "Seek ye therefore first the kingdom of God and his justice; and all these things shall be added unto you."[56] The man who is "light in the Lord"[57] and who walks as a "child of the light"[58] has a sure grasp of the fundamental demands of justice in all life's difficulties and complexities, obscured though they may be by so much individual, national and racial selfishness.

Animated, too, by the charity of Christ, he finds it impossible not to love his fellow men. He makes his own their needs, their sufferings and their joys. There is a sureness of touch in all his activity in every field. It is energetic, generous and considerate. For "charity is patient, is kind; charity envieth not, dealeth not perversely, is not puffed up, is not ambitious, seeketh not her own, is not provoked to anger, thinketh no evil; rejoiceth not in iniquity, but rejoiceth with the truth; beareth all things, believeth all things, hopeth all things, endureth all things."[59]

CONCLUSION

Living members of Christ's Mystical Body

258. In conclusion, venerable brethren, We would remind you of that sublime truth of Catholic doctrine: our incorporation as living members in Christ's Mystical Body, the Church, "For as the body is one and hath many members; and all the members of the body, whereas they are many, yet are one body; so also is Christ."[60]

259. We most earnestly beg all Our sons the world over, clergy and laity, to be deeply conscious of the dignity, the nobility, which is theirs through being grafted on to Christ as shoots on a vine: "I am the vine; you the branches."[61] They are thus called to a share in His own divine life; and since they are united in mind and spirit with the divine Redeemer even when they are engaged in the affairs of the world, their work becomes a continuation of His work, pene-

---

[56] *Matt.* 6, 33. [57] *Eph.* 5, 8. [58] Cf. *ibid.*
[59] *1 Cor.* 13, 4-7. [60] *1 Cor.* 12, 12. [61] *John* 15, 5.

trated with redemptive power. "He that abideth in me, and I in him, the same beareth much fruit."⁶²

Thus is man's work exalted and ennobled—so highly exalted that it leads to his own personal perfection of soul, and helps to extend to others the fruits of Redemption, all over the world. It becomes a means whereby the Christian way of life can leaven this civilization in which we live and work—leaven it with the ferment of the Gospel.

Era of immense possibilities

260. This era in which we live is in the grip of deadly errors; it is torn by deep disorders. But it is also an era which offers to those who work with the Church immense possibilities in the field of the apostolate. And therein lies our hope.

261. Venerable brethren and dear sons, We began with that wonderful encyclical of Pope Leo, and passed in review before you the various problems of our modern social life. We have given principles and directives which We exhort you earnestly to think over, and now, for your part, to put into effect. Your courageous cooperation in this respect will surely help to bring about the realization of Christ's Kingdom in this world, "a kingdom of truth and life; a kingdom of holiness and grace; a kingdom of justice, of love and of peace,"⁶³ which assures the enjoyment of those heavenly blessings for which we were created and for which we long most ardently.

Mother and Teacher

262. For here Our concern is with the doctrine of the Catholic and Apostolic Church. She is the Mother and Teacher of all nations. Her light illumines, enkindles and enflames. No age but hears her warning voice, vibrant with heavenly wisdom.

She is ever powerful to offer suitable, effective remedies for the increasing needs of men, and the sorrows and anxieties of this present life. Her words re-echo those of the Psalmist of old—words

---

⁶² *Ibid.* ⁶³ The Preface of *Christ the King.*

which never fail to raise our fainting spirits and give us courage: "I will hear what the Lord God will speak in me: for he will speak peace unto his people. And unto his saints: and unto them that are converted to the heart. Surely his salvation is near to them that fear him: that glory may dwell in our land. Mercy and truth have met each other: justice and peace have kissed. Truth is sprung out of the earth: and justice hath looked down from heaven. For the Lord will give goodness: and our earth shall yield her fruit. Justice shall walk before him: and shall set his steps in the way."[64]

May Christ reign

263. For some considerable time now, venerable brethren, Our solicitude for the Universal Church has been directed into the writing of this letter; and We wish to conclude it by voicing the following desires: May man's divine Redeemer "who of God is made unto us wisdom and justice and sanctification and redemption,"[65] reign and triumph gloriously throughout all ages, in all and over all. And, with the right ordering of human society, may all nations at last enjoy true prosperity, happiness and peace.

264. In earnest of these wishes, and as a pledge of Our fatherly goodwill, may the Apostolic Blessing, which We give in the Lord with all Our heart, descend upon you, venerable brethren, and upon all the faithful entrusted to your care, and especially upon those who respond with generosity to Our appeals.

Given at Rome, at St. Peter's, on the 15th day of May, in the year 1961, the third of Our Pontificate.

JOHN PP. XXIII

[64] *Ps.* 84, 9 *et seq.*
[65] 1 *Cor.* 1, 30.

A Commentary on

PACEM IN TERRIS

by Rev. John F. Cronin, S.S.

TO MOST OF THE world, the encyclical "Peace on Earth" was as unexpected as it was welcome. As a rule, Pope John found it difficult to conceal his enthusiasms. Thus, in early 1961, he announced that a social encyclical would be soon forthcoming even though it [*Mater et Magistra*] did not appear until nearly six months later. By contrast, the preparation of the peace encyclical was a closely held secret. It literally burst on the world on Holy Thursday, 1963, less than two months before the Pope's death. In fact, its preparation was quite likely prompted by the Cuban crisis of October, 1962, with its overtones of possible world nuclear war.

Historians will find it difficult to find a parallel to this document in terms of widespread and genuine acclaim. Certainly no comparable papal utterance was ever received with the sustained enthusiasm generated by this encyclical. If secular history is consulted for declarations of equally far-reaching import, one thinks in terms of the *Magna Carta* or the Declaration of Independence.

Protestant and Jewish comment was no less favorable than Catholic appraisals. The encyclical immediately sparked suggestions for a national or even international interreligious congress on peace, to be based primarily on the words of Pope John. The President of the United States greeted this message of peace, yet the Chairman of the Council of Ministers of the U.S.S.R. was likewise enthusiastic. The spirit of the encyclical permeated a major foreign-policy address given by President Kennedy shortly after it appeared. It may well have been a factor influencing the 1963 test-ban treaty concluded by the major nuclear powers.

What are the causes of this unique reaction? Of course, the subject matter had much to do with the worldwide approval. The love of peace is a common human trait, and this yearning is deeply reinforced by knowledge of the consequences of nuclear war. When the Communists of the Soviet Union were compelled to air their dispute with the Chinese Communists, their reply to Peiping was in terms of the fearful consequences of atomic strife. Because global war is unthinkable today, peace is more than ever the common language of mankind.

But other popes have spoken eloquently of peace. Pope Pius XII treated the subject at such length and with such insight that he was often called the Pope of Peace. Surely this encyclical owes much to the writings of Pope Pius, as even a casual glance at the footnotes will show. Yet even the magnificent Christmas addresses of Pope Pius did not evoke the enthusiasm which greeted *Pacem in Terris.*

One of the unique qualities of this encyclical was its literary excellence. Even when it was restating and summarizing traditional Catholic teaching on peace and human rights, it did this with a clarity, simplicity, and eloquence rarely found in pontifical documents. Its treatment is orderly and unified. Because of its simplicity, it was not too difficult to achieve very readable translations. (It should be noted, however, that the various English translations circulating in this country differ among themselves in quite a few key points. At least part of this is due to the fact that, because of subsequent changes in the official Latin text, the Italian version itself differed from the Latin—and some of the English translations circulating in this country were based almost exclusively on the Italian. The translation used here was prepared directly from the official Latin text.)

Literary style, important as it is, must be considered of secondary importance in the present context. The greatness of this encyclical must rest primarily upon its content. Two aspects of this content are outstanding. First of all, the encyclical is a majestic summary of the moral and religious ideals that should underlie society. It presents the citizen, the state, and world society as seen in a context of truth, justice, love, and freedom. This is a beautiful blueprint for peace, and its appeal to all men of good will is understandable.

The second major feature of the encyclical is the new initiative which it opens in man's quest for peace. It was an important part of the effort to make the Church a fourth force in the modern world. We may consider as two major forces in our time the protagonists of the Cold War, disregarding for the moment the difference on this subject between the U.S.S.R. and the Chinese People's Republic. Then there is the so-called neutralist bloc, which for political reasons tries to remain aloof from the power struggle of the atomic giants. Pope John would also have the Church neutral in this conflict, but for moral rather than political reasons. He wants the Church to be able to promote peace in season and out of season. Moral judgments which religion must pronounce upon the system of communism should not impede religious leaders from promoting peaceful initiatives with Communist powers.

The Moral Basis of Society

The reception given to this encyclical by the Communist world is a source of continuing amazement to those familiar with its contents. One might have expected a selective endorsement of certain passages, such as those advocating disarmament, discouraging nuclear war, and suggesting a possible détente with Communist nations and leaders. But it was difficult to foresee the comparative silence—almost acquiescence by default—in regard to the first three parts of this document. Here the Pope lays the foundation for subsequent discussions of peace among nations. And these foundations are exclusively spiritual!

Order in the universe proclaims the greatness of God. In contrast to the astonishing rule of law in the physical world, there is disunity among individuals and among nations. But this disunity does not reflect the absence of law. The law which governs man is of an entirely different type from the law governing the physical world. Man is ruled by moral law, equally binding in its directives, but subject to the requirement that man must choose freely to follow God's law. When men choose to disregard the moral law, we have disorder, strife, and war.

To study human society, one must learn God's purpose in creating man as a social being. This study begins with the human person, intelligent and free in his nature. Consequently man has rights and duties flowing from this nature, and enhanced by the higher order of grace making men "sons and friends of God, and heirs to eternal glory." (No. 10) The encyclical enumeration of these rights is thorough. The Pope begins with the right to life and the economic and social consequences of this fundamental right. In effect, man has a moral claim upon society to the opportunity to work and to earn his livelihood. When through no fault of his own he is deprived of the means for earning his living, society should look after his needs.

Higher than social and economic rights are those associated with the intellectual and spiritual aspects of man's nature. Man has the right to be respected and to keep his good name, to seek the truth, to freedom of speech, and "to be accurately informed about public events." (No. 12) He has a moral claim to share in the benefits of culture, to receive a good general and technical education, and to advance in life in keeping with natural talent and acquired skill.

Then there is the right "to worship God in accordance with the right dictates of his own conscience, and to profess his religion both in private and in public." (No. 14) The translation used here differs from those widely circulated in the United States: "according to the dictates of an upright conscience" (Vatican Press) and "according to the sincere dictates of his own conscience." (N.C.W.C. edition) This translation divergence highlights a point of controversy among churchmen in their discussions of freedom of conscience. Reduced to its essentials the question would seem to be this: Under what circumstances and to what degree, if any, does a person with erroneous but sincere convictions have a strict "right" to pursue these convictions, and what duties if any does this impose on others? The Latin literally translated has an element of obscurity (perhaps calculated) in regard to this question. One might hazard the guess that the Pope favored the more modern view in this matter but did not wish to make a final decision while it was before Vatican Council II.

Other rights enumerated are the right to choose one's state in life, whether married or single, the rights of the family including parental control over support and education of children, and various economic rights which are closely associated with family living. Man must be given the opportunity to work and the chance to exercise personal initiative in his occupation. Working conditions should be suitable for health and welfare. The job must be suited to a worker's degree of responsibility. It should pay a living wage. Man has the right to own property, but also a social responsibility in this ownership.

As a social being, man has the right of association. Such associations should be free and permit initiative on the part of their members. Indeed, a wide variety of societies are essential for the safeguarding of man's freedom and dignity. Social life also demands freedom of movement, and this includes the right to emigrate. Man must be allowed to take an active part in public life. He is entitled to full legal protection of his rights.

Since rights are founded in nature, it follows that the rights of one man give rise to corresponding duties in other men: "That men should recognize and perform their respective rights and duties is imperative to a well ordered society." (No. 31) In the economic sphere, such a society should provide men with abundant resources. A morally ordered society will be founded on truth, justice, love, and freedom. It will be primarily a spiritual reality.

By its means enlightened men can share their knowledge of the truth, can claim their rights and fulfill their duties, receive encouragement in their aspirations for the goods of the spirit, share their enjoyment of the wholesome pleasures of the world, strive continually to pass on to others all that is best in themselves, and make their own the spiritual riches of others. (No. 36)

When society is formed on a basis of rights and duties, men have an immediate grasp of spiritual and intellectual values, and have no difficulty in understanding what is meant by truth, justice, love and freedom. . . . Inspired by such principles, they attain to a better knowledge of the true God—a personal God transcending human nature. They recognize that their relationship with God forms the very foundation of their life—the interior life of the spirit, and the life which they live in the society of their fellows. (No. 45)

Such is the ideal basis of human society. It is not often that this ideal is fully realized in any part of the world. But it does make a real difference when men strive in this direction, even if such striving may not be explicitly based on spiritual values. Instinctive natural goodness may lead this way. Religious creeds may help, even when a given faith may make no allowances for natural law. The greatest enemy to a society of this nature is a philosophical creed that denies human dignity and rejects the concept of rights and duties. In our times, Nazism, fascism, and communism have virtually denied individual rights and have deified the state or the ruling forces in society.

If we grant man's yearning for truth, then Pope John has done mankind a signal service in presenting so well the real foundations of society. Even when men fail to live up to these ideals, possibly through weakness or selfishness, they can at least acknowledge the truth and hope one day to live up to its demands. By contrast, if their ruling philosophy rejects the doctrine of natural rights, it will take longer for truth to prevail and for the leaders of society to recognize the false premises upon which they have built. Part II of the encyclical deals with problems of this type.

The Individual and the State

The discussion of man and society presupposes the true nature of society, as a rich texture of interrelated associations, capped by the civil state as its highest natural organ. By nature man forms many societies. He achieves order and unity in society through civil government, which exists to provide for the welfare of individuals and the lesser social groups. Since this civil society is necessary for orderly and peaceful human existence, it can be said that civil authority is a product of man's nature and hence of God who created this nature. Civil authority is spiritual in origin and moral in nature. It has the right to use force to carry out its legitimate decrees, but its primary appeal is to the consciences of citizens.

> Governmental authority, therefore, is a postulate of the moral order and derives from God. Consequently, laws and decrees passed in contravention of the moral order, and hence of the divine will, can have no binding force in conscience. . . . (No. 51)

Of course, the fact that authority comes from God does not preclude our democratic right to choose rulers and determine the proper procedures of government. Thus we may choose our rulers democratically, but then must obey their just decrees as binding in conscience.

Under civil society men, both as individuals and members of lesser organizations, contribute to the general welfare. They harmonize their own interests with the needs of others. Civil authority has primary responsibility for seeking the common good of the community, which means the welfare of the state and of each of its citizens. "It is generally accepted that the common good is best safeguarded when personal rights and duties are guaranteed." (No. 60) This must not be interpreted in the *laissez-faire*, individualistic sense of "classical liberalism" (corresponding to the extreme right today). On the contrary, civil government must see that social progress accompanies economic development, so that no citizen suffers from extreme disparity in relation to those who are well off.

This is most likely to happen under democratic government. While Pope John reiterates the classic teaching that the Church favors no particular form of government, provided only it is just, there is little doubt that for the modern world he prefers constitutional democracy. He spells out such details as the threefold division of authority; executive, legislative, and judicial. Public officials should be appointed for limited terms. The basic constitution should contain a bill of rights. Men have a right to take an active part in government, although this right may be affected by the degree of political development of a state.

To summarize, the Pope comes just short of saying that democracy is the ideal form of government, and other forms can be tolerated as concessions to human weakness. A citizenry may lack the economic, educational, and cultural background for democratic rule. But this is a weakness that should be remedied. Drastic as this approach may seem, in view of traditional Catholic political teaching and the political encyclicals of Pope Leo XIII, it is not novel. The political views of St. Thomas Aquinas and St. Robert Bellarmine were basically democratic. Pope Pius XII, in his 1944 Christmas message, came out strongly for a democratic form of government. It is only fair to state that the democratic tradition has always had strong backers within the Church. What seemed to be opposite trends can usually be explained in terms of special historical conditions.

Relations Between States

Having built up an imposing structure of moral order in describing human society and the relationship between man and the state, it is only natural that a similar basis will be urged for dealings among states. This follows from the fact that rulers of states are still human persons, bound by the moral law. Moreover, God's law is as valid in relations between states as it is between individuals. There is a universal common good that affects states, just as there is a common good within individual governments. Accordingly, we can assert that truth, justice, love, and freedom must also prevail among the nations of the world.

This conclusion leads to important practical consequences. Among the more notable are these:

1) Nations are equal in natural dignity. Cultural and other differences are no excuse for any nation feeling superior to another. Rather the more fortunate nations should help those who may lack certain advantages.

2) The rights of minorities should be respected. But these minorities in turn must play their proper role in the nation in which they dwell.

3) Political refugees should be given asylum and every opportunity to develop a new life in the country to which they have fled.

4) Atomic armament presents a monstrous threat to mankind. Nuclear testing for war purposes should cease; nuclear weapons should be banned; and there should be a "suitable disarmament program, with an effective system of mutual control." (No. 112) True and lasting peace does not hinge upon balanced deterrents, but rather upon mutual trust. The value of such a peace is the strongest argument in favor of its feasibility.

> In their deliberations together, let men of outstanding wisdom and influence give serious thought to the problem of achieving a more human adjustment of relations between states throughout the world. It must be an adjustment that is based on mutual trust, sincerity in ne-

gotiation, and the faithful fulfilment of obligations assumed. Every aspect of the problem must be examined, so that eventually there may emerge some point of agreement from which to initiate treaties which are sincere, lasting, and beneficial in their effects. (No. 118)

5) Developing nations should be aided by wealthier peoples, so that they may enjoy their proper place in the modern world.

Of these points, by far the most controversial is the call for disarmament and mutual negotiations. Those who dismiss this plea as impractical and utopian misread the mind of the Pope. He is not seeking some vague future time in which nations will live together in real peace and harmony. He is convinced that the time is now, and that sincere negotiations will gradually build up trust. He even dares to state that "love, not fear, must dominate the relationship between individuals and between nations." (No. 129)

There are signs that powerful world leaders are beginning cautiously to agree with Pope John. When leaders of the Western world approach the Soviet Union today, they do this with full awareness of the difficulties they confront. They are not naive pacifists, nor do they assume that good will alone is enough in dealing with the political realists of the Kremlin. But they feel that grounds exist today to hope that a real détente meets the mutual needs of both sides in the Cold War.

A World Political Community

No less optimistic is the encyclical's call for a world political community. On the assumption that the existing system of divergent national sovereignties is inadequate to meet the pressing needs of security and peace in the world, there is need for a world government with adequate power to confront these urgent needs.

> Today the universal common good presents us with problems which are world-wide in their dimensions; problems, therefore, which cannot be solved except by a public authority with power, organization, and means coextensive with these problems, and with a world-wide sphere of activity. Consequently the moral order itself demands the establishment of some such general form of public authority. (No. 137)

Such an authority must be established by mutual consent, not by force. It must respect the rights of the human person and also the sovereignty of its member states. It should not interfere with their internal problems, but only deal with those issues which "because of their extreme gravity, vastness, and urgency must be considered too difficult for the rulers of individual states to solve with any degree of success." (No. 140)

After discussing the abstract need for world government, the Pope praised the work of the United Nations and specifically, with mild reservations, the Universal Declaration of Human Rights. He concludes this section with the clear wish that the U.N. may develop into the world government described earlier. "May the day be not long delayed when every human being can find in this organization an effective safeguard of his personal rights. . . ." (No. 145)

Once again there is the reaction on the part of some that the Pope is entirely utopian in his hopes. When the encyclical was written, the U.N. was faced with both political and financial difficulties, and many feared that it would not survive. But Pope John felt that what must be done, would be done. Since the world cannot afford to break up into competing blocs, with the danger of thermonuclear war always in the offing, it must overcome present difficulties and move toward a real, effective community of nations.

All these endeavors offer a real challenge for the apostolic Catholic. The pastoral exhortations regarding this challenge largely parallel those of *Mater et Magistra.*

> What has so far been achieved is insufficient compared with what needs to be done; all men must realize that. Every day provides a more important, a more fitting enterprise to which they must turn their hands —industry, trade unions, professional organizations, insurance, cultural institutions, the law, politics, medical and recreational facilities, and other such activities. The age in which we live needs all these things. It is an age in which men, having discovered the atom and achieved the breakthrough into outer space, are now exploring other avenues, leading to almost endless horizons. (No. 156)

As always, the emphasis of Pope John is on the positive and the constructive. He is much happier showing people opportunities to do good than warning them of evils and dangers.

WORKING WITH THOSE WHO DIFFER FROM US

Obviously this apostolic work is not to be done exclusively within the Catholic community. There is to be co-operation with others who are also Christian and with non-Christians who are reasonable men, men of natural moral integrity. Such persons differ from us in belief. Differences may involve judgments on both sides that others are partially in error, yet this should not dissuade sincere men from warm-hearted cooperation. One distinguishes between error and the person who falls into error. We can rightly assume that he too seeks the truth and hope that he will find it. Hence, far from being diffident about such cooperation, we should rather consider this an important part of our apostolic mission.

In the same manner, we distinguish between a philosophy of life which happens to be false, and "economic, social, cultural, and political undertakings, even when such undertakings draw their origin and inspiration from that philosophy." (No. 159) The philosophy may remain the same, but movements change, even when expressly based on false philosophy. There can be good and commendable elements in such movements. Accordingly, contacts with such sources may offer unexpected fruit, granted that we must be prudent in these matters and docile to directives of ecclesiastical authority.

These instructions are cryptic and there is no universal agreement as to their meaning. It is widely held that they apply to contacts with the Communist world and supply the *rationale* for the negotiations between the Holy See and Communist nations which were being conducted as the encyclical was written. But the principles as given in the encyclical are general in nature, and we cannot quarrel with those who also see in them reference to anticlerical movements in Europe and Latin America, or the "opening to the left" in Italian politics, Spanish fascism, or any similar accommodation with historic antagonists.

Those who consider these passages as directed primarily at Communist nations find them in complete harmony with the peace message of the encyclical. While Vatican negotiations with Communist powers can have a legitimate short-range objective of securing better conditions for believers behind the Iron Curtain, it is almost certain that broader aims are also envisaged. It is a fact that conditions have changed within Communist countries. Communist Russia is not the same as Communist China, nor are conditions exactly the same in Poland, Hungary, and Rumania. All that is said in this encyclical about the power of truth, justice, love, and freedom may, in the long run, be applicable to these powers. This is not only a conclusion of Christian optimism, but it also follows from a careful reading of history. Revolutions founded on false philosophy have, in the past, lost their original coloration as reason and common sense triumphed over erroneous dogma.

But we must remember that the papal suggestions, as interpreted here, are precisely and carefully formulated. There is no basis to the view, spread in some American circles, that the Church has gone soft on communism. Nor are these principles meant to give *carte blanche* for indiscriminate co-operation with Communists or united-front activities with them. We hope that Communists will change their principles; we do not assert that a radical change has already taken place. But civilized, Christian dialogue is more likely to promote such change than is the use of invective and the adoption by us of the worst tactics of Leninism.

Conclusion

We conclude this analysis with two sublime quotations from the encyclical, this time, for literary reasons, using part of the Vatican Press translation:

> "There is an immense task incumbent upon all men of good will, namely, the task of restoring the relations of the human family in truth, in justice, in love, and in freedom: the relations among individual human beings; among citizens and their own countries, among nations themselves; and finally among individuals, families, intermediate associations, and nations on the one hand, and the world community on the other. This is a most exalted task, for it is the task of bringing about true peace in the order established by God." (No. 163)

The Pope calls for an increase in the number of those devoted to this task: "For it is an imperative of duty; it is a requirement of love. Every believer in this world of ours must be a spark of light, a center of love, a vivifying leaven amidst his fellow men: and he will be this all the more perfectly the more closely he lives in communion with God in the intimacy of his own soul." (No. 164)

PACEM IN TERRIS

An Encyclical of Pope John XXIII
to the Whole World

- *Natural dignity of human beings*
- *Mutual rights and duties*
- *Individuals and government*
- *Relations between states*
- *Refugees, disarmament, mutual aid*
- *A world authority*
- *Error and the errant*

PEACE ON EARTH—which man throughout the ages has so longed for and sought after—can never be established, never guaranteed, except by the diligent observance of the divinely established order.

Order in the universe

2. That a marvelous order predominates in the world of living beings and in the forces of nature, is the plain lesson which the progress of modern research and the discoveries of technology teach us. And it is part of the greatness of man that he can appreciate that order, and devise the means for harnessing those forces for his own benefit.

3. But what emerges first and foremost from the progress of scientific knowledge and the inventions of technology is the infinite greatness of God Himself, who created both man and the universe. Yes; out of nothing He made all things, and filled them with the fullness of His own wisdom and goodness. Hence, these are the words

the holy psalmist uses in praise of God: "O Lord, our Lord: how admirable is thy name in the whole earth!"[1] And elsewhere he says: "How great are thy works, O Lord! Thou hast made all things in wisdom."[2]

Moreover,[2a] God created man "in His own image and likeness,"[3] endowed him with intelligence and freedom, and made him lord of creation. All this the psalmist proclaims when he says: "Thou hast made him a little less than the angels: thou hast crowned him with glory and honor, and hast set him over the works of thy hands. Thou hast subjected all things under his feet."[4]

Order in human beings

4. And yet there is a disunity among individuals and among nations which is in striking contrast to this perfect order in the universe. One would think that the relationships that bind men together could only be governed by force.

5. But the world's Creator has stamped man's inmost being with an order revealed to man by his conscience; and his conscience insists on his preserving it. Men "show the work of the law written in their hearts. Their conscience bears witness to them."[5] And how could it be otherwise? All created being reflects the infinite wisdom of God. It reflects it all the more clearly, the higher it stands in the scale of perfection.[6]

6. But the mischief is often caused by erroneous opinions. Many people think that the laws which govern man's relations with the State are the same as those which regulate the blind, elemental forces of the universe. But it is not so; the laws which govern men are quite different. The Father of the universe has inscribed them in man's nature, and that is where we must look for them; there and nowhere else.

7. These laws clearly indicate how a man must behave toward

---

[1] *Ps.* 8, 1.   [2] *Ps.* 103, 24.
[2a] In the Latin text this paragraph is part of the preceding one, hence we have not assigned it a number. For format reasons we have broken paragraphs down in a few places but have kept our numbering system keyed to the Latin paragraphs.—Ed.
[3] Cf. *Gen.* 1, 26.   [4] *Ps.* 8, 6-8.
[5] *Rom.* 2, 15.   [6] Cf. *Ps.* 18, 8-11.

his fellows in society, and how the mutual relationships between the members of a State and its officials are to be conducted. They show too what principles must govern the relations between States; and finally, what should be the relations between individuals or States on the one hand, and the world-wide community of nations on the other. Men's common interests make it imperative that at long last a world-wide community of nations be established.

PART I

ORDER BETWEEN MEN

Every man is a person with rights and duties

8. We must devote our attention first of all to that order which should prevail among men.

9. Any well-regulated and productive association of men in society demands the acceptance of one fundamental principle: that each individual man is truly a person. His is a nature, that is, endowed with intelligence and free will. As such he has rights and duties, which together flow as a direct consequence from his nature. These rights and duties are universal and inviolable, and therefore altogether inalienable.[7]

10. When, furthermore, we consider man's personal dignity from the standpoint of divine revelation, inevitably our estimate of it is incomparably increased. Men have been ransomed by the blood of Jesus Christ. Grace has made them sons and friends of God, and heirs to eternal glory.

RIGHTS

The right to life and to a worthy standard of living

11. But first We must speak of man's rights. Man has the right to live. He has the right to bodily integrity and to the means necessary for the proper development of life, particularly food, clothing, shelter, medical care, rest, and finally, the necessary social services.

---

[7] Cf. Pius XII's broadcast message, Christmas 1942, *AAS* 35 (1943) 9-24; and John XXIII's sermon, Jan. 4, 1963, *AAS* 55 (1963) 89-91.

In consequence, he has the right to be looked after in the event of ill-health; disability stemming from his work; widowhood; old age; enforced unemployment; or whenever through no fault of his own he is deprived of the means of livelihood.[8]

Rights pertaining to moral and cultural values

12. Moreover, man has a natural right to be respected. He has a right to his good name. He has a right to freedom in investigating the truth, and—within the limits of the moral order and the common good—to freedom of speech and publication, and to freedom to pursue whatever profession he may choose. He has the right, also, to be accurately informed about public events.

13. He has the natural right to share in the benefits of culture, and hence to receive a good general education, and a technical or professional training consistent with the degree of educational development in his own country. Furthermore, a system must be devised for affording gifted members of society the opportunity of engaging in more advanced studies, with a view to their occupying, as far as possible, positions of responsibility in society in keeping with their natural talent and acquired skill.[9]

The right to worship God according to one's conscience

14. Also among man's rights is that of being able to worship God in accordance with the right dictates of his own conscience, and to profess his religion both in private and in public. According to the clear teaching of Lactantius, "this is the very condition of our birth, that we render to the God who made us that just homage which is His due; that we acknowledge Him alone as God, and follow Him. It is from this *ligature* of piety, which binds us and joins us to God, that religion derives its name."[10]

Hence, too, Pope Leo XIII declared that "true freedom, freedom worthy of the sons of God, is that freedom which most truly safeguards the dignity of the human person. It is stronger than any

---

[8] Cf. Pius XI's encyclical *"Divini Redemptoris," AAS* 29 (1937) 78; and Pius XII's broadcast message, Pentecost, June 1, 1941, *AAS* 33 (1941) 195-205.
[9] Cf. Pius XII's broadcast message, Christmas 1942, *AAS* 35 (1943) 9-24.
[10] *Divinae Institutiones*, lib. IV, c.28.2; *PL* 6,535.

violence or injustice. Such is the freedom which has always been desired by the Church, and which she holds most dear. It is the sort of freedom which the Apostles resolutely claimed for themselves. The apologists defended it in their writings; thousands of martyrs consecrated it with their blood."[11]

The right to choose freely one's state in life

15. Human beings have also the right to choose for themselves the kind of life which appeals to them: whether it is to found a family—in the founding of which both the man and the woman enjoy equal rights and duties—or to embrace the priesthood or the religious life.[12]

16. The family, founded upon marriage freely contracted, one and indissoluble, must be regarded as the natural, primary cell of human society. The interests of the family, therefore, must be taken very specially into consideration in social and economic affairs, as well as in the spheres of faith and morals. For all of these have to do with strengthening the family and assisting it in the fulfilment of its mission.

17. Of course, the support and education of children is a right which belongs primarily to the parents.[13]

Economic rights

18. In the economic sphere, it is evident that a man has the inherent right not only to be given the opportunity to work, but also to be allowed the exercise of personal initiative in the work he does.[14]

19. The conditions in which a man works form a necessary corollary to these rights. They must not be such as to weaken his physical or moral fibre, or militate against the proper development of adolescents to manhood. Women must be accorded such condi-

---

[11] Encyclical *"Libertas praestantissimum,"* Acta Leonis XIII, VIII, 1888, pp. 237-38.
[12] Cf. Pius XII's broadcast message, Christmas 1942, AAS 35 (1943) 9-24.
[13] Cf. Pius XI's encyclical *"Casti connubii,"* AAS 22 (1930) 539-92, and Pius XII's broadcast message, Christmas 1942, AAS 35 (1943) 9-24.
[14] Cf. Pius XII's broadcast message, Pentecost, June 1, 1941, AAS 33 (1941) 201.

tions of work as are consistent with their needs and responsibilities as wives and mothers.[15]

20. A further consequence of man's personal dignity is his right to engage in economic activities suited to his degree of responsibility.[16] The worker is likewise entitled to a wage that is determined in accordance with the precepts of justice. This needs stressing. The amount a worker receives must be sufficient, in proportion to available funds, to allow him and his family a standard of living consistent with human dignity. Pope Pius XII expressed it in these terms:

"Nature imposes work upon man as a duty, and man has the corresponding natural right to demand that the work he does shall provide him with the means of livelihood for himself and his children. Such is nature's categorical imperative for the preservation of man."[17]

21. As a further consequence of man's nature, he has the right to the private ownership of property, including that of productive goods. This, as We have said elsewhere, is "a right which constitutes so efficacious a means of asserting one's personality and exercising responsibility in every field, and an element of solidity and security for family life, and of greater peace and prosperity in the State."[18]

22. Finally, it is opportune to point out that the right to own private property entails a social obligation as well.[19]

The right of meeting and association

23. Men are by nature social, and consequently they have the right to meet together and to form associations with their fellows. They have the right to confer on such associations the type of organization which they consider best calculated to achieve their

---

[15] Cf. Leo XIII's encyclical *"Rerum novarum,"* Acta Leonis XIII, XI, 1891, pp. 128-29.
[16] Cf. John XXIII's encyclical *"Mater et Magistra,"* AAS 53 (1961) 422; see p. 271 above.
[17] Cf. Pius XII's broadcast message, Pentecost, June 1, 1941, AAS 33 (1941) 201.
[18] John XXIII's encyclical *"Mater et Magistra,"* AAS 53 (1961) 428; see p. 278 above.
[19] Cf. *ibid.,* p. 430; see p. 280 above.

objectives. They have also the right to exercise their own initiative and act on their own responsibility within these associations for the attainment of the desired results.[20]

24. As We insisted in Our encyclical *Mater et Magistra,* the founding of a great many such intermediate groups or societies for the pursuit of aims which it is not within the competence of the individual to achieve efficiently, is a matter of great urgency. Such groups and societies must be considered absolutely essential for the safeguarding of man's personal freedom and dignity, while leaving intact a sense of responsibility.[21]

The right to emigrate and immigrate

25. Again, every human being has the right to freedom of movement and of residence within the confines of his own State. When there are just reasons in favor of it, he must be permitted to emigrate to other countries and take up residence there.[22] The fact that he is a citizen of a particular State does not deprive him of membership in the human family, nor of citizenship in that universal society, the common, world-wide fellowship of men.

Political rights

26. Finally, man's personal dignity involves his right to take an active part in public life, and to make his own contribution to the common welfare of his fellow citizens. As Pope Pius XII said, "man as such, far from being an object or, as it were, an inert element in society, is rather its subject, its basis and its purpose; and so must he be esteemed."[23]

27. As a human person he is entitled to the legal protection of his rights, and such protection must be effective, unbiased, and strictly just. To quote again Pope Pius XII: "In consequence of that juridical order willed by God, man has his own inalienable

---

[20] Cf. Leo XIII's encyclical *"Rerum novarum," Acta Leonis XIII,* XI, 1891, pp. 134-142; Pius XI's encyclical *"Quadragesimo anno,"* AAS 23 (1931) 199-200; and Pius XII's encyclical *"Sertum laetitiae,"* AAS 31 (1939) 635-44.
[21] Cf. AAS 53 (1961) 430; TPS, VII, 318.
[22] Cf. Pius XII's broadcast message, Christmas 1952, AAS 45 (1953) 36-46.
[23] Cf. Pius XII's broadcast message, Christmas 1944, AAS 37 (1945) 12.

right to juridical security. To him is assigned a certain, well-defined sphere of law, immune from arbitrary attack."[24]

DUTIES

Rights and duties necessarily linked in the one person

28. The natural rights of which We have so far been speaking are inextricably bound up with as many duties, all applying to one and the same person. These rights and duties derive their origin, their sustenance, and their indestructibility from the natural law, which in conferring the one imposes the other.

29. Thus, for example, the right to live involves the duty to preserve one's life; the right to a decent standard of living, the duty to live in a becoming fashion; the right to be free to seek out the truth, the duty to devote oneself to an ever deeper and wider search for it.

Reciprocity of rights and duties between persons

30. Once this is admitted, it follows that in human society one man's natural right gives rise to a corresponding duty in other men; the duty, that is, of recognizing and respecting that right. Every basic human right draws its authoritative force from the natural law, which confers it and attaches to it its respective duty. Hence, to claim one's rights and ignore one's duties, or only half fulfill them, is like building a house with one hand and tearing it down with the other.

Mutual collaboration

31. Since men are social by nature, they must live together and consult each other's interests. That men should recognize and perform their respective rights and duties is imperative to a well ordered society. But the result will be that each individual will make his whole-hearted contribution to the creation of a civic order in which rights and duties are ever more diligently and more effectively observed.

[24] Cf. Pius XII's broadcast message, Christmas 1942, *AAS* 35 (1943) 21.

32. For example, it is useless to admit that a man has a right to the necessities of life, unless we also do all in our power to supply him with means sufficient for his livelihood.

33. Hence society must not only be well ordered, it must also provide men with abundant resources. This postulates not only the mutual recognition and fulfillment of rights and duties, but also the involvement and collaboration of all men in the many enterprises which our present civilization makes possible, encourages or indeed demands.

An attitude of responsibility

34. Man's personal dignity requires besides that he enjoy freedom and be able to make up his own mind when he acts. In his association with his fellows, therefore, there is every reason why his recognition of rights, observance of duties, and many-sided collaboration with other men, should be primarily a matter of his own personal decision. Each man should act on his own initiative, conviction, and sense of responsibility, not under the constant pressure of external coercion or enticement. There is nothing human about a society that is welded together by force. Far from encouraging, as it should, the attainment of man's progress and perfection, it is merely an obstacle to his freedom.

Social life in truth, justice, charity and freedom

35. Hence, before a society can be considered well-ordered, creative, and consonant with human dignity, it must be based on truth. St. Paul expressed this as follows: "Putting away lying, speak ye the truth every man with his neighbor, for we are members one of another."[25] And so will it be, if each man acknowledges sincerely his own rights and his own duties toward others.

Human society, as We here picture it, demands that men be guided by justice, respect the rights of others and do their duty. It demands, too, that they be animated by such love as will make them feel the needs of others as their own, and induce them to share their

---

[25] *Eph.* 4, 25.

goods with others, and to strive in the world to make all men alike heirs to the noblest of intellectual and spiritual values. Nor is this enough; for human society thrives on freedom, namely, on the use of means which are consistent with the dignity of its individual members, who, being endowed with reason, assume responsibility for their own actions.

36. And so, dearest sons and brothers, we must think of human society as being primarily a spiritual reality. By its means enlightened men can share their knowledge of the truth, can claim their rights and fulfill their duties, receive encouragement in their aspirations for the goods of the spirit, share their enjoyment of all the wholesome pleasures of the world, and strive continually to pass on to others all that is best in themselves and to make their own the spiritual riches of others. It is these spiritual values which exert a guiding influence on culture, economics, social institutions, political movements and forms, laws, and all the other components which go to make up the external community of men and its continual development.

God and the moral order

37. Now the order which prevails in human society is wholly incorporeal in nature. Its foundation is truth, and it must be brought into effect by justice. It needs to be animated and perfected by men's love for one another, and, while preserving freedom intact, it must make for an equilibrium in society which is increasingly more human in character.

38. But such an order—universal, absolute and immutable in its principles—finds its source in the true, personal and transcendent God. He is the first truth, the sovereign good, and as such the deepest source from which human society, if it is to be properly constituted, creative, and worthy of man's dignity, draws its genuine vitality.[26] This is what St. Thomas means when he says: "Human reason is the standard which measures the degree of goodness of the human will, and as such it derives from the eternal law, which is divine reason . . . Hence it is clear that the goodness of the human

---

[26] Cf. Pius XII's broadcast message, Christmas 1942, *AAS* 35 (1943) 14.

will depends much more on the eternal law than on human reason."[27]

Characteristics of the present day

39. There are three things which characterize our modern age.

40. In the first place we notice a progressive improvement in the economic and social condition of working men. They began by claiming their rights principally in the economic and social spheres, and then proceeded to lay claim to their political rights as well. Finally, they have turned their attention to acquiring the more cultural benefits of society.

Today, therefore, working men all over the world are loud in their demands that they shall in no circumstances be subjected to arbitrary treatment, as though devoid of intelligence and freedom. They insist on being treated as human beings, with a share in every sector of human society: in the socio-economic sphere, in government, and in the realm of learning and culture.

41. Secondly, the part that women are now playing in political life is everywhere evident. This is a development that is perhaps of swifter growth among Christian nations, but it is also happening extensively, if more slowly, among nations that are heirs to different traditions and imbued with a different culture. Women are gaining an increasing awareness of their natural dignity. Far from being content with a purely passive role or allowing themselves to be regarded as a kind of instrument, they are demanding both in domestic and in public life the rights and duties which belong to them as human persons.

42. Finally, we are confronted in this modern age with a form of society which is evolving on entirely new social and political lines. Since all peoples have either attained political independence or are on the way to attaining it, soon no nation will rule over another and none will be subject to an alien power.

43. Thus all over the world men are either the citizens of an independent State, or are shortly to become so; nor is any nation nowadays content to submit to foreign domination. The long-standing

[27] *Summa Theol.* Ia-IIae, q. 19, a.4; cf. a.9.

inferiority complex of certain classes because of their economic and social status, sex, or position in the State, and the corresponding superiority complex of other classes, is rapidly becoming a thing of the past.

Equality of men

44. Today, on the contrary, the conviction is widespread that all men are equal in natural dignity; and so, on the doctrinal and theoretical level, at least, no form of approval is being given to racial discrimination. All this is of supreme significance for the formation of a human society animated by the principles We have mentioned above, for man's awareness of his rights must inevitably lead him to the recognition of his duties. The possession of rights involves the duty of implementing those rights, for they are the expression of a man's personal dignity. And the possession of rights also involves their recognition and respect by other people.

45. When society is formed on a basis of rights and duties, men have an immediate grasp of spiritual and intellectual values, and have no difficulty in understanding what is meant by truth, justice, charity and freedom. They become, moreover, conscious of being members of such a society. And that is not all. Inspired by such principles, they attain to a better knowledge of the true God—a personal God transcending human nature. They recognize that their relationship with God forms the very foundation of their life—the interior life of the spirit, and the life which they live in the society of their fellows.

PART II

RELATIONS BETWEEN INDIVIDUALS AND THE PUBLIC AUTHORITIES WITHIN A SINGLE STATE

Necessity and divine origin of authority

46. Human society can be neither well-ordered nor prosperous without the presence of those who, invested with legal authority, preserve its institutions and do all that is necessary to sponsor actively the interests of all its members. And they derive their author-

ity from God, for, as St. Paul teaches, "there is no power but from God."[28]

In his commentary on this passage, St. John Chrysostom writes: "What are you saying? Is every ruler appointed by God? No, that is not what I mean, he says, for I am not now talking about individual rulers, but about authority as such. My contention is that the existence of a ruling authority—the fact that some should command and others obey, and that all things not come about as the result of blind chance—this is a provision of divine wisdom."[29]

God has created men social by nature, and a society cannot "hold together unless someone is in command to give effective direction and unity of purpose. Hence every civilized community must have a ruling authority, and this authority, no less than society itself, has its source in nature, and consequently has God for its author."[30]

47. But it must not be imagined that authority knows no bounds. Since its starting point is the permission to govern in accordance with right reason, there is no escaping the conclusion that it derives its binding force from the moral order, which in turn has God as its origin and end.

Hence, to quote Pope Pius XII, "The absolute order of living beings, and the very purpose of man—an autonomous being, the subject of duties and inviolable rights, and the origin and purpose of human society—have a direct bearing upon the State as a necessary community endowed with authority. Divest it of this authority, and it is nothing, it is lifeless. . . . But right reason, and above all Christian faith, make it clear that such an order can have no other origin but in God, a personal God, our Creator. Hence it is from Him that State officials derive their dignity, for they share to some extent in the authority of God Himself."[31]

An appeal to conscience

48. Hence, a regime which governs solely or mainly by means of threats and intimidation or promises of reward, provides men with

---

[28] *Rom.* 13, 1-6.
[29] *In Epist. ad Rom.* c. 13, vv. 1-2, homil. XXIII; *PG* 60, 615.
[30] Leo XIII's encyclical *"Immortale Dei,"* Acta Leonis XIII, V, 1885, p. 120.
[31] Cf. Pius XII's broadcast message, Christmas 1944, *AAS* 37 (1945) 15.

no effective incentive to work for the common good. And even if it did, it would certainly be offensive to the dignity of free and rational human beings. Authority is before all else a moral force. For this reason the appeal of rulers should be to the individual conscience, to the duty which every man has of voluntarily contributing to the common good. But since all men are equal in natural dignity, no man has the capacity to force internal compliance on another. Only God can do that, for He alone scrutinizes and judges the secret counsels of the heart.

49. Hence, representatives of the State have no power to bind men in conscience, unless their own authority is tied to God's authority, and is a participation in it.[32]

50. The application of this principle likewise safeguards the dignity of citizens. Their obedience to civil authorities is never an obedience paid to them as men. It is in reality an act of homage paid to God, the provident Creator of the universe, who has decreed that men's dealings with one another be regulated in accordance with that order which He Himself has established. And we men do not demean ourselves in showing due reverence to God. On the contrary, we are lifted up and ennobled in spirit, for to serve God is to reign.[33]

51. Governmental authority, therefore, is a postulate of the moral order and derives from God. Consequently, laws and decrees passed in contravention of the moral order, and hence of the divine will, can have no binding force in conscience, since "it is right to obey God rather than men."[34]

Indeed, the passing of such laws undermines the very nature of authority and results in shameful abuse. As St. Thomas teaches, "In regard to the second proposition, we maintain that human law has the *rationale* of law in so far as it is in accordance with right reason, and as such it obviously derives from eternal law. A law which is at variance with reason is to that extent unjust and has no longer the *rationale* of law. It is rather an act of violence."[35]

---

[32] Cf. Leo XIII's encyclical *"Diuturnum illud," Acta Leonis XIII*, II, 1881, p. 274.
[33] Cf. ibid., p. 278; also Leo XIII's encyclical *"Immortale Dei," Acta Leonis XIII*, V, 1885, p. 130.
[34] *Acts* 5, 29.
[35] *Summa Theol.* Ia-IIae, q.93, a.3 ad 2um; cf. Pius XII's broadcast message, Christmas 1945, *AAS* 37 (1945) 5-23.

52. The fact that authority comes from God does not mean that men have no power to choose those who are to rule the State, or to decide upon the type of government they want, and determine the procedure and limitations of rulers in the exercise of their authority. Hence the above teaching is consonant with any genuinely democratic form of government.[36]

Attainment of the common good is the purpose of the public authority

53. Men, both as individuals and as intermediate groups, are required to make their own specific contributions to the general welfare. The main consequence of this is that they must harmonize their own interests with the needs of others, and offer their goods and services as their rulers shall direct—assuming, of course, that justice is maintained and the authorities are acting within the limits of their competence. Those who have authority in the State must exercise that authority in a way which is not only morally irreproachable, but also best calculated to ensure or promote the State's welfare.

54. The attainment of the common good is the sole reason for the existence of civil authorities. In working for the common good, therefore, the authorities must obviously respect its nature, and at the same time adjust their legislation to meet the requirements of the given situation.[37]

Essentials of the common good

55. Among the essential elements of the common good one must certainly include the various characteristics distinctive of each individual people.[38] But these by no means constitute the whole of it. For the common good, since it is intimately bound up with human nature, can never exist fully and completely unless the human person is taken into account at all times. Thus, attention must be paid

---

[36] Cf. Leo XIII's encyclical *"Diuturnum illud,"* Acta Leonis XIII, II, 1881, pp. 271-3; and Pius XII's broadcast message, Christmas 1944, AAS 37 (1945) 5-23.
[37] Cf. Pius XII's broadcast message, Christmas 1942, AAS 35 (1943) 13, and Leo XIII's encyclical *"Immortale Dei,"* Acta Leonis XIII, V, 1885, p. 120.
[38] Cf. Pius XII's encyclical *"Summi Pontificatus,"* AAS 31 (1939) 412-53.

to the basic nature of the common good and what it is that brings it about.³⁹

56. We must add, therefore, that it is in the nature of the common good that every single citizen has the right to share in it—although in different ways, depending on his tasks, merits and circumstances. Hence every civil authority must strive to promote the common good in the interest of all, without favoring any individual citizen or category of citizen. As Pope Leo XIII insisted:

"The civil power must not be subservient to the advantage of any one individual, or of some few persons; inasmuch as it was established for the common good of all."⁴⁰

Nevertheless, considerations of justice and equity can at times demand that those in power pay more attention to the weaker members of society, since these are at a disadvantage when it comes to defending their own rights and asserting their legitimate interests.⁴¹

The spiritual, too

57. In this connection, We would draw the attention of Our own sons to the fact that the common good is something which affects the needs of the whole man, body and soul. That, then, is the sort of good which rulers of States must take suitable measure to ensure. They must respect the hierarchy of values, and aim at achieving the spiritual as well as the material prosperity of their subjects.⁴²

58. These principles are clearly contained in that passage in Our encyclical *Mater et Magistra* where We emphasized that the common good "must take account of all those social conditions which favor the full development of human personality."⁴³

59. Consisting, as he does, of body and immortal soul, man cannot in this mortal life satisfy his needs or attain perfect happiness. Thus, the measures that are taken to implement the common good

---

[39] Cf. Pius XI's encyclical *"Mit brennender Sorge,"* AAS 29 (1937) 159, and his encyclical *"Divini Redemptoris,"* AAS 29 (1937) 65-106.
[40] Leo XIII's encyclical *"Immortale Dei,"* Acta Leonis XIII, V, 1885, p. 121.
[41] Cf. Leo XIII's encyclical *"Rerum novarum,"* Acta Leonis XIII, XI, 1891, pp. 133-4.
[42] Cf. Pius XII's encyclical *"Summi Pontificatus,"* AAS 31 (1939) 433.
[43] AAS 53 (1961) 417; see pp. 266-7 above.

must not jeopardize his eternal salvation; indeed, they must even help him to obtain it.⁴⁴

Responsibilities of the public authority, and rights and duties of individuals

60. It is generally accepted today that the common good is best safeguarded when personal rights and duties are guaranteed. The chief concern of civil authorities must therefore be to ensure that these rights are recognized, respected, co-ordinated, defended and promoted, and that each individual is enabled to perform his duties more easily. For "to safeguard the inviolable rights of the human person, and to facilitate the performance of his duties, is the principal duty of every public authority."⁴⁵

61. Thus any government which refused to recognize human rights or acted in violation of them, would not only fail in its duty; its decrees would be wholly lacking in binding force.⁴⁶

Reconciliation and protection of rights and duties of individuals

62. One of the principal duties of any government, moreover, is the suitable and adequate superintendence and co-ordination of men's respective rights in society. This must be done in such a way (1) that the exercise of their rights by certain citizens does not obstruct other citizens in the exercise of theirs; (2) that the individual, standing upon his own rights, does not impede others in the performance of their duties; (3) that the rights of all be effectively safeguarded, and completely restored if they have been violated.⁴⁷

Duty of promoting the rights of individuals

63. In addition, heads of States must make a positive contribution to the creation of an over-all climate in which the individual

---

⁴⁴ Cf. Pius XI's encyclical *"Quadragesimo anno," AAS* 23 (1931) 215.
⁴⁵ Cf. Pius XII's broadcast message, Pentecost, June 1, 1941, *AAS* 33 (1941) 200.
⁴⁶ Cf. Pius XI's encyclical *"Mit brennender Sorge," AAS* 29 (1937) 159, and his encyclical *"Divini Redemptoris," AAS* 29 (1937) 79; and Pius XII's broadcast message, Christmas 1942, *AAS* 35 (1943) 9-24.
⁴⁷ Cf. Pius XI's encyclical *"Divini Redemptoris," AAS* 29 (1937) 81, and Pius XII's broadcast message, Christmas 1942, *AAS* 35 (1943) 9-24.

can both safeguard his own rights and fulfill his duties, and can do so readily. For if there is one thing we have learned in the school of experience, it is surely this: that, in the modern world especially, political, economic and cultural inequities among citizens become more and more widespread when public authorities fail to take appropriate action in these spheres. And the consequence is that human rights and duties are thus rendered totally ineffective.

64. The public administration must therefore give considerable care and thought to the question of social as well as economic progress, and to the development of essential services in keeping with the expansion of the productive system. Such services include road-building, transportation, communications, drinking-water, housing, medical care, ample facilities for the practice of religion, and aids to recreation. The government must also see to the provision of insurance facilities, to obviate any likelihood of a citizen's being unable to maintain a decent standard of living in the event of some misfortune, or greatly increased family responsibilities.

The government is also required to show no less energy and efficiency in the matter of providing opportunities for suitable employment, graded to the capacity of the workers. It must make sure that working men are paid a just and equitable wage, and are allowed a sense of responsibility in the industrial concerns for which they work. It must facilitate the formation of intermediate groups, so that the social life of the people may become more fruitful and less constrained. And finally, it must ensure that everyone has the means and opportunity of sharing as far as possible in cultural benefits.

Harmonious relations between public authority's two forms of intervention

65. The common welfare further demands that in their efforts to co-ordinate and protect, and their efforts to promote, the rights of citizens, the civil authorities preserve a delicate balance. An excessive concern for the rights of any particular individuals or groups might well result in the principal advantages of the State being in effect monopolized by these citizens. Or again, the absurd situation

can arise where the civil authorities, while taking measures to protect the rights of citizens, themselves stand in the way of the full exercise of these rights. "For this principle must always be retained: that however extensive and far-reaching the influence of the State on the economy may be, it must never be exerted to the extent of depriving the individual citizen of his freedom of action. It must rather augment his freedom, while effectively guaranteeing the protection of everyone's essential, personal rights."[48]

66. And the same principle must be adopted by civil authorities in their various efforts to facilitate the exercise of rights and performance of duties in every department of social life.

Structure and operation of the public authority

67. For the rest, it is not possible to give a general ruling on the most suitable form of government, or the ways in which civil authorities can most effectively fulfill their legislative, administrative, and judicial functions.

68. In determining what form a particular government shall take, and the way in which it shall function, a major consideration will be the prevailing circumstances and the condition of the people; and these are things which vary in different places and at different times.

We think, however, that it is in keeping with human nature for the State to be given a form which embodies a threefold division of public office properly corresponding to the three main functions of public authority. In such a State a precise legal framework is provided, not only for the official functions of government, but also for the mutual relations between citizens and public officials. This will obviously afford a sure protection to citizens, both in the safeguarding of their rights and in the fulfilment of their duties.

69. If, however, this juridical and political structure is to realize its potential benefits, it is absolutely essential that public officials do their utmost to solve the problems that arise; and they must do so by using policies and techniques which it is within their competence to

---

[48] John XXIII's encyclical *"Mater et Magistra,"* AAS 53 (1961) 415; see p. 264 above.

implement, and which suit the actual condition of the State. It is also essential that, despite constantly changing conditions, legislators never disregard the moral law or constitutional provision, nor act at variance with the exigencies of the common good. And as justice must be the guiding principle in the administration of the State, and executives must thoroughly understand the law and carefully weigh all attendant circumstances, so too in the courts: justice must be administered impartially, and judges must be wholly incorrupt and uninfluenced by the solicitations of interested parties. The good order of society also requires that individuals and subsidiary groups within the State be effectively protected by law in the affirmation of their rights and the performance of their duties, both in their relations with each other and with government officials.[49]

Law and conscience

70. There can be no doubt that a State juridical system which conforms to the principles of justice and rightness, and corresponds to the degree of civic maturity evinced by the State in question, is highly conducive to the attainment of the common good.

71. And yet social life is so complex, varied and active in this modern age, that even a juridical system which has been established with great prudence and foresight often seems inadequate to the need.

72. Moreover, the relations of citizens with each other, of citizens and intermediate groups with public authorities, and the relations between public authorities of the same State, are sometimes seen to be of so ambiguous and explosive a nature, that they are not susceptible of being regulated by any hard and fast system of laws.

In such cases, if the authorities want to preserve the State's juridical system intact—in itself and in its application to specific cases—and if they want to minister to the principal needs of society, adapt the laws to the conditions of modern life and seek solutions to new problems, then it is essential that they have a clear idea of the nature and limits of their own legitimate spheres of action. Their calmness, integrity, clear-sightedness and perseverance must be

[49] Cf. Pius XII's broadcast message, Christmas 1942, *AAS* 35 (1943) 21.

such that they will recognize at once what is needed in a given situation, and act with promptness and efficiency.[50]

Citizens' participation in public life

73. A natural consequence of men's dignity is unquestionably their right to take an active part in government, though their degree of participation will necessarily depend on the stage of development reached by the political community of which they are members.

74. For the rest, this right to take part in government opens out to men a new and extensive field of opportunity for service. A situation is created in which civic authorities can, from the greater frequency of their contacts and discussions with the citizens, gain a clearer idea of what policies are in fact effectual for the common good; and in a system which allows for a regular succession of public officials, the authority of these officials, far from growing old and feeble, takes on a new vitality in keeping with the progressive development of human society.[51]

Characteristics of the present day

75. There is every indication at the present time that these aims and ideals are giving rise to various demands concerning the juridical organization of States. The first is this: that a clear and precisely worded charter of fundamental human rights be formulated and incorporated into the State's general constitution.

76. Secondly, each State must have a public constitution, couched in juridical terms, laying down clear rules relating to the designation of public officials, their reciprocal relations, spheres of competence and prescribed methods of operation.

77. The final demand is that relations between citizens and public authorities be described in terms of rights and duties. It must be clearly laid down that the principal function of public authorities is to recognize, respect, co-ordinate, safeguard and promote citizens' rights and duties.

78. We must, however, reject the view that the will of the indi-

---

[50] Cf. Pius XII's broadcast message, Christmas 1944, *AAS* 37 (1945) 15-16.
[51] Cf. Pius XII's broadcast message, Christmas 1942, *AAS* 35 (1943) 12.

vidual or the group is the primary and only source of a citizen's rights and duties, and of the binding force of political constitutions and the government's authority.[52]

79. But the aspirations We have mentioned are a clear indication of the fact that men, increasingly aware nowadays of their personal dignity, have found the incentive to enter government service and demand constitutional recognition for their own inviolable rights. Not content with this, they are demanding, too, the observance of constitutional procedures in the appointment of public authorities, and are insisting that they exercise their office within this constitutional framework.

Part III

RELATIONS BETWEEN STATES

Subjects of rights and duties

80. With respect to States themselves, Our predecessors have constantly taught, and We wish to lend the weight of Our own authority to their teaching, that nations are the subjects of reciprocal rights and duties. Their relationships, therefore, must likewise be harmonized in accordance with the dictates of truth, justice, willing co-operation, and freedom. The same law of nature that governs the life and conduct of individuals must also regulate the relations of political communities with one another.

81. This will be readily understood when one reflects that it is quite impossible for political leaders to lay aside their natural dignity while acting in their country's name and in its interests. They are still bound by the natural law, which is the rule that governs all moral conduct, and they have no authority to depart from its slightest precepts.

82. The idea that men, by the fact of their appointment to public office, are compelled to lay aside their own humanity, is quite inconceivable. Their very attainment to this high-ranking office was due

---

[52] Cf. Leo XIII's apostolic letter *"Annum ingressi,"* Acta Leonis XIII, XXII, 1902-1903, pp. 52-80.

to their exceptional gifts and intellectual qualities, which earned for them their reputation as outstanding representatives of the body politic.

83. Moreover, a ruling authority is indispensable to civil society. That is a fact which follows from the moral order itself. Such authority, therefore, cannot be misdirected against the moral order. It would immediately cease to exist, being deprived of its whole *raison d'être*. God Himself warns us of this: "Hear, therefore, ye kings, and understand: learn, ye that are judges of the ends of the earth. Give ear, you that rule the people, and that please yourselves in multitudes of nations. For power is given you by the Lord, and strength by the Most High, who will examine your works, and search out your thoughts."[53]

84. And lastly one must bear in mind that, even when it regulates the relations between States, authority must be exercised for the promotion of the common good. That is the primary reason for its existence.

An imperative of the common good

85. But one of the principal imperatives of the common good is the recognition of the moral order and the unfailing observance of its precepts. "A firmly established order between political communities must be founded on the unshakable and unmoving rock of the moral law, that law which is revealed in the order of nature by the Creator Himself, and engraved indelibly on men's hearts . . . Its principles are beacon lights to guide the policies of men and nations. They are also warning lights—providential signs—which men must heed if their laborious efforts to establish a new order are not to encounter perilous storms and shipwreck."[54]

In truth

86. The first point to be settled is that mutual ties between States must be governed by truth. Truth calls for the elimination of every

[53] *Wisd.* 6, 2-4.
[54] Cf. Pius XII's broadcast message, Christmas 1941, *AAS* 34 (1942) 16.

trace of racial discrimination, and the consequent recognition of the inviolable principle that all States are by nature equal in dignity.

Each of them accordingly has the right to exist, to develop, and to possess the necessary means and accept the primary responsibility for its own development. Each is also legitimately entitled to its good name and to the respect which is its due.

87. As we know from experience, men frequently differ widely in knowledge, virtue, intelligence and wealth, but that is no valid argument in favor of a system whereby those who are in a position of superiority impose their will arbitrarily on others. On the contrary, such men have a greater share in the common responsibility to help others to reach perfection by their mutual efforts.

88. So, too, on the international level: some nations may have attained to a superior degree of scientific, cultural and economic development. But that does not entitle them to exert unjust political domination over other nations. It means that they have to make a greater contribution to the common cause of social progress.

89. The fact is that no one can be by nature superior to his fellows, since all men are equally noble in natural dignity. And consequently there are no differences at all between political communities from the point of view of natural dignity. Each State is like a body, the members of which are human beings. And, as we know from experience, nations can be highly sensitive in matters in any way touching their dignity and honor; and with good reason.

The question of propaganda

90. Truth further demands an attitude of unruffled impartiality in the use of the many aids to the promotion and spread of mutual understanding between nations which modern scientific progress has made available. This does not mean that people should be prevented from drawing particular attention to the virtues of their own way of life, but it does mean the utter rejection of ways of disseminating information which violate the principles of truth and justice, and injure the reputation of another nation.[55]

[55] Cf. Pius XII's broadcast message, Christmas 1940, *AAS* 33 (1941) 5-14.

In justice

91. Relations between States must furthermore be regulated by justice. This necessitates both the recognition of their mutual rights, and, at the same time, the fulfilment of their respective duties.

92. States have the right to existence, to self-development, and to the means necessary to achieve this. They have the right to play the leading part in the process of their own development, and the right of their good name and due honors. Consequently, States are likewise in duty bound to safeguard all such rights effectively, and to avoid any action that could violate them. And just as individual men may not pursue their own private interests in a way that is unfair and detrimental to others, so too it would be criminal in a State to aim at improving itself by the use of methods which involve other nations in injury and unjust oppression. There is a saying of St. Augustine which has particular relevance in this context: "Take away justice, and what are kingdoms but mighty bands of robbers?"[56]

93. There may be, and sometimes is, a clash of interests among States, each striving for its own development. When differences of this sort arise, they must be settled in a truly human way, not by armed force nor by deceit or trickery. There must be a mutual assessment of the arguments and feelings on both sides, a mature and objective investigation of the situation, and an equitable reconciliation of opposing views.

The treatment of minorities

94. A special instance of this clash of interests is furnished by that political trend (which since the nineteenth century has become widespread throughout the world and has gained in strength) as a result of which men of similar ethnic background are anxious for political autonomy and unification into a single nation. For many reasons this cannot always be effected, and consequently minority peoples are often obliged to live within the territories of a nation of a different ethnic origin. This situation gives rise to serious problems.

95. It is quite clear that any attempt to check the vitality and

[56] *De civitate Dei,* lib. IV, c. 4; *PL* 41, 115; cf. Pius XII's broadcast message, Christmas 1939, *AAS* 32 (1940) 5-13.

growth of these ethnic minorities is a flagrant violation of justice; the more so if such perverse efforts are aimed at their very extinction.

96. Indeed, the best interests of justice are served by those public authorities who do all they can to improve the human conditions of the members of these minority groups, especially in what concerns their language, culture, ancient traditions, and their economic activity and enterprise.[57]

A cautionary note

97. It is worth noting, however, that these minority groups, in reaction, perhaps, to the enforced hardships of their present situation, or to historical circumstances, frequently tend to magnify unduly characteristics proper to their own people. They even rate them above those human values which are common to all mankind, as though the good of the entire human family should subserve the interests of their own particular group. A more reasonable attitude for such people to adopt would be to recognize the advantages, too, which accrue to them from their own special situation. They should realize that their constant association with a people steeped in a different civilization from their own has no small part to play in the development of their own particular genius and spirit. Little by little they can absorb into their very being those virtues which characterize the other nation. But for this to happen these minority groups must enter into some kind of association with the peoples in whose midst they are living, and learn to share their customs and way of life. It will never happen if they sow seeds of disaffection, which can only produce a harvest of evils, stifling the political development of nations.

Active solidarity

98. Since relationships between States must be regulated in accordance with the principles of truth and justice, States must further these relationships by taking positive steps to pool their material and spiritual resources. In many cases this can be achieved by all

---

[57] Cf. Pius XII's broadcast message, Christmas 1941, *AAS* 34 (1942) 10-21.

kinds of mutual collaboration; and this is already happening in our own day in the economic, social, political, educational, health and athletic spheres—and with beneficial results. We must bear in mind that of its very nature civil authority exists, not to confine men within the frontiers of their own nations, but primarily to protect the common good of the State, which certainly cannot be divorced from the common good of the entire human family.

99. Thus, in pursuing their own interests, civil societies, far from causing injury to others, must join plans and forces whenever the efforts of particular States cannot achieve the desired goal. But in doing so great care must be taken. What is beneficial to some States may prove detrimental rather than advantageous to others.

Contacts between races

100. Furthermore, the universal common good requires the encouragement in all nations of every kind of reciprocation between citizens and their intermediate societies. There are many parts of the world where we find groupings of people of more or less different ethnic origin. Nothing must be allowed to prevent reciprocal relations between them. Indeed such a prohibition would flout the very spirit of an age which has done so much to nullify the distances separating peoples. Nor must one overlook the fact that whatever their ethnic background, men possess, besides the special characteristics which distinguish them from other men, other very important elements in common with the rest of mankind. And these can form the basis of their progressive development and self-realization, especially in regard to spiritual values. They have, therefore, the right and duty to carry on their lives with others in society.

The proper balance between population, land and capital

101. As everyone is well aware, there are some countries where there is an imbalance between the amount of arable land and the number of inhabitants; others where there is an imbalance between the richness of the resources and the instruments of agriculture available. It is imperative, therefore, that nations enter into collabora-

tion with each other, and facilitate the circulation of goods, capital and manpower.[58]

102. We advocate in such cases the policy of bringing the work to the workers, wherever possible, rather than bringing workers to the scene of the work. In this way many people will be afforded an opportunity of increasing their resources without being exposed to the painful necessity of uprooting themselves from their own homes, settling in a strange environment, and forming new social contacts.

The problem of political refugees

103. The deep feelings of paternal love for all mankind which God has implanted in Our heart make it impossible for Us to view without bitter anguish of spirit the plight of those who for political reasons have been exiled from their own homelands. There are great numbers of such refugees at the present time, and many are the sufferings—the incredible sufferings—to which they are constantly exposed.

104. Here surely is our proof that, in defining the scope of a just freedom within which individual citizens may live lives worthy of their human dignity, the rulers of some nations have been far too restrictive. Sometimes in States of this kind the very right to freedom is called in question, and even flatly denied. We have here a complete reversal of the right order of society, for the whole *raison d'être* of public authority is to safeguard the interests of the community. Its sovereign duty is to recognize the noble realm of freedom and protect its rights.

The refugee's rights

105. For this reason, it is not irrelevant to draw the attention of the world to the fact that these refugees are persons and all their rights as persons must be recognized. Refugees cannot lose these rights simply because they are deprived of citizenship of their own States.

106. And among man's personal rights we must include his right

---

[58] Cf. John XXIII's encyclical *"Mater et Magistra," AAS* 53 (1961) 439; see pp. 289-90 above.

to enter a country in which he hopes to be able to provide more fittingly for himself and his dependents. It is therefore the duty of State officials to accept such immigrants and—so far as the good of their own community, rightly understood, permits—to further the aims of those who may wish to become members of a new society.

Commendable efforts

107. We therefore take this opportunity of giving Our public approval and commendation to every undertaking, founded on the principles of human solidarity or of Christian charity, which aims at relieving the distress of those who are compelled to emigrate from their own country to another.

108. And We must indeed single out for the praise of all right-minded men those international agencies which devote all their energies to this most important work.

Causes of the arms race

109. On the other hand, We are deeply distressed to see the enormous stocks of armaments that have been, and continue to be, manufactured in the economically more developed countries. This policy is involving a vast outlay of intellectual and material resources, with the result that the people of these countries are saddled with a great burden, while other countries lack the help they need for their economic and social development.

110. There is a common belief that under modern conditions peace cannot be assured except on the basis of an equal balance of armaments and that this factor is the probable cause of this stockpiling of armaments. Thus, if one country increases its military strength, others are immediately roused by a competitive spirit to augment their own supply of armaments. And if one country is equipped with atomic weapons, others consider themselves justified in producing such weapons themselves, equal in destructive force.

111. Consequently people are living in the grip of constant fear. They are afraid that at any moment the impending storm may break upon them with horrific violence. And they have good reasons for their fear, for there is certainly no lack of such weapons.

While it is difficult to believe that anyone would dare to assume responsibility for initiating the appalling slaughter and destruction that war would bring in its wake, there is no denying that the conflagration could be started by some chance and unforeseen circumstance. Moreover, even though the monstrous power of modern weapons does indeed act as a deterrent, there is reason to fear that the very testing of nuclear devices for war purposes can, if continued, lead to serious danger for various forms of life on earth.

Need for disarmament

112. Hence justice, right reason, and the recognition of man's dignity cry out insistently for a cessation to the arms race. The stock-piles of armaments which have been built up in various countries must be reduced all round and simultaneously by the parties concerned. Nuclear weapons must be banned. A general agreement must be reached on a suitable disarmament program, with an effective system of mutual control. In the words of Pope Pius XII: "The calamity of a world war, with the economic and social ruin and the moral excesses and dissolution that accompany it, must not on any account be permitted to engulf the human race for a third time."[59]

113. Everyone, however, must realize that, unless this process of disarmament be thoroughgoing and complete, and reach men's very souls, it is impossible to stop the arms race, or to reduce armaments, or—and this is the main thing—ultimately to abolish them entirely. Everyone must sincerely co-operate in the effort to banish fear and the anxious expectation of war from men's minds. But this requires that the fundamental principle upon which peace is based in today's world be replaced by an altogether different one, namely, the realization that true and lasting peace among nations cannot consist in the possession of an equal supply of armaments but only in mutual trust. And We are confident that this can be achieved, for it is a thing which not only is dictated by common sense, but is in itself most desirable and most fruitful of good.

[59] Cf. Pius XII's broadcast message, Christmas 1941, *AAS* 34 (1942) 17, and Benedict XV's exhortation to the rulers of the belligerent powers, August 1, 1917, *AAS* 9 (1917) 418.

Three motives

114. Here, then, we have an objective dictated first of all by reason. There is general agreement—or at least there should be—that relations between States, as between individuals, must be regulated not by armed force, but in accordance with the principles of right reason: the principles, that is, of truth, justice and vigorous and sincere co-operation.

115. Secondly, it is an objective which We maintain is most earnestly to be desired. For who is there who does not feel the craving to be rid of the threat of war, and to see peace preserved and made daily more secure?

116. And finally it is an objective which is rich with possibilities for good. Its advantages will be felt everywhere, by individuals, by families, by nations, by the whole human race. The warning of Pope Pius XII still rings in our ears: "Nothing is lost by peace; everything may be lost by war."[60]

A call to unsparing effort

117. We therefore consider it Our duty as the vicar on earth of Jesus Christ—the Saviour of the world, the Author of peace—and as interpreter of the most ardent wishes of the whole human family, in the fatherly love We bear all mankind, to beg and beseech mankind, and above all the rulers of States, to be unsparing of their labor and efforts to ensure that human affairs follow a rational and dignified course.

118. In their deliberations together, let men of outstanding wisdom and influence give serious thought to the problem of achieving a more human adjustment of relations between States throughout the world. It must be an adjustment that is based on mutual trust, sincerity in negotiation, and the faithful fulfilment of obligations assumed. Every aspect of the problem must be examined, so that eventually there may emerge some point of agreement from which to initiate treaties which are sincere, lasting, and beneficial in their effects.

---

[60] Cf. Pius XII's broadcast message, August 24, 1939, *AAS* 31 (1939) 334.

119. We, for Our part, will pray unceasingly that God may bless these labors by His divine assistance, and make them fruitful.

In liberty

120. Furthermore, relations between States must be regulated by the principle of freedom. This means that no country has the right to take any action that would constitute an unjust oppression of other countries, or an unwarranted interference in their affairs. On the contrary, all should help to develop in others an increasing awareness of their duties, an adventurous and enterprising spirit, and the resolution to take the initiative for their own advancement in every field of endeavor.

The evolution of economically under-developed countries

121. All men are united by their common origin and fellowship, their redemption by Christ, and their supernatural destiny. They are called to form one Christian family. In Our encyclical *Mater et Magistra*, therefore, We appealed to the more wealthy nations to render every kind of assistance to those States which are still in the process of economic development.[61]

122. It is no small consolation to Us to be able to testify here to the wide acceptance of Our appeal, and We are confident that in the years that lie ahead it will be accepted even more widely. The result We look for is that the poorer States shall in as short a time as possible attain to a degree of economic development that enables their citizens to live in conditions more in keeping with their human dignity.

123. Again and again We must insist on the need for helping these peoples in a way which guarantees to them the preservation of their own freedom. They must be conscious that they are themselves playing the major role in their economic and social development; that they are themselves to shoulder the main burden of it.

124. Hence the wisdom of Pope Pius XII's teaching: "A new order founded on moral principles is the surest bulwark against the

---

[61] *AAS* 53 (1961) 440-41; see pp. 290-91 above.

violation of the freedom, integrity and security of other nations, no matter what may be their territorial extension or their capacity for defense. For although it is almost inevitable that the larger States, in view of their greater power and vaster resources, will themselves decide on the norms governing their economic associations with smaller States, nevertheless these smaller States cannot be denied their right, in keeping with the common good, to political freedom, and to the adoption of a position of neutrality in the conflicts between nations. No State can be denied this right, for it is a postulate of the natural law itself, as also of international law. These smaller States have also the right of assuring their own economic development. It is only with the effective guaranteeing of these rights that smaller nations can fittingly promote the common good of all mankind, as well as the material welfare and the cultural and spiritual progress of their own people."[62]

125. The wealthier States, therefore, while providing various forms of assistance to the poorer, must have the highest possible respect for the latter's national characteristics and time-honored civil institutions. They must also repudiate any policy of domination. If this can be achieved, then "a precious contribution will have been made to the formation of a world community, in which each individual nation, conscious of its rights and duties, can work on terms of equality with the rest for the attainment of universal prosperity."[63]

Signs of the times

126. Men nowadays are becoming more and more convinced that any disputes which may arise between nations must be resolved by negotiation and agreement, and not by recourse to arms.

127. We acknowledge that this conviction owes its origin chiefly to the terrifying destructive force of modern weapons. It arises from fear of the ghastly and catastrophic consequences of their use. Thus, in this age which boasts of its atomic power, it no longer

[62] Cf. Pius XII's broadcast message, Christmas 1941, *AAS* 34 (1942) 16-17.
[63] John XXIII's encyclical *"Mater et Magistra," AAS* 53 (1961) 443; see p. 294 above.

makes sense to maintain that war is a fit instrument with which to repair the violation of justice.

128. And yet, unhappily, we often find the law of fear reigning supreme among nations and causing them to spend enormous sums on armaments. Their object is not aggression, so they say—and there is no reason for disbelieving them—but to deter others from aggression.

129. Nevertheless, We are hopeful that, by establishing contact with one another and by a policy of negotiation, nations will come to a better recognition of the natural ties that bind them together as men. We are hopeful, too, that they will come to a fairer realization of one of the cardinal duties deriving from our common nature: namely, that love, not fear, must dominate the relationships between individuals and between nations. It is principally characteristic of love that it draws men together in all sorts of ways, sincerely united in the bonds of mind and matter; and this is a union from which countless blessings can flow.

PART IV

RELATIONSHIP OF MEN AND OF POLITICAL COMMUNITIES WITH THE WORLD COMMUNITY

Interdependence of political communities

130. Recent progress in science and technology has had a profound influence on man's way of life. This progress is a spur to men all over the world to extend their collaboration and association with one another in these days when material resources, travel from one country to another, and technical information have so vastly increased. This has led to a phenomenal growth in relationships between individuals, families and intermediate associations belonging to the various nations, and between the public authorities of the various political communities. There is also a growing economic interdependence between States. National economies are gradually becoming so interdependent that a kind of world economy is being born from the simultaneous integration of the economies of individ-

ual States. And finally, each country's social progress, order, security and peace are necessarily linked with the social progress, order, security and peace of every other country.

131. From this it is clear that no State can fittingly pursue its own interests in isolation from the rest, nor, under such circumstances, can it develop itself as it should. The prosperity and progress of any State is in part consequence, and in part cause, of the prosperity and progress of all other States.

Inadequacy of modern States to ensure the universal common good

132. No era will ever succeed in destroying the unity of the human family, for it consists of men who are all equal by virtue of their natural dignity. Hence there will always be an imperative need —born of man's very nature—to promote in sufficient measure the universal common good; the good, that is, of the whole human family.

133. In the past rulers of States seem to have been able to make sufficient provision for the universal common good through the normal diplomatic channels, or by top-level meetings and discussions, treaties and agreements; by using, that is, the ways and means suggested by the natural law, the law of nations, or international law.

134. In our own day, however, mutual relationships between States have undergone a far-reaching change. On the one hand, the universal common good gives rise to problems of the utmost gravity, complexity and urgency—especially as regards the preservation of the security and peace of the whole world. On the other hand, the rulers of individual nations, being all on an equal footing, largely fail in their efforts to achieve this, however much they multiply their meetings and their endeavors to discover more fitting instruments of justice. And this is no reflection on their sincerity and enterprise. It is merely that their authority is not sufficiently influential.

135. We are thus driven to the conclusion that the shape and structure of political life in the modern world, and the influence exercised by public authority in all the nations of the world are unequal to the task of promoting the common good of all peoples.

Connection between the common good and political authority

136. Now, if one considers carefully the inner significance of the common good on the one hand, and the nature and function of public authority on the other, one cannot fail to see that there is an intrinsic connection between them. Public authority, as the means of promoting the common good in civil society, is a postulate of the moral order. But the moral order likewise requires that this authority be effective in attaining its end. Hence the civil institutions in which such authority resides, becomes operative and promotes its ends, are endowed with a certain kind of structure and efficacy: a structure and efficacy which make such institutions capable of realizing the common good by ways and means adequate to the changing historical conditions.

137. Today the universal common good presents us with problems which are world-wide in their dimensions; problems, therefore, which cannot be solved except by a public authority with power, organization and means co-extensive with these problems, and with a world-wide sphere of activity. Consequently the moral order itself demands the establishment of some such general form of public authority.

Public authority instituted by common consent and not imposed by force

138. But this general authority equipped with world-wide power and adequate means for achieving the universal common good cannot be imposed by force. It must be set up with the consent of all nations. If its work is to be effective, it must operate with fairness, absolute impartiality, and with dedication to the common good of all peoples. The forcible imposition by the more powerful nations of a universal authority of this kind would inevitably arouse fears of its being used as an instrument to serve the interests of the few or to take the side of a single nation, and thus the influence and effectiveness of its activity would be undermined. For even though nations may differ widely in material progress and military strength, they are very sensitive as regards their juridical equality and the excellence of their own way of life. They are right, therefore, in

their reluctance to submit to an authority imposed by force, established without their co-operation, or not accepted of their own accord.

The universal common good and personal rights

139. The common good of individual States is something that cannot be determined without reference to the human person, and the same is true of the common good of all States taken together. Hence the public authority of the world community must likewise have as its special aim the recognition, respect, safeguarding and promotion of the rights of the human person. This can be done by direct action, if need be, or by the creation throughout the world of the sort of conditions in which rulers of individual States can more easily carry out their specific functions.

The principle of subsidiarity

140. The same principle of subsidiarity which governs the relations between public authorities and individuals, families and intermediate societies in a single State, must also apply to the relations between the public authority of the world community and the public authorities of each political community. The special function of this universal authority must be to evaluate and find a solution to economic, social, political and cultural problems which affect the universal common good. These are problems which, because of their extreme gravity, vastness and urgency, must be considered too difficult for the rulers of individual States to solve with any degree of success.

141. But it is no part of the duty of universal authority to limit the sphere of action of the public authority of individual States, or to arrogate any of their functions to itself. On the contrary, its essential purpose is to create world conditions in which the public authorities of each nation, its citizens and intermediate groups, can carry out their tasks, fulfil their duties and claim their rights with greater security.[64]

[64] Cf. Pius XII's address to Young Members of Italian Catholic Action, Rome, Sept. 12, 1948, *AAS* 40 (1948) 412.

Modern developments

142. The United Nations Organization (U.N.) was established, as is well known, on June 26, 1945. To it were subsequently added lesser organizations consisting of members nominated by the public authority of the various nations and entrusted with highly important international functions in the economic, social, cultural, educational and health fields. The United Nations Organization has the special aim of maintaining and strengthening peace between nations, and of encouraging and assisting friendly relations between them, based on the principles of equality, mutual respect, and extensive co-operation in every field of human endeavor.

143. A clear proof of the farsightedness of this organization is provided by the Universal Declaration of Human Rights passed by the United Nations General Assembly on December 10, 1948. The preamble of this declaration affirms that the genuine recognition and complete observance of all the rights and freedoms outlined in the declaration is a goal to be sought by all peoples and all nations.

144. We are, of course, aware that some of the points in the declaration did not meet with unqualified approval in some quarters; and there was justification for this. Nevertheless, We think the document should be considered a step in the right direction, an approach toward the establishment of a juridical and political ordering of the world community. It is a solemn recognition of the personal dignity of every human being; an assertion of everyone's right to be free to seek out the truth, to follow moral principles, discharge the duties imposed by justice, and lead a fully human life. It also recognized other rights connected with these.

145. It is therefore Our earnest wish that the United Nations Organization may be able progressively to adapt its structure and methods of operation to the magnitude and nobility of its tasks. May the day be not long delayed when every human being can find in this organization an effective safeguard of his personal rights; those rights, that is, which derive directly from his dignity as a human person, and which are therefore universal, inviolable and inalienable. This is all the more desirable in that men today are taking an ever more active part in the public life of their own na-

tions, and in doing so they are showing an increased interest in the affairs of all peoples. They are becoming more and more conscious of being living members of the universal family of mankind.

Part V

PASTORAL EXHORTATIONS

Duty of taking part in public life

146. Here once more We exhort Our sons to take an active part in public life, and to work together for the benefit of the whole human race, as well as for their own political communities. It is vitally necessary for them to endeavor, in the light of Christian faith and with love as their guide, to ensure that every institution, whether economic, social, cultural or political, be such as not to obstruct but rather to facilitate man's self-betterment, both in the natural and in the supernatural order.

Scientific competence, technical capacity and professional experience

147. And yet, if they are to imbue civilization with right ideals and Christian principles, it is not enough for Our sons to be illumined by the heavenly light of faith and to be fired with enthusiasm for a cause; they must involve themselves in the work of these institutions, and strive to influence them effectively from within.

148. But in a culture and civilization like our own, which is so remarkable for its scientific knowledge and its technical discoveries, clearly no one can insinuate himself into public life unless he be scientifically competent, technically capable, and skilled in the practice of his own profession.

Apostolate of a trained laity

149. And yet even this must be reckoned insufficient to bring the relationships of daily life into conformity with a more human standard, based, as it must be, on truth, tempered by justice, motivated by mutual love, and holding fast to the practice of freedom.

150. If these policies are really to become operative, men must first of all take the utmost care to conduct their various temporal activities in accordance with the laws which govern each and every such activity, observing the principles which correspond to their respective natures. Secondly, men's actions must be made to conform with the precepts of the moral order. This means that their behavior must be such as to reflect their consciousness of exercising a personal right or performing a personal duty. Reason has a further demand to make. In obedience to the providential designs and commands of God respecting our salvation and not neglecting the dictates of conscience, men must conduct themselves in their temporal activity in such a way as to effect a thorough integration of the principal spiritual values with those of science, technology and the professions.

Integration of faith and action

151. In traditionally Christian States at the present time, civil institutions evince a high degree of scientific and technical progress and possess abundant machinery for the attainment of every kind of objective. And yet it must be owned that these institutions are often but slightly affected by Christian motives and a Christian spirit.

152. One may well ask the reason for this, since the men who have largely contributed—and who are still contributing—to the creation of these institutions are men who are professed Christians, and who live their lives, at least in part, in accordance with the precepts of the gospels. In Our opinion the explanation lies in a certain cleavage between faith and practice. Their inner, spiritual unity must be restored, so that faith may be the light and love the motivating force of all their actions.

Integral education

153. We consider too that a further reason for this very frequent divorce between faith and practice in Christians is an inadequate education in Christian teaching and Christian morality. In many places the amount of energy devoted to the study of secular subjects

is all too often out of proportion to that devoted to the study of religion. Scientific training reaches a very high level, whereas religious training generally does not advance beyond the elementary stage. It is essential, therefore, that the instruction given to our young people be complete and continuous, and imparted in such a way that moral goodness and the cultivation of religious values may keep pace with scientific knowledge and continually advancing technical progress. Young people must also be taught how to carry out their own particular obligations in a truly fitting manner.[65]

Constant endeavor

154. In this connection We think it opportune to point out how difficult it is to understand clearly the relation between the objective requirements of justice and concrete situations; to define, that is, correctly to what degree and in what form doctrinal principles and directives must be applied in the given state of human society.

155. The definition of these degrees and forms is all the more difficult in an age such as ours, driven forward by a fever of activity. And yet this is the age in which each one of us is required to make his own contribution to the universal common good. Daily is borne in on us the need to make the reality of social life conform better to the requirements of justice. Hence Our sons have every reason for not thinking that they can relax their efforts and be satisfied with what they have already achieved.

156. What has so far been achieved is insufficient compared with what needs to be done; all men must realize that. Every day provides a more important, a more fitting enterprise to which they must turn their hands—industry, trade unions, professional organizations, insurance, cultural institutions, the law, politics, medical and recreational facilities, and other such activities. The age in which we live needs all these things. It is an age in which men, having discovered the atom and achieved the breakthrough into outer space, are now exploring other avenues, leading to almost limitless horizons.

[65] Cf. John XXIII's encyclical *"Mater et Magistra," AAS* 53 (1961) 454; see pp. 306-07 above.

Relations between Catholics and non-Catholics in social and economic affairs

157. The principles We have set out in this document take their rise from the very nature of things. They derive, for the most part, from the consideration of man's natural rights. Thus the putting of these principles into effect frequently involves extensive co-operation between Catholics and those Christians who are separated from the Apostolic See. It even involves the co-operation of Catholics with men who may not be Christians but who nevertheless are reasonable men, and men of natural moral integrity. "In such circumstances they must, of course, bear themselves as Catholics, and do nothing to compromise religion and morality. Yet at the same time they should show themselves animated by a spirit of understanding and unselfishness, ready to co-operate loyally in achieving objects which are good in themselves, or conducive to good."[66]

Error and the errant

158. It is always perfectly justifiable to distinguish between error as such and the person who falls into error—even in the case of men who err regarding the truth or are led astray as a result of their inadequate knowledge, in matters either of religion or of the highest ethical standards. A man who has fallen into error does not cease to be a man. He never forfeits his personal dignity; and that is something that must always be taken into account. Besides, there exists in man's very nature an undying capacity to break through the barriers of error and seek the road to truth. God, in His great providence, is ever present with His aid. Today, maybe, a man lacks faith and turns aside into error; tomorrow, perhaps, illumined by God's light, he may indeed embrace the truth.

Catholics who, in order to achieve some external good, collaborate with unbelievers or with those who through error lack the fullness of faith in Christ, may possibly provide the occasion or even the incentive for their conversion to the truth.

---

[66] *Ibid.,* p. 456; see p. 308 above.

Philosophies and historical movements

159. Again it is perfectly legitimate to make a clear distinction between a false philosophy of the nature, origin and purpose of men and the world, and economic, social, cultural, and political undertakings, even when such undertakings draw their origin and inspiration from that philosophy. True, the philosophic formula does not change once it has been set down in precise terms, but the undertakings clearly cannot avoid being influenced to a certain extent by the changing conditions in which they have to operate. Besides, who can deny the possible existence of good and commendable elements in these undertakings, elements which do indeed conform to the dictates of right reason, and are an expression of man's lawful aspirations?

160. It may sometimes happen, therefore, that meetings arranged for some practical end—though hitherto they were thought to be altogether useless—may in fact be fruitful at the present time, or at least offer prospects of success.

But whether or not the moment for such co-operation has arrived, and the manner and degree of such co-operation in the attainment of economic, social, cultural and political advantages—these are matters for prudence to decide; prudence, the queen of all the virtues which rule the lives of men both as individuals and in society.

As far as Catholics are concerned, the decision rests primarily with those who take a leading part in the life of the community, and in these specific fields. They must, however, act in accordance with the principles of the natural law, and observe the Church's social teaching and the directives of ecclesiastical authority. For it must not be forgotten that the Church has the right and duty not only to safeguard her teaching on faith and morals, but also to exercise her authority over her sons by intervening in their external affairs whenever a judgment has to be made concerning the practical application of this teaching.[67]

---

[67] *Ibid.*, p. 456; see p. 308 above; cf. Leo XIII's encyclical *"Immortale Dei,"* *Acta Leonis XIII*, V, 1885, p. 128; Pius XI's encyclical *"Ubi arcano,"* *AAS* 14 (1922) 698; and Pius XII's address to the Union of International Sodalities of Catholic Women, Rome, Sept. 11, 1947, *AAS* 39 (1947) 486.

Little by little

161. There are indeed some people who, in their generosity of spirit, burn with a desire to institute wholesale reforms whenever they come across situations which show scant regard for justice or are wholly out of keeping with its claims. They tackle the problem with such impetuosity that one would think they were embarking on some political revolution.

162. We would remind such people that it is the law of nature that all things must be of gradual growth. If there is to be any improvement in human institutions, the work must be done slowly and deliberately from within. Pope Pius XII expressed it in these terms: "Salvation and justice consist not in the uprooting of an outdated system, but in a well designed policy of development. Hotheadedness was never constructive; it has always destroyed everything. It has inflamed passions, but never assuaged them. It sows no seeds but those of hatred and destruction. Far from bringing about the reconciliation of contending parties, it reduces men and political parties to the necessity of laboriously redoing the work of the past, building on the ruins that disharmony has left in its wake."[68]

An immense task

163. Hence among the very serious obligations incumbent upon men of high principles, We must include the task of establishing new relationships in human society, under the mastery and guidance of truth, justice, charity and freedom—relations between individual citizens, between citizens and their respective States, between States, and finally between individuals, families, intermediate associations and States on the one hand, and the world community on the other. There is surely no one who will not consider this a most exalted task, for it is one which is able to bring about true peace in accordance with divinely established order.

164. Considering the need, the men who are shouldering this responsibility are far too few in number, yet they are deserving of the highest recognition from society, and We rightfully honor them

[68] Cf. Pius XII's address to Italian workers, Rome, Pentecost, June 13, 1943, *AAS* 35 (1943) 175.

with Our public praise. We call upon them to persevere in their ideals, which are of such tremendous benefit to mankind. At the same time We are encouraged to hope that many more men, Christians especially, will join their cause, spurred on by love and the realization of their duty. Everyone who has joined the ranks of Christ must be a glowing point of light in the world, a nucleus of love, a leaven of the whole mass. He will be so in proportion to his degree of spiritual union with God.

165. The world will never be the dwelling-place of peace, till peace has found a home in the heart of each and every man, till every man preserves in himself the order ordained by God to be preserved. That is why St. Augustine asks the question: "Does your mind desire the strength to gain the mastery over your passions? Let it submit to a greater power, and it will conquer all beneath it. And peace will be in you—true, sure, most ordered peace. What is that order? God as ruler of the mind; the mind as ruler of the body. Nothing could be more orderly."[69]

The Prince of Peace

166. Our concern here has been with problems which are causing men extreme anxiety at the present time; problems which are intimately bound up with the progress of human society. Unquestionably, the teaching We have given has been inspired by a longing which We feel most keenly, and which We know is shared by all men of good will: that peace may be assured on earth.

167. We who, in spite of Our inadequacy, are nevertheless the vicar of Him whom the prophet announced as the *Prince of Peace*,[70] conceive of it as Our duty to devote all Our thoughts and care and energy to further this common good of all mankind. Yet peace is but an empty word, if it does not rest upon that order which Our hope prevailed upon Us to set forth in outline in this encyclical. It is an order that is founded on truth, built up on justice, nurtured and animated by charity, and brought into effect under the auspices of freedom.

[69] *Miscellanea Augustiniana* . . . St. Augustine, *Sermones post Maurinos reperti*, Rome, 1930, p. 633.
[70] Cf. *Is.* 9, 6.

168. So magnificent, so exalted is this aim that human resources alone, even though inspired by the most praiseworthy good will, cannot hope to achieve it. God Himself must come to man's aid with His heavenly assistance, if human society is to bear the closest possible resemblance to the kingdom of God.

169. The very order of things, therefore, demands that during this sacred season we pray earnestly to Him who by His bitter passion and death washed away men's sins, which are the fountainhead of discord, misery and inequality; to Him who shed His blood to reconcile the human race to the heavenly Father, and bestowed the gifts of peace. "For He is our peace, who hath made both one . . . And coming, He preached peace to you that were afar off; and peace to them that were nigh."[71]

170. The sacred liturgy of these days re-echoes the same message: "Our Lord Jesus Christ, after His resurrection, stood in the midst of His disciples and said: Peace be upon you, alleluia. The disciples rejoiced when they saw the Lord."[72] It is Christ, therefore, who brought us peace; Christ who bequeathed it to us: "Peace I leave with you: my peace I give unto you: not as the world giveth, do I give unto you."[73]

171. Let us, then, pray with all fervor for this peace which our divine Redeemer came to bring us. May He banish from the souls of men whatever might endanger peace. May He transform all men into witnesses of truth, justice and brotherly love. May He illumine with His light the minds of rulers, so that, besides caring for the proper material welfare of their peoples, they may also guarantee them the fairest gift of peace.

Finally, may Christ inflame the desires of all men to break through the barriers which divide them, to strengthen the bonds of mutual love, to learn to understand one another, and to pardon those who have done them wrong. Through His power and inspiration may all peoples welcome each other to their hearts as brothers, and may the peace they long for ever flower and ever reign among them.

---

[71] *Eph.* 2, 14-17.
[72] Responsory at Matins, Feria VI within the Octave of Easter.
[73] *John* 14, 27.

172. And so, dear brothers, with the ardent wish that peace may come upon the flocks committed to your care, for the special benefit of those who are most lowly and in the greatest need of help and defense, lovingly in the Lord We bestow on you, on Our priests both secular and regular, on religious both men and women, on all the faithful and especially those who give wholehearted obedience to these Our exhortations, Our Apostolic Blessing. And upon all men of good will, to whom We also address this encyclical, We implore from God health and prosperity.

173. Given at Rome, at St. Peter's, on Holy Thursday, the eleventh day of April, in the year 1963, the fifth of Our Pontificate.

JOHN PP. XXIII

THE SPIRIT OF "PACEM IN TERRIS"

Reflections on the Encyclical, from Five Addresses by Pope John XXIII

On the eve of the encyclical's publication, Pope John appeared before television cameras to sign five copies for Church archives, and to read a brief commentary:

THE ENCYCLICAL LETTER *Pacem in terris* is about to travel the broad highways of the world, and Our spirit is understandably taken with the deepest emotion: first because of the document's subject matter—peace—which answers the deepest longing of the human family, and then because of the date We have chosen to give it—Holy Thursday, the day of *Coena Domini*.[1]

Oh, how sweet-sounding the words of Jesus to His disciples before His passion and death, *pro mundi vita*,[2] for the redemption and salvation of all men!

The encyclical's visage reflects the light of divine revelation, which supplies the living substance of its thought. But its doctrinal lines also are derived from the most profound demands of human nature, and, for the most part, belong to the sphere of natural law. This explains an innovation appropriate to this document—that it is directed not only to the hierarchy of the universal Church, to the clergy and faithful of the whole world, but also "to all men of good will." Universal peace is a blessing which interests everyone without exception, and so We have opened Our heart and mind to everyone.

The encyclical is made up of five parts: relations between individuals; those of individuals with public authority; those between nations; those of individual men and individual nations with the world community; and finally, in the fifth section, pastoral norms that can readily be grasped.

In this manner not only have We sought to point up the founda-

---

[1] The Lord's Supper.   [2] For the life of the world.

tion of the structure of peace—that is, respect for the order established by God and protection of human dignity—but We also have indicated the different levels on which to build this structure and, almost, the very stones necessary for its construction, excluding no one from the invitation to make a personal contribution. But, with apostolic zeal and fervently echoing Christ's command, "Go and teach," We say first of all to the sons of the Church: "Carry peace with you, spread its benefits."

We nurture the trust that men will joyfully welcome the message of *Pacem in terris,* and open their hearts to it. In the meantime We will follow its course with Our prayers and with deep affection that reaches out to all nations.

—April 9, 1963

"Pacem in terris" is dated Holy Thursday, 1963. At the close of a Mass on that day for the Vatican diplomatic corps, Pope John told of his hopes for the encyclical:

. . . Today, even as yesterday, the Church summons men unceasingly to the unity of charity. This is the message We wanted to reiterate audibly and clearly to all men through Our encyclical *Pacem in terris.* We are pleased that it should appear on this day when Christ spoke the divine words, "Love one another."[3] For Our primary aim was to send the people of today a great call to love. May they be quick to acknowledge the common origin which makes them brothers, and unite together in love. May charity provide a new vitality to the actions of governments. May it help them to accept God's presence in history, His laws, and the practical consequences entailed. May all their actions be inspired by the spirit of obedience to a law which transcends individuals. In this spirit may they not overlook anything which will enhance the growth of the human person and insure a social order solidly rooted in truth, justice, peace, and liberty!

Our only wish, Our only design, in this solemn document of Our magisterium was to humbly re-echo the message of Christ, to communicate His intimate conversation on Holy Thursday. . . .

—April 11, 1963

[3] *John* 13, 34.

In his 1963 Easter message, Pope John noted a special bond between his new social encyclical and "Mater et Magistra":

... A cause of excitement these days is the encyclical *Pacem in terris,* which is dedicated to the right ordering of society in order to achieve the priceless blessing of peace.

The letter expounds the Church's thought on this subject, outlining in the light of the Gospel all the elements that conduce to true peace for the individual, the family, and the community. Oh, peace! More than a balance of external forces, peace is a divine gift, a pledge of the love of Christ who reconciles souls to the heavenly Father and establishes them in His grace. Interior order based on good will assures a tranquil external order; otherwise the external is unstable, dependent as it is on human prudence.

This new document, which is linked with *Mater et Magistra,* sums up the teachings of Our predecessors from Leo XIII to Pius XII on the subject of peace. During the last seventy years the popes have directed a considerable volume of teaching, exhortations, and serious warnings toward preserving or regaining this inestimable gift.

Pacem in terris is meant to be Our Easter gift for the year of our Lord 1963. It is an expression of that ardent desire which inflames Our soul as universal shepherd of Holy Church, a reflection of the heart of Christ. "He is our peace," says the Apostle Paul, "and, coming, he preached peace to you that were afar off; and peace to them that were nigh. For by him we have access both in one Spirit to the Father."[4] There you have a heavenly vision! Peace with God in the fulfilment of His will; peace among men in respect for each one's rights, for upon each is signed the glory of the Most High;[5] peace in families where husbands and wives collaborate with the Lord in transmitting life, and children grow as olive branches around the table.[6]

Peace within nations, in careful attention to the ordered development of civil life. Peace, finally, in the mutual relations of nations, in loyalty and in determination to end suspicions, misunderstandings, and threats.

The two documents *Mater et Magistra* and *Pacem in terris* offer

[4] *Eph.* 2, 14, 17-18.   [5] Cf. *Ps.* 4, 7.   [6] Cf. *Ps.* 127, 3.

new reasons for serious reflection on socio-economic and political problems with a view to reaching solutions based on respect and love for those immutable and universal laws written in the heart of every man.

We are certainly not deceiving Ourself that any of this is easy. But, with God's help and with the sincere tribute of submission to Him, true progress in brotherhood and peace is possible. A good start has already been made, and this encourages one to continue and to have trust. . . .

—April 13, 1963

At a general audience Pope John acknowledged that echoes of support for his encyclical had reached him from every part of the world:

. . . We feel the sacred obligation of spreading . . . peace from this center of Catholic unity through the entire world, and it comforts Us in the depths of Our being to see how Providence in its goodness blesses Our efforts. The encyclical *Pacem in terris* has everywhere met with a favorable response; for this We are profoundly grateful. . . .

We gave the encyclical the date of Holy Thursday—the day on which the divine Redeemer, about to conclude His public life and set forth to Calvary to die "for our salvation and that of the whole world,"[7] entrusted to His disciples the testament of these lovely and memorable words: "Peace I leave you, my peace I give you."[8] On that day the Redeemer shed a great light on the world, a light which the apostles of the Gospel have spread over the whole earth.

Echoing the divine commandments, We have lit from that flame a torch for the men of today. You can imagine Our heartfelt joy in seeing its light spread, gradually making its way into minds and hearts. . . .

—April 24, 1963

Shortly before confinement by his last illness, Pope John, in ceremonies for his reception of the Balzan peace prize, spoke these words:

. . . The edifice of peace must be built day by day, and on solid foundations. Here, under the vaults of the Vatican basilica, we see

[7] Roman Liturgy for Holy Thursday.   [8] *John* 14, 27.

Michelangelo's peerless dome rising in the Roman sky. Surely we do not forget that it rests on four imposing pillars driven deep into the earth to rest on rock: that rock cited at the end of the Sermon on the Mount: ". . . the winds blew and beat upon that house, but it did not fall; it was founded upon rock."[9]

Peace, then, is a house, the house of all. It is the arch which joins earth to heaven. But to rise so high it must rest on four solid pillars: those We pointed out in Our encyclical *Pacem in terris*.

"Peace," We said, "is but an empty word, if it does not rest upon that order which Our hope prevailed upon Us to set forth in outline in this encyclical. It is an order that is founded on truth, built on justice, nurtured and animated by charity, and brought into effect under the auspices of freedom."

These four principles supporting the entire edifice belong to natural law, which is written in each man's heart. And so We addressed Our exhortation to all humanity. In the light of past experience and with objective and serene appreciation for the language of the Church, We are convinced that in years to come the doctrine it offers to the world will prevail by its very clarity. Presented to our contemporaries without partisan slant, it cannot but foster the growth in the world of those who worthily and with glory will be called builders and makers of peace. . . .

—May 10, 1963

[9] *Matt.* 7, 25.

VI

*The Great Council
of Renewal
and Reunion*

Vatican Council II is still in progress as this book goes to press. The full extent and impact of its doctrinal and administrative decrees will not soon be known and it is no part of our intention here to appraise the Council as such. Beyond all doubt, however, the "fact" of the Council and the impact of this "fact" on the Church and the world, with the rubbing of elbows which took place, is at least partially measurable already—and this gigantic result we can credit to Pope John himself.

We present here a few key messages of Pope John dealing with the Council, indicating his plans and hopes for it, together with a brief analysis prepared by our own staff of the part this great Council played in Pope John's life and pontificate.—Ed.

A Commentary on

POPE JOHN AND THE COUNCIL

by The Editors

AS HE LOOKED out over the 2,540 Fathers assembled in St. Peter's basilica for the opening of the Second Vatican Council, Pope John XXIII surely must have felt a sense of great personal achievement. For of all twenty-one ecumenical councils of the Catholic Church none was more clearly the work of one man. From its very conception, through the three years of preparation, the actual sessions, and even into the sessions after his death, the spirit of Pope John has pervaded its every moment. So true is this that it has come to be known as "Pope John's Council."

It was he, and he alone, who conceived the idea of holding a council at this point in history. We know this from his own words: "The decision to hold an ecumenical council came to Us in the first instance in a sudden flash of inspiration. We communicated this decision, without elaboration, to the Sacred College of Cardinals on that memorable January 25, 1959." Thus, it was not an idea that had emerged from committee meetings or that had been in the air for even a short time. Indeed, its originality and unexpectedness is attested to by the surprise— in fact, the shock—expressed by so many of the Pope's advisors. As he himself more than once remarked, there was even a certain amount of opposition to his idea from men more timid, less visionary.

It would, of course, be wrong to say that he alone was responsible for the *aggiornamento* which was so manifest in the Council. Earlier popes, notably Pius XII, had made ready the ground and sown the seed. As one writer said, "the *aggiornamento,* which was Pope John's great legacy to the Church, would have been inconceivable had the groundwork not been prepared by Pius XII with his liturgical and pastoral reforms." Pope John, well aware of the efforts of his predecessors, saw that the moment was right for a Council, that it was the best instrument for bringing into sharp focus and into solution the many new problems and needs which had been gradually emerging.

Once committed to the idea of a council, Pope John made it the center of his pontificate. He prayed for its success continuously, in public and in private, and implored the prayers of all the world for it. He addressed a special message to nuns, for example, on the spiritual contribution they could make to the success of the Council. He scarcely ever gave an address without mentioning the Council, and scores of his talks were entirely devoted to it. Penance as a means to the Council's success was the subject of an entire encyclical, *"Paenitentiam agere."*

It was from John that the Council received its goals, its direction. He said over and over, nowhere more explicitly than in his opening address to the Council, that the Council was to be pastoral in its aims. He told the Fathers that they were not gathered in council merely to safeguard Catholic doctrine or to restate in greater detail the fundamental teaching of the Church. Rather, they were to see to it that Catholic doctrine "shall be more widely known, more deeply understood, and more penetrating in its effects on men's moral lives." Catholic teaching must "be studied afresh and reformulated in contemporary terms." He said, "We must work out ways and means of expounding these truths in a manner more consistent with a predominantly pastoral view of the Church's teaching office."

Another, related purpose of the Council was summed up in Pope John's favorite term, *"aggiornamento,"* a word whose literal meaning is "a bringing up to date." For the Holy Father this *"aggiornamento"* was to have two dimensions: first, an internal renewal of the Church that would bring out sharply the features it had when it first came from the hands of Christ; second, a revitalization in the Church's approach to the modern world, which would make the Church better understood and more attractive, and put her in a position to bring the Gospel more effectively to twentieth-century man.

While a pastoral quality and the goal of renewal were Pope John's general directions for the Council, he often expanded upon them, citing certain specific hopes for it:

> We are expecting really great things from this council, which aims at bringing a greater vigor to faith, to doctrine, to Church discipline, and to religious and spiritual life. Furthermore, it aims at making a great contribution toward a reaffirmation of the principles of Christian law that serve as the basis and the framework for the developments of civil, economic, political, and social life.

On another occasion he said this of his hopes for the Council:

> ... the aim of the Council is to make the clergy on every level shine with a new holiness; to bring the main points and precepts of Christian

doctrine to the people of God in the best possible way; to give young people, the fresh seeds whose growth holds the hope of a better age, sound training in how to live as they should; to foster the activities of the social apostolate; and to nourish a deep missionary spirit, the kind of spirit that will make it clear to everyone that each and every person is our brother and our friend.

One, perhaps distant, result of the Council's *aggiornamento* that Pope John foresaw was the reunion of divided Christianity. The Council, he said, would bring the Church "a new and fuller splendor in these disturbed times and raise a new hope" that separated Christians would one day be united in the one Church of Christ. His most immediate hopes seemed to be for the reunion of the Eastern and Western Churches.

> A determined step toward a reunion between the Eastern and Western brethren, within the one and only fold of Christ, the eternal Shepherd, would be a marvelous occurrence and a lovely flower of human and heavenly charity. That should be one of the most valuable achievements of the coming Second Vatican Ecumenical Council.

Of course, his hopes for the reunion not only of East and West but of all separated Christians he expressed many times. And when he did his words were characteristically warm and personal. In a special talk to the non-Catholic observers at the Council he recalled the opening day with these words:

> From time to time my eye ranged over the multitude of sons and brothers, and when my glance rested upon your group, on each of you personally, I drew a special comfort from your presence . . . if you would read my heart, you would perhaps understand much more than words can say.

To facilitate communication between the Church and separated Christians Pope John established for the Council a secretariat for Christian unity, a body he later raised to the status of a conciliar commission, thus emphasizing its importance in the Council.

In addition to calling the Council into being and defining its goals, Pope John gave the actual meetings the stamp of his personality: a marvelous quality of openness and freedom. One bold move toward openness was his invitation to non-Catholic observers to attend all the general sessions, hear all the arguments, know at once of all the decisions. No longer was an ecumenical council to be a private meeting, with all its problems kept "within the family." The effect of this innovation was entirely good. The observers were astonished at the freedom of debate, the easy airing of a wide range of views. This experience changed their long-held notion—and the world's—that the Catholic Church is a dictatorial monolith within which only one, authorized view can be expressed. Pope John declared that the differences of opinion amongst the Fathers demonstrated to the world the "existence in the Church of the holy freedom of the sons of God." And the mere act of inviting observers did incalculable good by its clear affirmation of Pope John's love for all mankind and his eagerness to initiate a movement toward reunion of all Christians.

The freedom of debate at the Council was in large measure the wish and achievement of Pope John. As one writer said, the Pope believed deeply in the "law of dialogue":

> John XXIII's pedagogy, a pedagogy fitted to a Church of world-wide dimensions, was to gather together for a common undertaking men of intelligence and of the most diversely oriented points of view. Persistence in processing this method . . . has resulted in the institution of face to face discussions on all levels in all sectors—structured dialogue of the Church with separated Christians; dialogue between the bishops and the Roman congregations, first within the dimensions of the preparatory commissions, then of the Central Commission, and, finally, of the entire assembly of the Council. And this dialogue has proved contagious. It has extended across the world, far beyond official organizations—into dioceses, between the bishops, their clergy, and their faithful; between priests, between laymen, between Catholics and non-Catholics—pulling down man-made partitions, sweeping aside prejudices and conventions. (René Laurentin, *Cross Currents*, Fall 1963)

Except for his opening and closing addresses, Pope John absented himself from all sessions of the Council, though he is said to have followed it on a special communications circuit. He made it eminently clear that the assembled bishops were to discuss everything freely and at length, and that they would not have to feel subject to any possible pressure that the Supreme Pontiff's presence might cause.

Only when the progress and good order of the Council were at stake did Pope John intervene directly. For example, when a majority of the Fathers voted to reject the schema on the sources of revelation but failed to get the required two-thirds vote, John intervened in favor of the majority and remanded the schema to a joint committee which he organized on the spot. He intervened again, in the final days of the first session, during the debate on the schema concerning the nature of the Church. This time he directed that in the nine-month interim before the second session not only this schema but all the schemata—particularly those already discussed in Council—were to be revised by mixed commissions and sent to the bishops for their comments. To harmonize the work of these commissions, he created a new central coordinating committee. It should be noted that in neither instance did Pope John try to force his own views on the Fathers; rather, he continued the dialogue among them, shifting it from the whole Council to the arena of special commissions on which both sides of the debate were represented.

No one can say yet what will be the full effect of Pope John's Council. We know, of course, that at the time of this writing it has already resulted in specific decrees which have produced sweeping changes in the liturgy and that additional decrees will no doubt be forthcoming. We know, too, that it has rid the world of its illusion that the Church is an archaism, closed to all change. But above all else, Pope John's great achievement was the Council itself, the very fact of bishops from all over the world meeting each other, rubbing elbows, exchanging views, seeing the Church Universal face to face. And this "fact" is entirely attributable to Pope John.

Proclamation of the Second Vatican Council

The Apostolic Constitution "Humanae Salutis"

- *Disturbed condition of the world*
- *Church's response to change*
- *Hopes for unity*
- *Formal convocation of the Council*
- *An appeal to separated Christians*

BEFORE CHRIST JESUS, who had reopened the way to salvation for mankind, ascended into heaven, He gave the Apostles He had chosen a command to carry the light of the Gospel to all nations, and He willingly made a promise to them that would confer authority and stability upon the office He had committed to them: *Behold I am with you all days, even to the consummation of the world.*[1]

There has never been a time when this constant, joyful presence of Christ has failed to show itself alive and at work in the holy Church, but it has shone forth most clearly at times when mankind and society were being buffeted by unusually fierce storms. It is at times like these that the Bride of Christ has most clearly shown that she is the teacher of truth and the minister of salvation, and has proved in full view of everyone just how much power there is to be found in charity, in the offering up of devout prayers, in bearing with troubles and hardships through the grace of God; also just what heavenly safeguards she possesses, and how unconquerable they are, since they are the same ones her divine Founder was employing when He said, at the great hour of His life: *Have confidence, I have overcome the world.*[2]

---

[1] *Matt.* 28, 20.   [2] *John* 16, 33.

A disturbed society

In this age of ours, the Church sees a human society that is seriously disturbed and looking toward a complete change. And while human society is being carried along toward a new order, far-reaching tasks remain for the Church; as we have learned, this has been the case in every period of great distress. The Church is now called upon to take the perennial, vital divine power of the Gospel and inject it into the veins of the human society of today, which glories in its recent scientific and technological advances, at the same time that it is suffering damage to its social order, which some people have tried to repair without God's assistance.

And so We might note that the men of our day have not made the same progress in goods of the soul as they have in external goods. As a result, they are more careless about seeking the things that will not perish; instead, they often long for the passing pleasures of the world, which technical advances have made so easy to obtain; and finally—this is something new and frightening—there has arisen a whole party of men who deny the existence of God and are organized on what amounts to a military basis, and it has extended its influence to many nations.

Light from darkness

These causes of sorrow and anxiety that come to mind should point up the need for vigilance and make every individual aware of his own responsibilities. We know that the over-all picture of these evils has disturbed some people to such an extent that they can see nothing but darkness and shadows, and feel that the world has been completely covered by them.

But We prefer to place Our unshakeable trust in the divine savior of the human race, who has not deserted the human beings whom He has redeemed. As a matter of fact, in keeping with the advice of Christ the Lord who urged us to recognize the *signs . . . of the times*,[3] we can, in the midst of all the hideous clouds and darkness, perceive a number of things that seem to be omens portending a better day for the Church and for mankind.

[3] *Matt.* 16, 4.

For the murderous wars that have followed one after the other in our times, as well as the great harm inflicted on souls by many ideas and notions, and the great hardships and sufferings that too many men have experienced for such a long time—all these things have been a kind of warning as well. And the very scientific and technical progress that has supplied men with the power to produce fearful arms aimed at their own destruction has given rise to a great deal of anxiety and concern.

The result of this has been that men are now gripped by a real interest and concern, that they are more ready to admit that their own abilities and powers are limited, that they long for peace, that they are weighing the importance of the goods of the soul, and finally that they are trying to accelerate that course of social life which it must be said human society has already entered upon, even if with uncertain steps. It is a course of affairs that impels individual men, various classes of society and whole nations to work together in friendly fashion more and more and offer each other the mutual help that will round out and improve each other's efforts.

This will be of immense help toward carrying on the apostolic activity of the Church more easily and more effectively; for many men, who may well have been unaware of the Church's lofty mission up to the present, seem to be more inclined to accept her admonitions now that they have learned so much more fruitfully from their own experience.

Continuing concern of the Church

As far as the Church is concerned, she has never remained indifferent to the course of events in nations, to scientific and technical progress, to the changing conditions of human society; rather, she has kept a constant watch over them; she has resisted with all her strength the teaching of those who reduce everything to matter or try to undermine the foundations of the Catholic faith; and she has drawn the richest of fruits from her bosom to inspire people to enter into the sacred apostolate, into works of devotion, into her activity in all fields of human endeavor.

This applies first of all to the work carried on by the clergy, who have shown themselves better prepared in learning and virtue to meet their responsibilities; and secondly to the work of laymen, who have gained a greater awareness of the role entrusted to them in the Church, and especially of the responsibility of each one of them to offer a helping hand to the hierarchy of the Church.

Besides this, you have the fact that the hardships of immense proportions with which many communities of Christians find themselves bitterly afflicted today are resulting in a truly admirable multitude of bishops, priests, and laymen enduring attacks and insults of all kinds because of their unshakeable loyalty to the Catholic faith, and producing examples of Christian fortitude that may rightly be compared with the ones recorded in the letters of gold in the annals of the Church.

And so, while we see how completely changed the face of human society is, so too the Catholic Church presents itself to our eyes as clothed with a greatly changed and more perfect form: evidencing a firmer unity of structure, developed by the help of a richer doctrine and more beautifully resplendent with the brightness of sanctity, so that she stands forth completely prepared to fight the holy battles of the faith.

Decision to call a council

We have had in Our mind's eye this twofold picture: on the one hand, human society laboring under a great need for spiritual goods; on the other, the Church of Christ flourishing with a fullness of life. This picture has been before Our eyes since the very beginning of Our supreme pontificate, to whose heights We were raised despite Our unworthiness by the most gracious plan of God in His providence.

As We gazed upon this picture, We considered it a serious responsibility of Our apostolic office to direct Our thoughts toward having the Church, through the cooperation of all Our sons, show herself better and better fitted to solve the problems of the men of this age. For this reason, in response to an inner voice that arose from a kind of heavenly inspiration, We felt that the time was ripe for Us to give the Catholic Church and the whole human family the gift of a new ecumenical council, which would continue that series of twenty synods which have been of such great value for the growth of heavenly grace in the souls of the faithful and for the progress of Christianity in the course of the centuries.

The great outpouring of joy with which the announcement of this was greeted by Catholics throughout the whole world; the ardent prayers that the whole Church poured forth to God so eagerly for this intention and which have not let up; the eager and steady efforts devoted to preparing for this council, which have exceeded Our fondest hopes; and finally the devoted interest, or, We might even say, the expectation, full of respect, with which this council is being followed by those who are not Christians or who are separated from the Roman Church—all of these things, We say, offer the clearest proof that the enormous importance and greatness of this event has escaped no one.

Changing, yet unchanged

The coming ecumenical synod is, fortunately, taking place at a time when the Church is burning with a more ardent eagerness to add new strength and power to her faith and to restore gently the wonderful vision of her unity, while at the same time she more urgently feels that she is bound by her office not only to make her power and force more vital and more effective and to promote the holiness of her sons, but also to bring about a growth in the diffusion of Christian truth and of her institutions.

This will bring out clearly that holy mother Church is always alive and flourishing with perpetual youth, always involved in human events, and always, in the course of the centuries, adorned with a fresh appearance, radiating new glories, bearing new palms, even while remaining always the same perfect picture of that form which her divine Spouse, who loves and protects her, We mean Christ Jesus, willed her to have.

Christian unity

At a time when we can see increasingly frequent attempts in various parts of the world by more and more people (who are pursuing this goal with all their strength) to re-establish a visible unity among all Christians, which will fully satisfy the desires and wishes of the divine Saviour, it seems altogether fitting to have the forthcoming council point up such aspects of doctrine and show such an example of fraternal charity as will enkindle among Christians separated from the Apostolic See a keener enthusiasm for that unity and, in a sense, prepare the way for its achievement.

Plans for peace

Finally, as far as the whole human family is concerned, which, much beset by threats of fearful struggles, is kept anxious, upset and uncertain, the coming ecumenical council will furnish all men of good will with an opportunity for entering into and promoting plans and proposals for peace. This peace in the true sense can and must be generated by goods of a spiritual and supernatural nature, and by the minds and consciences of men, taking their light and their lead from God, the Creator and Redeemer of the human race.

Need for preparation

But these fruits, which We so ardently desire to see come from the ecumenical synod and which We have discussed so willingly and so often, require that in preparing for a project of such tremendous importance planning, steady effort, and hard work be employed. Questions that have to do with the doctrines of faith and with practical life are being brought up; proposals are being made to adapt Christian institutions and apply Christian precepts perfectly to the many aspects of daily living, and to have them be of greater service to the mystical body of Christ and its sacred responsibilities and functions, which have to do with the supernatural order. All these things touch on sacred scripture, sacred tradition, the sacraments and prayers of the Church, morals and discipline, the organizations devoted to the practice of charity and care of the needy, the lay apostolate, missionary undertakings.

Influence of the Church

But the heavenly order must have as much influence as possible on that other order, limited by the boundaries of time, which unfortunately is often the only one that occupies the care and anxious concern of men.

For in the area of temporal affairs, too, the Church shows herself a *Mother and Teacher,* in the words used by Our predecessor of happy memory, Innocent III, when the Fourth Ecumenical Council of the Lateran was held. Even though the main goal toward which the Church is striving is not an earthly one, still, as she journeys along her path, she cannot ignore the questions that have to do with temporal goods or pay no attention to the labors that produce these goods. She is well aware of the precise benefit that can be conferred on immortal souls by whatever serves to make a little more human the lives of individual men, whose eternal salvation she is seeking. She realizes that when she sheds the light of Christ upon men, she is helping them to know themselves better. For she leads them to understand what they really are, what dignity they enjoy, what goal they must pursue.

As a result, at the present time the Church is, either officially or unofficially, playing a role in international organizations and has developed an organized social teaching which touches on families, schools, employment, human society and its various ties, and all questions of this kind; and because of this doctrine, the Church has achieved so lofty a pinnacle of prestige that her solemn pronouncements are treated with the highest respect by all prudent men, who regard her as a spokesman and defender for morality and a vindicator of the rights and duties of individuals and of nations.

And so We feel sure that the decisions made in the ecumenical synod will have the effect not only of shedding the light of Christian wisdom and supplying strength and ardor to the hearts and minds of individuals but also of permeating the whole range of human activities.

It was on January 25, 1959, that We first announced that an ecumenical council would be celebrated.[4] When We did so, it seemed as if We were throwing out a tiny seed, with an anxious mind and hand. With the support of God's help, We then moved on to the many different kinds of serious preparation that a project of this size demanded.

Almost exactly three years have passed since that day, and in the

---

[4] Cf. p. 22 above.

intervening time, We have seen that tiny seed grow, with the help of heavenly grace, into a great and noble tree. As We look at the long, hard road that has been covered, We offer the greatest of thanks to God, Who has bountifully bestowed upon Us the help to enable everything to move along as it should, in harmonious fashion.

The preparatory stage

Before deciding upon what subjects were to be treated in the council, We first of all sought the wise and prudent counsel of the cardinals, all the bishops of the Catholic world, the sacred congregations of the Roman Curia, the generals of religious orders and congregations, Catholic universities and ecclesiastical faculties. A whole year was spent in poring over their suggestions, vast in number; and this process made clear the main subjects to which study ought to be devoted.

Then various commissions were set up to prepare for the council, and We gave them the arduous task of suggesting outlines for decrees concerning faith and morals, from among which We would choose the ones to be taken up in the general sessions of the council.

It gives Us the greatest of joy to inform you that these preparations, which were so eagerly undertaken and to which cardinals, bishops, prelates, theologians, canon lawyers, and learned men and experts from the whole world have contributed their distinguished cooperative efforts, are on the verge of being concluded.

And so, with full confidence in the help of the divine Redeemer, who is the beginning and end of all things, and in the prayer of His august mother, the Most Blessed Virgin Mary, and of St. Joseph, to whose patronage We have committed this very important event from its very beginning, it is Our judgment that the time has come to convoke the second Ecumenical Council of the Vatican.

The council convoked

And so, after listening to the opinions of the cardinals of the Holy Roman Church upon this matter, by the authority of Our Lord Jesus Christ, of the Holy Apostles Peter and Paul, and Our own, We announce, We proclaim, We convoke, for this coming year of 1962, the second Sacred Ecumenical and universal Council of the Vatican, which will be celebrated in the Patriarchal Basilica of the Vatican, on the days which God in His great providence shall have given [Us] to decide.

And so We desire and We command that Our beloved sons, the cardinals of the Holy Roman Church, Our venerable brethren, the patriarchs, primates, archbishops, and bishops, both residential and titular, as well as all the churchmen who must by law be present at an ecumenical council, be present at the ecumenical council being convoked by Us from all parts of the world.

A call for prayers

Finally, We ask each of the faithful and the Christian people as a whole to devote every effort to the council and to pour forth great prayers to Almighty God graciously to sustain this great undertaking that is now imminent and to strengthen it with His virtue and power, and to grant that it will take place with fitting dignity. May these common prayers flow steadily from faith as from a living font; may they be accompanied by voluntary bodily mortification to make them more acceptable to God and supremely effective; may they also be enriched by an unselfish effort to live a Christian life, which would be a sign that all are already prepared to carry out the precepts and decrees that eventually will be laid down by this council.

We address these suggestions to Our most loving sons of the secular and the religious clergy, wherever they reside, and to all the faithful of every degree. We address them in a special way to children, the great value of whose innocence and prayers to God is known to everyone, and to the sick and the suffering, for We are convinced that their pains, their lives, so very much like that of a sacrificial victim, are, through the power of the Cross of Christ, turned into an effective plea, into salvation, into a source of holy life for the universal Church.

Interest of separated Christians

Last of all, We earnestly ask all Christians who are separated from the Catholic Church to plead with God: for the council will redound to their benefit too. For We know very well that many of these sons have a desire to achieve unity and peace, according to the teaching of Christ, and according to the prayer He addressed to the heavenly Father; nor has it escaped Us that when they heard the news of the council, not only did they receive it with great joy, but a number of them even promised they would pray to God that things might turn out well and successfully and had high hopes that some representatives of their groups would be sent to inform them of what was done in the council. All these things brought Us immense hope and consolation; and We set up a special office, called a secretariat, to deal with this matter and carry on these contacts more easily and more effectively.

Would that the Christian family of this time might have the same experience we read of in the times of the Apostles, after the ascension of Christ into heaven: when the whole Church, so recently born, with perfect harmony of minds and hearts, directed its attention to Peter, the Pastor of the lambs and the sheep, and prayed with him and for him. And may the adorable Spirit of God, acceding to the most ardent wishes and hopes of everyone, accept this prayer, which is lifted up to Him daily from all parts of the world:

"Renew Thy wonderful works in this age of ours through a new Pentecost, as it were, and grant to Holy Church that, persevering in ardent prayer in union with Mary the Mother of Jesus and under the leadership of the Blessed Peter, she may spread the kingdom of the divine Saviour, the kingdom of truth and of justice, the kingdom of love and of peace. Amen."[5]

Formal conclusion

We desire this constitution to take effect now and to remain in effect permanently; and to have the things decreed in it observed religiously by those whom it concerns, and thus obtain their full force. No contrary prescriptions of any kind may interfere with the force of this constitution since We countermand them all by this constitution. And so, if anyone, no matter what his authority, knowingly or unknowingly, does anything contrary to what We

---

[5] *AAS* 51 (1959) 832. From a prayer to the Holy Ghost for the success of the ecumenical council. This indulgenced prayer, dated September 23, 1959, was published by the Sacred Penitentiary.—Ed.

have decreed, We command that his action be regarded as invalid and have no effect. Again, no one may rescind or alter these documents which contain Our will, or this constitution; and exactly the same authority is to be attributed to any copies of it, whether printed or handwritten, that bear the seal of some person in ecclesiastical office and that are countersigned by some public notary, as would be to this if it were to be displayed. And if anyone disregards or detracts from these decrees We have laid down for all, let him know that he will suffer the penalties established by law for those who have not carried out the commands of the supreme pontiffs.[6]

Given at Rome, at St. Peter's, on December 25th, the Nativity of Our Lord Jesus Christ, in the year 1961, the fourth of Our Pontificate.

I, JOHN,
Bishop of the Catholic Church

[6] This paragraph is a technical, canonical conclusion to an apostolic constitution. —Tr.

PENANCE FOR SUCCESS OF THE COUNCIL

The Encyclical "Paenitentiam Agere"
to Catholic Bishops

- *Biblical precedents*
- *Renewal of the Church through penance*
- *Earlier councils*
- *A call for prayer and penance*
- *Kinds of penance*

DOING PENANCE for one's sins is a first step towards obtaining forgiveness and winning eternal salvation. That is the clear and explicit teaching of Christ, and no one can fail to see how justified and how right the Catholic Church has always been in constantly insisting on this. She is the spokesman for her divine Redeemer. No individual Christian can grow in perfection, nor can Christianity itself gain in vigor, except it be on this basis of penance.

That is why in Our apostolic constitution officially proclaiming the Second Ecumenical Vatican Council and urging the faithful to make a worthy spiritual preparation for this great event by prayer and other acts of Christian virtue, We included a warning to them not to overlook the practice of voluntary mortification.[1]

A request repeated

And now, as the day for the opening of the Second Vatican Council draws nearer, We wish to repeat that request of Ours and dwell on it at greater length. In doing so We are confident that We

[1] Cf. Apostolic constitution *"Humanae salutis,"* AAS 54 (1962) 12. (See p. 386 above.)

are serving the best interests of this most important and solemn assembly. For while admitting that Christ is present to His Church "all days, even unto the consummation of the world,"[2] we must think of Him as being even closer to men's hearts and minds during the time of an ecumenical council, for He is present in the persons of His legates, of whom He said quite emphatically, "He who hears you, hears me."[3]

The Ecumenical Council will be a meeting of the successors of the Apostles, men to whom the Saviour of the human race gave the command to teach all nations and urge them to observe all His commandments.[4] Its manifest task, therefore, will be to reaffirm publicly God's rights over mankind, whom Christ's blood has redeemed, and to reaffirm the duties of redeemed mankind towards its God and Saviour.

Calls to penance in the Bible

Now we have only to open the sacred books of the Old and New Testament to be assured of one thing: it was never God's will to reveal Himself in any solemn encounter with mortal men—to speak in human terms—without first calling them to prayer and penance. Indeed, Moses refused to give the Hebrews the tables of the Law until they had expiated their crime of idolatry and ingratitude.[5]

So too the Prophets; they never wearied of exhorting the Israelites to make their prayers acceptable to God, their supreme Overlord, by offering them in a penitential spirit. Otherwise they would bring about their own exclusion from the plan of divine Providence, according to which God Himself was to be the King of His chosen people.

The most deeply impressive of these prophetic utterances is surely that warning of Joel which is constantly ringing in our ears in the course of the Lenten liturgy: "Now therefore, says the Lord, be converted to me with all your heart, in fasting and in weeping and in mourning. And rend your hearts and not your garments. . . . Between the porch and the altar the priests, the Lord's ministers,

---

[2] *Matt.* 28, 20. [3] *Luke* 10, 16.
[4] Cf. *Matt.* 28, 19-20. [5] Cf. *Exod.* 32, 6-35, and *1 Cor.* 10, 7.

shall weep and say: Spare, O Lord, spare thy people, and give not thy inheritance to reproach, that the heathen should rule over them."[6]

Nor did these calls to penance cease when the Son of God became incarnate. On the contrary, they became even more insistent. At the very outset of his preaching, John the Baptist proclaimed: "Do penance, for the kingdom of heaven is at hand."[7] And Jesus inaugurated His saving mission in the same way. He did not begin by revealing the principal truths of the faith. First He insisted that the soul must repent of every trace of sin that could render it impervious to the message of eternal salvation: "From that time Jesus began to preach and to say, 'Do penance, for the kingdom of heaven is at hand.' "[8]

He was even more vehement than were the Prophets in His demands that those who listened to Him should undergo a complete change of heart and submit in perfect sincerity to all the laws of the Supreme God. "For behold," He said, "the kingdom of God is within you."[9]

Indeed, penance is that counterforce which keeps the forces of concupiscence in check and repels them. In the words of Christ Himself, "the kingdom of heaven has been enduring violent assault, and the violent have been seizing it by force."[10]

The apostles held undeviatingly to the principles of their divine Master. When the Holy Spirit had descended on them in the form of fiery tongues, Peter expressed his invitation to the multitudes to seek rebirth in Christ and to accept the gifts of the most holy Paraclete in these words: "Do penance and be baptized, every one of you, in the name of Jesus Christ, for the remission of your sins. And you will receive the gift of the Holy Spirit."[11] Paul too, the teacher of the Gentiles, announced to the Romans in no uncertain terms that the kingdom of God did not consist in an attitude of intellectual superiority or in indulging the pleasures of sense. It consisted in the triumph of justice and in peace of mind. "For the kingdom of God does not consist in food and drink, but in justice and peace and joy in the Holy Spirit."[12]

[6] *Joel* 2, 12-13 and 17.   [7] *Matt.* 3, 2.   [8] *Ibid.* 4, 17.
[9] *Luke* 17, 21.   [10] *Matt.* 11, 12.   [11] *Acts* 2, 38.   [12] *Rom.* 14, 17.

Penance and baptismal innocence

However, a rude awakening is in store for the person who thinks that penance is necessary only for those aspiring to membership in the kingdom of God. He who is already a member of Christ must learn of necessity to keep a rein upon himself. Only so will he be able to drive away the enemy of his soul and keep his baptismal innocence unsullied, or regain God's grace when it is lost by sin.

To become a member of Holy Church by baptism is to be clothed in the beauty with which Christ adorns His beloved Bride. "Christ loved the Church and delivered himself up for her; that he might sanctify her, cleansing her in the bath of water by means of the word of life; in order that he might present to himself the Church in all her glory, not having spot or wrinkle or any such thing; but that she might be holy and without blemish."[13]

This being so, well may those sinners who have stained the white robe of their sacred baptism fear the just punishments of God. Their remedy is "to wash their robes in the blood of the Lamb"[14]—to restore themselves to their former splendor in the sacrament of Penance—and to school themselves in the practice of Christian virtue. Hence the Apostle Paul's severe warning: "A man making void the law of Moses dies without any mercy on the word of two or three witnesses; how much worse punishments do you think he deserves, who has trodden under foot the Son of God, and has regarded as unclean the blood of the covenant through which he was sanctified, and has insulted the Spirit of grace? . . . It is a fearful thing to fall into the hands of the living God."[15]

The Bride of Christ, holy and unsullied

Certainly, venerable brethren, when one views the faith which distinguishes the Church, the sacraments which nourish and perfect her, the universal laws and precepts which govern her, the unfailing glory that is hers by reason of the heroic virtue and constancy of so many of her elect, there can be no doubt that the Bride of Christ, so dear to her divine Redeemer, has always kept herself holy and unsullied.

[13] *Eph.* 5, 25-27.   [14] Cf. *Apoc.* 7, 14.   [15] *Heb.* 10, 28-29 and 31.

Her forgetful children

But of her children there are some who nevertheless forget the greatness of their calling and election. They mar their God-given beauty, and fail to mirror in themselves the image of Jesus Christ. We cannot find it in Us to threaten or abuse them, for the love We bear them is a father's love. Instead We appeal to them in the words of the Council of Trent—the best restorative for Catholic discipline. "When we put on Christ in baptism (*Gal.* 3, 27), we become in Him an entirely new creature and obtain the full and complete remission of every sin. It is only with great effort and with great compunction on our part that we can obtain the same newness and sinlessness in the sacrament of penance, for such is the stipulation of divine justice. That is why the holy Fathers called penance 'a laborious kind of baptism'."[16]

Penance in the prayers of the Church

The very frequency with which this call to penance is reiterated makes it imperative for Christians to recognize it as coming from the divine Redeemer for the purpose of bringing about their purification and spiritual renewal. It is transmitted to us by the Church, in her sacred liturgy, in the teaching of the Fathers and the precepts of the councils. "Make our souls to glow in Thy sight with desire of Thee."[17] "Help us to repress our worldly appetites, that we may the more easily obtain the blessings of heaven."[18] That is how the Catholic Church prays to God's Supreme Majesty in these ancient prayers from the Lenten liturgy.

Earlier councils and calls to penance

Can we wonder, then, that Our predecessors, when they were preparing the ground for an ecumenical council, made a point of exhorting the faithful to perform salutary acts of penance?

---

[16] Council of Trent, Sess. XIV, *doctrina de Sacramento Paenitentiae*, ch. 2; cf. St. Greg. Naz., *Orat.* 39, 17: *PG* 36, 356; St. John Dam., *De fide orthod.* 4, 9: *PG* 94, 11, 24.
[17] Collect for Tuesday in the first week in Lent.
[18] Collect for Wednesday in the fourth week in Lent.

Consider, for example, the words of Innocent III before the Fourth Lateran Council: "To your praying add fasting and almsgiving. It is on these wings that our prayers fly the more swiftly and effortlessly to the holy ears of God, that He may mercifully hear us in the time of need."[19]

Before the Second Ecumenical Council of Lyons, Gregory X wrote to all his prelates and chaplains commanding them to observe a three-day fast.[20]

And finally, Pius IX exhorted all the faithful to prepare themselves worthily and joyously for the First Vatican Council by ridding their souls of every stain of sin and the punishment due to sin. "It is certain," he said, "that men's prayers are more pleasing to God if they go up to Him from a pure heart; from souls, that is, that are free from all sin."[21]

Prayer and penance for the coming council

We too, venerable brethren, on the example of Our predecessors, are most anxious that the whole Catholic world, both clerical and lay, shall prepare itself for this great event, the forthcoming council, by ardent prayer, good works, and the practice of Christian penance.

Clearly the most efficacious kind of prayer for gaining the divine protection is prayer that is offered publicly by the whole community; for our Redeemer said: "Where two or three are gathered together for my sake, there am I in the midst of them."[22]

The situation, therefore, demands that Christians today, as in the days of the early Church, shall be of "one heart and one soul,"[23] imploring God with prayer and penance to grant that this great assembly may measure up to all our expectations.

The salutary results we pray for are these: that the faith, the love, the moral lives of Catholics may be so re-invigorated, so intensified,

---

[19] *Epist. ad Concil. Later. IV spectantes,* Epist. 28 ad fideles per Moguntinas provincias constitutos, Mansi, *Amplissimi Coll. Concil.* 22, Paris and Leipzig, 1903, col. 959.
[20] Cf. Mansi, *loc. cit.* 24, col. 62.
[21] Cf. *Act. et Decr. Sacr. Concil. Recent., Coll. Lac.* tom. VII, Frieburg im Breisgau, 1890, col. 10.
[22] *Matt.* 18, 20.   [23] *Acts* 4, 32.

that all who are at present separated from this Apostolic See may be impelled to strive actively and sincerely for union, and enter the one fold under the one Shepherd.[24]

Specific steps to be taken

To achieve greater unanimity in this prayer, venerable brethren, We would have you organize a solemn novena to the Holy Spirit in all the parishes of your diocese immediately preceding the Ecumenical Council. The object of this novena will be to beg for an abundance of heavenly light and supernatural aid for the Fathers in council. To all who join in this novena We impart from the Church's treasury a plenary indulgence, obtainable on the usual conditions.

Then, too, a public act of prayer and propitiation might fittingly be arranged in every diocese and, in conjunction with it, a special course of sermons, to serve as a fervent invitation to the faithful to redouble their works of mercy and penance. By this means they may hope to propitiate Almighty God and thus obtain by their prayers that renewal of Christian life which is one of the principal aims of the coming Council. As Our predecessor Pius XI so aptly observed: "Prayer and penance are the two potent inspirations sent to us at this time by God, that we may bring back to Him our wayward human race that wanders aimlessly without a guide. They are the inspirations that will disperse and remedy the first and foremost cause of all rebellion and unrest, man's revolt against God."[25]

Internal repentance

Our first need is for internal repentance; the detestation, that is, of sin, and the determination to make amends for it. This is the repentance shown by those who make a good confession, take part in the Eucharistic Sacrifice and receive Holy Communion. The faithful should be specially encouraged to do this during the novena to the Holy Spirit, for external acts of penance are quite obviously

---

[24] Cf. *John* 10, 16.
[25] Encyclical *"Caritate Christi compulsi," AAS* 24 (1932) 191.

useless unless accompanied by a clear conscience and the detestation of sin. Hence Christ's severe warning: "Unless you repent you will all perish in the same manner."[26] God forbid that any of Our sons and daughters succumb to this danger.

Outward acts of penance

But the faithful must also be encouraged to do outward acts of penance, both to keep their bodies under the strict control of reason and faith, and to make amends for their own and other people's sins. St. Paul was caught up to the third heaven—he reached the summit of holiness—and yet he had no hesitation in saying of himself, "I chastise my body and bring it into subjection."[27] On another occasion he said: "They who belong to Christ have crucified their flesh with its passions and desires."[28] St. Augustine issued the same insistent warning: "It is not enough for a man to change his ways for the better and to give up the practice of evil, unless by painful penance, sorrowing humility, the sacrifice of a contrite heart and the giving of alms he makes amends to God for all that he has done wrong."[29]

External penance includes particularly the acceptance from God in a spirit of resignation and trust of all life's sorrows and hardships and of everything that involves inconvenience and annoyance in the conscientious performance of the obligations of our daily life and work and the practice of Christian virtue. Penance of this kind is in fact inescapable. Yet it serves not only to win God's mercy and forgiveness for our sins, and His heavenly aid for the Ecumenical Council, but also sweetens, one might almost say, the bitterness of this mortal life of ours with the promise of its heavenly reward. For "the sufferings of the present time are not worthy to be compared with the glory to come that will be revealed in us."[30]

Voluntary acts as part of external penance

But besides bearing in a Christian spirit the inescapable annoyances and sufferings of this life, the faithful ought also take the initiative in doing voluntary acts of penance and offering them to

---

[26] *Luke* 13, 5. [27] *1 Cor.* 9, 27. [28] *Gal.* 5, 24.
[29] Serm. 351, 5, 12; *PL* 39, 1549. [30] *Rom.* 8, 18.

God. In this they will be following in the footsteps of our divine Redeemer who, as the Prince of the Apostles said, "died once for sins, the Just for the unjust; that he might bring us to God. Put to death indeed in the flesh, he was brought to life in the spirit."[31] "Since, therefore, Christ has suffered in the flesh," it is only fitting that we be "armed with the same intent."[32]

It is right, too, to seek example and inspiration from the great saints of the Church. Pure as they were, they inflicted such mortifications upon themselves as to leave us almost aghast with admiration. And as we contemplate their saintly heroism, shall not we be moved by God's grace to impose on ourselves some voluntary sufferings and deprivations, we whose consciences are perhaps weighed down by so heavy a burden of guilt?

And who does not know that this sort of penance is the more acceptable to God in that it springs not from the natural infirmities of soul or body, but from a free and generous resolve of the will, and as such is a most welcome sacrifice in God's sight?

A share in the work of eternal salvation

Finally, the object of the Ecumenical Council, as everyone knows, will be to render more effective that divine work which our Redeemer accomplished. Christ our Lord accomplished it by being "offered . . . because it was his own will."[33] He accomplished it not merely by teaching men His heavenly doctrine, but also, and more especially, by pouring out His most precious blood for their salvation. Yet each of us can say with St. Paul: "I now rejoice in my sufferings . . . and fill up those things that are wanting of the sufferings of Christ, in my flesh, for his body, which is the Church."[34]

Let us then be alert and generous, and take full advantage of this opportunity of offering up our sorrows and sufferings to God "for building up the body of Christ,"[35] the Church. No fairer, no more desirable fate could befall us than to be given a share in that work which has as its object the eternal salvation of men who have strayed far too often from the right path of truth and virtue.

---

[31] *1 Peter* 3, 18.   [32] Cf. *ibid.*, 4, 1.   [33] *Isa.* 53, 7.
[34] *Col.* 1, 24.   [35] *Eph.* 4, 12.

A necessary repudiation

Jesus Christ taught us self-discipline and *self-denial* when He said: "If anyone wishes to come after me, let him deny himself and take up his cross daily and follow me."[36] Yet there are many people, alas, who join instead the immoderate quest for earthly pleasures, thus debasing and weakening the nobler powers of the human spirit. It is all the more necessary, therefore, for Christians to repudiate this unworthy way of life which gives frequent rein to the turbulent emotions of the soul and seriously endangers its eternal salvation. They must repudiate it with all the energy and courage displayed by the martyrs and those heroic men and women who have been the glory of the Church in every age of her history. If everyone does this, each in his own station in life, he will be enabled to play his individual part in making this Second Ecumenical Vatican Council, which is especially concerned with the refurbishing of Christian morality, an outstanding success.

Preparing to receive the good seed

So much for the subject of Our letter, venerable brethren, and it is Our confident hope that both you yourselves and, at your instigation, all Our sons throughout the world, both clerical and lay, will give a whole-hearted and generous response to Our fatherly appeals. Everyone wants the forthcoming ecumenical council to give all possible impetus to the spread of Christianity. It must give louder and louder utterance to that "word by which the kingdom is preached" mentioned in the parable of the sower,[37] and help to bring about the wider extension of "the kingdom of God" in the world. But all this must depend to a large extent on the dispositions of the souls which the Council will be endeavoring to inspire to truth and virtue, to the worship of God both in private and in public, to a disciplined life and to missionary zeal.

Do your utmost, venerable brethren; explore every avenue that is open to you; have no hesitation in mustering all your authority and available resources in an effort to persuade the faithful under

[36] *Luke* 9, 23.   [37] *Matt.* 13, 19.

your charge to purify their souls by penance and to enkindle them with the fervor of piety. The "good seed" which the Council will scatter far and wide over the Church in those days must not be allowed to go to waste; it must find its way into hearts that are ready and prepared, loyal and true. If such is the case, then the forthcoming council will indeed be for the faithful, a fruitful source of eternal salvation.

"Behold, now is the acceptable time; behold, now is the day of salvation."[38] These are words which We consider most applicable to that period of time which will shortly be upon us when the Ecumenical Council is in session. But when God in His Providence decrees to give His supernatural gifts to men, He does so in the measure of their own individual desires and dispositions. Hence Our long-continued insistence on the spiritual preparation of Christians for this great event. Hence, too, the supreme importance of giving heed to this final invitation of Ours addressed to those who are willing to be guided by Our demands.

High hopes

We, venerable brethren, must lead the way; and may all the faithful—especially priests, monks and nuns, children, the sick and the afflicted—join us in praying and doing penance, that God may give His Church the abundance of light and grace that is so necessary for her at this time. For will not Almighty God surely be lavish with His gifts, after receiving so many gifts from His children; gifts which breathe the scent of myrrh, the sweet fragrance of their filial devotion?

Then, too, what a wonderful, what a heartening spectacle of religious fervor it will be to see the countless armies of Christians throughout the world devoting themselves to assiduous prayer and voluntary self-denial in response to Our appeals! This is the sort of religious fervor with which the Church's sons and daughters should be imbued. May their example be an inspiration to those who are so immersed in the affairs of this world as to be neglectful of their duties towards God.

[38] *2 Cor. 6, 2.*

If you can implement these desires of Ours; if when you leave your dioceses to come to Rome for the Council, you can come laden with such spiritual riches as these, then we may hope indeed to see the dawning of a new and fairer age for the Catholic Church throughout the world.

A blessing

Buoyed up by this assurance, venerable brethren, We lovingly impart to you and to all the clergy and faithful committed to your loyal care, that pledge of heaven's graces, that earnest of Our fatherly good will, Our Apostolic Blessing.

Given at Rome, at St. Peter's, on the 1st day of July, the Feast of the Most Precious Blood of Our Lord Jesus Christ, in the year 1962, the fourth of Our Pontificate.

JOHN PP. XXIII

THE CONTRIBUTION OF NUNS TO SUCCESS OF THE COUNCIL

A Letter to All Women in Religious Life

- *Prayer life*
- *Poverty, chastity, obedience*
- *Apostolic work*

THE LARGEST TEMPLE in Christendom is getting ready to welcome the Fathers of the Second Ecumenical Council of the Vatican. October 11th will mark the opening of the great event toward which the prayerful expectation of all Catholics is being directed; for that matter, we can say the expectation of all men of good will. This is a solemn hour in the history of the Church: what we are seeking is to give a new fervor to the effort of spiritual renewal that she is always carrying on, and thus give a new impetus to the works and institutions that are a part of that life of hers that stretches back over the centuries.

Response from various states in life

The clergy are already reciting the Breviary in union with Us every day for the success of the Ecumenical Council.[1] The laypeople (the children, the sick and the old people in particular), who have been invited a number of times to offer up their prayers and sacrifices for this intention, are responding to the invitation promptly and generously. Everyone wants to make his own contribution toward transforming the Council "into a kind of new Pentecost."[2]

---

[1] Apostolic exhortation *"Sacrae Laudis,"* Jan. 6, 1962, *AAS* 54 (1962) 66-75. *TPS*, VIII, 63-9.
[2] Prayer for the Council: cf. *AAS* 51 (1959) 832.

It is only natural to expect that, in the midst of this atmosphere of intense preparation, those who have offered themselves completely to God and who have become familiar with the practice of prayer and of the most fervent charity will be bound to stand out.

The contribution expected from religious

Beloved daughters. The Church has gathered you under her protective mantle, has approved your constitutions, has defended your rights, has benefited from and is still benefiting from your works. And so you deserve to have the words of the Apostle Paul applied to you as an expression of gratitude for what you have done up to now and as a most cheerful wish for the future: "We pray for you to the Lord, that He may give you the spirit of wisdom and of revelation to know him well. May he choose to enlighten the eyes of your mind so that you may know what hope he has called you to, and what a wealth of glory his inheritance among the Saints is reserving for you."[3]

Make this letter the object of your thoughtful consideration; and listen to all that the Divine Master wants to suggest to each one of you in the message of the lowly Vicar of Christ. Preparation for the Council demands that souls who are consecrated to the Lord according to the forms approved by canon law think back over what their vocation commits them to, with renewed fervor. In this way, at the proper time, their reply to the directives issued by the Council will be prompt and whole-hearted, since the way will have been prepared for it by a more intensive effort at personal sanctification.

If a life consecrated to God is to correspond better with the desire of the divine Heart, it must really be: 1) a life of prayer; 2) a life of example; 3) a life of apostolate.

---

[3] Cf. *Eph.* 1, 16-18. The above translation is a literal version of the Holy Father's Italian. The Confraternity edition of the New Testament gives: "I . . . do not cease to give thanks for you, making mention of you in my prayers, that the God of our Lord Jesus Christ, the Father of glory, may grant you the spirit of wisdom and revelation in deep knowledge of him: the eyes of your mind being enlightened, so that you may know what is the hope of his calling, what the riches of the glory of his inheritance in the saints."

I. LIFE OF PRAYER

Our thoughts go first of all to the nuns and sisters who are leading a contemplative and penitential life.

Pre-eminence of the interior life

On February 2, 1961, the feast of the Presentation of Jesus in the Temple, as We were passing on the gift of candles We had received that day, We said: "The first destination of the candles, religious houses with the strictest rules of mortification and penance, is meant to affirm once more the pre-eminence of the duties of worship and of total consecration to a life of prayer over any other form of apostolate; at the same time it is meant to emphasize the loftiness of, and the necessity for, vocations to this way of life."[4] The Church will always encourage her daughters who have chosen to give themselves to the contemplative life in order to conform in a more perfect way to the call of the Divine Master.

This corresponds to a truth that is universally valid, even for sisters whose life is pre-eminently an active one: that the interior life alone is the soul and the foundation of any apostolate. Meditate on this truth, all of you, beloved daughters, who are rightly called *quasi apes argumentosae*,[5] because you are constantly practicing the fourteen works of mercy in fraternal communion with your fellow-sisters. Even those of you who are consecrated to God in secular institutes must draw all the force and effectiveness of your undertakings from prayer.

A life offered to the Lord carries with it difficulties and sacrifices, just as does every other form of life with others. And only prayer wins the gift of joyful perseverance. The good works to which you dedicate yourselves are not always crowned with success: disappointments, misunderstandings, ingratitude are lying in wait for you. Without the help of prayer, you will not be able to stand firm on the rigorous path. And do not forget that an ill-advised

---

[4] *Discorsi, Messaggi, Colloqui di Sua Santità Giovanni XXIII*, III, 143. *TPS*, VII, 7-22.
[5] like busy bees.

dynamism might make you fall into that "heresy of action" that was rejected by Our predecessors. Once you have overcome this danger, you can have confidence in being genuine cooperators in the salvation of souls and you will add merits to your crown.

The meaning of "a life of prayer"

All of you, whether you are dedicated to the contemplative life or the active life, understand the expression, "the life of prayer." It does not mean a mechanical repetition of formulas; rather, it is the indispensable means that permits you to enter into intimacy with the Lord, to have a better understanding of your dignity as daughters of God, as spouses of the Holy Spirit, and a better knowledge of the *"dulcis hospes animae"*[6] who speaks to anyone who knows how to listen to Him in recollection.

Nourishing the life of prayer

Let your prayer be nourished at the fonts of a profound knowledge of the Sacred Scriptures and especially of the New Testament; and then of the liturgy and of the teaching of the Church in all its fullness. Holy Mass ought to be the center of the day, so that every action converges upon it either as preparation or as thanksgiving; let Holy Communion be the daily food that sustains, and comforts and strengthens. In this way, you will not run the danger—as happened to the foolish virgins in the parable—of letting the oil run down in your lamp, and you will always find yourselves ready for anything—for glory and for ignominy, for health and for sickness, to carry on your work and to die: "Behold the bridegroom cometh, go ye forth to meet him."[7]

And right here is a good place to remind you, as We have done so often, of the three devotions that We consider to be fundamental even for the simple faithful of the laity: "There is nothing better for enlightening and encouraging adoration of Jesus than meditating on Him and invoking Him in the threefold light of His Name, His Heart, His Blood."[8]

---

[6] sweet guest of the soul.
[7] *Matt.* 25, 6.
[8] Discourse at the conclusion of the Roman Synod, *AAS* 52 (1960) 305. Summary in *TPS*, VI, 161-3.

The Name, the Heart, the Blood of Jesus: here you have the substantial nourishment for a solid life of piety.

Nomen Jesu![9] Truly *"nil canitur suavius—nil auditur jucundius —nil cogitatur dulcius—quam Jesus Dei Filius:* there is nothing sweeter to sing of, nothing more pleasant to hear, nothing more lovable to think of than Jesus, the Son of God."[10]

Cor Jesu![11] Pius XII of venerable memory has this to say in his encyclical *Haurietis Aquas,* issued on May 15, 1956, which We recommend that you go back over and meditate upon attentively: "If the evidence on which devotion to the wounded Heart of Jesus is based is rightly weighed, it will have to be clear to all that we are dealing here not with an ordinary form of piety which anyone may at his discretion esteem less than other devotions, or regard lightly, but with a form of worship that is supremely well-fitted for the attainment of Christian perfection."[12]

Sanguis Christi![13] "It is the loftiest sign of His redeeming sacrifice, which is renewed mystically and really in the Holy Mass and gives meaning and direction to the life of a Christian."[14]

II. Life of Example

The message of Jesus: "I have given you an example, that as I have done to you, so you do also."[15] Souls which desire to follow faithfully in the footsteps of the Lord are presented with the practice of the evangelical counsels, which is "the royal road to Christian holiness."[16]

A) Evangelical Poverty

Jesus was born in a stable; during his public life, he did not have a place to lay his head at night;[17] and he died on a bare cross.

---

[9] The name of Jesus.
[10] Hymn at Vespers on the feast of the Holy Name of Jesus.
[11] The heart of Jesus.
[12] *AAS* 48 (1956) 346. *TPS,* III, 115-49.
[13] The blood of Christ.
[14] Discourse to members of the Society of the Precious Blood and members of the Sodality, June 2, 1962: cf. *L'Osservatore Romano,* June 3, 1962.
[15] *John* 13, 15.
[16] Encyclical *"Sacerdotii Nostri primordia,"* Aug. 1, 1959; *AAS* 51 (1959) 550-51. (See p. 73 above.)
[17] Cf. *Matt.* 8, 20.

This is the first condition that he lays down for anyone who wants to follow him: "If thou wilt be perfect, go sell what thou hast, and give to the poor, and thou shalt have treasure in heaven."[18]

The significance of poverty

You have been attracted by the example and teaching of the Divine Master, and you have offered Him everything: *laetus obtuli universa.*[19] In the light of imitation of the poor Christ, your vow takes on its full meaning and value; it makes us be satisfied day by day with what we absolutely need; it makes us bestow what is left over upon the poor and upon good works, out of obedience; and with regard to the unforeseen things of tomorrow, with regard to sickness and old age, it entrusts us to the care of divine providence, without excluding prudence and foresight.

Detachment from the goods of this world attracts the attention of everyone and shows all of them that poverty does not mean misery and meanness, nor, for that matter, avarice; and it makes them give more serious thought to the divine words: "What doth it profit a man, if he gain the whole world, and suffer the loss of his own soul?"[20]

Live to the full the vow or promise that makes you resemble Him who although He was rich became poor so that we might become rich from His poverty.[21]

Temptations against poverty

In this regard, there will be no shortage of temptations, like the desire for little conveniences, satisfaction in food, or in the use of goods. Poverty, as you know, has its thorns, which ought to be loved, so that they may become roses in heaven.

At other times, the need for renovations and modernizations that are certainly justifiable may be extended too far and result in an ostentation in buildings and furnishings that has at times stirred up unfavorable comment, even if these new items have nothing to do with the modest quarters of the sisters. You understand what

---
[18] *Matt.* 19, 21.
[19] I have joyfully offered all these things. (*1 Par.* 29, 17)
[20] *Matt.* 16, 26.   [21] Cf. *2 Cor.* 8, 9.

We mean, beloved daughters: We have no intention of saying that anything that is indispensable for physical health and for wise and suitable recreation is opposed to the vow of poverty. But We would like to trust that the eye of the Divine Master may never, as it were, come to be saddened by a kind of affectation that may also have a negative influence on the interior life of persons consecrated to God, when they live in quarters that lack an air of austerity. Let poverty be held in great honor among all of you.

Indigent nuns

We would like to say a special word of comfort and consolation to the cloistered nuns for whom sister poverty often becomes "sister indigence." Jesus, the Son of God who made Himself poor, will come to console you. Meanwhile, in His name, We Ourself want to hold out a hand in your behalf to your fellow-sisters who are in a better economic position and to generous benefactors as well; and We want to encourage the enterprises in this direction that have been undertaken by the Federation of Cloistered Monasteries, under the Sacred Congregation for Religious, reminding all of the divine promise: "Blessed are ye poor, for yours is the kingdom of God."[22]

B) ANGELIC CHASTITY

You read in the Gospel how much Jesus has suffered; what injuries have been inflicted upon Him. But from Bethlehem to Calvary, the splendor that radiates from His divine purity grows ever greater and conquers the crowds. This shows how great were the austerity and the enchanting attraction of His conduct and bearing.

Chastity, a social virtue

May it be so with you, beloved daughters. May God bless the delicate efforts, the mortifications, the renunciations with which you strive to make this virtue, about which Pius XII wrote a memorable encyclical,[23] ever more radiant and splendid. Live up to the teachings of that letter: let your conduct prove to everyone that chastity

---

[22] *Luke* 6, 20.
[23] Encyclical *"Sacra Virginitas,"* Mar. 25, 1954, *AAS* 46 (1954) 161. *TPS* I, 101-123.

is not only an attainable virtue, but a social virtue, and is to be ardently defended through prayer, vigilance and mortification of the senses.

Let your example demonstrate that your heart is not shut up in some kind of sterile selfishness but rather that it has chosen the one thing that is indispensable for opening itself out to the needs of its neighbor with a deep interest and care. With this in view, be attentive to the rules of good taste—We repeat it—be attentive to them and apply them. Do not pay any attention to those who want to bring into your life any kind of conduct or attitude not in keeping with proper reserve and with the things you are supposed to observe.

Erroneous theories

In your apostolic activities, push aside the theories of those who wish to hear little or no mention of modesty and shame, and instead wish to introduce into educational methods standards and approaches that are opposed to the teaching of the Sacred Books and of Catholic tradition.

A cause for serenity

Even though materialism in theory or practice is threatening on the one hand, and hedonism and corruption are trying to break through every dike on the other, Our mind remains serene and confident as it beholds the angelic legions who have offered the Lord their chastity and who, with prayer and sacrifice, are winning miracles of divine mercy for those who have gone astray, and are offering propitiation that wins pardon for the sins of individuals and of whole nations.

C) Spirit of Obedience

The Apostle St. Paul develops the notion of the humiliation of Jesus who became obedient even unto His death on the cross.[24] In order to follow the Divine Master better, you have bound yourselves to Him with a vow or a promise of obedience.

[24] *Phil.* 2, 8.

This constant immolation of your "ego," this annihilation of yourselves can cost a great deal; but it is also true that here lies victory,[25] for this spiritual crucifixion carries with it heavenly graces for you and for mankind.

Obedience and the person

The teaching of the Church on the inalienable rights of the human person is clear and precise. The special endowments of each man must be allowed to develop properly so that each may live up to the gifts he has received from God. All this is clearly understood. But once you move on from respect for the person to exaltation of the personality and to the affirmation of personalism, then the dangers become serious. Let the words of Pius XII in his exhortation *Menti Nostrae* be a valuable indication of this for you too: "In an age like ours, when the principle of authority is being seriously shaken, it is absolutely necessary for the priest, who is firmly rooted in the principles of the faith, to look upon authority and accept it not just as the bulwark of the social and religious order, but also as the foundation for his own personal sanctification."[26]

To those in authority

At this point, We want to continue Our instruction with some words for those who have to direct others and who hold positions of responsibility.

Demand the most whole-hearted obedience to the rules; and at the same time be understanding toward your fellow-sisters; do all you can to help each one develop her natural aptitudes. It is the duty of superiors to make obedience lovable, not to achieve an observance that is merely external, and all the less to impose unbearable burdens.

St. Catherine of Siena

Beloved daughters. We exhort all of you to live according to the spirit of this virtue, which is nourished on profound humility,

[25] Cf. *Prov.* 21, 28.   [26] *AAS* 42 (1950) 662-3.

on absolute disinterestedness, on complete detachment. If obedience has become your way of life in all things, you will be able to understand the words of St. Catherine of Siena: "How sweet and glorious this virtue is, for all the other virtues are in it! O, obedience, which dost sail thy course without growing tired, and dost reach the port of salvation without danger! Thou dost conform thyself to the only-begotten Word . . .; thou dost rise in the bark of the Most Holy Cross, and bring thyself to sustain but never go beyond the obedience of the Word nor dost thou ever wander from his teaching . . . Thou are great with long perseverance and so great that thou dost extend from Heaven to earth, because through thee the gates of heaven are opened."[27]

III. LIFE OF APOSTOLATE

St. Paul teaches that the mystery revealed to us by God is the plan set out from all eternity in Christ, to be realized in Him in the fullness of time; and that is: "to re-establish all things in Christ that are in heaven and on earth."[28]

Cloistered nuns and the apostolate

No soul that is consecrated to the Lord is dispensed from the sublime task of carrying on the salvific mission of the divine Redeemer.

The Church expects a great deal from those who live in the silence of the cloister, and from them in particular. They, like Moses, are holding their arms lifted up on high in prayer, fully aware that this attitude of supplication is the way to win the victory. The contribution of sisters of the contemplative life to the apostolate is so important that Pius XI chose as the co-patroness of the missions—and hence a partner of St. Francis Xavier—not a sister of the active life, but a Carmelite, St. Therese of the Child Jesus.

---

[27] *Dialogues,* c. 155.
[28] *Eph.* 1, 10. The translation given above is from the Confraternity Edition of the New Testament; a literal translation of the Italian version quoted by the Holy Father would read: "to re-establish all things that are in heaven and on earth in a single head, Christ."—Transl.

An interest in all things

Yes, you have to be spiritually involved in all the needs of the Church militant. Let no misfortune, no tragedy or calamity find you a stranger to it; let no scientific discovery, no cultural meeting or social and political gathering make you think: "these are things that have nothing to do with us." Let the Church militant feel your presence wherever your spiritual contribution is needed for the good of souls and also for true human progress and universal peace. Let the souls in purgatory enjoy the benefit of your prayers and offerings for their repose, so that the beatific vision may come to them more quickly. In union with the chorus of the angels and the saints, keep on repeating the eternal *Alleluja* to the August Trinity.

Those in the active life

Let all those who are devoting themselves to the active life remember that not only prayers but works as well are needed if the new direction being taken by society is to draw its nourishment from the Gospel; and let all be for the glory of God; for the salvation of souls.

And since the scholastic, charitable and welfare fields cannot use people who are unprepared to meet the increased demands imposed by present-day regulations, devote your efforts, in accordance with obedience, to completing your studies and gaining the diplomas that will put you in a position to overcome all difficulties. In this way, even aside from the proven capacity you must have, your spirit of dedication, of patience and of sacrifice will come to be better appreciated.

Needs of new nations

In addition, there are further needs and demands being expressed in the new countries that have just entered into the family of free nations. Without any lessening of our affection for our own countries, the whole world has become, more so than in the past, everybody's country. Many sisters have already listened to this appeal and reminder. The field is immense. It is useless to complain that the children of this world get there before the apostles of Christ. Complaining solves nothing: we have to get moving, to get ready for the future, to have trust.

In this task, not even those sisters devoted to contemplation are to be excluded. In some areas of Africa and of the Far East, the people are attracted more by the contemplative life, which is more in keeping with the way in which their civilization has developed. Some of the more educated social classes complain, as it were, that the dynamic life of the missionaries may be having less influence on their way of conceiving religion and of adhering to Christianity.

Meetings of superiors

You can see, beloved daughters, how many reasons there are to encourage the meetings of superiors-general sponsored by the Sacred Congregation of Religious, on both the national and international levels. In this way, you can better keep up to date on present-day conditions, benefit from each other's experiences, and gain new strength and comfort from the realization that the Church has a valiant corps of souls who are ready and able to face any obstacle.

Secular institutes

The consecrated souls in the new Secular Institutes know that their work is appreciated too and that We want to encourage them to make their contribution to having the Gospel penetrate into every aspect of the modern world.

Some of them may attain positions of great importance and responsibility. It would be well for them to make themselves appreciated for their competence, their hard work, their sense of responsibility, as well as for those virtues that are raised to a lofty level by grace. This will help to avoid the dominance of those who rely almost exclusively on human cleverness and on the power of economic, scientific and technical means. *Nos autem in nomine Domini Dei nostri fortes sumus.*[29]

[29] But we are strong in the name of the Lord our God. (*Ps.* 19, 8)

Fraternal charity

We invite all of you souls consecrated to the Lord in the contemplative or in the active life to draw closer to each other in fraternal charity. May the spirit of Pentecost alight upon your elect Families and bring them together in that fusion of souls that could be seen in the Cenacle, where, along with the Mother of God and the Apostles, certain pious women were present.[30]

Conclusion

These are Our wishes, Our prayers, Our hopes. On the eve of the Vatican Council, the Church has called upon all of the faithful and asked of each of them an act that will show his support, his witness, his courage.

Daily resolution

May you be among the first to foster a holy enthusiasm, beloved daughters. The *Imitation of Christ* has some moving words on this point: "It is fitting for us to renew our good resolution every day, and to stir ourselves up to fervor, as if we had just been converted, and to say: Help me, O Lord God, in my good resolution and in thy holy service; and make today begin perfectly, for I have done nothing up to now."[31]

Mary, Joseph, and patron saints

May the Mother of Jesus and our Mother enkindle new fervor in you! Trust in this heavenly Mother; and at the same time, keep close to her Spouse St. Joseph, who is also the Patron of the Second Vatican Council; and pray to the saints who are held in special honor in your individual communities as well, that they may unite their effective intercession to bring it about that "the holy Church, reunited in a unanimous, more intense prayer around Mary, the Mother of Jesus, and guided by Peter, may spread the kingdom of the divine Savior, which is a kingdom of truth, of justice, of love and of peace."

---

[30] Cf. *Acts* 1, 14.   [31] I, 19, 1. Translation by C. Guasti.

A blessing

The most ample Apostolic Blessing that We pour forth upon all religious communities and upon each and every soul consecrated to God, is intended as a pledge of heavenly favors and an encouragement to a good life and to good work *in Ecclesia et in Christo Jesu.*[32]

From the Apostolic Palace of the Vatican, July 2, 1962, the fourth year of Our Pontificate.

JOHN PP. XXIII

[32] in the Church and in Christ Jesus. (*Eph.* 3, 21)

Opening Address to the Council

An Address of Pope John XXIII

- *The Church's teaching office*
- *The decision to hold a council*
- *Keeping up to date*
- *A council more pastoral than doctrinal*
- *The right attitude toward error*
- *A world unified by Christianity*

TODAY, VENERABLE BRETHREN, is a day of joy for Mother Church: through God's most kindly providence the longed-for day has dawned for the solemn opening of the Second Vatican Ecumenical Council, here at St. Peter's shrine. And Mary, God's Virgin Mother, on this feast day of her noble motherhood, gives it her gracious protection.

The Church in Council

A positive proof of the Catholic Church's vitality is furnished by every single council held in the long course of the centuries—by the twenty ecumenical councils as well as by the many thousands of memorable regional and provincial ones emblazoned on the scroll of history.

And now the Church must once more reaffirm that teaching authority of hers which never fails, but will endure until the end of time. For that was Our reason for calling this most authoritative assembly, and We address you now as the humble successor, the latest born, of this Prince of Apostles. The present Council is a special, world-wide manifestation by the Church of her teaching office, exercised in taking account of the errors, needs and opportunities of our day.

A history of triumph . . .

We address you, therefore, as Christ's vicar, and We naturally begin this General Council by setting it in its historical context. The voice of the past is both spirited and heartening. We remember with joy those early popes and their more recent successors to whom we owe so much. Their hallowed, momentous words come down to us through the councils held in both the East and the West, from the fourth century to the Middle Ages, and right down to modern times. Their uninterrupted witness, so zealously given, proclaims the triumph of Christ's Church, that divine and human society which derives from its divine Redeemer its title, its gifts of grace, its whole dynamic force.

. . . *and of adversity*

Here is cause indeed for spiritual joy. And yet this history has its darker side too, a fact which cannot be glossed over. These nineteen hundred years have reaped their harvest of sorrow and bitterness. The aged Simeon's prophecy to Mary, the Mother of Jesus, proves true in every age: "Behold, this child is destined for the fall and for the rise of many in Israel, and for a sign that shall be contradicted."[1] Jesus, too, when grown to manhood, made it quite clear that men in times to come would oppose Him. We remember those mysterious words of His: "He who hears you, hears me."[2] St. Luke, who records these words, also quotes Him later as saying: "He who is not with me is against me; and he who does not gather with me scatters."[3]

To be with Christ or against Him

Certain it is that the critical issues, the thorny problems that wait upon men's solution, have remained the same for almost twenty centuries. And why? Because the whole of history and of life hinges on the person of Jesus Christ. *Either* men anchor themselves on Him and His Church, and thus enjoy the blessings of light and joy, right order and peace; *or* they live their lives apart from

---

[1] *Luke* 2, 34.   [2] *Ibid.* 10, 16.   [3] *Ibid.* 11, 23.

Him; many positively oppose Him, and deliberately exclude themselves from the Church. The result can only be confusion in their lives, bitterness in their relations with one another, and the savage threat of war.

A pastoral function

But the function of every ecumenical council has always been to make a solemn proclamation of the union that exists between Christ and His Church; to diffuse the light of truth; to give right guidance to men both as individuals and as members of a family and a society; to evoke and strengthen their spiritual resources; and to set their minds continually on those higher values which are genuine and unfailing.

No study of human history during these twenty centuries of Christendom can fail to take note of the evidence of this extraordinary teaching authority of the Church as voiced in her general councils. The documents are there, whole volumes of them; a sacred heritage housed in the Roman archives and in the most famous libraries of the world.

The Decision to Hold the Second Vatican Council

A sudden inspiration

As regards the immediate cause for this great event which gathers you here together at Our bidding, it is sufficient for Us to put on record once more something which, though trifling in itself, made a deep impression on Us personally. The decision to hold an ecumenical council came to Us in the first instance in a sudden flash of inspiration. We communicated this decision, without elaboration, to the Sacred College of Cardinals on that memorable January 25, 1959, the feast of St. Paul's Conversion, in his patriarchal basilica in the Ostien Way.[4] The response was immediate. It was as though some ray of supernatural light had entered the minds of all present: it was reflected in their faces; it shone from their eyes. At once the world was swept by a wave of enthusiasm, and men everywhere began to wait eagerly for the celebration of this Council.

[4] See pp. 20-23 above.

Arduous preparation

For three years the arduous work of preparation continued. It consisted in making a detailed and accurate analysis of the prevailing condition of the faith, the religious practice, and the vitality of the Christian, and particularly the Catholic, body.

We are convinced that the time spent in preparing for this Ecumenical Council was in itself an initial token of grace, a gift from heaven.

Hope for spiritual enrichment

For We have every confidence that the Church, in the light of this Council, will gain in spiritual riches. New sources of energy will be opened to her, enabling her to face the future without fear. By introducing timely changes and a prudent system of mutual co-operation, We intend that the Church shall really succeed in bringing men, families and nations to the appreciation of supernatural values.

Thus the celebration of this Council becomes a compelling motive for whole-hearted thanksgiving to God, the giver of every good gift, and for exultantly proclaiming the glory of Christ the Lord, the triumphant and immortal King of ages and peoples.

The Timing of This Council

And now, venerable brethren, there is another point that We would have you consider. Quite apart from the spiritual joy we all feel at this solemn moment of history, the very circumstances in which this Council is opening are supremely propitious. May We go on record as expressing this conviction openly before you now in full assembly.

Pessimistic voices

In the daily exercise of Our pastoral office, it sometimes happens that We hear certain opinions which disturb Us—opinions expressed by people who, though fired with a commendable zeal for religion, are lacking in sufficient prudence and judgment in their evaluation of events. They can see nothing but calamity and disaster in the present state of the world. They say over and over that this modern age of ours, in comparison with past ages, is definitely deteriorating. One would think from their attitude that history, that great teacher of life, had taught them nothing. They seem to imagine that in the days of the earlier councils everything was as it should be so far as doctrine and morality and the Church's rightful liberty were concerned.

We feel that We must disagree with these prophets of doom, who are always forecasting worse disasters, as though the end of the world were at hand.

A basis for optimism

Present indications are that the human family is on the threshold of a new era. We must recognize here the hand of God, who, as the years roll by, is ever directing men's efforts, whether they realize it or not, towards the fulfillment of the inscrutable designs of His providence, wisely arranging everything, even adverse human fortune, for the Church's good.

Civil intervention eliminated

As a simple example of what We mean, consider the extremely critical problems which exist today in the political and economic spheres. Men are so worried by these things that they give scant thought to those religious concerns which are the province of the Church's teaching authority. All this is evil, and we are right to condemn it. But this new state of affairs has at least one undeniable advantage: it has eliminated the innumerable obstacles erected by worldly men to impede the Church's freedom of action. We have only to take a cursory glance through the annals of the Church to realize that even those ecumenical councils which are recorded there in letters of gold, were celebrated in the midst of serious difficulties and most distressing circumstances, through the unwarranted intervention of the civil authority. Such intervention was sometimes dictated by a sincere intention on the part of the secular princes to protect the Church's interests, but more often than not their motives were purely political and selfish, and the resultant situation was fraught with spiritual disadvantage and danger.

Earnest prayer for absent bishops

We must indeed confess to you Our deep sorrow over the fact that so many bishops are missing today from your midst. They suffer imprisonment and every kind of disability because of their faith in Christ. The thought of these dear brothers of Ours impels Us to pray for them with great earnestness. Yet We are not without hope; and We have the immense consolation of knowing that the Church, freed at last from the worldly fetters that trammelled her in past ages, can through you raise her majestic and solemn voice from this Vatican Basilica, as from a second Apostolic Cenacle.

The Council's Principal Duty:
The Defense and Advancement of Truth

The major interest of the Ecumenical Council is this: that the sacred heritage of Christian truth be safeguarded and expounded with greater efficacy.

That doctrine embraces the whole man, body and soul. It bids us live as pilgrims here on earth, as we journey onwards towards our heavenly homeland.

Man's twofold obligation

It demonstrates how we must conduct this mortal life of ours. If we are to achieve God's purpose in our regard we have a twofold obligation: as citizens of earth, and as citizens of heaven. That is to say, all men without exception, both individually and in society, have a life-long obligation to strive after heavenly values through the right use of the things of this earth. These temporal goods must be used in such a way as not to jeopardize eternal happiness.

Seeking the kingdom of God

True enough, Christ our Lord said: "Seek first the kingdom of God and His justice,"[5] and this word "first" indicates what the pri-

[5] *Matt.* 6, 33.

mary direction of all our thoughts and energies must be. Nevertheless, we must not forget the rest of Our Lord's injunction: "and all these things shall be given you besides."[6] Thus the traditional as well as the contemporary Christian approach to life is to strive with all zeal for evangelical perfection, and at the same time to contribute toward the material good of humanity. It is from the living example and the charitable enterprise of such Christians as these that all that is highest and noblest in human society takes its strength and growth.

Contributing to society

If this doctrine is to make its impact on the various spheres of human activity—in private, family and social life—then it is absolutely vital that the Church shall never for an instant lose sight of that sacred patrimony of truth inherited from the Fathers. But it is equally necessary for her to keep up to date with the changing conditions of this modern world, and of modern living, for these have opened up entirely new avenues for the Catholic apostolate.

Beyond science

The Church has never been stinting in her admiration for the results of man's inventive genius and scientific progress, which have so revolutionized modern living. But neither has she been backward in assessing these new developments at their true value. While keeping a watchful eye on these things, she has constantly exhorted men to look beyond such visible phenomena—to God, the source of all wisdom and beauty. Her constant fear has been that man, who was commanded to "subject the earth and rule it,"[7] should in the process forget that other serious command: "The Lord thy God shalt thou worship, and Him only shalt thou serve."[8] Real progress must not be impeded by a passing infatuation for transient things.

Bringing Home the Church's Teaching to the Modern World

From what We have said, the doctrinal role of this present Council is sufficiently clear.

[6] *Ibid.* [7] Cf. *Gen.* 1, 28. [8] *Matt.* 4, 10; *Luke* 4, 8.

Transmitting the truth fearlessly

This twenty-first Ecumenical Council can draw upon the most effective and valued assistance of experts in every branch of sacred science, in the practical sphere of the apostolate, and in administration. Its intention is to give to the world the whole of that doctrine which, notwithstanding every difficulty and contradiction, has become the common heritage of mankind—to transmit it in all its purity, undiluted, undistorted.

It is a treasure of incalculable worth, not indeed coveted by all, but available to all men of good will.

And our duty is not just to guard this treasure, as though it were some museum-piece and we the curators, but earnestly and fearlessly to dedicate ourselves to the work that needs to be done in this modern age of ours, pursuing the path which the Church has followed for almost twenty centuries.

Nor are we here primarily to discuss certain fundamentals of Catholic doctrine, or to restate in greater detail the traditional teaching of the Fathers and of early and more recent theologians. We presume that these things are sufficiently well-known and familiar to you all.

A fresh approach

There was no need to call a council merely to hold discussions of that nature. What is needed at the present time is a new enthusiasm, a new joy and serenity of mind in the unreserved acceptance by all of the entire Christian faith, without forfeiting that accuracy and precision in its presentation which characterized the proceedings of the Council of Trent and the First Vatican Council. What is needed, and what everyone imbued with a truly Christian, Catholic and apostolic spirit craves today, is that this doctrine shall be more widely known, more deeply understood, and more penetrating in its effects on men's moral lives. What is needed is that this certain and immutable doctrine, to which the faithful owe obedience, be studied afresh and reformulated in contemporary terms. For this deposit of faith, or truths which are contained in our time-honored teaching is one thing; the manner in which these truths are set forth (with their meaning preserved intact) is something else.

Opening Address to the Council

This, then, is what will require our careful, and perhaps too our patient, consideration. We must work out ways and means of expounding these truths in a manner more consistent with a predominantly pastoral view of the Church's teaching office.

THE RIGHT WAY TO SUPPRESS ERROR

In these days which mark the beginning of this Second Vatican Council, it is more obvious than ever before that the Lord's truth is indeed eternal. Human ideologies change. Successive generations give rise to varying errors, and these often vanish as quickly as they came, like mist before the sun.

The Church has always opposed these errors, and often condemned them with the utmost severity. Today, however, Christ's Bride prefers the balm of mercy to the arm of severity. She believes that present needs are best served by explaining more fully the purport of her doctrines, rather than by publishing condemnations.

Contemporary repudiation of godlessness

Not that the need to repudiate and guard against erroneous teaching and dangerous ideologies is less today than formerly. But all such error is so manifestly contrary to rightness and goodness, and produces such fatal results, that our contemporaries show every inclination to condemn it of their own accord—especially that way of life which repudiates God and His law, and which places excessive confidence in technical progress and an exclusively material prosperity. It is more and more widely understood that personal dignity and true self-realization are of vital importance and worth every effort to achieve. More important still, experience has at long last taught men that physical violence, armed might, and political domination are no help at all in providing a happy solution to the serious problems which affect them.

A loving mother

The great desire, therefore, of the Catholic Church in raising aloft at this Council the torch of truth, is to show herself to the world as the loving mother of all mankind; gentle, patient, and full of tenderness and sympathy for her separated children. To the human race oppressed by so many difficulties, she says what Peter once said to the poor man who begged an alms: "Silver and gold I have none; but what I have, that I give thee. In the name of Jesus Christ of Nazareth, arise and walk."[9] In other words it is not corruptible wealth, nor the promise of earthly happiness, that the Church offers the world today, but the gifts of divine grace which, since they raise men up to the dignity of being sons of God, are powerful assistance and support for the living of a more fully human life. She unseals the fountains of her life-giving doctrine, so that men, illumined by the light of Christ, will understand their true nature and dignity and purpose. Everywhere, through her children, she extends the frontiers of Christian love, the most powerful means of eradicating the seeds of discord, the most effective means of promoting concord, peace with justice, and universal brotherhood.

Promoting Unity of the Christian and Human Family

The Church's anxiety to promote and defend truth springs from her conviction that without the assistance of the whole of revealed doctrine man is quite incapable of attaining to that complete and steadfast unanimity which is associated with genuine peace and eternal salvation. For such is God's plan. He "wishes all men to be saved and to come to the knowledge of the truth."[10]

Unhappily, however, the entire Christian family has not as yet fully and perfectly attained to this visible unity in the truth. But the Catholic Church considers it her duty to work actively for the fulfillment of that great mystery of unity for which Christ prayed so earnestly to His heavenly Father on the eve of His great sacrifice. The knowledge that she is so intimately associated with that prayer is for her an occasion of ineffable peace and joy. And why should she not rejoice sincerely when she sees Christ's prayer extending its salvific and ever increasing efficacy even over those who are not of her fold?

Reflection of that unity sought by Christ

Indeed, if we consider well the unity for which Christ prayed on behalf of His Church, it would seem to shine, as it were, with a

[9] *Acts* 3, 6.   [10] *1 Tim.* 2, 4.

threefold ray of supernatural, saving light. There is first of all that unity of Catholics among themselves which must always be kept steadfast and exemplary. There is also a unity of prayer and ardent longing prompting Christians separated from this Apostolic See to aspire to union with us. And finally there is a unity which consists in the esteem and respect shown for the Catholic Church by members of various non-Christian religions.

Universality and unity

It is therefore an overwhelming source of grief to us to know that, although Christ's blood has redeemed every man that is born into this world, there is still a great part of the human race that does not share in those sources of supernatural grace which exist in the Catholic Church. And yet the Church sheds her light everywhere. The power that is hers by reason of her supernatural unity redounds to the advantage of the whole family of men. She amply justifies those magnificent words of St. Cyprian: "The Church, radiant with the light of her Lord, sheds her rays over all the world, and that light of hers remains one, though everywhere diffused; her corporate unity is not divided. She spreads her luxuriant branches over all the earth; she sends out her fair-flowing streams ever farther afield. But the head is one; the source is one. She is the one mother of countless generations. And we are her children, born of her, fed with her milk, animated with her breath."[11]

Blazing a trail

Such, venerable brethren, is the aim of the Second Vatican Council. It musters the Church's best energies and studies with all earnestness how to have the message of salvation more readily welcomed by men. By that very fact it blazes a trail that leads toward that unity of the human race which is so necessary if this earthly realm of ours is to conform to the realm of heaven, "whose king is truth, whose law is love, whose duration is eternity."[12]

---

[11] *De Catholicae Ecclesiae Unitate*, 5.
[12] St. Augustine, *Ep.* 138, 3.

Conclusion

Thus, venerable brethren in the episcopate, "our heart is wide open to you."[13] Here we are assembled in this Vatican Basilica at a turning-point in the history of the Church; here at this meeting-place of earth and heaven, by St. Peter's tomb and the tomb of so many of Our predecessors, whose ashes in this solemn hour seem to thrill in mystic exultation.

A radiant dawn

For with the opening of this Council a new day is dawning on the Church, bathing her in radiant splendor. It is yet the dawn, but the sun in its rising has already set our hearts aglow. All around is the fragrance of holiness and joy. Yet there are stars to be seen in this temple, enhancing its magnificence with their brightness. You are those stars, as witness the Apostle John;[14] the churches you represent are golden candlesticks shining round the tomb of the Prince of Apostles.[15] With you We see other dignitaries come to Rome from the five continents to represent their various nations. Their attitude is one of respect and warm-hearted expectation.

Saints, faithful, and Council Fathers

Hence, it is true to say that the citizens of earth and heaven are united in the celebration of this Council. The role of the saints in heaven is to supervise our labors; the role of the faithful on earth, to offer concerted prayer to God; your role, to show prompt obedience to the supernatural guidance of the Holy Spirit and to do your utmost to answer the needs and expectations of every nation on earth. To do this you will need serenity of mind, a spirit of brotherly concord, moderation in your proposals, dignity in discussion, and wisdom in deliberation.

God grant that your zeal and your labors may abundantly fulfill these aspirations. The eyes of the world are upon you; and all its hopes.

---

[13] *2 Cor.* 6, 11.   [14] *Apoc.* 1, 20.   [15] *Ibid.*

Prayer for divine assistance

Almighty God, we have no confidence in our own strength; all our trust is in you. Graciously look down on these Pastors of your Church. Aid their counsels and their legislation with the light of your divine grace. Be pleased to hear the prayers we offer you, united in faith, in voice, in mind.

Mary, help of Christians, help of bishops; recently in your church at Loreto, where We venerated the mystery of the Incarnation,[16] you gave us a special token of your love. Prosper now this work of ours, and by your kindly aid bring it to a happy, successful conclusion. And do you, with St. Joseph your spouse, the holy apostles Peter and Paul, St. John the Baptist and St. John the Evangelist, intercede for us before the throne of God.

To Jesus Christ, our most loving Redeemer, the immortal King of all peoples and all ages, be love, power and glory for ever and ever. Amen.

—October 11, 1962

[16] Cf. *TPS,* VIII, 273-8.

TO THE OBSERVER DELEGATES

An Address of Pope John XXIII to Non-Catholics at the Council

- *His own reliance on the Lord*
- *Special comfort from their presence*
- *Patient hopefulness for unity*

GENTLEMEN, today's most welcome meeting, friendly and confidential in tone, is to be marked with respect and simplicity as well. The first word which rises up in my heart is a prayer taken from the 67th Psalm, which has a lesson for all: *Benedictus Dominus per singulos dies: portat onera nostra Deus, salus nostra.* Blessed be the Lord, day after day: God, our salvation, bears our burdens![1]

When in 1952 Pope Pius XII most unexpectedly asked me to become the Patriarch of Venice, I told him that I did not need to reflect very long before accepting the appointment. My will, in fact, did not figure at all in this proposal; there was no desire in my heart of being appointed to one office or ministry rather than to another. My episcopal motto fully provided my answer: *Obedientia et Pax!*[2]

And so when after thirty years in the direct service of the Holy See, I prepared myself to begin a new kind of life and found myself shepherd of the flock of Venice, which I was to tend for the next six years, I reflected and meditated upon those words of the Psalm: *Portat onera nostra Deus,* God bears our burdens. He supports us, as we are and with what we possess; with His treasure in us and with our miseries.

This same thought was with me four years ago when I accepted

---

[1] *Ps.* 67, 20. [2] Obedience and peace.

the succession of St. Peter,³ and it has been so in all that has followed right up to the announcement and the preparation of the Council.

Insofar as my humble person is concerned, I would not like to claim any special inspiration. I abide by the sound doctrine which teaches that everything comes from God. In this very sense I have considered as a heavenly inspiration the idea for the Council which began on October 11th. I confess to you that it was for me a day of great emotion.

On that providential and historic occasion, I devoted particular attention to my immediate duty of meditating, praying, and giving thanks to God. But from time to time my eye ranged over the multitude of sons and brothers, and when my glance rested upon your group, on each of you personally, I drew a special comfort from your presence.

Without wishing to encroach upon the future, let us content ourselves today with stating the fact. *Benedictus Deus per singulos dies!* Yet, if you would read my heart, you would perhaps understand much more than words can say.

Experience with non-Catholics

How could I forget the ten years spent in Sofia? Or the ten more at Istanbul and Athens? They were twenty happy and satisfying years, during which I became acquainted with venerable persons and with young people of great generosity. I looked upon them with affection, even though my work as representative of the Holy Father in the Near East was not explicitly concerned with them.

Then again at Paris, which is one of the crossroads of the world —and was especially so immediately after the last war—I had frequent meetings with Christians of various denominations.

Never, in my knowledge, was there confusion among us over principles, nor any disagreement on the plane of charity in the common work of helping those in need, which the circumstances of the time made necessary. We did not haggle, we talked together; we did not have arguments, but bore each other good will.

One day long ago I gave to a venerable and aged prelate of an

³ Cf. *TPS,* V, 142.

oriental church, not in communion with Rome, a medal of the pontificate of Pius XI. This gesture was meant to be, and was, a simple act of friendly courtesy. Not long after, on the point of closing his eyes to this world's light, the old man requested that at his death the medal of the Pope be put on his breast. I saw it myself and the memory of it still moves me. I have mentioned this episode purposely, because in its touching simplicity it is like a flower of the field which the return of spring allows one to pluck and offer. May the Lord always thus accompany our steps with His grace.

A burning intention

Your welcome presence here and the emotion of my priestly heart—the heart of *episcopus Ecclesiae Dei*,[4] as I said Thursday before the Council assembly—the emotion of my fellow workers and, I am certain of it, your own emotion too, prompt me to confide to you that there burns in my heart the intention of working and sacrificing to hasten the hour when for all men the prayer of Jesus at the Last Supper will have reached its fulfillment. But the Christian virtue of patience must not hinder the equally fundamental virtue of prudence.

And so I say again: *Benedictus Deus per singulos dies*: *Blessed be God day after day.* For today, let that suffice. The Catholic Church is now engaged in a work of calmness and generosity; you, in your endeavor of observing, with renewed and benevolent attention.

May the heavenly grace which inspires, moves hearts and rewards good works be upon all things and all men.

—October 13, 1962

[4] a bishop of the Church of God.

Toward a New Pentecost

An Address of Pope John XXIII at the Close of the Council's First Session

- *Memories of the opening day*
- *Orientation of the bishops*
- *Good beginnings*
- *Continuation of work during recess*
- *The long road ahead*

THE FIRST SESSION of the Second Ecumenical Vatican Council, begun on the feast of the Blessed Virgin Mary's divine motherhood, comes to an auspicious end on this holy feast day of her Immaculate Conception, in the radiant splendor of the Mother of God and men.

It is as though some mystic, heavenly rainbow joined this present solemn assembly of ours with that resplendent, inaugural gathering held here on October 11th.[1] Certain it is that these two liturgical festivities provide for us a joyous occasion of heartfelt thanksgiving to God.

The deep significance of this event is all the more striking when we remember that it was on this feast day that Our predecessor Pius IX inaugurated the First Vatican Council.

Mary's protection

It is worthwhile pondering these coincidences, for they make us realize that the Church's historic events invariably take place beneath the kindly influence of Mary's maternal protection.

---

[1] Cf. *TPS*, VIII, 207-16.

The Word was made flesh of the Virgin Mary. Such was the divine Redeemer's plan; and what is a council, if not an act of faith in God, of obedience to His laws, and of sincere endeavor to cooperate with His plan of redemption? We are overjoyed, therefore, to be celebrating today the immaculate stem which bore the flower *of Jesse's root,*[2] for we see this flower blossoming more and more as the sacred season of Advent rushes by.

You, the bishops of the five continents, will soon be leaving this hall of St. Peter to return to your beloved dioceses and continue the pastoral guidance of your flocks. Let us then reflect on what has so far been accomplished, so that during this time of waiting we can draw strength from past achievements, and map out our future policy for the successful completion of this great enterprise.

What We have to say will fall under three main headings: the first phase of this Ecumenical Council, its continuation, and its anticipated results, namely, the spread of faith, holiness and apostolic endeavor in the Church and in the world.

Opening ceremony recalled

We still retain vivid memories of the opening of this Ecumenical Council, and the sight of that solemn assembly of bishops from every part of the world, a gathering unique in history. *The one, holy, catholic and apostolic Church* was revealed to all mankind in the shining splendor of her perennial mission, in the solidity of her structure, in the persuasiveness and attractiveness of her teaching.

It is with pleasure, too, that We recall the fact that the governments of very many nations sent delegates to represent them at the Council's inaugural ceremony. Allow Us to express once again Our gratitude for the admiring interest shown by Our contemporaries in the opening of this General Council. Sympathetic assurances of extraordinary goodwill, respect and esteem have reached Us from all over the world.

[2] Cf. *Is.* 11, 1.

I

THE FIRST PHASE OF THE COUNCIL

That memorable October 11th initiated the closely co-ordinated work of the Fathers-in-council. Today concludes the first phase of that work, and it is well to reflect for a while on what has been accomplished.

Orientation required

The first session was like the slow and majestic prelude to a great masterpiece. The Fathers settled themselves to enter wholeheartedly into the very nature and purpose of the work that lay ahead, and to penetrate the divine plan. They had come together from far and wide as brothers to this ancient See, and obviously they had first to become acquainted. To understand one another's hearts, they had to look at each other squarely. To achieve a balanced and profitable interchange of views on pastoral matters, they had to describe their own experiences, gleaned under the most varied conditions of the apostolate in different parts of the world.

Differing views

Understandably, in an assembly of this magnitude, a few days were needed to arrive at an agreement on matters about which there existed, in all charity, a sharp divergence of views. Such difference of opinion can be disturbing at times, but it is no cause for surprise. In fact it was providential, for it served to clarify issues, and to demonstrate to the world the existence in the Church of the holy freedom of the sons of God.

Schema on sacred liturgy

It was no accident that the first *schema* to be considered was the one dealing with the sacred liturgy. The liturgy has to do with man's relationship with God. This relationship is of the utmost importance. It must be based on the solid foundation of revelation and apostolic teaching, so as to contribute to man's spiritual good;

and that, with a broadness of vision which avoids the superficiality and haste so often characterizing relationships between men.

A good beginning—a firm foundation

Then five more *schemata* were presented. These provoked discussions and expressions of opinion which We consider most useful for working out acceptably the final and definitive form of the individual constitutions. It is therefore right to conclude that a good beginning has been made, and a firm foundation laid for future discussions.

II
The Continuation of the Council

And now, venerable brethren, We turn Our attention to that phase of the work which will engage us during the coming interval of nine months, after you have returned to your respective Sees. It will be a hidden, silent work, but nonetheless important.

The thought of each one of you in his own diocese fills Us with pleasure, for We know that on your return from the City you will bring your people the shining torch of confidence and charity, and remain closely united with Us in prayer. We are reminded of the wonderful words of Ecclesiasticus about the high priest Simon: "He himself stood by the altar, and about him was the ring of his brethren."[3]

All our strength, as you see, derives from this union of prayer and purpose.

Council's work continues...

Today's celebrations do not ring the curtain down on our combined activities. Indeed, there is work to be done by all of us during this recess, and this work is certainly of greater weight and importance than was the case during the recesses of any previous ecumenical council. Under modern conditions of life we find no difficulty in remaining constantly in touch with every kind of issue—be they personal issues or those relating to the apostolate.

[3] *Ecclus.* 50, 13.

. . . under special supervision

Furthermore, the newly-constituted representative commission of cardinals and bishops will ensure that the work of the Council continues without intermission. The object of this commission is to direct and supervise the work of the Council during these coming months, and, along with the various conciliar commissions, to lay a firm foundation for the ultimate success of the Ecumenical Council. Thus, in spite of the nine-month recess, the active work of the Council will continue.

Hope for conclusion by Christmas, 1963

Each bishop, for all his preoccupation with pastoral administration, will continue to study and investigate the *schemata* so far provided, and any other material which may be sent later. Thus when the Fathers of the Council reconvene in Rome next September, the new session will proceed without obstacle, and all the more expeditiously for the experience gained in this first session. We may therefore hope that the conclusion awaited by our dearest people may be reached next Christmas, the fourth centenary of the end of the Ecumenical Council of Trent, amid the joys that derive from the vision and worship of the glory of the incarnate Word of God.

III

The Expected Results of the Council

The glorious vista of the vast sphere of influence of our combined labors which confidently opens out before Our prophetic gaze, fills Us with ardent expectation. We greatly long for the realization of those aims for which We called the Council: "that the Church, rooted in faith, strong in hope, ardent in charity, may flourish with new and youthful vigor, and, fortified by holy laws, may be more energetic and swift to spread Christ's kingdom."[4]

Benefits for all—Christian and non-Christian

Even though the Ecumenical Council has not yet promulgated its decrees—these, of course, must wait until the labors of the Council

[4] *Letter to the German Hierarchy,* Jan. 11, 1962.

have reached completion—it is nonetheless consoling to look forward even at this stage to the real benefits which will result from it. In God's providence, it will not merely be the sons of the Catholic Church who will reap these benefits, but all those brothers of ours who rejoice in the name of Christian, and those countless children of ancient and glorious civilizations on whom the light of Christianity has not yet dawned. Indeed, these people have nothing to fear from the light of the Gospel. On the contrary—as has so often happened in the past—it will contrive to nurture and bring to fruition those fertile seeds of religious faith and human progress which are already planted in their midst.

Such is the vista that opens out before Us, venerable brethren, and We know that you share Our longing.

Implementing the decrees

When that time comes, all the decisions of this Ecumenical Council will have to be implemented in every field of the Church's striving, not excluding the social field; and the laws established by the Council will have to be obeyed with promptness and generosity.[5]

This, clearly, will be the most important phase of the work. It will demand a gigantic, composite effort on the part of pastors in preaching sound doctrine and skillfully applying the conciliar decrees. It will need the co-operation of the diocesan and regular clergy, of religious institutes, and of the laity, each in accordance with his own station in life and his own ability. Their common endeavor must be to ensure that the acts of the Ecumenical Council meet with the generous and loyal response of the faithful.

The dawn of the new Pentecost

Then, doubtless, will dawn that new Pentecost which is the object of our yearning—a Pentecost that will increase the Church's wealth of spiritual strength and extend her maternal influence and saving power to every sphere of human endeavor. Then will we see the extension of Christ's kingdom on earth, and throughout the world will re-echo more clearly, more eloquently, the good news of man's

[5] Cf. *Prayer to the Holy Spirit for the Council.*

redemption; confirming the kingship of almighty God, strengthening the bonds of fraternal love among men, and establishing that peace which was promised in this world to men of good will.

These, venerable brethren, are the emotions which spur Us on, which nourish Our boundless hopes and Our prayers. The work of this session is completed, and you are soon to return to the beloved flocks entrusted to your care. In wishing you Godspeed, We request that you convey to your priests and people the greatness of Our affection, that you be eloquent messengers of Our greetings and good wishes.

A greeting of peace

We wish to reiterate those words of greeting which Our predecessor Pius IX addressed to the bishops of the First Vatican Council: "See, dearest brothers, how blessed and joyful it is to live together in harmony in God's house. May you always so live. And as our Lord Jesus Christ gave peace to His apostles, so I also, His unworthy vicar, give you peace in His name. Peace, as you know, casts out fear; peace shuts its ears to uninformed talk. May this peace be with you all the days of your life."[6]

In these past months of companionship here together, we have experienced that wonderful joy to which Pius IX has borne such eloquent testimony.

The road ahead

A long road still lies ahead of us, but you know that the Church's Supreme Shepherd has each one of you constantly in his thoughts and in his heart as you go about your pastoral duties, which are in no way dissociated from the earnest preoccupations of this Council.

We have outlined for you today the threefold sphere of our combined operations, and this We did for your encouragement. The glorious opening of the Council was the prelude to the mighty enterprise. In the coming months work and thought will go on unflaggingly; and the effect of all this will be that the Ecumenical Council will one day bestow on all mankind those benefits of faith, hope and

---

[6] *Mansi*, 1869-70, p. 765, 158.

charity which are so ardently expected of it. This threefold character clearly shows the unique importance of this Council.

A heavy responsibility rests upon our shoulders, but God Himself will sustain us on the way.

May the Immaculate Virgin Mary be with us always. May Joseph, her most chaste spouse and patron of the Ecumenical Council, whose name from today onwards shines in the Canon of the Mass, accompany us on our journey, as he accompanied and supported the Holy Family of Nazareth at God's bidding. And may we likewise enjoy the patronage of St. Peter and St. Paul, St. John the Baptist, and all the popes, bishops and doctors of God's Church.

Glory to the Saviour

We are gathered here in the heart of Christendom, in the basilica and at the tomb of the Prince of Apostles. But We recall with pleasure that the cathedral of the diocese of Rome is the Lateran Basilica, the mother and center of all churches, dedicated to Jesus the divine Saviour. "To Him, therefore, who is the immortal and invisible King of all ages and peoples, be glory and power forever and ever."[7]

In this hour of heartfelt joy, the heavens open above us and all the splendor of the heavenly court shines down, filling us with confident assurance, a more than human steadfastness of faith, and joy and peace beyond compare.

In the radiance of this supernatural light We look forward to your return, venerable brethren, and salute you "with a holy kiss."[8] We call down upon you the wealth of God's favors, pledged and promised by this, Our Apostolic Blessing.

—December 8, 1962

[7] Cf. *1 Tim.* 1, 17; *Apoc.* 1, 6.
[8] Cf. *Rom.* 16, 16.

Thoughts for the Council's Recess

A Letter Sent to Each
of the Fathers of the Council

- *Importance of contacts among bishops in the interim*
- *The new co-ordinating commission*
- *Responsibilities of bishops*
- *Help from the laity*
- *Concern for all humanity*

VENERABLE AND dearest brother. We still retain vivid memories of that magnificent gathering of bishops in St. Peters' for the opening of the first session of the Second Vatican Council.[1] And though We sent these bishops home again after celebrating the feast of the Blessed Virgin Mary's Immaculate Conception[2] and the canonization of Bl. Peter Julian Eymard, Anthony Pucci, and Francis of Camporosso,[3] We still remain united with them in the spiritual bonds of love.

The year ahead

Today, however, is a turning-point in the year. It marks the transition from the wonderful mystery enacted in Bethlehem's cave to the glorious Epiphany of that Lord who is the glorious and immortal King of ages and nations. Hence Our most urgent desire is to take up again in thought and in word the serious and sacred theme of the Council. The whole of this present year is going to be devoted to it. It is going to be the single, unifying, focal point of the minds and hearts and voices of all men the wide world over.

All those engaged in this work will realize that these months of

---

[1] Cf. *TPS*, VIII, 207-16.   [2] *Ibid.*, 398-403.   [3] *Ibid.*, 372-7.

1963 which come between the Epiphany, January 6, and Our Lady's birthday, September 8, are in very truth a continuation of the present Council so auspiciously inaugurated last October. The doctrinal expositions, the appeals to pastoral experience, the free and withal respectful discussions of the past few weeks, have all helped to hammer out a clearly defined procedural plan, in accordance with which the subsequent work of the Council will proceed on more rapid and expeditious lines.

CONTINUATION OF THE ECUMENICAL COUNCIL

The Council is not now in abeyance; that must be clearly understood. It is true that Our brothers in the episcopate—who, together with Us, the Sovereign Pontiff, constitute this General Council— have left Rome for the time being in order to devote themselves to their pastoral duties. But, though absent in body, they must consider themselves, and show themselves throughout the course of this year, very present in mind.

Necessity for episcopal unity

In these times, as you know, the possibilities of fruitful association, even from a great distance, have enormously increased, and it is not only permissible, it is imperative, that we do our utmost to bring this advance in communications to bear on the service of holy Church throughout the world. Above all, it is important to ensure that the bishops, who together with the Sovereign Pontiff, constitute the very soul and center of the Council's activity, remain closely knit together, as it were, in perfect unity. This rule must certainly obtain in Rome—in the administrative offices of the Vatican where the central government of the whole Church is conducted in a dedicated and businesslike spirit, and in those seats of sacred learning, of prayer and good works, which exist, so to speak, beneath the very eyes of the vicar of Jesus Christ. But it must also obtain in every part of the world where the sacred hierarchy holds sway, and where these same ends are pursued in perfect spiritual union with the Roman Pontiff, and in the power of the Holy Spirit who "has placed you as bishops, to rule the Church of God."[4]

[4] *Acts* 20, 28.

Basic Considerations Proposed

While awaiting the further progress of the Council, We would draw your attention to certain points which, in view of Our experience of the general congregations held so far,[5] and of Our conversations with the Council Fathers both individually and collectively, We consider of supreme importance. These points apply to the interim period of eight months during which the commissions are engaged in their hidden and unostentatious, though none the less useful and efficient work, and afterwards to what We hope will be the concluding period in Rome, from September until the Council ends.

During the recess

For the sake of clarity and precision, We give you these points under four headings. They have special reference to these eight months which precede the feast of Our Lady's birthday. Further directives will be given as the opportunity arises.

The main headings are these:

I. The Commission of Cardinals for co-ordinating and directing the work of the Council, which was announced on December 6, 1962, and formally set up on December 17 under the presidency of Our venerable brother, Amleto Giovanni Cardinal Cicognani.

II. The lively interest with which those bishops who live at a distance from the City must keep in touch with the work that is going on at the center.

III. The co-operation of clergy and laity in the Council, manifested by an ever increasing resolve to interest themselves in its work, pray for its success, and lead holy and sanctified lives.

IV. The wide scope of this Twenty-first Ecumenical Council, embracing, as it does, the many varied aims and ambitions of Christ's Church.

I

The New Commission of Cardinals

We have co-opted the Church's highest dignitaries on the Commission for continuing, co-ordinating, and directing the work of the

[5] Cf. "A Guide to the Congregations and the Projects," *TPS*, VIII, 304-27.

Council during these eight months, even though some of them live outside the holy Vatican City. We did so partly out of respect for the Cardinals in question, but also because of the knowledge and experience they have already derived from working on the other commissions which have gone into the making of this Council.

Relationship to the regular Council commissions

It is not envisioned that this latest and principal commission will in any way lessen or depreciate the work of the others. It is intended rather to co-ordinate their work, and to determine more clearly what direction that work shall take, having regard to the general aims and intentions of the Council as a whole.

It will be aided in its work by the General Secretariat, that is, by the General Secretary, the five sub-secretaries, and their assistants. We have already had experience of the thoroughness with which these men do their work. Theirs is a purely executive work, we know, but it is one which is nevertheless of great practical importance, and requiring a considerable degree of prudence.

II

Contacts with Bishops Living Away from Rome

Duties of the Roman Pontiff and of the bishops

The Ecumenical Council must clearly receive its general directive from the Roman Pontiff who convoked it, but it is within the bishops' competence to determine the manner in which the Council shall freely proceed within this general framework.

The decisions of the Council will, of course, be submitted to the Church's supreme pastor for approval, for it is from his apostolic authority that, ultimately, all decrees must derive their legal force. It is nevertheless the duty of the Council Fathers to put forward all such decrees, deliberate on them, decide on their final form, and eventually subscribe to them together with the Roman Pontiff.

The Council of Jerusalem—and episcopal authority

In this matter We would commend to the Fathers a careful consideration of the events of the Council of Jerusalem described in the fifteenth chapter of the *Acts of the Apostles,* concluding with the embassy to Antioch of Paul and Barnabas with Judas Barsabas and Silas.[6] In this simple narrative, written nearly twenty centuries ago, we are given a perfect example of a council. This first council plainly illustrates the nature of the episcopal authority, and the serious obligations which every ecumenical synod, from the Council of Jerusalem to the present Second Vatican Council, places on the bishops who take part in it.

Conciliar responsibilities of every bishop

An enthusiastic involvement in the work of the Council is a sacred duty so far as bishops are concerned, since for them pastoral solicitude is a matter of their vocation. This duty demands not only their attendance at the forthcoming congregations in the Vatican Basilica, but also their remaining in the closest bond of spiritual union with their brother bishops during this interim period of eight months. They must co-operate with the commission presided over by Our Cardinal Secretary of State by replying promptly to any written requests for information. Promptness in dealing with the issues involved and in supplying the necessary information will ensure that the Council is directed on its course by policies of wisdom. It will also hasten the longed-for completion of this magnificent enterprise which is claiming the attention of the entire world.

The bishops' assistants in Council matters

This year conciliar business will be regarded by every bishop as "the apple of his eye." His lively concern for the speedy and proper completion of the work will prompt him to make full use of the collaboration and assistance of learned, virtuous priests who are experts in the various branches of ecclesiastical learning. He may thus avail himself of the services of men whose names are already well known in Rome and who have worked on the Conciliar commissions, or of priests and religious universally famed for their learning and practical wisdom. The Secretary General should be

[6] Cf. *Acts* 15, 1-22.

notified of their names, since circumstances may arise in which their assistance will be of the greatest value. The bishop's collaborators should be few in number, scrupulous in the matter of observing secrecy concerning conciliar business, worthy of the nobility of the work they are called upon to assist, and able to contribute to its efficacy and prestige.

III

Clerical and Lay Co-operation

Growing interest and enthusiasm of Christians

The enthusiasm with which Christians are following the Council's progress is happily increasing each day. Indeed, the energy and activity displayed by the Church in recent months has exceeded all expectations. Such is the joyful and consoling news that reaches Us daily from all quarters of the globe. It is indicative of the Church's abundant vitality.

A familiar and refreshing thought comes to Our mind—that of the first Pentecost; and a text which sums up, as it were, the principal characteristics of our daily liturgy: "For the spirit of the Lord fills the world, is all embracing, and knows man's utterance."[7]

Certainly the entire Catholic world, in this continent and beyond the seas, received the news of the calling of a council, and later its inauguration, with the most respectful attention and the keenest interest. Gradually hope and confidence grew, inspired by the vision of a better future.

Christians everywhere are anxious to join together in common prayer—especially those of the faithful who show in their lives a high degree of moral integrity, patience, purity, and holiness—realizing that the success of the Council will help to procure for the human race a just and ordered prosperity, as well as that sure peace which is an earthly foretaste of the joys of heaven.

Difficulties to be avoided

There are some well-intentioned and sincerely religious people who are constantly advocating the introduction of new forms of pri-

[7] *Wis.* 1, 7.

vate and public devotions. They are intent on the wide diffusion throughout the Catholic world of forms of prayer adapted to the particular circumstances, countries, languages, and traditions of the people.

It is not in the least necessary to introduce new and special forms of prayer at the present time. The approved and time-honored forms are perfectly adequate for the purpose.

The Catholic Church is the queen who stands in the sight of the nations at the right hand of God, "in gilded clothing: surrounded with variety."[8] The Church's marvelously unified structure, founded on the primacy of the Roman Pontiff, and consisting of dioceses and parishes, is embellished with a variety of liturgies and devotions, some of great antiquity, others more modern. Hers, therefore, is a structure which is at once solid and compact, and yet admits of variety and multiplicity in the forms of her private and public prayer.

Opportunities for the faithful to collaborate

In virtue of his sacred office, the ruler of each diocese is its bishop. All matters of doctrine, administration, and divine worship come under his surveillance. These various matters are most conscientiously attended to by bishops and prelates, each in his own diocese and in accordance with his own particular sphere of duty. Priests and religious, monks and nuns, and the laity themselves, have the Mass, the Office, and the Rosary. These are the most powerful and efficacious means whereby the world-wide Christian family can, in private and in public, beg God's aid for the Ecumenical Council.

Above all—enthusiasm for prayer

But what is of greatest importance is that people shall be fired with a burning enthusiasm for prayer, and spread the warmth of that flame to others, with that zeal and self-sacrifice which Romans express in the words: *instanter, instantius, instantissime*.[9] Such is the prayer required of a Christian people: a prayer full of confident assurance, looking forward with joy to the wealth of God's grace.

[8] Cf. *Ps.* 44, 10.   [9] earnestly, more earnestly, most earnestly.

IV

THE COUNCIL'S AIMS FOR CHRISTIANS AND THE ENTIRE HUMAN FAMILY

The Council's impact on the world

We wish to make one or two further points, venerable brother, before concluding this spiritual address. Information comes to Us from all quarters concerning the confidence with which, since the Council's inception, public opinion has veered toward a peaceful and Christian settlement of the major issues of the day. It is the Council that has aroused these expectations, for it has spoken in no half-hearted terms, but with resounding eloquence and realism.

True, Our plan to call the Second Vatican Council did not at first seem to arouse much speculation from the world at large. But after three years of preparation, and particularly since the first session, from October 11 to December 8 last year, the Council has evoked such universal respect even among men of differing religions, ideologies, and political persuasions, that one may well believe that the light of heavenly grace has cast its rays closer and closer to men's minds, impelling them by slow degrees towards Jesus Christ and His holy, motherly Church.

Non-Catholic observers invited to the Council

To note but one instance: We invited our separated brethren—men who are proud to call themselves Christian—to send representatives as observers to the Vatican Council. These invitations, We are glad to say, have met with an overwhelmingly favorable and encouraging response.

The deference with which these invitations were received is surely something almost unique in the history of the Church and her Councils. For Our part, We are driven to the conclusion that this favorable attitude is indeed a sign that many people are already beginning to appreciate the true significance of the prayer which Jesus Christ prayed to His Father on the sacred eve of His passion: "Father, the hour has come! Glorify thy Son, that thy Son may glorify thee. .... I pray ... for those whom thou hast given me, because they are thine. .... Holy Father, keep in thy name those whom thou hast given me, that they may be one even as we are."[10]

The world-wide concern of the Council

In a certain measure, this is already beginning to come true before our very eyes. The immediate concern of the Council is, of course, with the members of the one, true, catholic, and apostolic Church. It was they We had principally in mind when We convoked the Council. But if we confined ourselves exclusively to our own individual concerns and those of Catholics, entrenched behind the ramparts of the Catholic Church, we would surely be inadequate (or so it has always seemed to Us) to the demands of our divine Redeemer, who, according to the beloved disciple, "is a propitiation for our sins, not for ours only—but also for those of the whole world."[11]

Are we not convinced that the divine Redeemer is indeed the light of the world? The same evangelist says of Him: "It was the true light that enlightens every man who comes into the world."[12]

Salvation meant for all

And was it not with the inspiration of the Holy Spirit that St. Luke wrote, "All flesh shall see the salvation of God"[13]?

St. Paul, who justly claimed to be an apostle and a prophet, had this to say to the Romans: "But glory and honor and peace shall be awarded to everyone who does good, to Jew first and then to Greek. Because with God there is no respect of persons."[14]

Consider the joy with which St. Paul summed up in a few words the whole nature and purpose of the mystery of man's salvation: "The grace of God our Saviour has appeared to all men."[15]

Let Us conclude these texts with a sentence from that most authoritative and most eloquent of St. Paul's commentators, St. John Chrysostom. It is a sentence which from the days of Our youth has never failed to inspire Us: "Remember, brothers, that you must

[10] *John* 17, 1, 9, 11.   [11] *1 John* 2, 2.   [12] *John* 1, 9.
[13] *Luke* 3, 6.   [14] *Rom.* 2, 10-11.   [15] *Tit.* 2, 11.

give an account not only of your own lives, but of the whole world."[16]

Encouraging signs

That many of our separated brethren view the Ecumenical Council with so much respect and good will, certainly gives cause for considerable satisfaction. But how much greater cause for hope shall we have, and how incalculably richer will be our reward of heavenly grace, if these men who have been called with us to the same faith and to the same salvation in Christ and His one fold, shall learn from experience the greater extent of our genuine charity in their regard, as we bear witness to the truth in all its fullness.

One fold, one shepherd

This is what God has ordained in the hidden designs of His providence. In this we are invited to discern the early dawning of that longed-for day, the coming of which was hailed by Christ the Lord with such confidence, such ardent longing, when He said: "And other sheep I have that are not of this fold. Them also I must bring . . . and there shall be one fold and one shepherd."[17] What a joy it would be for Us to be able to have these "sheep" around Us and to read with them these wonderful words of our Lord. What a joy it would be to be able to consider with them the marvelous images contained in the tenth chapter of St. John's Gospel, especially where Christ says, "I am the door," the door through which the sheep must enter. "If anyone enter by me he shall be safe, and shall go in and out, and shall find pastures."[18]

To benefit the whole brotherhood of men

These then are Our desires; confidently We repeat them. By God's grace may this Second Vatican Council, which is now happily launched on its course, arouse such a potential of spiritual energy in the Church, may it so extend the field of the Catholic apostolate, that men everywhere, led by the Spouse of Christ, may

---

[16] Homily XV on St. Matthew.   [17] *John* 10, 16.   [18] *John* 10, 9.

attain their loftiest and most ambitious aims, which till now have eluded their grasp.

A magnificent hope indeed! It concerns not only the Church, but the whole brotherhood of men.

We, the bishops of God's Church, have some rethinking to do on the serious responsibilities of our pastoral office. True, by God's grace we have safeguarded, and continue to safeguard, the integrity of Catholic doctrine as taught by the holy Gospels, revered tradition, the Fathers of the Church, and the Roman pontiffs. That much is to our credit. But it is not enough. God's command goes further: "Go, therefore, and make disciples of all nations."[19] And again, in the Old Testament: "He gave to every one of them commandment concerning his neighbor."[20]

Exhortations and Good Wishes

Venerable brother, it is with great joy that We address Our thoughts to you on this evening of the Ephiphany of our Lord Jesus Christ.

Work resumed by the commissions

We are glad to be able to inform you that the commissions of the Second Vatican Council have energetically resumed their work; the Secretary of the Council will shortly be sending to the Council Fathers in the rank of the episcopate information regarding the preparation and study of the *schemata* that are being drafted by the various commissions.

They are supported in their ardent endeavors by the prayer of the entire clergy and of the religious, both men and women, scattered throughout every part of the world. God grant that these labors of theirs may be blessed with unfailing pastoral wisdom; and may they bring to birth fruits laden with the promise of the joy and salvation of the whole human race. Such is the grace of Jesus Christ. He came "to cast fire upon the earth,"[21] to set the world alight with the glow of faith and the radiance of love.

[19] *Matt.* 28, 19.   [20] *Ecclus.* 17, 12.   [21] Cf. *Luke* 12, 49.

St. Paul's words to the Colossians

No words of Ours could be more inspiring to Our brothers in the episcopate than the words of St. Paul to the Colossians. None could rival them in eloquence. The Apostle of the Gentiles—and how truly is he called a "vessel of election"!—intent on arousing in others that generosity which reaches for the noblest of ambitions and is undaunted in the face of toil, proclaimed as his motto: "Christ is all things and in all."[22] He added: "Put on, therefore, as God's chosen ones, holy and beloved, a heart of mercy, kindness, humility, meekness, patience. Bear with one another and forgive one another, if anyone has a grievance against any other; even as the Lord has forgiven you, so also do you forgive. But above all these things have charity, which is the bond of perfection. And may the peace of Christ reign in your hearts; unto that peace, indeed, you were called in one body. Show yourselves thankful. Let the word of Christ dwell in you abundantly: in all wisdom teach and admonish one another by psalms, hymns and spiritual songs, singing in your hearts to God by his grace. Whatever you do in word or in work, do all in the name of the Lord Jesus, giving thanks to God the Father through him."[23]

With such sentiments as these, venerable brother, and spurred on by our sense of duty, let us in lightness of mind and joy of heart, and putting all our trust in the help of divine grace, take up once more our share in the common, sacred task for the good of God's holy Church. And to gain for our desires and longings the abundant light and help of God's grace, lovingly in the Lord We bestow upon you, venerable brother, and your entire flock, Our Apostolic Blessing.

Given at Rome, at St. Peter's, on the sixth day of January, the feast of the Lord's Epiphany, in the year 1963, the fifth of Our pontificate.

JOHN PP. XXIII

[22] *Col.* 3, 11.
[23] *Col.* 3, 12-17.

VII

A Spiritual Testament

The interest the world takes in any pope as spiritual leader of hundreds of millions of souls is naturally very great. But there was something extraordinary about the interest in Pope John. It derived not only from the fact that he was the Pope but from the fact that he was in himself a remarkable person. Men everywhere were fascinated by him, perhaps most of all by the apparent contrast between the man and the office he held. To the world the papacy is unique in its claims to spiritual power, outstanding in even its temporal eminence. Yet John himself was a simple man, garrulously friendly and proudly aware of his peasant origins.

The letters and speeches thus far in the book, though frequently reflecting the personality of this unusual man, have all been connected in some way with his office as Supreme Pontiff. This section of the book presents something different: the intimate thoughts of Pope John XXIII, once Angelo Roncalli.

There is a letter to his family, written eighteen months before his death; his last will and testament, a spiritual document drafted and re-drafted over a period of forty years; notes made when on retreat and random reflections jotted down at no specified time.

These personal, interesting, and moving documents are filled with examples of his simple piety, his deep love for his family, his serene trust in God, his resignation in the face of old age and physical pain, and, everywhere, his natural, unselfconscious humility. We learn too what it feels like to be a pope and what John thought a pope should be.

As old age brought with it the pain and suffering that were to mark his final years of life, he remained at all times serene and uncomplaining, accepting all as the will of God and declaring that suffering was good schooling for a pope. His references to it were always brief and in passing, never morbid or self-pitying. He lived a life that was an example and a consolation for a suffering world.

His personal attributes are difficult to capture in print, but we have selected those materials available that give some inkling of the spirit of this great man. It is altogether fitting that we end this book of tribute and memorial to Pope John in this way. Truly, Pope John has left us, in his words and example, in his whole life as well as his pontificate, a priceless spiritual testament.—Ed.

A LETTER TO HIS FAMILY

From Pope John XXIII to His Brother, Intended for All the Roncalli Family

- *A rare letter*
- *A famous family*
- *Happy poverty*
- *The living and the dead*

MY DEAR BROTHER Severo. Today is the feast of your great patron—he of your true and proper name, St. Francis Xavier, as our dear "barba"[1] was called and now, happily, our nephew Zaverio.

I think it is three years since I stopped using a typewriter, as I liked so much to do; and if I have decided today to resume the practice and to employ a new machine that is all my own, it is because I have reached the age of eighty. But I continue to be well; and I am starting out again along the good path still in good health, although some little disturbance makes me say that 80 is not 60 nor 50. For now, at least, I can continue the good service of the Lord and of the Holy Church.

A message to all Roncallis

This letter which I have chosen to address to you, my dear Severo, as a message intended for everyone—Alfredo, Giuseppino, Assunta, sister-in-law Caterina, your dear Maria, Virgino, and Angelo Ghisleni, as well as all our relatives—I want to be an expression of my affection for all of you, affection ever keen and

[1] Apparently a nickname for his uncle Zaverio.

ever fresh. Though I am engaged, as you know, in a very important service, a service toward which the eyes of the whole world are directed, I cannot forget my beloved relatives, to whom my thoughts turn from day to day.

It gives me pleasure to tell you that since you cannot correspond personally with me as you once could, you can confide everything to Msgr. Capovilla, who is very fond of you and to whom you can say everything just as you would to me.

A worthwhile sacrifice

Please remember that this is one of the very few private letters I have written to any of my family during the past three years of my pontificate; and please sympathize with me if I can do no more, not even with those of my own blood. This sacrifice which I impose upon myself in my relations with you does more honor to you and to me and gains more respect and understanding than you could believe or imagine.

Now the great displays of reverence and affection for the Pope on the occasion of his 80th birthday are coming to an end, and I am glad because I prefer to the praise and best wishes of men the mercy of the Lord who has chosen me for a task so great that I desire Him to sustain me to the end of my life.

Personal tranquility of the Pope

My personal tranquility, which makes so great an impression on the world, consists completely in this: to persevere in obedience as I always have, and not to desire or pray to live longer, not even for one day beyond the time when the angel of death will come to call me and take me to Paradise, as I am confident he will.

That does not keep me from thanking the Lord for having decided to find in Brusico and Colombera[2] the man destined to be called the direct successor of so many popes through 20 centuries, and to take the name of Vicar of Jesus Christ on earth.

[2] Brusico and Colombera are the names of the two houses in which Pope John lived as a boy.

To persevere in humility

Through this call the name Roncalli was brought to the attention, sympathy, and respect of the whole world. And you do well to hold fast to your humility, as I also strive to do, and not to allow yourselves to be carried away by the follies and wiles of the world. The world is interested only in making money—enjoying life and having its way at all cost, even if unfortunately this requires force.

To be prepared for death

The 80 years that have gone by tell me, and you too, dear Severo, and all of our dear ones, that what counts most is to keep ourselves always well prepared to pass away suddenly; for this is the most important thing: to assure ourselves of eternal life by trusting in the goodness of the Lord, who sees all and provides for all.

I want to express these sentiments to you, my most dear Severo, so that you may pass them on to all our close relatives from Colombera, Gerole, Bonate, Medolago, and wherever they may be, and to those whose exact town I do not know. I leave to your discretion how to go about it. I think that Enrica could help you and Don Battista as well.

Continue loving one another, all you Roncallis who make up new families, and please try to understand if I cannot write to each family. Our Giuseppino is right when he says to his brother the Pope: "Here you are a prisoner of luxury and you cannot do all that you would like."

Remembrance of the suffering

It gives me joy to recall the names of those who are suffering most among you: dear Maria, your blessed wife, and good Rita, who with her sufferings has assured Paradise for herself and for you two who have helped her with so much charity; sister-in-law Caterina, who always reminds me of her, and our Giovanni who looks down upon us from heaven, together with our Roncalli relatives and other close relatives like those who emigrated to Milan.

The honor of a pope

I know that you will have to endure some mortification from those who choose to jump to conclusions without good judgment. So it is to have in the family a Pope, to whom the respectful gaze of the whole world turns, and to have his relatives living so modestly, remaining in their social position. But then many know that the Pope, son of humble but honorable people, does not forget anyone, and has and shows a good heart for all his closest relatives; that, besides, his condition is that of nearly all his recent predecessors; and that the honor of a pope is not to make his relatives rich, but only to help them with charity according to their needs and each one's condition.

This is and will be one of the finest and most prized titles of Pope John and of his Roncalli family.

At my death I will not lack the tribute that so honored the holiness of Pius X: *born poor and died poor.*

A chorus of souls

It is only natural that since I have reached the age of 80, all the others are coming along behind me. Courage, courage! We are in good company. I always keep close by my bed the photograph that gathers together all our dead, with their names written on marble: grandfather Angelo, uncle Zaverio, our venerable parents, our brother Giovanni, sisters Teresa, Ancilla, Maria, and Enrica. Oh, what a wonderful chorus of souls is waiting for us and praying for us! I am always thinking of them. To remember them in prayer gives me courage and fills me with joy in trustful expectation of being united with them all in heavenly and eternal glory.

I bless all of you together, recalling the wives who have come to gladden the Roncalli family or have gone to increase the joy of new families of different names but the same feelings. Oh, the children, the children! What a treasure, and what a blessing!

JOHN PP. XXIII
— December 3, 1961

LAST WILL AND TESTAMENT

The Spiritual Testament and Last Wishes of Pope John XXIII

- *Profession of faith*
- *His poverty*
- *Bequests*
- *A farewell to family*

Venice, June 29, 1954

MY SPIRITUAL TESTAMENT AND LAST WISHES

ON THE POINT OF presenting myself before the One and Triune Lord who created me, redeemed me, chose me to be his priest and bishop, and covered me with unending graces, I entrust my poor soul to His mercy; I humbly ask pardon for my sins and deficiencies. I offer Him the little good, although petty and imperfect, that with His aid I have succeeded in doing, for His glory, for the service of Holy Church, for the edification of my brethren, begging Him finally to receive me, like a good and kind father, with His Saints into eternal happiness.

A profession of faith

I profess once again with all my heart my entire Christian and Catholic faith, my adherence and subjection to the Holy Apostolic and Roman Church, and my complete devotion and obedience to her August Head, the Supreme Pontiff, whom it was my great honor to represent for long years in various regions of the East and West, who at the end chose to have me come to Venice as Cardinal and Patriarch, and whom I have always followed with sincere affection, aside from and above and beyond any dignity conferred upon me. The sense of my own littleness and nothingness has always been my good companion, keeping me humble and calm, and making me employ myself to the best of my ability in a constant exercise of obedience and charity for souls and for the interests of the Kingdom of Jesus, my Lord and my all. To Him be all glory; for me and for my merit, His mercy. *Meritum meum miseratio Domini. Domine, tu omnia nosti: tu scis quia amo Te.*[1] This alone is enough for me.

A request for pardon

I ask pardon of those whom I have unwittingly offended, of all to whom I have not been a source of edification. I feel that I have nothing to forgive anyone, for all who have known and dealt with me—including those who have offended me, scorned me, held me in bad esteem (with good reason, for that matter), or have been a source of affliction to me—I regard solely as brothers and benefactors, to whom I am grateful and for whom I pray and always will pray.

The grace of poverty

Born poor, but of honorable and humble people, I am particularly happy to die poor, having given away, in accordance with the various demands and circumstances of my simple and modest life, for the benefit of the poor and of the Holy Church that had nurtured me, all that came into my hands—which was little enough, as a matter of fact—during the years of my priesthood and episcopacy. Outward appearances of ease and comfort often veiled hidden thorns of distressing poverty and kept me from giving with all the largesse I would have liked. I thank God for this grace of poverty which I vowed in my youth, poverty of spirit as a priest of the Sacred Heart, and real poverty. This grace has sustained me in never asking for anything, neither positions, nor money, nor favors—never, not for myself, nor for my relatives or friends.

[1] My merit is the mercy of the Lord. Lord thou has known all things. Thou knowest that I love Thee.

To the Pope's own family

To my beloved family *secundum sanguinem*[2]—from whom, in fact, I have received no material wealth—I can leave only a wholehearted and most special blessing, inviting it to maintain that fear of God that always made it so dear and beloved to me, simple and modest as it was, without my ever feeling ashamed of it: this is its true title to honor. I have also helped it at times in its more serious needs, as one poor man with the other poor, but without ever removing it from the honorable poverty with which it was content. I pray and always will pray for its prosperity; I am happy to see in its new, vigorous offshoots that strength and loyalty to their fathers' religious tradition which will always be its fortune. My most fervent wish is that none of my relatives and dear ones may miss the joy of that last eternal reunion.

Departing, as I trust, for the roads of Heaven, I salute and thank and bless the many who formed my spiritual family at Bergamo, at Rome, in the East, in France, and at Venice, and who were my fellow townsmen, benefactors, colleagues, students, aides, friends and acquaintances, priests and laymen, Brothers and Sisters, and for whom, by the disposition of Providence, I was, no matter how unworthy, a colleague, a father, or a pastor.

To all his benefactors

The goodness directed toward my poor person by all whom I met along my path made my life serene. As I face death, I recall each and every one—those who have preceded me in taking the final step, those who will survive me and who will follow me. May they pray for me. I will repay them from Purgatory or from Paradise, where I hope to be received, I repeat it once again, not because of my merits, but because of the mercy of my Lord.

To his children of Venice

I remember all and will pray for all. But my children of Venice —the last ones the Lord placed around me, as a final consolation

---

[2] by blood

and joy for my priestly life—I want especially to mention as a sign of my admiration, my gratitude, my very special tenderness. I embrace them all in spirit, clergy and laity without exception, as I have loved them without exception as members of the same family, the object of one paternal and priestly care and love. *Pater sancte, serva eos in nomine tuo quos dedisti mihi: ut sint unum sicut et nos.*[3]

A final reminder

At the moment for saying farewell, or better still, *arrivederci*, I once more remind everyone of what counts most in life: blessed Jesus Christ, His Holy Church, His Gospel; and in the Gospel, above all, the *Pater noster*[4] in the spirit and heart of Jesus and the Gospel, the truth and goodness, the goodness meek and kind, active and patient, victorious and unbowed.

My children, my brethren, *arrivederci*.[5] In the name of the Father, of the Son, of the Holy Spirit. In the name of Jesus, our love; of Mary, our and His most sweet Mother; of St. Joseph, my first and specially loved Protector. In the name of St. Peter, St. John the Baptist, St. Mark, St. Lawrence Justinian, and St. Pius X. Amen.

Cardinal Angelo Giuseppe Roncalli, patriarch.

(The following additions to the text were all made in his own handwriting.)

. . . The pages that I have written are valid as an attestation of my absolute will in case of my sudden death.

Venice, September 17, 1957
Angelo Giuseppe Cardinal Roncalli

And they are valid also as a spiritual testament to be added to the provisions of the will joined here under the date of April 30, 1959.

JOHN PP. XXIII
From Rome, December 4, 1959.

---

[3] *John* 17, 11. "Holy Father, keep them in thy name whom thou hast given me; that they may be one, as we also are."
[4] Our Father.
[5] Till we meet again.

My Testament

Castelgandolfo, September 12, 1961

Under the dear and trusting auspices of Mary, my heavenly Mother, to whose name is dedicated today's liturgy, and in the eightieth year of my age, I hereby lay down and renew my testament, annulling every other declaration concerning my will made and written prior to this a number of times.

I await and will accept with simplicity and joy the arrival of sister death in all the circumstances with which it will please the Lord to send her to me.

For God's forgiveness

First of all, I ask forgiveness of the Father of mercies *pro innumerabilibus peccatis, offensionibus et negligentiis meis,*[6] as I have so often said and repeated in offering my daily Sacrifice.

For this first grace of Jesus' pardon for all my faults, and of my soul's introduction into blessed and eternal Paradise, I recommend myself to the prayers of all who have followed me and known me during the whole of my life as priest, bishop, and most humble and unworthy Servant of the Servants of the Lord.

Renewal of faith

Next, my heart leaps with joy to make a fervent, whole-hearted renewal of my profession of Catholic, apostolic, and Roman faith. Among the various forms and symbols with which the faith is usually expressed, I prefer the priestly and pontifical "Credo of the Mass" because of its more vast, more sonorous elevation as in union with the universal Church of every rite, of every age, of every region—from the *"Credo in unum Deum, patrem omnipotentem"*[7] to the *"et vitam venturi saeculi."*[8]

---

[6] for my countless sins, offenses and negligences.
[7] "I believe in one God, the father almighty."
[8] "and the life of the world to come."

RETREAT NOTES

Selections from Notes of Pope John XXIII Made
on Several Retreats During His Pontificate

- *A "confession" of failings*
- *Memories of childhood*
- *Virtues for a pope*
- *On growing old*
- *Maxims of perfection*
- *Devotion to Mary*

Castelgandolfo, Aug. 10-15, 1961

I HAVE IMPOSED silence and stopped the ordinary activities of my ministry. My only companion Msgr. Cavagna, my regular confessor.

At dawn on the feast of St. Lawrence—5:45 in the morning—I recite the Divine Office on the terrace looking toward Rome.

I think back [over the past] with tenderness, on this the anniversary of the date of my ordination to the priesthood—August 10, 1904—in the church of Santa Maria in Monte Santo on the Piazza del Popolo: with Msgr. Ceppetelli, the Vice-regent of Rome, an archbishop and the titular patriarch of Constantinople, as the ordaining prelate. The whole scene is before me even at a distance of 57 years.

From that day to this, how my nothingness has been confounded: *Deus meus misericordia mea.*[1]

[1] *My God my mercy.* (Footnote italics in these Retreat Notes indicate *Latin* words underlined in original text. See bibliographic note, p. 508.—Ed.)

Thursday, August 10, 1961

This kind of spiritual retreat goes beyond the ordinary rules. My memory is gladdened with all the grace of the Lord, in spite of the mortification of having cooperated so poorly, with an employment of energies that was in no way proportionate to the gifts received. It is a mystery that makes me tremble and at the same time moves me deeply.

After my first Mass at the tomb of St. Peter, there were the hands of the Holy Father Pius X resting upon my head in a blessing that was full of best wishes for me and for my life in the priesthood that was just beginning. And after more than half a century (57 years to be exact) here are my own hands opened upon the Catholics—and not just the Catholics—of the whole world, in a gesture of universal fatherliness, as successor of that same Pius X, who has been proclaimed a Saint, and as one living on in his priesthood and that of his predecessors and successors, who had been placed, like St. Peter, over the governing of the whole Church of Christ, which is *one, holy, catholic and apostolic.*

These are all sacred words. They go beyond any implication of personal exaltation of my own that I could ever imagine: and they leave me in the depths of my nothingness raised up to the heights of a ministry that surpasses the loftiness of every human honor.

When on October 28, 1958, the Cardinals of the Holy Roman Church chose me at the age of 77 for the supreme responsibility of governing the universal flock of Christ Jesus, the conviction was widespread that I would be an interim Pope during a transitional period. Instead, here I am now on the eve of the fourth year of [my] Pontificate, in the midst of carrying out an extensive program with the whole world watching it expectantly. As for myself, my attitude is like that of St. Martin: *nec mori timuit, nec vivere recusavit.*[2]

I must always stay ready: to die, perhaps suddenly; and to live for as long as the Lord may be pleased to leave me here below. Yes: always. On the threshold of my 80th year, I must stay ready: to die or to live: in the one case or the other to make provision

---

[2] *He was not afraid to die, but neither did he refuse to live.*

for my sanctification. *I must be and I want to be truly* what I am called everywhere, and what is my principal title, "Holy Father."

My Sanctification

I am a long way off from actually possessing it yet: but the desire for it and the will to succeed in this regard are keen and determined on my part.

This *special sanctification of my own* is pointed out to me here at Castello by a page and by a picture.

The page I came across unexpectedly is in a little book called "*Christian perfection. Some ascetical writings of Antonio Rosmini*".[3] *In what holiness consists.* "Keep in mind the great thought that holiness consists in a taste for being contradicted and humiliated, rightly or wrongly: in a taste for obeying: in a taste for waiting with great tranquillity: in being indifferent to what pleases Superiors; and in being truly without any will: in recognizing benefits that are received and one's own unworthiness; in having a great gratitude, in respect for the person of others and especially for the Ministers of God: in genuine charity, tranquillity, resignation and gentleness, desire to do good to all and a spirit of hard work. I am about to depart and I can say no more, but this is enough."[4]

To my edification, these are the ordinary applications of my own motto, which was taken from Baronio: *Oboedientia et pax.*[5] O Jesus: you remain with me always. I thank you for this doctrine which follows me everywhere.

The picture. It is in the oldest and innermost chapel of this apostolic palace. Yesterday I showed it to my spiritual director, Msgr. Alfredo Cavagna. It is the hidden and most precious jewel of this summer residence. It dates from the time of Urban VIII (1626-1634). And it was the object of his devotion, as it was for Pius IX, who would say Mass there, and then after his own, attend that of his secretary in the little oratory alongside that you can still

---

[3] Under the auspices of Sciacca (Soc. Ed. Int.) Turin 1955, p. 591. (See bibliographic note, p. 508.—Ed.)
[4] Stresa, 6, IX, 940. (See bibliographic note, p. 508.—Ed.)
[5] *Obedience and peace.*

see there. The whole was decorated by the painter Lagi Simone, "painter and gilder." At the altar there is a quite devotional canvas: *The pietà: Jesus dead and Mary in sorrow.* No other indication: pictures and decorations. Around about, all scenes of the sufferings of Jesus: a permanent school for the exercise of every pontificate.

All this—words and pictures—has come to confirm me in the doctrine of suffering. Of all the mysteries of the life of Jesus, this is the best adapted and most familiar to the permanent devotion of the Pope: *pati et contemni pro Christo et cum Christo.*[6]

This is the first light from this study that I am undertaking as a practice of perfection in preparation for my entry into old age. *Voluntas Dei: san[c]tificatio mea in Xsto.*[7] O Jesus: *"Factus es adjutor meus: in umbra alarum tuarum exulto. Adheret anima mea tibi: me sustentat dextera tua.*[8]

August 11, 1961[8a]

Before all else: *Confiteor Deo Omnipotenti.*[9]

Throughout the whole of my life, I have always been faithful to my weekly confession. On a number of occasions during my lifetime, I have made a general confession. On this occasion, I have rested content with a general review without going into great detail: but still following the words of the Offertory of each day's Mass, "*pro innumerabilibus peccatis, et offensionibus et negligentiis meis*":[10] all of them already confessed, each in its turn, but still, as always, regretted and detested.

Peccata: circa castitatem[11] in relations with myself, in the form of immodest actions: nothing serious, *never*.

Then in relations with others, *oculis, contactibus, sive in tempore*

---

[6] *to suffer and be despised for Christ and with Christ.*
[7] *The will of God: my sanctification in Christ.*
[8] *Ps. 62. O you are my help, and in the shadow of your wings I shout for joy. My soul clings fast to you; your right hand upholds me.*
[8a] The entries for August 11 and 12, 1961, appeared separately in a later issue of *Osservatore Romano.* We have placed them here in chronological order.
[9] *I confess to almighty God.*
[10] *for my countless sins, offenses and negligences.*
[11] Sins against *chastity.*

pubertatis, vel juventutis, vel maturitatis, vel senectutis, neque in lecturis librorum, vel ephemeridorum, vel conspiciendo figuras, vel imagines, gratia Dei, gratia Dei numquam permisit tentationes et jacturam, nunquam, nunquam: sed semper adjuvavit me, cum magna et infinita misericordia: in quo confido me semper servaturum usque ad finem vitae meae.[12]

Circa oboedientiam.[13] I have never had and never experienced temptations against obedience, and I thank the Lord for not having allowed any, not even when this obedience cost me a great deal, as I am suffering from it now: *factus,*[14] as I am, *servus servorum Dei*[15] . . . .

Circa humilitatem.[16] I have [kept] alive devotion to it and the external practice of it, too. This does not do away with my inner feelings when it seems as if some lack of regard has been shown me. But I even rejoice about it before God as an exercise of patience and as a hidden hair-shirt for my sins and to obtain the Lord's pardon for the sins of the whole world.

Circa caritatem.[17] This is the practice that costs me least: and yet despite this, at times, it causes me sacrifice and tempts me and stirs me to some impatience that may perhaps, as far as I know, cause someone to suffer.

Offensiones.[18] Who knows how many, many times against the law of the Lord and against the laws of Holy Church! *Innumerabilis numerus.*[19] But this is always aside from Church regulations and never matter for mortal or venial sin. I feel love for the rules and regulations and loyalty to all this Church law in my heart and in my mind, and it is a regular motive for keeping me alert, especially *ad exemplum et ad aedificationem clericorum et fidelium.*[20]

---

[12] *the grace of God, the grace of God never allowed temptations and a fall, through looks, touch, either in the time of my boyhood, or of my teens, or of my adulthood, or of my old age, neither through the reading of books or magazines, or through looking at pictures or images, never, never: instead He has always helped me with great and infinite mercy: in which I trust I will continue to persevere to the end of my life.*
[13] On *obedience.*
[14] *having been made.*
[15] *servant of the servants of God.*
[16] On *humility.*
[17] On *charity.*
[18] *Offenses.*
[19] *A countless number.*
[20] *for the example and the edification of the clergy and the faithful.*

I have confessed all these *offensiones* too: but all of them together and with a purpose of amendment, adding, as I grow older, a daily effort at excellence and perfection.

Negligentiae.[21] These have to be looked into with regard to the whole series of various functions involved in my pastoral life, for its spirit *eminere debet*[22] in an apostle and a successor of St. Peter, which is how everyone regards me today.

The keen remembrance of the failings of my long life stretching over 80 years—"*innumerabilibus peccatis, offensionibus et negligentiis*"[22a] was the general matter for the Holy Confession that I made once again this morning to my spiritual director, Msgr. Alfredo Cavagna, here in my bedroom, where my predecessors Pius XI and Pius XII slept and where Pius XII died as well on October 9, 1958, the only pope up to now to die in the summer residence at Castello.

O Lord Jesus, continue to have mercy upon me, a poor sinner, so that I may feel sure of thy great and eternal pardon.

Again, August 11

Afternoon of Forgiveness

Holy Confession every week on Friday or Saturday after careful preparation is still, as always, a solid basis for progress toward holiness: and it is still a sight that brings peace and calm and that encourages the habit of keeping yourself prepared to die a good death at any hour and any moment of the day! This tranquillity I possess, and this feeling that I am ready to go and to present myself to the Lord at the slightest hint from Him seems to me to be such a pledge of trust and of love as to merit for me the final display of his mercy from Jesus, whose Vicar upon earth I am called.

And so, let's always keep moving toward him as if he were ever awaiting me with open arms. . . .

---

[21] *Negligences.*
[22] *must be outstanding.*
[22a] See footnote 10, p. 473.

Saturday, August 12

Jesus Crucified
and His Dear Mother in Sorrow

This retreat of mine has, then, as its aim to succeed in marking progress in my efforts toward my *personal* sanctification: not just as a Christian, a priest and a bishop, but as Pope, as the *bonus pater omnium Christianorum*,[23] as the *bonus pastor*,[24] which is what the Lord has chosen me to be, despite all my littleness and unworthiness.

On many other occasions, I think back over the mystery of the *Precious Blood* of Jesus, devotion to which I felt should inspire me right from the beginning as Supreme Pontiff, along with that to the *Name* and *Heart* of Jesus, which are quite well known and widespread, as I said.

I confess it: this was a sudden and unexpected inspiration for me. From the time I was a boy, little more than an infant, I saw a private devotion to the Most Precious Blood of Jesus in my old grand-uncle Zaverio—the oldest of the five Roncalli brothers, and as a matter of fact *the first one to train me in the religious practice that soon blossomed forth, and I would say spontaneously, in the form of my vocation to the priesthood.* I recall the devotional books in his kneeling-bench: and among them the "Most Precious Blood," which he used during the month of July. Oh! sacred and blessed memories of my childhood. How precious they are to me in the light of this eventide of my life, clarifying basic points with regard to my sanctification and providing a consoling vision of what—as I humbly trust—awaits me in my eternity. *Crucifix and eternity: Passion of Christ in the light of never-ending eternity.* Oh! Oh! what delights: oh! what foundations and ever more so: the life that I still have to live here below ought to be a peace brought to life: at the foot of the cross of Jesus Crucified which has been bathed in His most precious Blood; and in the most bitter tears of the Sorrowful Mother of Jesus and of mine. . . .

---

[23] *good father of all Christians.*
[24] *good shepherd.*

Suggestions for a Good Apostolate[24a]

To treat everyone with respect, with prudence and with Gospel simplicity.

There is common belief in and approval for the idea that the Pope's language, even in ordinary conversations, ought to savor of the mysterious and of a circumspect awesomeness. Instead what is more in keeping with the example of Jesus is the most attractive simplicity, along with the prudence of the wise men and the saints who are helped by God. Simplicity may stir up not exactly contempt but less consideration on the part of the supposedly learned. The supposedly learned do not matter very much and no one should pay any attention to whether or not they may be able to inflict some form of humiliation by their judgments or their attitude: it will all result in harm and confusion for themselves. The man who is *simplex rectus et timens Deum*[25] is always the worthiest and the strongest. Always naturally sustained by a wise and gracious prudence. A man is simple if he is not ashamed to confess the Gospel before men who look upon it as nothing but a sign of weakness and a childish affair—and to confess each and every part of it and on all occasions and in the presence of anyone—if he doesn't let himself be deceived or turned against people by his neighbor, and if he doesn't lose his peace of mind because of any attitude that others may adopt toward him.

A man is *prudent* if he knows how to keep quiet about some part of the truth that it would be inopportune to make known, as long as keeping quiet about it will not ruin the part of the truth that he speaks, by falsifying it; if he knows how to reach the good goals that he has set for himself by choosing the most effective means to make decisions and to act; if he always knows how to foresee and measure the difficulties and the opposition that will stand in the way and to choose the road that involves lesser difficulties and dangers; if he never loses sight of a good, noble, great goal once he has decided upon it, and succeeds in overcoming all

---

[24a] We are following *Osservatore Romano* in placing the next several pages of text under the entry date of August 12, 1961.—Ed.
[25] *simple, upright, and God-fearing.*

obstacles and going on to a successful conclusion; if in all matters he draws a clear distinction between what is essential and what is not and does not let himself get embroiled with minor matters, but rather keeps all his energies directed systematically toward a successful outcome; if at the root of all this, he looks to God alone for success, and trusts in Him, and realizes even when he has not succeeded in whole or in part that he has done well by relating everything to the will and to the greater glory of God.

Simplicity has nothing in it that contradicts *prudence,* nor vice versa. Simplicity is love, prudence is thought. Love prays: intelligence keeps watch. *Vigilate et orate.*[26] Perfect reconciliation. Love is like a cooing dove: the mind in action is like a serpent who never falls to the ground, and is never dashed against anything because he goes along probing all the high spots and the low spots along his path with his head.

To Remain Calm
in the Face of Everything That Happens

The Lord Jesus who founded the Holy Church is the one who governs all events with his wisdom, his power and his indescribable goodness and directs them according to his good pleasure and for the greater good of his chosen ones who make up his beloved mystical spouse.

No matter how events may seem to be going against the good of the Church, I ought to enjoy perfect tranquillity: which doesn't of course dispense me from longing and from praying that *fiat voluntas sua sicut in coelo et in terra.*[27]

I must guard myself against the rashness of those who are either mentally blind or deceived by hidden pride and presume to do some good without being called by God in his Church, as if the Divine Redeemer had any need of their miserable cooperation or that of any man whatsoever. . . .

What counts is to cooperate with God toward the salvation of souls and of the whole world. . . .

[26] *Watch and pray.*
[27] *His will be done on earth as it is in heaven.*

In omnibus respice finem.[28] This doesn't mean the conclusion of a man's life: but rather the goal, the *divine vocation* to which the Pope was raised up through a mysterious disposition of Providence.

This vocation is expressed in a threefold burst of light: *personal holiness* of the Pope that makes his life glorious; *love for the universal Church* according to the measure of that heavenly grace which alone can set one on the road to *glory* and ensure it: finally the condition of the will of Jesus Christ, who alone directs the Church through the Pope and governs it according to His own good pleasure in view of the glory that is the greatest on earth and in the eternal heavens.

The sacrosanct duty of the lowly Pope is to purify all his intentions in this light of glory and to live in conformity of doctrine and of grace in such a way as to merit for himself the greater honor of growing to resemble Christ in grace, as his Vicar: Christ Crucified, at the price of his Blood, Redeemer of the world: Christ the Rabbi, teacher, the one true Teacher of ages and nations.

THOUGHTS (I)

USEFULNESS OF TRIBULATIONS

As I turn my attention inward to myself and go back over the various events of my humble life, I have to admit that up to now the Lord has excused me from those tribulations that make the service of truth, justice, and charity difficult and not welcome for so many souls. I passed through the period of infancy and boyhood without taking any notice of poverty, without any family disturbances or any troubles with studies or difficulties arising from dangerous situations like, for example, military service at the age of 20, and during the World War, from 1915 to 1921.

Always a warm welcome

Small and lowly as I realize I was, I received nothing but warm welcomes in the environment that greeted me, in the seminaries of Bergamo and, later on, Rome, and during my 10 years as a priest

[28] *In all things, look to the end.*

alongside my Bishop and in my home town: then from 1921 down to the present (1961), that is from Rome to Rome and finally to the Vatican. O dear God, how can I ever thank you for the kind receptions that always awaited me wherever I *went* in your name and *always out of pure obedience,* not to my will, but to yours?

Quid retribuam, Domine, pro omnibus quae tribuisti mihi?[29] I well see that my answer to myself and to the Lord is always *"calicem salutarem accipere et nomen Domini invocare."*[30]

As I have already indicated in these pages: if and when *magna mihi tribulatio advenerit,*[31] to accept it well; and if this be a while yet in coming, then to continue to drink the *blood of Jesus* along with that combination of small or great tribulations that the Lord in His goodness may choose to set around it. I have always been deeply impressed—and still am—by that little Psalm 130 which says: *O Lord, my heart is not proud, nor are my eyes haughty; I busy not myself with great things, nor with things too sublime for me. Imo composui et pacavi animam meam. Sicut parvulus in gremio matris suae, ita in me est anima mea.*[32] Oh! how dear these words are! But if I should have to be upset toward the end, Lord Jesus mine, thou shalt comfort me in tribulation. Thy Blood, thy Blood, which I will continue to drink from thy chalice, which is the same as saying from thy Heart, will be to me a pledge of salvation and of eternal joy. *"Quod est in praesenti, momentaneum et leve tribulationis nostrae, supramodum in sublimitate aeternum gloriae pondus operatur in nobis."*[33]

THOUGHTS (II)

To be satisfied with each day's apostolate: not to waste time on predictions of the future.

Christus heri et hodie, ipse et saecula.[34]

---

[29] *What shall I give back, O Lord, for all that you have given to me?*
[30] *to take up the chalice of salvation and call upon the name of the Lord.*
[31] *great tribulation comes upon me.*
[32] *Nay rather, I have stilled and quieted my soul like a weaned child. Like a weaned child on its mother's lap, so is my soul within me.*
[33] *For that which is at present momentary and light of our tribulation worketh for us above measure exceedingly an eternal weight of glory. (2 Cor. 4, 17)*
[34] *Christ yesterday and today, and forever.*

Not to make predictions and not to give any assurances about the future is the *rule of conduct* that comes from the *spirit of tranquillity and of firmness* that the Pope, as the first among priests, must bestow upon the faithful and upon his fellow-workers for their enlightenment and encouragement. . . .

A basic rule for the Pope's conduct is this one of always resting content with his *present* state, and not getting all tangled up with the *future* but instead leaving it in the Lord's hands without making too many plans or merely human provisions, and being careful not to speak of it with any ease and assurance to anyone whatsoever.

The experience of these three years of my service as Pope, which I accepted *tremens et timens*[35] out of pure obedience to the will of the Lord as it was expressed to me by the voice of the Sacred College of Cardinals in conclave, is a stirring and lasting witness to and motive for my spirit's fidelity to this maxim: absolute abandonment to God as far as the present is concerned and perfect tranquillity with regard to the future.

All of the various undertakings of a pastoral nature that have been interspersed through this first effort of Ours at carrying out the pontifical mission of apostolate have come from absolute calm and from a loving—I would even say a silent—inspiration of the Lord to this poor servant of his, who with no merits of his own, or rather that very simple merit of not questioning, but simply agreeing and obeying, has turned out to be a not unprofitable instrument of honor to Jesus and of edification for many souls.

The first contacts with the lowly and with the great: some of the charitable visits here and there: meekness and humility in approach and clarity in ideas along with fervent encouragement: the Lenten visits to new parishes, the celebration of the diocesan synod with unexpected success, the drawing closer of its Father to the whole of Christendom through the many creations of cardinals and of bishops from every nation and every race and color: and now the vast movement—of imposing proportions that go beyond all expectations—of the Ecumenical Council, all this confirms the value of the principle to wait and to express with faith, with modesty,

---

[35] *in fear and trembling.*

with trusting fervor the good inspiration of the grace of Jesus, who watches over the governing of the world, and leads it to the loftiest goals of the creation, the redemption, the final and eternal glorification of souls and of nations.

Sunday, August 13

Exercise of prudence by the Pope and the bishops.

Faith, hope and charity are the three stars of episcopal glory. The Pope *in capite et in exemplum*[36] and the bishops, all the bishops of the Church with him.

The sublime, holy and divine task of the Pope for the whole Church and of the bishops for their own dioceses is to preach the Gospel, to lead men to eternal salvation: with the caution of working to see to it that no other earthly matter gets in the way of or becomes intertwined with or upsets this primary ministry. The intertwining can arise in particular from differences of human opinions on matters of politics that come to oppose each other in the form of various thoughts and attitudes. Over and above all the opinions and parties that stir up and afflict society and the whole of mankind rises the Gospel. The Pope reads it and along with the bishops comments on it, with both the one and the others acting not as participants in the worldly interests of anyone whatsoever, but rather as dwellers in the city of peace that is undisturbed and happy and from which comes the divine rule that can well guide the earthly city and the whole world.

As a matter of fact *this is* what sensible men are looking for from the Church: and nothing else.

A clear conscience with regard to my conduct as new Pope during these three years calms me, and I beg the Lord to help me keep myself faithful to this good beginning.

It is quite important to insist upon the bishops [in this matter of prudence] so that everyone may do as much: and may the example of the Pope be a lesson and an encouragement to everyone. To preach to all men, equally and in a general way, justice, charity,

[36] *at the head and as a model.*

humility, meekness, gentleness and the other Gospel virtues, defending the rights of the Church in the proper way when they are violated or compromised.

At all times, but especially in these times, it is up to the bishop to spread the balm of gentleness over the wounds of mankind (and so he must guard against any rash judgment, any word that will injure anyone whatsoever, any flattery that is motivated by fear, any connivance with evil that may be suggested to him with the hope of helping someone); to maintain a bearing that will be serious, reserved and firm; to be careful to carry on a conversation with all that will be gentle and loving and at the same time to be able to distinguish between good and evil with holy doctrine, but without any vehemence.

Any efforts or intrigues of human making will be worth very little in these affairs of worldly interest.

Instead, by more constant and intense prayer to diligently promote divine worship among the faithful, along with the practices of piety, the frequenting of the Sacraments, which will be preached well and administered well, and, above all, religious instruction: this will contribute toward solving problems, including those of a temporal nature, much better than other human schemes will ever succeed in doing. This will draw down the blessings of God upon the people, keep them from many evils, and call wandering minds back to a more correct way of thinking. Help comes down from on high: and the heavenly light scatters the darkness.[37]

And this is my thought and my pastoral concern today as it must be for always.

Monday, August 14

Six Maxims of Perfection

As for the goal to be reached in my life, I must:

1) Desire only to be *justus et sanctus*,[38] and in this *way* to please God.

---

[37] Cf. A. Rosmini from Villa Albani (Rome) Nov. 23, 1848: *op. cit., passim*, 19-21. (See bibliographic note, p. 508.—Ed.)
[38] *just and holy*.

2) Direct everything, thoughts and actions, toward the growth, the service, the glory of Holy Church.

3) Feeling that I am called by God, and precisely for this [reason], remain perfectly calm about all that happens not only with regard to me, but also with regard to the Church, while still laboring always in her behalf and suffering with Christ for her.

4) Remain always resigned to divine Providence.

5) Recognize myself always in my nothingness.

6) Always plan my day with clear vision and perfect order.

My life as a priest, indeed—as people quite often say to my honor and confusion—as prince of the whole priesthood of Christ, in His name and by His power, stands before and beneath the eyes of my divine Master, the great lawgiver. He watches me, bloodied, beaten, hanging from the Cross. He looks at me with breast pierced, with hands and feet pierced, and invites me always to look at Him in turn. Justice has led Him directly to charity; and charity has immolated Him. This must be my lot: *non est discipulus super magistrum.*[39]

O Jesus, languishing and dying for me, here I am before you. Old now, on the way toward the end of my service, of my life. Keep me very close to your heart, and make its beat one with mine. I would like to feel myself inseparably bound to You with a chain of gold, made up of fine and graceful links.

First: *the justice* that forces me always to find my God in all things.

Second: *the providence and goodness* that will guide my steps.

Third: inexhaustible and most patient *charity toward neighbor.*

Fourth: *the sacrifice* that must be my companion and that I want to and ought to taste at all times.

Fifth: *the glory* that Jesus assures me of for this life and for eternal life.

O Jesus Crucified *amor meus et misericordia mea nunc et in saecula.*[40]

---

[39] *The disciple is not greater than the master.*
[40] *my love and my mercy now and forever.*

Pater, si vis transfer calicem istum a me: verumtamen non mea voluntas sed tua fiat.[41]

August 15, 1961

FEAST OF THE ASSUMPTION

Here we are at one of the most solemn and most beloved celebrations of religious devotion. My immediate predecessor, Pope Pius XII, proclaimed it a dogma of faith—November 1, 1950. I was one of the fortunate ones who was present in St. Peter's square for that ceremony, as Nuncio to France. . . .

The phrase that expresses the main thought of this closing of [the retreat] is the common, and yet very precious one: *Ad Jesum per Mariam.*[42]

As a matter of fact, this life of mine that is turning toward its sunset could not be better dissolved than in my concentrating completely on Jesus, who is the Son of Mary and who is offered to me from her arms for the comfort and delight of my soul.

For this reason, I will take very special care to pay attention with a profound and serene joy to these three splendid words that must stand as the summing up of my effort at perfection: *Pietas, mansuetudo, charitas.*[43]

I will keep on devoting myself to the exercises of piety toward perfection: *the Holy Mass, the Breviary, the whole of the Rosary:* and great and constant intimacy with Jesus, as He is contemplated in the mind's eye as Infant and Crucified; as adored in the Sacrament. The Breviary keeps my mind in constant elevation; the Holy Mass immerses it in the *name,* the *heart,* the *blood of Christ.* Oh! what tenderness and delight lie in this morning Mass of mine!

The Rosary which I have pledged myself to recite with devotion whole and entire, *since the beginning of 1958,* has become a

---

[41] *Father, if thou wilt, remove this chalice from me: but yet not my will, but thine be done. Luke 22, 42.*
[42] *To Jesus through Mary.*
[43] *Devotion, meekness, charity.*

tranquil daily practice of meditation and contemplation, that keeps my mind open to the very vast field of my teaching office and ministry as supreme Pastor of the Church and universal father of souls.

As this spiritual retreat of mine draws nearer to a close, I perceive ever more clearly the living substance of the task that Jesus, either by permitting it or by planning it, has entrusted to my life.

Vicarius Xsti?[44] Ah! I am not worthy of this title, poor son of Battista and Marianna Roncalli, two good Christians, it's true: but so modest and humble. *Vicarius Xsti*: hence my task is there: *Sacerdos et victima*.[45] The priesthood exalts me, but the sacrifice that the priesthood lets one endure makes me tremble.

Blessed Jesus, God and man. I confirm my consecration to you, for life, for death, for eternity.

From a consideration of all that happens in life and of all that surrounds me, it is easy for me to pause often over Calvary: to talk there with the dying Jesus and with His Mother, and to go down from Calvary to the holy Tabernacle, the dwelling place of Jesus in the Sacrament. The Breviary becomes more pleasing to me and I enjoy it best at my regular work-table: but the Rosary and the meditating on the mysteries, along with the intentions that for some time I have liked to add to each decade, is something I enjoy more on my knees close by the sacred veil of the Eucharist.

As a reminder of the fervor and the happy inspirations of these days, I would like to fix the three most clear-cut points of my daily conversations with Jesus:

1) In the morning, Holy Mass after having recited the Breviary —before Mass—up to Sext. After Mass: Sext and None and the first part of the rosary.

2) After dinner, I will never omit *a brief visit* as soon as I have come out of the dining room, and a brief rest.

3) In the afternoon hours and after the brief rest—never in bed, but rather in an easy-chair—recitation of Vespers and of Compline, and the second part of the Rosary, the sorrowful mysteries. This form of prayer can well be as efficacious as a visit to the Blessed Sacrament for me.[46]

[44] *Vicar of Christ?*   [45] *Priest and victim.*
[46] The words "valermi come visita" can also mean "count for a visit."—Translator.

4) In the evening, at 7:30, the third part of the Rosary in common with the pontifical family: secretary, sisters, and domestics. If it be convenient, a final visit to the Blessed Sacrament to recommend to Him the hours of night.

As for the practice of *meekness,* I will not add any words. I thank the Lord for His goodness in helping me in the practice of the *mitis et humilis corde, ore et opere.* . . .[47]

By the grace of the Lord, I have not yet entered into the *senueris:*[48] but with the 80 years that I have now completed, I find myself at the door. And so I must keep ready for this last stage of my life where limitations and sacrifices are waiting for me, right up to the sacrifice of bodily life and the opening up of eternal life. Oh Jesus: here I am ready to extend my hands that are now weak and trembling: to let others help me get dressed and support me along the way.

O Lord, thou hast added to Peter *"et duces quo tu non vis."*[49]

Oh! after all the many graces lavished upon me during my long life, there is nothing more that I want. Thou hast revealed the way to me, O Jesus: *sequar Te quocumque ieris:*[50] to sacrifice, to mortifications, to death.

Post mortem reliquos mors pia consecrat.
Palmamque emeritos gloria suscipit.[51]

The thought of a death that may be very near and that certainly is not far off, reminds me of my dear St. Joseph, who is with good reason venerated, among other ways, as the protector of the dying, because Jesus and Mary were present at his blessed and happy passing, just as his whole life had been spent in their company.

The Church's hymn goes on with this reminder: *Tu vero superis par frueris Deo mira sorte beatior.*[52]

Oh! how it delights me to mark the final notes of this spiritual

---

[47] *meek and humble of heart, in word and deed.*
[48] *Thou shalt be old.*
[49] *And lead thee whither thou wouldst not.*
[50] *I will follow thee wherever thou goest.*
[51] *A happy lot uplifts other men after death, and glory rears in bliss those who have won the palm.* From Hymn for First Vespers for Feast of St. Joseph, March 19. Translation from Mulcahy's *The Hymns of the Roman Breviary and Missal,* Dublin, Brown and Nolan, 1938, p. 130.
[52] *Thou, like the blest above, e'en here, dost God enjoy, wondrous happy thy destiny. Ibid.*

retreat of mine with the last verse of the liturgical hymn that the Holy Church dedicates to the Most Blessed Trinity and from which comes, in the commemoration of St. Joseph the spouse of Mary, every blessing and every assurance of resplendent and eternal life:

> *Nobis, summa Trias, parce precantibus*
> *Da Joseph meritis sidera scandere*
> *Ut tandem liceat nos tibi perpetim*
> *Gratum promere canticum. Amen.*[53]

Nov. 26-Dec. 2, 1961

Brief Notes

1) I recall all that I meditated on and wrote for the occasion of my eightieth birthday, in the solitude of Castel Gandolfo with my confessor, Msgr. Alfredo Cavagna. *Cf.* manuscript of my *Soliloquies*.

2) Having entered upon and now completed my eightieth year doesn't disturb me; instead it keeps me calm and confident. We are where We usually are: I desire nothing more nor less than what the Lord continues to give me. I thank Him and I bless Him *per singulos dies*:[54] ready for anything.

3) I am aware of the beginning of a certain disturbance in my body that must be natural for an old man. I bear with it calmly, even if it does give me a little annoyance at times and even in spite of the fact that it makes me fear that it may be growing worse. It is not pleasant to think about it a good deal; but once again, I feel prepared for anything.

4) I enjoy the satisfaction that comes from remaining faithful to my religious practices: Office, triple *Prayer of Meditation on the Rosary*: constant union with God and with spiritual things.

5) The practice of saying things that are substantial and not

---

[53] *Spare us, great Trinity, humbly imploring Thee,*
By Joseph's merits grant we may to heav'n attain,
So may we there at last, pay thee unceasingly
Grateful joyous chants, hymn of praise.—Ibid.
[54] *every day.*

empty makes me desire a greater closeness to what was written by the great pontiffs of ancient times. During these months, St. Leo the Great and Innocent III have become familiar to me. Unfortunately, few priests bother with them despite the fact that they are rich in theological and pastoral doctrine. I will never grow tired of drawing upon these invaluable fonts of sacred knowledge and of lofty and delightful poetry.

6) But above all, I want to insist on attention to holy intimacies with the Lord: on keeping myself in a tranquil and loving conversation with Him. *Verbum Patris caro factum;*[55] center and life of the Mystical Body; and in continuation of divine brotherhood—*divine and human*—through whom I am his brother by adoption, and with him son of Mary His Mother.

7) In this relationship you find the task and the dignity of Supreme Pontiff of the Holy Catholic Church and of *"Vicarius Christi,"*[56] as I am recognized. Oh! how I feel the meaning and the tenderness of each morning's *"Domine non sum dignus,"*[57] with the Sacred Host in hand, seal of humility and of love.

8) The expectation of the Second Ecumenical Council of the Vatican absorbs a great part of my daily activities. It stirs up in my mind the thought and the desire to draw around my own daily prayer the prayer of all the Catholic clergy, secular and regular, and of the religious congregations of women, in a form that is official and universal. . . .

[55] *The Word of the Father made flesh.*
[56] Vicar of Christ.
[57] *Lord I am not worthy.*

DIARY PAGES
AND FINAL REFLECTIONS

Excerpts from the Diary of Pope John XXIII
and Some Random Meditative Notes

- *His daily routine*
- *Personal reactions*
- *Hints of suffering*
- *Attitude toward his office*
- *Interior life*

Tuesday, January 1, 1963

Sit nomen Domini benedictum: ex hoc nunc et usque in saeculum.[1]

MY RISING, as usual, at *4 o'clock*. A quiet morning of prayer and good work. Preparation of the letter to the bishops on the Council.[2]

In the afternoon, Cardinal Testa: exchange of New Year's wishes. Reminder of Msgr. Cerasola and plan for a gathering of the Bergamese living in Rome.

In the evening, at the Clementine, Christmas music with the children of three charitable institutions: Gnocchi, Orionites, Nazareth. Two newly-weds from Medolago were present too: Virgilio Ghisleni, son of the other Virgilio who is dead now, my nephew through my sister Teresa. The bride is a Carminati from Medolago. They offer great promise for the future.

I note, with joy and gratitude to the Lord, that this first day of 1963 has begun well—from my own physical point of view as well.

---

[1] *May the name of the Lord be blessed: henceforth, now and forever.* (See bibliographic note, p. 508.)
[2] Cf. p. 447.

Friday, January 4

A wonderful audience in the Clementine with those taking part in the National Congress of the College Graduates' Movement of Catholic Action. I read a good allocution to them, and I believe they were both satisfied and encouraged.

During the day, I continued the laborious preparation of my "*epistola episcopalis*"[3] on the Council. . . .

Sunday, January 20

A cheerful feast of the spirit on the occasion of the canonization of St. Vincent Pallotti—a Roman priest—in St. Peter's. In the central nave from the Confessional to the Chair and in the two vast side naves, a *multitudo innumerabilis*[4] of devout Romans and of Catholics who had come from the north of Europe, under the inspiration of the Pallottine Fathers and Sisters: a world that was created by a "Roman priest" and that blossomed forth with great prosperity elsewhere.

The weather though was very ugly and it would have made hearts sad, had they not been alive and filled with the thought of the wonders of grace. The Pope was very happy about this canonization. It brought great joy and encouragement to the clergy. My prayers to the new saint, asking him to be a valiant patron of the Ecumenical Council, are intense and unremitting.

Tuesday, January 22

A very cold day. But a day of triumph at Sant'Andrea della Valle because of the dense crowd of pilgrims from all over Europe who had come to Rome for the canonization of St. Vincent Pallotti, and who gathered at Sant'Andrea around the body of the new saint, the man who conceived the idea and then became the apostle of the special celebration of the Octave of the Epiphany. All the pastors of Rome were there, along with the prelates and aides from the Vicariate, gathered with great fervor—*in plenitudine exultationis* —around the lowly successor of Pius IX, who on January 13, 1847,

---

[3] *episcopal letter.*   [4] *countless number.*

went there unexpectedly to do honor to what Father Pallotti had instituted. Connections in history: and a return of brilliant horizons. My talk was a little long: but it certainly corresponded to something mysterious that is hovering over our heads and perhaps knocking at many hearts. . . .

Sunday, February 10

This morning, I got up at 3 to finish the words that I had to deliver . . . A day that was unforgettable for three reasons: 1) The blessing of the cornerstone for the new building—the third—that will house the Pontifical Lombard Seminary. 2) The introduction of the cause for beatification and canonization of Cardinal Andrea Ferrari (d. 1921), Archbishop of Milan: a great event and a great kindness on the Lord's part in reserving this honor for me. Who would ever have imagined it? That this great privilege would go to the lowly secretary of Msgr. Radini Tedeschi. And as I carried it out, it's true, I was moved to the point of tears. 3) The arrival and the reception of the Metropolitan of the Ukraines, Msgr. Slipyi, after 18 years of imprisonment, in the presence of Cardinals Amleto Cicognani and Testa. Oh! the words of the "Imitation of Christ" are true and touching: *"Felix hora, quando Iesus vocat de lacrymis ad gaudium spiritus."*[5]

Tuesday, February 19

A large gathering of priests of a pastoral nature aimed at the orientation of the clergy in health and resort areas. Cardinal Traglia presented the participants in the Clementine. My talk a little bit long: but with a spiritual vigor that could not help but make an impression. I was very happy then to greet a good-sized group of priests from Venice. They were for me a reminder full of holy affection and of spiritual tenderness of my six happy years as patriarch of Venice, which I couldn't forget and which I will always carry in my heart.

Another wonderful visit, that of Msgr. Bortignon, the Bishop of

---

[5] *Happy is the hour when Jesus calls one from tears to joy of spirit.* **Book II, chap. 8.**

Padua, who is very familiar to me; and that of Cardinal Confalonieri and other Cardinals of the Sacred Congregation of Rites along with the Prefect, during which the signing of the document on the heroic virtues of Pauline Jaricot took place, which gave me the idea of making some extended remarks about this holy woman.

Saturday, February 23

A good night for practicing patience. A morning that was recollected, with the office up to Vespers.

Holy Mass on the *anniversary of the "Fiducia"*[6] in her chapel at St. John's, along with all the seminarians. A most devout Mass at 8 o'clock. At 9:30, everything was over and had turned out well. . . .

In the afternoon, a long talk here with my confessor, Msgr. Cavagna.

Sunday, March 17

In St. Peter's: solemn *beatification* of Elizabeth Seton that the whole American world has been longing for so much. Two events that were outstanding successes. In the morning, solemn Mass after the proclamation of the decrees: from which the Pope was absent, in keeping with ceremonial custom. In the afternoon, I attended the Benediction of the Most Blessed Sacrament imparted by the Archbishop of Baltimore.

This was followed by my talk from the Confessional facing toward the Chair. Very fine: a section at a time, the Pope and then the Cardinal of New York in English: a very large and exuberant crowd of Americans. They had applauded the Pope earlier at the time of the noon *Angelus* in the square.

The evening ever more vibrant both inside and outside the Basilica. . . .

Monday, April 15

I came away from Easter content: but actually not feeling well as far as my stomach trouble is concerned. A peaceful Holy Mass at

---

[6] The picture of Our Lady of Trust in the Lateran Seminary, to which Pope John had special devotion.—Translator.

home and then abandonment to God. Yesterday St. Peter's Square was simply *triumphal* as on only the rarest of occasions: with a solid unison of greetings and best wishes to the Pope as he appeared on the balcony. The final greetings in 27 languages: a diffusion of peace and of triumphant joy. The encyclical *"Pacem in terris"* acclaimed as perhaps never before. This yesterday.

Today a little rest at home, but with a great deal of distraction: long audience with Cardinal Testa; disturbances continuing so as to make me think seriously about my condition. . . .

Wednesday, May 1

. . . The vigil has brought me many plans, which I entrust to Mary to whom I wish to do honor. First of all a search for greater spiritual intimacy: between Mary and the Council, concerning which I must bring myself up to date. Today I spent two hours at the Tower of St. John, and I want to go back there, going over the "Acts" that are being prepared for prompt delivery to the Bishops of the Council. Then there is the whole matter of a consecration that I have begun to put into effect today; and to which I will direct the merit of the physical pains that hardly ever leave me.

My presence and my words—*Our Lady; St. Joseph; the Holy Church*—in the great audience of this morning in St. Peter's, may, I hope, be the notes of my reverent and resounding declaration of my homage to Mary.

Friday, May 10

We have reached the two days that will mark the glorification of poor Pope John for his accomplishments as *princeps pacis*.[7] This morning, the peace prize of the Stephen Balzan foundation was conferred upon me in the Sala Regia in the Vatican. . . .

Saturday, May 11

Noctem quietam et finem perfectum concedat nobis Dominus Omnipotens.[8] These words of the liturgy put a fitting conclusion

---
[7] *Prince of peace.*
[8] *May the Almighty Lord grant us a peaceful night and a perfect end.*

to the success of these last few days in proclaiming the triumph of peace, from here at the center of the world. Yesterday's double ceremony in the *sala Regia* and in the Vatican, and this evening's visit of the Pope to the Quirinal, with the accompanying talks of the two presidents Gronchi and Segni, and of the Pope, mark two historical and useful days in the course of my life and of my service to the Holy See and to Italy. In thinking about it, even I—who am always a little cold in these matters—have not suppressed my emotion and my gratitude to the Lord *"qui respexit humilitatem servi sui . . . et fecit mihi magna qui potens est."*[9] Who would ever have thought that these mysterious words that are suffused with so much grace would be applied precisely to my weakness?

Monday, May 20

O dear saint of mine, Bernardine, beloved among all my saints: with the sweetness of thy feast-day, thou hast brought me several signs of the continuation of a great physical pain that does not leave me, and that makes me think and suffer a great deal.

This morning for the third time *I rested content with* receiving *Holy Communion* in bed, instead of enjoying the celebration of Holy Mass: patience: patience. Still I could not give up receiving the farewell visit of Cardinal Wyszynski, primate of Poland, Archbishop of Gniezno and Warsaw, with four of his bishops who are on their way back to their homeland. The rest of the day in bed with several particularly painful episodes. I am helped, and always with great charity, by those who are close to me: Cardinal Cicognani, Msgr. Capovilla, Frater Federico Belotti, and the servants.

Undated[10]

List of great graces bestowed on someone who has little regard for himself: but who receives inspirations to good and puts them into practice with humility and trust.

First Grace. Accepting the honor and the burden of the pontifi-

---
[9] *who has regarded the humility of his servant . . . and he that is mighty has done great things to me.*
[10] Internal evidence indicates that these words were written shortly before the Second Vatican Council opened on Oct. 11, 1962.—Ed.

cate with simplicity and with the joy of being able to say that I have done nothing to bring it on; absolutely nothing; instead I have made definite, conscious efforts not to attract any attention to myself.

Second Grace. Making it seem simple for me to carry out immediately certain ideas that were in no way complex and in fact were extremely simple, but that had vast significance and consequences for the future—and with immediate success. What words these are: to accept the Lord's inspirations to good: *simpliciter et confidenter!*[11]

To put forth, in a conversation with my Secretary of State on January 20, 1959, without ever having thought of it beforehand, mention of an ecumenical council, of a diocesan synod, and of a revision of the Code of Canon Law—without ever having thought of it before, and contrary to anything I had ever supposed or imagined in this regard.

The first person to be surprised by this proposal of mine was myself, and no one had ever even hinted to me about these matters.

And to say that everything then seemed very natural to me in its immediate and later continual development.

After three years of laborious, continuous, but also happy and tranquil preparation, here we are now at the foot of the holy mountain.

May the Lord sustain us in bringing everything to a successful conclusion!

Undated[12]

. . . This bed is an altar. ! An altar calls for a victim. Here I am ready. I have before me the clear vision of my soul, of my priesthood, of the Council, of the universal Church.

. . . The Lord is quite right in adding the cross to the manifestation of infinite mercy of which He had given me signs during these last months in particular.

. . . I am at peace. My desire has been always to do the will

---

[11] *with simplicity and trust.*
[12] These selections *as a whole* seem to have been arranged in *Osservatore Romano* with the thought of giving a picture of John XXIII's mind as he lay dying.—Translator.

of God, always, always. I pray for the Church, for children, for priests and bishops that they may be holy, for the whole world.

. . . Having come forth from the poverty and littleness of Sotto il Monte, I tried never to separate myself from it. What great grace the Lord has granted me: holy parish-priests, model parents; a strong Christian tradition; a poverty that was serene and contented.

. . . I want to die without knowing whether I own anything of my own. Poverty has often embarrassed me, especially when I was not able to help my own who were very poor, or some brother priest. But I have never regretted it!

. . . My devotions as a child, at home, in the parish, alongside of uncle Saverio: Jesus in the Blessed Sacrament and the Sacred Heart, the Precious Blood, our blessed Lady, St. Joseph, the three Francises: of Assisi, Xavier and de Sales, St. Charles, St. Gregory Barbarigo, the Guardian Angel, the Dead. . .

. . . The Council. God knows that I have opened my little soul to this great inspiration with simplicity. Will He choose to let me finish it? May He be blessed. Will He not let me do it? . . . . I will see its successful conclusion from heaven where I hope—even more, I am sure—that the divine mercy will choose to draw me.

. . . What reverberations from this *Pacem in terris!* What is mine in this document is above all the humble example that I have tried to give during all my poor life: *De bono homine pacifico*.[13]

The world has awakened. Little by little, the most pure doctrine of the encyclical, a doctrine proposed in the right way, will find its way into consciences.

. . . No, I am not upset over what has been written and said about me. It is all too little if you compare it with the sufferings and cares of Jesus, the Son of God, during His life and on the cross.

. . . Every so often, during the recitation of the Rosary, along with the familiar intentions, I add some others. At those times I go back over the course of my life. I pray for my Bergamo, for the dear brethren of Bulgaria (Oh! those ten years); for the Turks and the Greeks. I see once again the eight years of my stay among the French who have been so good to me and whom I have

---

[13] *On the good peace-making man. Imitation of Christ,* book II, Chapter III.

loved so much and still do. I see once again Venice, my Venice, which is always on my lips and in my heart. And then here I am, here, alongside of St. Peter and the Lateran. In the early days of this pontifical service, I didn't fully realize all that it meant to be the Bishop of Rome and, as a result, the Shepherd of the universal Church. Then, week by week, a full understanding has come. And I have felt at home, as if I had never done anything else for the whole of my life.

Oh! what great consolations are the contacts with the crowds and the audiences.

And I cannot think of the trip to Loreto and Assisi without growing sentimental. And the dear people of Rome! I will always love them, and from heaven I will go on protecting them.

. . . My Roman seminary, with the sacred [picture of] Our Lady of Trust; Propaganda Fide (oh, those very happy years from '21 to '25!), the great monastic orders (I wanted so much to go to Montecassino and who knows, who knows?); the countless circle of priests, brothers, nuns, sisters, and missionaries: this is the treasure of the Church.

. . . Catholic action. It was begun by Msgr. Radini, my bishop (there was a man really worthy to become Pope!) and it has remained faithful to those teachings . . .

. . . The sick, the imprisoned, the poor, the refugees . . .

. . . I have read back over what I wrote in my book in the midst of the World War in 1916. The last days of Msgr. Radini, his final invocation: peace, peace . . . I would like it to be my last prayer as Pope too, as the lowly Pope John.

Appendix and Index

APPENDIX

A. Bibliographic Data and Notes

Almost all the Pope's public messages are printed in the Vatican City daily newspaper, *L'Osservatore Romano*. They are printed in the language in which they were given (Latin, French, English, German, Italian, etc.); occasionally an Italian translation is published at the same time. Some weeks later a few of these messages (together with an occasional message which never appeared in *L'Osservatore Romano*) are selected for inclusion in the official publication of the Holy See, the *Acta Apostolicae Sedis*. Normally the text as it appears in *L'Osservatore Romano* is identical with the text as it appears in the *Acta*. Occasionally, however, some changes are made and once in a great while the change is of a substantive nature. The text in the *Acta*, of course, is the official text.

With a few exceptions (for example, *Mater et Magistra* and *Pacem in Terris*) the translations which appear in this book are based on the *L'Osservatore Romano* text. This is because all but two of the translations (namely *Retreat Notes* and *Diary Pages*) originally appeared in *The Pope Speaks Magazine* and in most cases the dictates of time required the use of the *Osservatore* text. In any event the editors have no reason to believe that the translations would differ in any substantial way had they been prepared directly from the *Acta*. In this bibliographic section we are indicating both the *Osservatore* and *Acta* references as well as a reference to *The Pope Speaks Magazine*. We are also indicating the opening words of the original language text, which is the normal way to identify papal messages. The English language title in almost all cases is one which has been selected by the editors and has no official status. The individual messages are listed in the order in which they appear in this book.

Principal abbreviations used here and elsewhere in this book are as follows:

AAS —Acta Apostolicae Sedis;
NCWC—National Catholic Welfare Conference;
OR —L'Osservatore Romano;
TPS —The Pope Speaks Magazine.

Part I

THE NAME "JOHN." (*Vocabor Ioannes*) Oct. 28, 1958. On the day of his election to the papacy Angelo Cardinal Roncalli surprised the world by

502 *Appendix*

selecting the name "John XXIII" for his pontificate. He explained the reasons for his selection in a private audience with the College of Cardinals. Latin text in *Osservatore Romano*, Oct. 30, 1958, and in *AAS* 50 (1958) 878-9. Translation by Martin F. Connor (*TPS* V, 134).

THIS ANXIOUS HOUR. (*Hac trepida hora*) Oct. 29, 1958. Elected Pope on the afternoon of Oct. 28, Pope John delivered this address to the College of Cardinals in the Sistine Chapel the following day. Latin text in *Osservatore Romano*, Oct. 30, 1958, and in *AAS* 50 (1958) 838-41. Translation by Martin F. Connor (*TPS* V, 135-8).

POPE AND PASTOR. (*Venerabiles Fratres*) Nov. 4, 1958. Pope John broke with precedent and delivered this homily at the Solemn Pontifical Mass that preceded his coronation as Sovereign Pontiff. Latin text in *Osservatore Romano*, Nov. 5, 1958, and in *AAS* 50 (1958) 884-8. Translation by Martin F. Connor (*TPS* V, 139-42).

ANNOUNCEMENT OF ECUMENICAL COUNCIL. (*Questa festiva*) Jan. 25, 1959. This excerpt is from an address delivered by Pope John to 17 Roman Cardinals in the cloister of the Benedictine Monastery adjoining the basilica of St. Paul-Outside-the-Walls after they had attended a solemn Mass in the Basilica Ostiensis. (The title of this message in *The Pope Speaks Magazine* was "Announcement of Ecumenical Council and Roman Synod.") Italian text in *AAS* 51 (1959) 65-9. Translation by Louciana G. M. Rose (*TPS* V, 398-401).

TRUTH, UNITY, AND PEACE. (*Ad Petri Cathedram*) June 29, 1959. The first encyclical letter of Pope John XXIII, it was addressed to all bishops, priests, and faithful of the Catholic Church, and was subtitled: "On the advance of truth, unity, and peace in a spirit of charity." (In *The Pope Speaks Magazine* the title of this message was "The Encyclical Letter, Ad Petri Cathedram.") Latin text in *Osservatore Romano*, July 3, 1959, and in *AAS* 51 (1959) 497-531. Translation by Martin F. Connor (*TPS* V, 359-83).

DEVOTION TO THE ROSARY. (*Grata recordatio*) Sept. 26, 1959. His third encyclical, this was addressed to all bishops and was subtitled, "On piously reciting the rosary, especially during the month of October." (The title of this message in *The Pope Speaks Magazine* was "The Encyclical Letter, Grata Recordatio." A slight change has been made in the translation since it appeared in *TPS*.) Latin text in *Osservatore Romano*, Sept. 30, 1959, and in *AAS* 51 (1959) 673-8. Translation by Martin F. Connor (*TPS* VI, 68-72).

Part II

ST. JOHN VIANNEY, MODEL FOR PRIESTS. (*Sacerdotii Nostri Primordia*) Aug. 1, 1959. This, his second encyclical, was addressed to all bishops "On the first centennial of the most holy death of St. John Mary Baptist Vianney."

Appendix 503

(The title of this message in *The Pope Speaks Magazine* was "The Encyclical Letter, Sacerdotii Nostri Primordia.") Latin text in *Osservatore Romano*, Aug. 1, 1959, and in *AAS* 51 (1959) 545-79. Translation by Rev. Austin Vaughan (*TPS* VI, 7-33).

COUNSELS FOR SEMINARIANS. (*Un vivo desiderio*) Jan. 28, 1960. This address was given to seminarians from the various ecclesiastical colleges, seminaries, and houses of study in Rome. The Pope addressed the seminarians in Italian but gave a number of Scriptural quotes in Latin. For the convenience of the reader we have printed the English translation of these Scriptural quotes directly in the body of the message, rather than in the footnotes which is our usual policy. The actual Latin quotations, however, are shown in the footnotes. Text in *Osservatore Romano*, Jan. 30, 1960, and in *AAS* 52 (1960) 271-7. Translation by Louciana G. M. Rose (*TPS* VI, 363-9).

THE ROMAN SYNOD AND THE PRIEST. (*Da quando*) Nov. 24, 1960. In this address Pope John speaks as Bishop of Rome to the priests and seminarians of his diocese. The Roman Synod had been held in January 1960 and the diocesan code of 755 regulations resulting from it had been promulgated on June 29, 1960. On both occasions Pope John had addressed the clergy of Rome. (The title of this message in *The Pope Speaks Magazine* was "The Synod and the Priest.") Italian text in *Osservatore Romano*, Nov. 25, 1960, and in *AAS* 52 (1960) 967-79. Translation by Rev. Austin Vaughan (*TPS* VII, 10-22).

THE ART OF SPIRITUAL DIRECTION. (*Questo incontro precede*) Sept. 9, 1962. This address was given to spiritual directors of seminaries participating in a course sponsored by the Sacred Congregation of Seminaries and Universities. The theme of the course was "The spiritual formation of candidates for the priesthood." Italian text in *Osservatore Romano*, Sept. 10-11, 1962, and in *AAS* 54 (1962) 673-8. Translation by Rev. Austin Vaughan (*TPS* VII, 259-64).

Part III

ONE FOLD, ONE SHEPHERD. (*Vi siamo grati*) Dec. 23, 1958. This excerpt is from the first Christmas message of Pope John. It was in reply to an address by Eugene Cardinal Tisserant, Dean of the College of Cardinals, conveying the Christmas greetings of the cardinals to the Holy Father. (The title of this message in *The Pope Speaks Magazine* was "The Legacy of Pius XII.") Italian text in *Osservatore Romano*, Dec. 24, 1958, and in *AAS* 50 (1959) 5-12. Translation by *TPS* staff based on one issued by N.C.W.C. News Service (*TPS* V, 131-2).

ST. LEO THE GREAT AND CHURCH UNITY. (*Aeterna Dei Sapientia*) Nov. 11, 1961. This encyclical, his sixth, addressed to all the bishops of the world, was issued in commemoration of the 15th centenary of the death of St. Leo the Great, Pope and Doctor of the Church. The translation is by Rev. H. E. Winstone and is printed with permission of the Catholic Truth Society, London. This, the American edition of Fr. Winstone's translation (*TPS* VIII, 7-22), may differ in some respects from the edition published in England. Latin text in *Osservatore Romano*, Dec. 9-10, 1961, and in *AAS* 53 (1961) 785-803.

ONE, HOLY, CATHOLIC, APOSTOLIC. (*La belleza*) Nov. 13, 1960. This talk was given at the close of a Byzantine Rite Mass celebrated in Old Slavonic in St. Peter's basilica. Pope John had presided over the rites and throughout the ceremony had intoned the principal blessings in Old Slavonic. Italian text in *Osservatore Romano*, Nov. 14-15, 1960, and in *AAS* 52 (1960) 958-64. Translation by Rev. Austin Vaughan (*TPS* VII, 64-9).

THE MISSIONS. (*Princeps Pastorum*) Nov. 28, 1959. His fourth encyclical, this was addressed to all bishops "in the 40th year since Benedict XV issued the apostolic letter 'Maximum illud.'" (In *The Pope Speaks Magazine* the title of this message was "The Encyclical Letter, Princeps Pastorum.") Latin text in *Osservatore Romano*, Nov. 29, 1959, and in *AAS* 51 (1959) 833-64. Translation by Louciana G. M. Rose (*TPS* VI, 123-45).

Part IV

TRUE CHRISTIAN PEACE. (*Eccoci a Natale*) Dec. 23, 1959. This broadcast was made a few moments after the traditional exchange of Christmas greetings between the Holy Father and the College of Cardinals. (The title of this message in *The Pope Speaks Magazine* was "Peace on Earth.") Italian text in *Osservatore Romano*, Dec. 24, 1959, and in *AAS* 52 (1960) 27-35. Translation by *TPS* staff, based on one issued by N.C.W.C. News Service (*TPS* VI, 200-07).

THE WAY TO PEACE. (*L'Apostolo Pietro*) Sept. 10, 1961. This radio address was delivered from his summer residence at Castelgandolfo. Broadcast over Vatican Radio and Italian radio and television networks, it was immediately translated and beamed in various languages into Eastern Europe by Radio Free Europe. (The title of this message as it appeared in *The Pope Speaks Magazine* was "A Call to Peace.") Italian text in *Osservatore Romano*, Sept. 11-12, 1961, and in *AAS* 53 (1961) 577-82. Translation by *TPS* staff, based on one issued by N.C.W.C. News Service (*TPS* VII, 251-6).

THE FIFTH COMMANDMENT. (*Votre joyeuse présence*) June 3, 1962. This address was given at an audience in the Vatican Basilica during a time of strife in Africa. (The title of this message as it appeared in *The Pope Speaks Magazine* was "Thou Shalt Not Kill.") French text in *Osservatore Romano*,

June 4-5, 1962, and in *AAS* 54 (1962) 447-8. Translation by *TPS* staff based on one issued by N.C.W.C. News Service (*TPS* VIII, 143-5).

A CALL FOR NEGOTIATIONS. (*Seigneur, écoute*) Oct. 25, 1962. This was a radio address to the world at a time of several international crises, particularly the missile crisis in Cuba and the invasion of northern India by Chinese Communist troops. French text in *Osservatore Romano*, Oct. 26, 1962, and in *AAS* 54 (1962) 861-2. Translation by *TPS* staff, based on one issued by N.C.W.C. News Service (*TPS* VIII, 227-8).

The Picture Essay

The 23-page "picture essay," an attempt to capture the "spirit" of Pope John in pictures and his own words, is the work of Mrs. Elizabeth McPherson and Miss Jacqueline Meyer of the *TPS* editorial board, and originally appeared in *TPS* IX, 49-71. The pictures are by Felici, Giordani and RNS.

Part V

A PREVIEW OF MATER ET MAGISTRA. (*La vostra presenza*) May 14, 1961. This address was given to an audience of 90,000 workers from 46 countries gathered in St. Peter's Square. (In *The Pope Speaks Magazine*, this message was entitled "Christianity and Social Problems: Preview of a New Encyclical.") Italian text in *Osservatore Romano*, May 15-16, 1961. Translation by Rev. Austin Vaughan (*TPS* VII, 103-12).

MATER ET MAGISTRA. (*Mater et Magistra*) May 15, 1961. This, the fifth encyclical letter of Pope John, was addressed to the clergy and faithful of the entire Catholic world. It was subtitled, "A re-evaluation of the social question in the light of Christian teaching." The translation was prepared by Rev. H. E. Winstone and reviewed by a team of American scholars, and is printed here with permission of the Catholic Truth Society, London, England. The American edition of this translation (*TPS* VII, 295-343) differs in certain respects from the edition published in England. Latin text in *Osservatore Romano*, July 15, 1961, in *AAS* 53 (1961) 501-64, and in *TPS* VII, 370-403.

PACEM IN TERRIS. (*Pacem in terris*) April 11, 1963. This encyclical, his eighth and last, was addressed not only to the clergy and faithful of the Catholic world but to all men of good will. It was subtitled, "On establishing universal peace in truth, justice, charity, and freedom." The translation was prepared by Rev. H. E. Winstone and reviewed by a team of American scholars, and is printed here with permission of the Catholic Truth Society of London, England. The American edition (*TPS* IX, 13-48) may differ in some respects from the edition published in England. Latin text in *Osservatore Romano*, April 11, 1963, and in *AAS* 54 (1963) 257-304.

THE SPIRIT OF "PACEM IN TERRIS." These are excerpts from the following five addresses, given in the weeks following the appearance of the encyclical:

———. On the Encyclical "Pacem in Terris." (*La lettera enciclica*) April 9, 1963. This address was delivered immediately after he had signed the encyclical "Pacem in Terris." Italian text in *Osservatore Romano*, April 10, 1963. Translation by *TPS* staff, based on one issued by N.C.W.C. News Service (*TPS* IX, 72-76).

———. The Lessons of Holy Thursday. (*La cérémonie du*) April 11, 1963. This address was given to the Vatican diplomatic corps at Holy Thursday Mass. French text in *Osservatore Romano*, April 13, 1963, and in *AAS* 55 (1963) 392-5. Translation by *TPS* staff, based on one issued by N.C.W.C. News Service (*TPS* IX, 73-4).

———. Easter Message to the World. (*Pax vobis: pace*) April 13, 1963. A radio address to the entire world. Italian text in *Osservatore Romano*, April 16-17, 1963, and *AAS* 55 (1963) 399-404. Translation by *TPS* staff, based on one issued by N.C.W.C. News Service (*TPS* IX, 74-5).

———. The Triumph of Peace. (*Una grande letizia*) April 24, 1963. This was an address to a general audience. Italian and French text in *Osservatore Romano*, April 25, 1963. Translation by *TPS* staff, based on one issued by N.C.W.C. News Service (*TPS* IX, 75).

———. Lessons of the "Magnificat." (*Il y a quelques*) May 10, 1963. This address was given in St. Peter's basilica after presentation of the Balzan Peace Prize to Pope John. French text in *Osservatore Romano*, May 11, 1963, and in *AAS* 55 (1963) 450-5. Translation by *TPS* staff, based on one issued by N.C.W.C. News Service (*TPS* IX, 76).

Part VI

PROCLAMATION OF THE SECOND VATICAN COUNCIL. (*Humanae salutis*) Dec. 25, 1961. This was an apostolic constitution formally directing that the Second Vatican Council be convoked in the year 1962. Some weeks later (Feb. 2, 1962) Pope John issued the apostolic letter *"Consilium diu Nostra,"* in which he named Oct. 11, 1962, as the precise day on which the Council was to open. (The title of this message in *The Pope Speaks Magazine* was "The Apostolic Constitution, Humanae Salutis.") Latin text in *Osservatore Romano*, Dec. 26-27, 1961, and in *AAS* 54 (1962) 5-13. Translation by Rev. Austin Vaughan (*TPS* VII, 353-61).

PENANCE FOR SUCCESS OF THE COUNCIL. (*Paenitentiam agere*) July 1, 1962. This, his seventh encyclical, was addressed to all the bishops of the Catholic Church and was subtitled "On doing penance for the success of the Second Vatican Council." (Its title in *The Pope Speaks Magazine* was "The Encyclical Letter, Paenitentiam Agere." The encyclical was made public on

Appendix 507

July 5, 1962, but was dated July 1, Feast of the Most Precious Blood. Latin text in *Osservatore Romano*, July 6, 1962, and in *AAS* 54 (1962) 481-91. Translation by Rev. H. E. Winstone (*TPS* VIII, 111-19).

THE CONTRIBUTION OF NUNS TO SUCCESS OF THE COUNCIL. (*Il tempio massimo*) July 2, 1962. This letter was addressed to cloistered nuns, congregations of sisters, and women in secular institutes. Pope John had already made appeals to the clergy and laity to prepare themselves spiritually for the coming Council. Italian text in *Osservatore Romano*, July 8, 1962, and in *AAS* 54 (1962) 508-17. Translation by Rev. Austin Vaughan (*TPS* VIII, 153-62).

OPENING ADDRESS TO THE COUNCIL. (*Gaudet Mater Ecclesia*) Oct. 11, 1962. Pope John opened the Second Vatican Council with this address to the 2,540 Council Fathers in St. Peter's basilica. (The title of this message in *The Pope Speaks Magazine* was "The Council—At the Threshold of a New Era." A slight change has been made in the translation since it appeared in *TPS*.) Latin text in *Osservatore Romano*, Oct. 12, 1962, and in *AAS* 54 (1962) 786-96. Translation by Rev. H. E. Winstone (*TPS* VIII, 207-16).

TO THE OBSERVER DELEGATES. (*Notre rencontre de*) Oct. 13, 1962. This address was delivered to non-Catholic observers attending the Council. The meeting was held in the Vatican's Consistory Hall, where the Holy Father sat in an armchair rather than the usual throne and did not use the formal "We" to refer to himself. He shook hands with all of them and was obviously overjoyed at their presence. French text in *Osservatore Romano*, Oct. 15-16, 1962, and in *AAS* 54 (1962) 814-16. Translation by TPS staff, based on one issued by N.C.W.C. News Service (*TPS* VIII, 225-7).

TOWARD A NEW PENTECOST. (*Prima sessio*) Dec. 8, 1962. Pope John delivered this address at ceremonies closing the first session of the Second Vatican Council. He had been ailing almost two weeks and appeared in the Council hall only to give this talk. Latin text in *Osservatore Romano*, Dec. 10-11, 1962, and in *AAS* 55 (1963) 35-41. Translation by Rev. H. E. Winstone (*TPS* VIII, 398-403).

THOUGHTS FOR THE COUNCIL'S RECESS. (*Mirabilis ille*) Jan. 6, 1963. This letter was personally addressed by Pope John to each of the Fathers of the Second Vatican Council. Latin text in *Osservatore Romano*, Feb. 8, 1963, and in *AAS* 55 (1963) 149-59. Translation by Rev. H. E. Winstone (*TPS* VIII, 342-51).

Part VII

A LETTER TO HIS FAMILY. (*Oggi è la festa*) Dec. 3, 1961. Although addressed to his brother Zaverio Roncalli, this letter was intended for the entire Roncalli family. It was not made public until after Pope John's death. The letter has a very personal tone throughout. He addresses his brother by the nickname "Severo," and discards the usual papal "We" for the more intimate "I." Italian text in *Osservatore Romano*, June 8, 1963. Translation by Rev. Austin Vaughan (*TPS* IX, 194-97).

LAST WILL AND TESTAMENT. (*Sul punto*) June 29, 1954—Sept. 12, 1961. The first draft of this document was dated 1925 and was subsequently brought up to date in turn at Istanbul, Paris, and Venice, as Bishop Roncalli was transferred to new posts. The text that appears here was drawn up in Venice in 1954. Additional confirmatory notes were appended in 1957 and 1959. Then, in 1961, a "renewal" of his testament was added by the Holy Father. Italian text in *Osservatore Romano*, June 7, 1963. Translation by Rev. Austin Vaughan (*TPS* IX, 198-201).

RETREAT NOTES. Aug. 1961 and Nov.-Dec. 1961. This material was published in *Osservatore Romano*, June 5, 13, and 16, 1963. It was identified as notes made by Pope John during two retreats in the above mentioned months. These *Retreat Notes* were written in Italian, but there were a number of Latin quotations and other words and phrases in Latin interspersed throughout. Many of the words (both Italian and Latin) were underlined in the manuscript. In our text we have italicized all the words which the Pope himself underlined (as indicated in the *Osservatore* text). But we have also italicized even those *Latin* words which were not underlined in the original text. (This is in keeping with standard editorial policy to italicize foreign language words when they appear in a text.) To permit the reader, however, to know which of these Latin words were underlined in the original text, we have indicated the underlining by italics in the *footnote* translations of these words. For format purposes we have also moved into the footnotes certain bibliographic references which were in the body of the text as printed in the *Osservatore* (e.g., footnotes 3, 4 and 37). Italian text translated by Rev. Austin Vaughan.

DIARY PAGES AND FINAL REFLECTIONS. Fall 1962-Spring 1963. These "diary" pages and random notes were published after Pope John's death. The Italian texts appeared in *Osservatore Romano* for June 5 and June 6, 1963, and for July 4, 1963. No information was provided about the precise source of the various texts and in some cases the material bore no date. As in the *Retreat Notes* there were many words (both Latin and Italian) underlined in the original text. We have followed the same footnote-italic technique which we employed in the *Retreat Notes* (see previous note) to permit the reader to know which Latin words were underlined in the original text. (Actually, in this case, unlike *Retreat Notes*, all the Latin words were underlined.) Translation by Rev. Austin Vaughan.

B. The Commentators and Editors

Rev. John F. Cronin, S.S., noted sociologist, is Assistant Director of the Social Action Department at The National Catholic Welfare Conference. He has written extensively in the field of contemporary political problems.

Rev. Francis X. Murphy, C.SS.R., is Professor of Patristic Moral Theology at Academia Alphonsina, Rome, and Staff Editor for Early Christian and Oriental History on the New Catholic Encyclopedia. A well-known Church historian, among his writings is a biography of Pope John XXIII.

Rev. Ferrer Smith, O.P., noted moral theologian, is Regent of Studies, Dominican House of Studies, Washington, D.C. His writings have been principally in the field of psychology and moral theology.

The Pope Speaks (whose staff provided the running commentary and otherwise edited and prepared this book for publication) is a quarterly magazine published in Washington, D. C., devoted primarily to publishing the talks and letters of the Holy Father. It has an advisory board composed of well-known churchmen and scholars, as well as an editorial board. The members of the advisory board are: Rev. Eugene Burke, C.S.P.; Rev. Eamon R. Carroll, O.Carm.; Very Rev. Francis J. Connell, C.SS.R.; Rev. John C. Ford, S.J.; Rev. Thomas Harte, C.SS.R.; Rev. William Hill, S.S.; Rt. Rev. Harry C. Koenig; Most Rev. Francis A. Marrocco; Very Rev. John P. McCormick, S.S.; Rev. Francis J. Powers, C.S.V.; Most Rev. Ambrose Senyshyn; Rt. Rev. Maurice S. Sheehy; Rev. Gerard S. Sloyan; Rev. Ferrer Smith, O.P.; Rev. James VanderVeldt, O.F.M.; Rev. Austin Vaughan; Mr. Eugene P. Willging.

The members of the editorial board (nearly all of whom played some part in the production of this book, with James Kearney as project manager) are: John O'Neil, editor and publisher; Frederick Dyer, Martin F. Connor, James Kearney, contributing editors; Elizabeth McPherson, managing editor; Sister M. Claudia, I.H.M., Rosalie L. Katkish, Rosabelle Kelp, Clara-Louise Kuehn, Henry Lefebure, Jacqueline Meyer, associate editors; Gloria Nowak, Joan Rowles, Alexandra Wolman, circulation.

INDEX

Ad Catholici Sacerdotii (Encyclical)
  Pope Pius XI on the priesthood, 70
Ad Petri Cathedram (Encyclical)
  Council, Comment on the, 4-5
  Pontifical program outlined, 8
  "Truth, unity, and peace:" Translation, 24-56
Aeterna Dei Sapientia (Encyclical)
  St. Leo the Great and Church unity, 140-159
Africa
  Prayers for peace in, 220
Agriculture
  Ancillary industries, Promotion of, 286
  Associations and social responsibilities of farmers, 287-288
  Depressed state of, 281-283
  Flight from the farm, 281-282
  Public services and rural areas, 283
  Remedies for depressed state of, 283-286
  Social conditions in rural communities, Amelioration of, 247
Agriculture. *See also* Farmers and farming
Apostolate
  Cloistered nuns and the, 418-419
  Lay, Education for the, 183-184
  Lay; Role in social education, 306, 307
  Pontifical mission, Reflections on the, 477-485
  Public life, Trained laymen in, 365-366, 369, 370-371
  Religious women, Opportunities for, 418-420
  Social action and the spiritual life, 248-249
  Social, Program for a, 237-239
  See also Catholic Action
Armaments
  Causes of the arms race, 355-356
Ars, France

Lourdes and Ars, Shrines of France, 100
Artisans
  Cooperative enterprises and, 271-272
Asceticism
  Priestly, St. John Vianney as model of, 72
Association
  Man's rights of, 332-333
Attila, King of the Huns
  Pope Leo the Great and, 140-141
Augustine, Saint, Bishop of Hippo
  De verbis Domini quoted, 121-123
  Schismatics, Invitation to, 41-42
Authority
  Divine origin of, 338-339
  Moral force, 339-341
Authority, Civil
  The common good and the exercise of, 341, 349, 362
  Responsibility toward individuals, 343-345, 347
  Structure and operation, 345-346
Authority, Public
  Common good, Promotion of the, 258, 259, 263, 264, 288-289
Authority, World
  Institution by consent, not force, 362-363
  Need for, and attributes of a, 323-324, 362-363

Benedict XIV, Pope
  Eulogy of St. Leo the Great, 147
Benedict XV, Pope
  Influence on Pope John's life, 3
  Maximum illud, Apostolic letter on the missions, 169, 171, 174, 180-181
Bible
  Nourishment from, 106-109
Birth control
  Poverty, Amelioration of, and, 248
  Underdeveloped areas and, 297-298

Bishops
  Conciliar responsibilities of, 448, 450, 451-452
  Priests and their, 98
  Thoughts for the Council's recess; Letter to Council Fathers, 446-458
Brotherhood of man
  Society, Prosperity of, and the, 29-30
Bulgaria
  Pope John as Apostolic Visitor to, 3
Byzantine rite
  Mass in, Address at, 160-167

Canon law
  Modernization of, Proposed, 22
Catechists
  Formation of, 188-189
  St. John Vianney as catechist, 92-94
Catholic Action
  Apostolate of, 48-49
  Mission countries, Adaptation to local conditions in, 189-190
  Public life, Christians in, 192-193
  Training for leadership in, 190-192
  See also Apostolate
Catholic Church
  Mother and teacher, 250-251, 314-315, 392
  Social teaching, Validity of her, 305-306
  See also The Church
Catholics
  Non-Catholics and; Cooperation in socio-economic affairs, 368
  Peace effort a duty of, 208-209
Chalcedon, Council of (451)
  St. Leo the Great and the, 145-146
Charity
  Mark of true Christian, 185-187
  Pacem in Terris, Call to love, 375
  Personal, Vast field for exercise of, 280-281
  Social problems and, 35
  Unity of Christians achieved through, 158
Charles Borromeo, Saint
  Pope John's devotion to, 3, 8
  Tridentine Council, Decrees of, and St. Charles' ministry, 18-19
Chastity
  Priest's chastity as help to others, 78
  St. John Vianney as model of, 76-78
  Social and personal virtue, 415-416

Christian life
  Renewal of, Appeal for, 54-56
Christian unity
  Movements toward union, 37, 390-391
  Promotion of; Duty of the Church, 432-433
Christianity
  Meeting point of heaven and earth, 250
Christians
  Attitude of, Counsels of St. Paul concerning, 214-215
  Citizens of two worlds, 55
  Non-Christians and; Cooperative efforts for world peace, 324-326
Christmas 1958
  Message (excerpt): One fold, One shepherd, 139
Christmas 1959
  Broadcast: True Christian peace, 201-211
Church, The
  Apostolicity of, 166
  Catholicity of, 165-166
  Developing nations, Church's contribution to, 295-296
  Holiness of, 163-164
  Mission countries, Needs of the Church in; Encyclical *Princeps Pastorum,* 168-197
  Mission: Sanctifying and teaching, 482
  Native cultures and, 177-179
  Universality of, 161-162, 180
  See also Catholic Church
Church history
  Holy men in, 164
Church unity. See Unity of the Church
Church. Teaching office
  Truth, Transmission of, to today's world, 430-431
Civilization, Modern
  Social problems today, 21-22, 243-246, 261-262, 387
Clergy
  Native, formation of, 171-176
Colonialism
  Developing nations and, 294
Common good
  Demands of, on national and world levels, 270-271

Communications media
    Truth and error, Presentation of, 27-28
Confession, Frequent
    Pius XII's recommendation, 96
Controversy, Religious
    Unity of the Church, Discussion as aid to, 39
Cooperative associations
    Artisans and, 271
Council Fathers
    Recess, Thoughts for the Council's; Letter to, 447-458
Councils, Ecumenical
    Pastoral function, 425
Craftsmen. *See* Artisans
Credit banks
    Farmers and, 284
Cuban Crisis
    Peace preserved through negotiations; Radio appeal to world leaders, 227-228
Cultural values
    Man's rights relative to, 330

Death
    Preparation for, 463
Detachment
    Secret of fruitfulness in apostolic activity, 104
Developing nations
    The Church's contribution to, 295-296
    Needs of, 247-248
    Responsibilities of economically developed nations toward, 234-235, 290-291, 292-293, 294-295, 358-359
Devotions
    Meditations on the Name, the Heart, and the Blood of Jesus, 412-413, 476
Dialogue, The
    Pope John and, 384
Diplomatic Corps
    Holy Thursday (1963) discourse to, on *Pacem in terris,* 375
Disarmament
    Obligations regarding, 356
Discrimination, Racial
    Equal dignity of men, of states, 350

Easter 1963
    Pacem in Terris as Easter gift, 376
Economic order
    Balanced development of the economy, 283-284, 288-289, 293
    Personal initiative and state intervention in the, 263-265
    Social progress and economic development, 269-271, 293
    True purpose of the economy, 269
Education
    Integration of religious with secular training, 366-367
    Man's right to, 330
Emigrants and refugees
    Duties of states toward, 354-355
    Ministry to, 52-53
Emigration and immigration
    Man's right to, 333
Encyclicals. *See* Social encyclicals
Ephesine Council (449)
    Condemned by St. Leo the Great, 144
Epiphany
    Octave celebration instituted by St. Vincent Pallotti, 135, 491
Error, Ideological
    Condemnation of, 51, 53
    The errant and; Judgments concerning, 368
Eucharist
    St. John Vianney's devotion to the, 83
Evangelical counsels
    Penance: Surest road to perfection, 73
Exiles
    Ministry to, 52-53

Faith
    Christian; Integration with action, 366
Family
    Foundation of, Respect for, 298-299
    Private property and the, 261
    Unity within the, 35-36
Farmers and farming
    Family farm as ideal farm unit, 286-287
    Nobility of farm work, 287, 288
    Problems, 233-234, 281-282
    Self-advancement of the farming community, 287-288
    See also Agriculture

Fatherhood
  Pope as universal father, 66-67
Ferrari, Andrea Cardinal, Abp. of Milan
  Beatification cause introduced, 492
France
  Pope John as Apostolic Delegate to, 3
Freedom
  Public authority and the individual, 343-345

Germany
  Social classes, Improved postwar relations among, 33
God
  Creator of the universe, 327-328
  Source of society's vitality, 336, 338
Good example
  Religious women, Lives of, 413-418
Good Shepherd
  Pope John's intention to be a, 16-17
  St. John Vianney, model of pastoral devotion, 88-89
Grata Recordatio (Encyclical)
  Rosary, The, 57-62
Greece
  Pope John as Apostolic Delegate to, 3

Haerent Animo (Apostolic Exhortation)
  St. Pius X on the priesthood, 70
Hedonism
  Disastrous attitude toward life, 307
Hierarchy
  Local, Development of, 171
Holiness, Personal. *See* Sanctity, Personal
Humanae Salutis (Apostolic Constitution)
  Proclamation of the 2nd Vatican Council, 386-396

Ignatius of Antioch, Saint
  Bishops, Submission of clergy to their, 45
Immigration and emigration
  Man's right to, 333
Industry
  Structure of, and the requirements of human dignity, 271-272

Interior life
  Pre-eminence of the, 411-412
International aid
  Obligations of wealthy nations, 290-293
International cooperation
  Disproportions in land, population, resources, and, 289-291
  Necessity for, and bases of, 300-303
International Labor Organization
  Work of the, 275-276
International relations
  Collaboration in pooling material and spiritual resources, 352-353, 353-354
  Freedom of individual states and, 358, 359
  Men, states, and the world community, 360-365
  Natural law the basis of right relations, 349
  Negotiations between nations, Need for, 357
  Propaganda, The question of, 350
Irenaeus, Saint
  Church unity, Appeal for, 156

Jerusalem, Council of
  Episcopal authority, 450-451
Jesus Christ
  Pontiffs to reflect the countenance of, 17-18
  Prince of Peace, 371-372
John XXIII, Pope
  Appearance, 5
  Balzan peace prize conferred, 494-495
  Bergamo, Service in, 2-3
  Biography, 1-6
  Confession, Practice of, 473-475
  Coronation address: "Pope and pastor," 15-19
  The Council and, 381-385
  Death, Readiness for, 471-472, 475
  Devotions, Favorite, 476
  Diary, Excerpts from his, 490-498
  Early life and education, 1-2
  Early writings, 2, 3
  Episcopal consecration on Feast of St. Charles Borromeo, 18
  Final reflections, 495-498

First 8 months as Pope, 24-25
First public address: "This anxious hour," 11-13
Goal of his pontificate, 5
Illness, Acceptance of, 488, 493-494, 495, 496
Inspirations received with simplicity and trust, 495-496
Joseph, St.; Devotion to, 487-488
Last will and testament, 465-469
Military service, 3
The name "John"; Reasons for choice, 6, 9-10
Non-Catholics, Experiences with, 437-438
Obedience as force in life of, 6
Personal influence, 65, 460
Piety, Exercises of; Reflections on, 485-487
Pontificate, Impact of his, 6, 460
Priestly life, Review of his, 470-471
Retreat notes, Selections from, 470-489
Roncalli family, Last letter to the, 461-464
Rosary, Devotion to, 8, 57-58, 485-487
Sanctification, Desire for, 472-473
Seminarian in Rome, 103
Task, The Pope's, 211
Tranquillity, Reflections on, 462

John Chrysostom, Saint
"Witnessing to the truth;" Quoted on, 185

John Vianney, Saint
Beatification and canonization of, 68-69
Model for priests; Encyclical *Sacerdotii Nostri Primordia*, 68-101
Pastoral life, 88-96

Joseph, Saint
John XXIII's devotion to, 487-488

Kingdom of God
Triumph of, Pray the Rosary for the, 61-62

Laity
Apostolate of a trained, 365-366, 369, 370-371
Missions, Aid to, 193-194

Native: Role in mission countries, 182-187, 192-193
Prayerful assistance to priests, The need for, 98-99
Social education, Role of the lay apostolate in, 306, 307
Social responsibility, 309

Leo I, the Great, Saint, Pope
Attila the Hun confronted by, 140-141
Church unity and; Encyclical *Aeterna Dei Sapientia*, 140-159
Council of Chalcedon (451) and, 145-146
Doctor of the Church, 146-148
Ephesine Council condemned by, 144
Incarnation, Letter to Flavian concerning, 143-144
Leonine Sacramentary, 143
Life, 141-142
Papacy, Authority and influence of; Teachings on, 150-154
Pontificate, Notable achievements of his, 142-146
Theodoret, Bsp. of Cyrus; Tribute to St. Leo the Great cited, 154

Leo XIII, Pope
Rerum novarum on social justice, 227-228, 237, 251-256
Rosary, Encyclicals on the, 57

Life
Eternal life as goal, 30
Laws of, Respect for, 298-300

Liturgy, Eastern
Expression of universality of the Church, 161-162

Living, Standard of
Man's right to a worthy, 329-330

Lourdes, France
Ars and Lourdes, Shrines of France, 100

Man
Associative rights, 332-333
Cultural values, Rights regarding, 330
Duties and responsibilities, 334-338
Education, Right to, 330
Emigration and immigration, Right to, 333
Equality of men, 338, 350
Life, Right to, 329-330

Moral values, Rights regarding, 330
Political rights, 333-334
Property rights, 332
Public life, Citizens in, 347
Religious liberty, Right to, 330-331
Standard of living, Right to a worthy, 329-330
Values, True hierarchy of, 309-310
Vocation, Right to choose, 331
Wages, Right to just, 332
Work rights, 331-332
Man, Brotherhood of. *See* Brotherhood of Man
Mass
 Priesthood and the, 85-88
Mater et Magistra (Encyclical)
 Christianity and social progress, 250-315
 Commentary on, 240-249
 Modernity of, 241, 249
 Preview, 232-236
 Response to, 226
 Social teaching of, 243-246
 The spirit of, 240-243
Materialism
 Degradation of man, 309-310
Menti Nostrae (Apostolic Exhortation)
 Pope Pius XII on the priesthood, 70
Migration
 Right of families to migrate, 261
Minority groups
 Rights and duties of, within the political community, 351-352
Missiology
 Importance of the study, 177
Missionaries
 Ambassadors of Christ, 46-47
 Foreign, Peace of, 173-174
Missionary countries
 Local hierarchies, Establishment of, 171
Missions
 Benedict XV on the, 169, 171, 174, 180-181
 Pius XII on the, 169
 Princeps Pastorum (Encyclical), Translation of, 168-197
Modern world. *See* Civilization, Modern
Moral order
 Interdependence of nations and the, 300-303
 Respect for the, 235-236
Moral values
 Man's rights in relation to, 330
Mystical Body of Christ
 Man's work a continuation of Christ's work, 313-314

Nationalism
 Native clergy and, 180-181
Nations. *See* State, The
Natural law
 Man's conscience reflects the, 328
 Man's rights and duties derive from, 334
 See also Order
Negotiations
 Peace preserved through; Radio message to world leaders during Cuban Crisis, 227-228
Non-Catholics. *See* Separated Christians
Non-Christians
 Christians and; Cooperative efforts for world peace, 324-326
Nuns
 Cloistered nuns, Apostolate of, 418-419
 Contribution of, to the success of the Council, 409-422
 Professional preparation for active life, 419

Obedience
 Holiness, Obedience as foundation and support of, 79-80
 St. John Vianney as model of, 79-80
 Sanctity and victory over self, 416-418
Order
 Human dignity as basis of, among men, 329-334
 Peace and, 327
 Universe reflects divine order, 327-328
 See also Natural law
Ownership
 Public, 279-280
 Shared ownership in firms, 269-270

Pacem in Terris (Encyclical)
 Commentary on, 316-326
 Purpose, 375

Reaction to, 316, 377
Spirit of; Reflections on the encyclical, 374-378
Summation of papal teaching on peace, 376
Translation, 327-373
Paenitentiam Agere (Encyclical)
Penitential preparation for the Council, 397-408
Papacy
Father, Pope as universal, 66-67
Image of, in the modern world, 6
Pastoral ministry
Pope John's, 16-17, 20
Venice, Pope John's patriarchate in, 3-4
Pastoral office
St. John Vianney's esteem for the, 89-91
Paul, Saint, Apostle
Christian attitudes; Counsels concerning, 214-215
Peace
Christian: Interior, social, and international appearance of, 202-204
Christmas 1959 broadcast, 201-211
Church's work for, 206-208
Errors of man in his search for, 205-206
External, based on interior peace, 14, 376
International, Truth the basis of, 204
Jesus Christ, Prince of Peace, 371-372
Mutual trust, not arms superiority, as basis of, 356-357
Negotiations, Peace preserved through, 227-228, 359-360
Pacem in Terris (Encyclical), 327-373
Papal pleas for, Recent, 212-213
Prayer for, 217-218
World rulers, Radio address to, on peace, 212-218
Peace of Christ
Unity of the Church and the, 42-44
Penance
Baptismal innocence and, 400-401
Calls to, in the Bible, 398-399
Council, Preparation for the; Encyclical *Paenitentiam agere*, 397-408

Perfection, Evangelical counsels as surest road to, 73
Sacrament of; St. John Vianney's administration of the, 94-95
Salvation, The work of, and penance, 405
Types, 403-405
Perfection
Evangelical counsel as surest road to, 73
Maxims (Six) of, 483-484
Persecuted Catholics
Mission communities, Perseverance of, 196-197
Prayers urged for, 53-54
Personality
Definition, 329
Social conditions and full development of, 342-343
Peter, Saint, Apostle
Letters recommended for study, 123-125
Philosophy
False philosophies irreconcilable with Christian teachings, 61
Pietà, The
Doctrine of suffering and, 472-473, 476
Piety
Excesses in pious practices, 114
Pius IX, Pope
At eighty (vignette), 128
Pius X, Saint, Pope
Haerent Animo, Apostolic exhortation on the priesthood, 70
Influence on Pope John's life, 2
On prayer, The priestly practice of, 83
On priestly sanctity, 98
St. John Vianney, Beatification of, 68, 69
Pius XI, Pope
Ad Catholici Sacerdotii, Encyclical on the priesthood, 70
Influence on Pope John's life, 3
Quadragesimo anno on social justice, 229-230, 237, 256-259
St. John Vianney designated patron of pastors, 69
Pius XII, Pope
Influence on Pope John's life, 2

Missions, Interest in the, 169
  On frequent confession, 96
  On obedience, 80
  On St. John Vianney, model for preachers, 93
  On the ideal Christian parish, 81
  Rosary, Encyclical *Ingruentium Malorum* on, 59
  Sempiternus Rex (Encyclical); 15th Centenary commemoration of Council of Chalcedon, 145
  Social justice, Teachings on, 230, 259-261
Politics
  Man's political rights, 333-334
Pontificate
  Pope's twofold role, 21
  Purpose of the office, 16
  Succession of popes unbroken, 58
Population increase
  Economic development and, 296-300
  Problem, 296-298
  See also Birth control
Poverty
  Economically developed and developing communities, Relationships between, 234, 290-291
  St. John Vianney and the use of possessions, 74-76
Poverty (Evangelical)
  Benefits of, and temptations against, 413-415
Prayer
  Eucharistic prayer, Benefits from, 84-85
  For peace, 217-218
  The habit of, 109
  Life of; Its meaning, 411-413
  Necessity of prayer life, 82-83
  St. John Vianney's devotion to, 81-88
  Weapon against spiritual enemies, 216-217
Preachers
  St. John Vianney as model for, 92-94
Present, The
  Providence, Trust in Divine, 480-481
Press
  Truth, Presentation of, and duties of the press, 27
Price protection
  Farmers and, 285-286

Priesthood
  Bishops and their priests, 98
  Chastity of priests as help to others, 78
  Christliness, formation of, in priests, 65-66
  Christ's friendship, 71
  Earlier popes on the, 70-71
  Evangelical counsels as surest road to perfection, 72-80
  Holiness, Priestly; Pope Pius XII on, 70-71
  The Mass and the, 85-88
  Personal sanctity the first duty of priests, 97, 98
  Reading, Priests', 121
  Roman Synod (1960) and priests, 112-128
  St. John Vianney, Model for priests; Encyclical *Sacerdotii Nostri Primordia*, 68-101
  Spiritual directors, A tribute to, 133-134
  Worldliness, Dangers of, for priests, 119-120
  See also Priestly life
Priestly life
  Activism, Tempering the excesses of, 122-123
  Altar the focus, 117
  Detachment, 119-123
  Immaculate life as mark of priest's mission, 116-117
  Kindly attitude as mark of the priest, 117
  Scriptures, Guidance from, 114-116
  Sources of danger, 120-121
  Serenity, 118-119
  Yoke of the Lord and peace of soul, 122
Priestly life. *See also* Priesthood
Priests. *See* Priesthood
Private enterprise
  Contribution to balanced internal economy, 289
Propagation of the Faith, Society for the
  Pope John's work with the, 3, 169
Property
  Private, Right of, 276-279, 332

Private, Social aspect of, 255, 257, 280-281
Use of material goods, 260
Providence, Divine
Pope John's sense of, 66-67
Trust in, 478, 481
Prudence
Definition and exercise of, 477-478, 482-483
Psalter
Study of, Recommended to seminarians, 108-109
Psalm 118: Precepts for priests, 115
Public life
Participation in, duty of Christians, 365

Quadragesimo Anno (Encyclical)
Christian social principles clarified in, 229-230, 237, 256-259
Social conditions at the time of the encyclical, 258

Races (of man)
Contacts between, encouraged, 353
Radini-Tedeschi, Giacomo, Bishop
Influence on Pope John's life, 2, 68-69
Refugees. *See* Emigrants and Refugees
Religious liberty
Man's right, 330-331
Religious life
Women in; Contributions to success of the Council, 409-422
Religious men
Vocation of, 45-46
Religious training
Secular and, Integration of, 366-367
Religious women
Vocation of, 47-48
Renewal
St. Charles Borromeo and post-Tridentine reforms, 18-19
Rerum Novarum (Encyclical)
Impact of, 251-252, 253-254
Social conditions at the time of the encyclical, 252-253
Synthesis of principles of social justice, 227-228, 237, 251, 254
Roman Synod (1960)
Announcement of, 22
Clergy of Rome and the; Address to, 112-128
Code for priestly life, 119
Pilot venture, 4
Promulgation of the, 112-113
Study encouraged, 114
Rome (city)
Spiritual greatness of, 153-154
Roncalli, Zaverio
Grand-uncle of Pope John; Memories of, 476
Pope John's letter to his brother Zaverio and family, 461-464
Rosary, The
Devotion to, 57-62, 485-487
Rulers (of nations)
Responsible for safeguarding peace, 13-14, 60-61, 213

Sacerdotii Nostri Primordia (Encyclical)
Translation, 68-101
Sacred Heart of Jesus
Love of the, and priestly chastity, 78
Sanctity, Personal
Basis: Prayer, example, and apostolic action, 410
The Mass and priestly sanctity, 86-88
Nature of, 472-473
Science and technology
God praised through scientific progress, 429
Secular institutes
Apostolate of women in, 420
Self-denial
Sanctification and, 406
Seminarians
The chosen few, 103-104
Contemporary difficulties in the training of, 131
Counsels for; Address to seminarians in Rome, 102-111
Papal affection for, 109
Sanctity, Growth in personal, 131-132
Spiritual direction of, 129-135
Training; Example of older priests, 133, 135
Vincent Pallotti, Saint, as example for, 134-135
Seminaries
Native teachers in, 175

Spiritual directors; Address to participants in a course for, 129-135
Separated Christians
   Christian unity; The 1958 Christmas message, 139
   Interest in the 2nd Vatican Council, 394-395
   Invited to 2nd Vatican Council, 454-455
   Reunion with, Desire for, 12-13, 40-42
Seton, Elizabeth Ann Bayley, Blessed
   Beatification ceremonies, 493
Sick, The
   Apostolate of, 49-50
Simplicity
   Definition, 477-478
Sin
   St. John Vianney's concern for sinners, 95-96
Slipyi, Josyf, Abp.
   Reception of, 492
Social classes
   Relations between, Based on human solidarity and Christian brotherhood, 256
Social conditions
   Material welfare of working classes, Regard for, 33-35
   Postwar improvement in relations among classes, 33
Social doctrine
   Catholic Church, Validity of her, 305-306
   Church's; Education for application of the, 306-308
   Ideologies, False, 303-304
   Practice, Suggestions for reduction into, 308-309
Social encyclicals
   Leo XIII to Pius XII; Review, 227-231, 251-261
Social insurance
   Farmers and, 285
Social justice
   Christian social teachings and improvements in social conditions, 50-52
   Rights of social classes, Protection of, 32
Social life
   Apostolate of a competent Christian laity, 365-366, 369, 370-371

Justice, Conformity to, a Christian imperative, 367
Social order
   Ideologies and establishment of true social order, 303-306
   Ramifications of social relationships, 265-267
   Rebuilding a new order of society, 303-313
Social problems
   Application of Catholic social teachings to, 246-247
   Mater et Magistra, Preview of; Address, 227-239
   Mater et Magistra (Encyclical), 250-315
Socialism
   Christian opposition to materialistic view of society, 258
Society
   Bases: Truth, justice, charity, and freedom, 335-336
   God the source of a society's vitality, 336, 338
   Moral basis of, 318-320
   A spiritual reality primarily, 336, 338
Spiritual direction
   The art of; Address to participants in a course for spiritual direction of seminarians, 129-135
State, The
   Common good its *raison d'etre,* 255
   Developing nations, Respect for national integrity of, 293, 294, 295-296
   Freedom of, and relations between, states, 358, 359
   Independence of the modern state, 337-338
   The individual and public authorities, Relationship between, 320-322, 338-348
   Interdependence of political communities, 360-361
   Minorities, Treatment of, 351-352
   Modern, Characteristics of, 347-348
   Obligations of the wealthy nations, 290-293
   Refugees, Duties of states toward, 354-355
   Relations between states, 322-323, 348-360

Index 521

Resources, The pooling of, by states, 352-353, 353-354
See also Developing Nations
Students
   Foreign, Charity toward, 194-195
Subsidiarity
   Principle of, applied to economic and social order, 263, 267, 279, 289
Suffering
   Apostolate of the, 49-50
   Sanctification and, 472-473
   Tribulations, Usefulness of, 479-480
Sunday
   Observance of Third Commandment, 310-311

Tardini, Domenico Cardinal
   Council, Holding of, proposed to, 4
Taxation
   Farmers and, 284
Teaching
   Priestly obligation to teach, 94
Theodoret, Bishop of Cyrus (5th century)
   Tribute to St. Leo the Great, 154
Theophilus, Patriarch, Abp. of Alexandria
   Schismatics, Invitation to, 40-41
Tranquillity
   Providence, Trust in, 478
Tribulation
   Usefulness of, 479-480
Truth
   Conduct of life and Christian truth, 25-29, 428-429
   Ignorance of, as source of evils, 25, 29
   Indifference to, destructive of religion, 28
   Natural and revealed, 25-26
   Rejection of revealed truth, Consequences of, 25-27
   Religious, Joy in the attainment of, 28-29
Turkey
   Pope John as Apostolic Delegate to, 3

Underdeveloped areas. *See* Developing nations
United Nations, The
   Aims and functions, 364
   Effectiveness of, 364
   Food and Agriculture Organization, 290
Unity
   International and domestic harmony the bases of peace and unity, 29-36
   Promoting harmony among men as Church's duty, 432-433
   Truth attained leads to, 29
Unity of the Church
   Achieved through charity, 158
   Aeterna Dei Sapientia (Encyclical) on, 140-159
   Christ's prayer for, 156-157
   Diversity of rites, 162-163
   Doctrine, organization, and worship, Unity of, as mark of Christ's Church, 37-40
   One fold, one shepherd, 456
   St. Leo the Great and: Encyclical *Aeterna Dei Sapientia*, 140-159
   Separated Christians, Invitation to, 36-44
   Single standard for the Church Militant, 159
Universal Declaration of Human Rights
   World community and the, 364

Vatican Council, Second
   Aims: Restore and reconstruct, 162, 428-429, 431-433, 454-457
   Announcement of, to the Roman cardinals; Address, 20-23
   Bishops' conciliar responsibilities, 448, 450, 451-452
   Church unity and, 155
   Cooperation, Lay and clerical, 452-453
   Coordinating Commission, Establishment of, 443, 449-450
   Decision to hold the, 425-426
   Goals defined by Pope John, 382-383
   Historical context, 423-425
   Holiness, Growth in, as preparation for the, 165
   Inspiration to hold the Council, 381
   Interim period, 1st and 2nd sessions, 447-458
   Leonine centenary, 15th, and, 148-154
   Observer delegates at the 1st session, 383-384, 436-438

Opening address to, 423-435
Penance for the; Encyclical *Paenitentiam Agere,* 397-408
Pentecost, Council as a new, 444-445
Preparatory phase, Beginning of, 161
Present time propitious for holding the, 426-428
Proclamation of the; Apostolic Constitution *Humanae Salutis,* 386-396
Resulting benefits envisioned, 443-444
Roman Synod (1960) as herald of, 127
Rosary recitation for Council's success, 62
Unity, Council as a spectacle of, 37
Vatican Council, Second. First Session (Oct. 11-Dec. 8, 1962)
Accomplishments summarized, 441-442
Closing ceremonies, Address at, 439-446
Venice
Pope John's patriarchate in, 3-4, 12
Vincent Pallotti, Saint
Canonization, 491-492
Spiritual director and apostle, 134-135
Vocation
Man's right to choose his own, 331
Pope's, 479
Vocation, Religious
Call for vocations, 99-100
Native vocations, Encouragement of, 173

Wages
Determination of just wages, 257, 267-269
Just, Man's right to, 332
War
Causes of, 207
Cuban Crisis; Radio appeal for negotiations to preserve peace, 227-228
Horrors of, 215-216
Wealth
Equitable distribution of, and national prosperity, 269
Women
Secular institutes: Contribution of women in religious life to Council's success, 409-422
Status in modern times, 337
Work
Advanced view of, 276
Man's rights regarding, 331-332
Perfection through daily work, 312-313
Remuneration of, 257, 267-269
Specifically human activity, 254-255, 260
Wages, Man's right to just, 332
Workers
Associations of, and the whole economy, 274-276
Associative rights, 256
Conditions improved in modern times, 337
Participation in management, 273-274
Work sites and, 354
Worldliness
Dangers of, for priests, 117-118, 119-120
Worship
Unity of, as mark of Christ's Church, 39-40